Nest Building and Bird Behavior

NICHOLAS E. COLLIAS AND ELSIE C. COLLIAS

Nest Building and Bird Behavior

PRINCETON UNIVERSITY PRESS / *Princeton, N.J.*

Copyright © 1984 by Princeton University Press
Published by Princeton University Press,
41 William Street, Princeton, New Jersey 08540
In the United Kingdom:
Princeton University Press, Guildford, Surrey

All Rights Reserved

Library of Congress Cataloging in Publication Data
will be found on the last printed page of this book
ISBN 0-691-08358-4 (cloth)
ISBN 0-691-08359-2 (pbk.)

This book has been composed in Linotron Aldus

Clothbound editions of Princeton University Press books
are printed on acid-free paper, and binding materials
are chosen for strength and durability.
Paperbacks, although satisfactory for personal collections,
are not usually suitable for library rebinding

Printed in the United States of America by
Princeton University Press
Princeton, New Jersey

To all the friends, colleagues, and assistants
who helped us in our research in field and aviary
on the fascinating weaverbirds

CONTENTS

LIST OF TABLES

THE nests of birds have always intrigued people, but only in recent years has their importance as guides in helping to understand the ecology and evolution of species come to be recognized. A considerable body of scientific literature on the biology of nest-building behavior has developed, but this material is widely scattered. We attempt to summarize and synthesize the more significant aspects of this literature on the uses, mechanisms, development, and evolution of nest building by birds. There is a slight amount of repetition so that each chapter, although related to the others and dealing with a different problem, can be referred to independently. Our emphasis throughout is on the relationship between nest building and other kinds of behavior. We hope the book will be of interest to the general reader, as well as of use to scientific investigators in ecology, ethology, sociobiology, evolution, and ornithology. Building of nests is a phenomenon of very general importance in the animal kingdom, as we previously tried to bring out in a volume of selected readings that we edited on "External Construction by Animals" (1976).

In 1956–1957, we spent a year in Africa observing and studying weaverbirds and their nests; the results were published in a monograph "The Evolution of Nest-building in the Weaverbirds (Ploceidae)" by the University of California Press (1964). Subsequently, we made several other field trips to Africa, as well as trips to Asia, Madagascar, the Seychelles, and Haiti. Various organizations and institutions, many friends, and many local guides generously aided our efforts to learn something of the nesting behavior of the birds of their countries.

We carried out long-term experiments on weaverbirds and their nests in aviaries at the University of California at Los Angeles. We were very fortunate to have many able young investigators assist us during the last two decades. We wish particularly to thank Janice K. Victoria, Catherine M. Jacobs, and Cathleen R. Cox. Others who participated in the research for one breeding season or more were the following, in chronological order: Richard Burrows, Donald S. Brooks, Peter J. Frumkies, Ronald J. Barfield, Brian S. Kahn, Edward S. Tarvyd, Herbert A. Brown, Donna F. Hardy, Ann Reisman, Martin Graham, Ellen Coutlee Jennrich, Lloyd Kiff, Robert J. Shallenberger, Carl Rischer, Michael Brandman, Jeffrey T. Fujimoto, Florence McAlary, and Thomas Haglund. We are most grateful to all of them.

We thank our colleagues and others who took time from their busy schedules to read one or more chapters and give us the benefit of their comments: Catherine H. Jacobs, Thomas R. Howell, George A. Bartholomew, Frank B. Gill, Jared M. Diamond, Elizabeth Flint, and Karen Collias. George H. Sines and William Klement, Jr., of the UCLA School of Engineering faculty kindly read the parts of the manuscript most closely related to engineering and gave valuable advice. We are of course solely responsible for all our statements.

We greatly appreciate the kindness of those persons who lent us photographs of bird nests, or other illustrations, and gave us permission to publish them. These persons are named in the credit line given with each illustration in the text. Photographs and drawings without credit lines were made by Nicholas E. Collias, except for figure 9.5, a photograph taken by Elsie C. Collias.

We thank the editors or publishers of the following journals or books, as well as other copyright holders, for permission to reproduce various photographs, excerpts, or other items: *Alauda. Revue internationale d'Ornithologie* (Organe de la Société d'Études Ornithologiques, France); American Museum of Natural History (Wesley E. Lanyon, Chairman, Department of Ornithology); *Animal Behaviour* (Balliere Tindall); *American Scientist* (journal of Sigma Xi, the Scientific Research Society); *American Zoologist* (American Society of Zoologists); *The Auk* (American Ornithologists' Union); "Comparative Psychology," third edition, edited by C. P. Stone (Prentice-Hall); *Condor* (Cooper Ornithological Society); *Ecology* (Ecological Society of America); *Emu* (Royal Australasian Ornithologists' Union); *Forma et Functio* (Friedr. Vieweg & Sohn, West Germany); *Ibis* (Journal of the British Ornithologists' Union); *Ostrich* (Southern African Ornithological Society); *Physiological Zoology* (copyright 1978 by the University of Chicago Press), University of California Publications in Zoology (University of California Press); and *The Wilson Bulletin* (Wilson Ornithological Society).

We thank correspondents who generously lent us unpublished manuscripts or sent copies of published articles that are difficult to obtain, or who helped with other materials: Mei-Fang Cheng, Mary LeCroy, Jared M. Diamond, Frances Hamerstrom, Klaus Immelmann, Pamela MacDonald, Austin J. MacInnis, June Baumer, and Fred N. White. Susan Grossman, Mary Seraydarian, and Phong Hua typed the manuscript, and we are happy to acknowledge their helpfulness.

Alfred E. Emerson, formerly Professor of Zoology at the University of Chicago, first interested one of us (N.E.C.) in the possibilities of a systematic study of birds' nests, weaverbird nests in particular. On our first visit to Africa, we were fortunate to have as our nearest neighbors, the noted ornithologist, James P. Chapin, and his wife, Ruth. Besides being a mine of information and a source of inspiration, they aided us in numerous practical matters.

The University of California at Los Angeles and the Natural History Museum of Los Angeles County have sponsored and aided our research, which over the years has been generously supported by a series of grants from the National Science Foundation, making the whole thing possible.

Los Angeles, California   NICHOLAS E. COLLIAS
October 1983   ELSIE C. COLLIAS

Nest Building and Bird Behavior

CHAPTER ONE

Introduction

THE object of this book is to describe the biology of nest-building behavior among birds. A nest is a special construction forming a bed or receptacle in which the eggs and young develop. Nests occur throughout the animal kingdom (N. Collias and Collias 1976), and are designed by evolution to help the parents meet the needs of their young. The type of nest built gives important insights into the life of each species, since nests focus the essential requirements of animals for reproduction. Nests are therefore very relevant to the science of ecology if we define ecology as the study of the relationship of living organisms to their environment.

F. H. Herrick (1911), one of the early pioneers in the scientific study of nests, or "caliology" as it was then called (C. Dixon 1902), stated that "it would be difficult indeed from the standpoint of the student of instinct and behavior, to find a more unsatisfactory class of scientific literature than that which deals with the nests of birds." The picture is now changing with the growing realization that nests provide clues to real and significant ecological relationships. Particularly during the last ten or fifteen years a large and important body of literature has grown up.

Bird nests include the best and the most highly evolved nests known among vertebrate animals. In relation to the nest there are two main types of birds, nidifugous ("nest fleeing") and nidicolous ("nest dwelling") birds (Nice 1962, Welty 1975, Skutch 1976). Nidifugous species have precocial young, which leave the nest soon after hatching. Examples are chickens and ducks. The young hatch covered with down, their eyes are open and alert, they can walk the day they hatch, and they are soon able to feed themselves. Nidicolous species generally have altricial young, which hatch in a helpless state—unable to stand, naked or nearly so, and with eyes closed. The young are completely dependent on the parents for food, comfort, and protection, and are unable to leave the nest for days, weeks, or even months, depending on the species. Nidicolous birds build the best nests among birds, and include the great majority of species. The most important examples are the passerine or perching birds, which comprise the largest order (Passeriformes) of birds and include more than half the living species.

Nests are of particular interest to the student of animal behavior. Nest-building behavior has traditionally been accepted as a classic example of instinct, a vague term that has served as a convenient label for species-typical behavior, without implying necessarily anything as to the causation of this behavior. The type of nest built is as much a property of a species, as is its behavior, appearance, morphology, or physiology. When a bird builds a nest it makes a more or less permanent record ("frozen behavior") of its behavior as related to its evolution.

PLAN OF TREATMENT

One can relate some important problems in the life of birds to the types of nests they build. These problems are the subjects of the various chapters and determine the general organization of this book. Comparisons of different kinds of nests (chap. 2), particularly within a group of related species or genera (chap. 3), give clues about the evolution of nest-building behavior. Sex differences in nest-building behavior are related to the type of mating system characteristic of the species and to the ability of a bird to attract and keep a mate (chap. 4). In male birds of some species the ability to manipulate materials has even become specialized in evolution and has been redirected solely to obtaining mates instead of to the task of building a receptacle for the eggs and the young (chap. 5).

Adaptation to the stress of the physical environment helps explain the nature of the nest site (chap. 6) and the type of nest (chap. 7). The diversity of competitors also helps explain the diversity of nest sites and construction in different species (chap. 8), while the form and strength of nests is often closely related to the need for security from different predators (chap. 9).

Just how a bird builds its nest (chap. 10) can be analyzed according to various sign-stimuli governing the acts and sequences of building behavior (chap. 11). The "play nests" built by immature birds of some species differ from the finished products turned out by the adults, and a comparison of the building behavior of young birds with that of mature birds gives an insight into the development of the ability to build (chap. 12). Changes in internal factors, particularly in the levels of secretion of different hormones, interacting systematically with behavioral factors, lead to the onset, increase, decline, and termination of nest building and of nesting motivation (chap. 13).

Finally, there are problems related to gregarious nesting (chap. 14). Many birds breed in groups or colonies. The degree of crowding of nests can be related to such problems as the distribution of food resources, predation, and stresses imposed by the physical environment. Gregarious nesting also increases the competition within the species. These negative aspects are balanced against the advantages of gregarious nesting, which include social facilitation of nest building and of breeding behavior.

There are about 9,000 known species of living and recently extinct birds in the world, variously classified in some 20 to 29 orders and 148 to 171 families (Mayr and Amadon 1951, Storer 1971, Welty 1975, Van Tyne and Berger 1976, Bock and Farrand 1980, Cracraft 1981). Appendix One gives a list of orders and families of the world's living birds with the general types of nests they build. Scientific and common names of birds referred to in the text are listed in the index.

Most birds are small, and in general small birds build the finest nests. In the Old World, the weaverbird family (Ploceidae) and the Old World warblers (Sylviidae), and in the New World, the tyrant flycatchers (Tyrannidae), ovenbirds (Furnariidae), and the orioles, caciques, and oropendolas (Icteridae) are noted for the great variety of complex nests they build.

Appendix Two lists some references that have excellent photographs of many kinds of nests. A selection of photographs showing some of the main types of nests is presented in the next chapter, especially in relation to the evolution of nest building. Other aspects of nest building are illustrated with photographs or drawings in subsequent chapters.

APPLICATION OF SCIENTIFIC METHODS TO THE STUDY OF NEST BUILDING

In general, we try to explain nest-building behavior among birds by applying the principle of evolution; Darwin's theories of natural selection and sexual selection; the principle of dynamic homeostasis; the basic engineering principle that function determines structure; as well as general ecological, ethological, and sociobiological principles.

We follow the common-sense, dictionary (Webster's) definition of scientific methods: "principles and procedures for the systematic pursuit of knowledge involving the recognition and formulation of a problem, the collection of data through observation and experiment, and the formulation and testing of hypotheses." We use all elements of this methodology in our book, but because this field of study has not been synthesized before in any really comprehensive way, we have had to place considerable emphasis on describing the facts of nest-building behavior and in formulating the basic problems. Nevertheless, hypotheses are not absent, as can be seen by inspecting particularly chapters 6 and 7 on the physical environment and the energetics of nest building, or the more experimental chapters 11, 12, and 13 on the analysis, development, and hormonal basis of nest building, or chapter 14 on gregarious nesting.

Our general method has been to analyze nest-building behavior by asking and attempting to answer a series of questions: What kinds of nests do birds build and why? What are the functions, causes, developmental and evolutionary aspects of the diverse types of building behavior? Hypotheses are really sophisticated guesses as to possible answers in a series of questions. Chapter 11 illustrates this process in some detail with one thoroughly analyzed case of nest-building behavior.

One must have some tolerance for the different ways in which scientists work. The results of a 1979 mail ballot to members of the Division of Ecology of the American Society of Zoologists indicated that "they thought the time was overdue for some significant effort at reopening lines of communication between theoretical and empirical ecologists." The response led to a symposium on "Theoretical Ecology" (Gordon 1981). The concluding address by Robert M. May on "The role of theory in ecology" develops the importance of theory to ecology, and May also states (1981, p. 909): "Naively simple formulations of The Way To Do Science—be they the Baconian Method of the Victorians or the extreme logical positivism of Popper today—are harmless in themselves, but have unfortunate consequences when they inspire doctrinaire vigilantes to ride the boundaries of a discipline, culling the sinners. The scrabbling, nonlinear way Darwin pursued his ends is typical of most good science. Writing about him, Ghiselin (1969, p. 236) says: 'Viewed from without, science appears to be a body of answers; from within it is a way of asking questions.' "

The preceding discussion emphasizes that in science the proper balance between inductive and deductive methods, or empirical and theoretical approaches, will vary with the stage of development and with the complexity of a particular discipline. There is presently a great need for the accurate description and synthesis of the widely scattered facts concerning nest building by birds, and we have tried to meet this need. The initial step in a scientific discipline is the precise description and classification of the phenomena of the subject, which are in fact the problems for investigation and which set the stage for further analysis. A good, basic inventory of reliable facts is the best source of scientific hypotheses for further analysis. This book includes some observations from our original research to help round out the picture, but the primary objective is synthesis of the extensive and scattered literature.

Bonner (1980) and Bartholomew (1982) have recently emphasized the importance to scientific progress of a proper balance between analysis and synthesis, that is, between reductionist and holistic approaches to scientific progress. As Bonner states (p. 9) "a holistic approach . . . is a necessary stage without which the reductionist progress could not be made," and "is the only way of describing the problems and grouping the facts." The first part of our book emphasizes synthesis—the evolution and functions or the significance of nest-building behavior. The second part emphasizes the analysis of nest-building behavior into its component mechanisms and into its physiological basis, in so far as they are known. The last chapter considers the relationship between individual and group behavior with reference to gregarious nesting.

CONCEPTUAL APPROACH

This comprehensive review of the biology of nest building in birds, the only one presently available, is written from a conceptual point of view based on principles of evolution, ethology, ecology, sociobiology, and physiology. Much of the conceptual contribution is as a synthesis—the insights provided by new ways in which facts and ideas related to nest-building behavior are grouped together. The most general conclusion of the book is that nests of birds play a key role in avian biology—far more than has generally been appreciated. In recent years, investigators have developed many relatively new concepts of nest-building behavior, of varying degrees of novelty, which are probably not very familiar to most ornithologists, ethologists, or general biologists; these we have presented in the summary at the end of each chapter.

An important feature of the work is the presentation of more adequate documentation to strengthen earlier tentative generalizations (N. Collias and Collias 1964). For example, table 2.1 gives the first comprehensive and adequate evidence from various parts of the world supporting the important assertion that domed and roofed nests are built by a much higher proportion of tropical species of passerine birds than of temperate-zone passerine birds. Another example is the concept that for birds the type of nest built may often be typical of the genus. Appendix One gives broad generalizations based for the first time on all the bird families of the world, for the type of nest built and the sex building it.

In our detailed application of evolutionary theory to the nest-building behavior of birds, we have relied for general orientation in modern evolutionary theory particularly on books by Mayr (1970), Wilson (1975), and Wright (1978).

CHAPTER TWO

Diversity of Nests and Major Evolutionary Trends in Nest Building

THE following classification of nests is based mainly on general trends or levels in the evolution of nest building. It is followed by a discussion of these evolutionary trends.

A CLASSIFICATION OF BIRD NESTS

A. Incubation by heat from the physical environment. Eggs buried in soil; heat from sun, volcanic activity, hot springs, or decomposition of vegetable matter. Mound builders, or megapodes (Megapodiidae).
B. Incubation by heat from physical environment and parental body heat.
   1. Eggs buried in sand for part of incubation period. Egyptian Plover.
   2. Eggs in nest; parent does not incubate during heat of day. Many Australian grass-finches (Estrildidae).
C. Incubation primarily by parent. The great majority of birds.
   1. No nest; eggs not laid in an enclosed cavity.
      a. Eggs laid in suitable habitat on ground, rock, or tree. Whip-poor-will, Common Murre or Guillemot, White Tern.
      b. Egg held on feet and incubated under a fold of belly skin. Emperor Penguin.
   2. Eggs laid in an enclosed cavity or burrow, usually with little nest lining.
      a. Bird uses a preformed cavity, as among rocks (Ashy Storm-Petrel), or in a tree (many hornbills, House Wren, Tree Swallow).
      b. Bird digs nest hole in the ground (many shearwaters), in a bank (European Bee-eater, Bank Swallow), or in a tree (most woodpeckers).
      c. Bird digs nest hole in ant or termite nest. Orange-fronted Parakeet, Rufous Woodpecker, and many species of kingfishers.
   3. Open nest, generally a scrape, simple platform, or cup.
      a. On the ground. Albatrosses, gulls, terns, many gallinaceous and grassland and passerine birds.

    b. On a cliff, on the side of a house, in a cave, or in a chimney. Cliff Swallow, House Martin, cave swiftlets (*Collocalia*), Chimney Swift.

    c. On water. Grebes, Black Tern.

    d. Fastened to herbaceous vegetation above ground or water. Red-winged Blackbird, Reed Warbler, bishop birds.

    e. In a shrub or a tree. Many species, with a great variety of nests, e.g., crude, simple nests (doves), mud cup (Australian Magpie-Lark), woven and suspended nests (orioles), and very small (many hummingbirds) to very large nests (Bald Eagle)

  4. Domed nest, particularly common in the tropics.

    a. In a tunnel in a bank or in a tree hole. Striated Diamondbird of Australia (Dicaeidae).

    b. Of various plant materials, placed on or near ground. Some rails, some pittas (Pittidae).

    c. Of mud (Cliff Swallow), of mud and cow dung (Rufous Ovenbird of South America).

    d. Of felted plant down or wool. Penduline Tit.

    e. Roofed with large leaf. Tailorbirds.

    f. Nonwoven, of plant materials bound together with spider or insect silk or fungal filaments (*Marasmius*). Sunbirds (Nectariniidae), Bushtit, many New World flycatchers.

    g. Thatched of dry grass stems or straws. Sparrow weavers (*Plocepasser*), East African social weavers (*Pseudonigrita*).

    h. Woven of green, flexible plant materials. True weaverbirds (Ploceinae).

  5. Compound nest, having two or more nesting compartments, genrally with a communal roof. Palmchat of Hispaniola, Monk Parakeet of Argentina, Buffalo Weaver of sub-Saharan Africa, Sociable Weaver of southwestern Africa.

D. Eggs laid in nest of other species.

  1. Parents care for own eggs and young. Great Horned Owl, Chestnut Sparrow.

  2. Brood parasites. Most cowbirds, viduine finches, honey-guides (Indicatoridae), many species of cuckoo.

Evolution of Nest Building

To maintain perspective and orientation in a discussion of nest evolution, it is necessary at the outset to keep certain principles in mind. Competition among species has often resulted in great differences in the habitats and nest sites occupied by related species. In turn, differences in the nature of the substrate for the nest has imposed special engineering requirements on nests with regard to materials, form, structure, and placement. Building a nest requires considerable expenditure of energy, and it is common for many birds to make a thousand or more trips to gather the necessary materials. Natural selection may therefore be expected generally to favor anything that tends to economize on effort, so long as undue sacrifice of any crucial advantage of the species is avoided.

Nests are so closely related to habitat and habits in any given species that there has been a tremendous amount of recurrent, convergent, and parallel evolution of nest types among birds, making it difficult to delineate particular phylogenies. In any particular line, evolution may lead to either an increasing complexity or, conversely, to an increasing simplification of nests, depending on conditions. We do not emphasize special family geneologies in this chapter, but rather we attempt to indicate the probable nature of the selection pressures that have led to the evolution of the main types of nests. Convergent evolution under similar conditions itself gives clues to these selection pressures.

The primary, basic, and most general functions of a nest are to help insure warmth and safety for the developing eggs and young. But growth and survival of the young depend on the total biology of the species, and to understand fully the forces in the evolution of the nest for any species, one must be familiar with other aspects of its life history as well. Conversely, selection of a given type of nest site influences other aspects of species behavior, as Cullen (1957) has shown for the Kittiwake Gull, and von Haartman (1957) for hole-nesting birds in general.

The problems of securing warmth and safety are most acute for small birds and their young. Small birds generally build nests that are more elaborate and better concealed than those of larger birds. Reduction in size and energy content of eggs has helped make possible the evolution of small body size in birds (Witschi 1956, W. R. Dawson and Evans 1960), but it has also required increased parental care of the young, which hatch in a helpless, well-nigh embryonic state. There are all degrees between precocial and altricial young and a parallel range of parental care (Nice 1962), related in a general way to nesting habits.

The fossil history of birds is poorly known compared with that of mammals, but some general sequences can be discerned (Brodkorb 1971, Feduccia 1980). The earliest known bird, *Archaeopteryx*, from the Jurassic period of the Mesozoic era (Age of Reptiles), had feathers but otherwise closely resembled certain fossil reptiles. Judging from its structure *Archaeopteryx* was arboreal, but we have no notion of its nesting behavior. The more primitive living arboreal birds, the Hoatzin (Opisthocomidae) and the guans (Cracidae), build rather crude nests of twigs in trees. Most fossil birds known from the Cretaceous period were water birds. During the Eocene and Paleocene epochs of the Tertiary period in the Cenozoic era (Age of Mammals and Birds), giant, flightless, running birds were relatively common, large size being perhaps correlated with effective defense of the nest against enemies by the parent, rather than with concealment. Another early Tertiary expansion was of puffbirds, rollers and their relatives—all hole-nesters today and some perhaps resembling the ancestors of the passerine birds (Order Passeriformes). The passerine birds are relatively small and many build elaborate nests. The songbirds (Suborder Passeres) had their great expansion from about mid-Tertiary to the present.

Origin of Nest Building in Birds

The ability of birds to maintain a high constant body temperature no doubt developed gradually, probably coincidently with evolution of the ability to fly. Even today, some birds pass into a state of torpor under certain conditions, when their body temperature falls drastically (Bartholomew et al. 1957). If birds became torpid during the cool nights of the breeding season, they could scarcely incubate their eggs effectively. During the transitional period of early avian evolution, when physiological temperature regulating mechanisms were being perfected, some birds probably continued to bury their eggs, leaving incubation to the sun or to decaying vegetation after the reptilian fashion, just as megapodes among living birds do today. The probability of low nocturnal body temperatures in ancestral birds is an argument in favor of the idea that in an early stage of avian evolution, incubation of the eggs may have depended in part or wholly upon some source of heat other than that furnished by the parental body.

Nests of Megapodes (Megapodiidae)

Nests of living megapodes show a tremendous range of variation (H. Frith 1962) (figs. 2.1, 2.2). The nest may vary from a simple, small pit dug in the sand, large enough for just one egg, to a gigantic mound of soil and decaying vegetation as much as thirty-five feet (10.7 m) in diameter and fifteen feet (4.6 m) high, perhaps the largest structure made by birds. Frith points out the striking parallel between reptile and bird on certain sunlit coral beaches where the turtles heave up out of the sea to dig holes on the beach in which to lay their eggs while the megapodes walk out of the bush to dig pits in the sand for their eggs. Similarly, in places where dark tropical forests fringe the rivers, female

Fig. 2.1. Male Mallee-fowl (*Leipoa ocellata*) scratching on his sandy mound (about 3 m diameter), Australia. (Photo: David and Carol Vleck)

Fig. 2.2. Male Brush-turkey (*Alectura lathami*) on his mound of brush and leaves, Australia. (Photo: David and Carol Vleck)

crocodiles build mounds of leaves for their eggs, in close proximity to the leafy mounds of megapodes.

A change in climate, especially toward the close of the Mesozoic era, from humid, tropical or subtropical to drier, cooler conditions with greater extremes of temperature, probably led in early avian evolution to two different ways of incubating the eggs. Some birds developed the modern method of incubation by direct application of body heat to the eggs. Other birds developed into mound builders, burying the eggs deep in the ground, safeguarding them from the harsh conditions, and at the same time evolving considerable efficiency in regulating the temperature of the mound around the eggs.

It is possible that modern megapodes once had ancestors that sat on their eggs as other birds now do and, instead of retaining the primitive reptilian mode, evolved their now seemingly peculiar mode of incubation by a sort of regressive evolution. Frith states that one thing is certain: megapodes, compared with any present-day reptiles, have greatly improved the ability to regulate the temperature of the mound. The Mallee-fowl (*Leipoa ocellata*) lives in arid regions of Australia where the temperatures may range from below freezing to above 38°C, and even in midsummer the night temperature may be 17° lower than the day temperature. Nevertheless this bird manages to maintain the incubation temperature next to the eggs buried in its mound relatively constant, between 32°C and 35°C.

Origin of Direct Parental Incubation of Eggs

The open nest may well have evolved in ancient birds from a nest like the simplest type built by modern megapodes. In some parts of Australia the Scrub-fowl (*Megapodius freycinet*) merely lays a single egg in a small pit in the sand or in a crevice in a rock, covers the egg with leaves, and departs, leaving the task of incubation to the sun (H. Frith 1962). When away from the nest, birds having open nests on the ground often cover their eggs with plant materials or downy feathers, or occasionally with earth.

As birds were evolving the ability to maintain a high, constant body temperature throughout the cool night independently of environmental temperatures, there was coincidentally a tremendous selection pressure favoring direct parental incubation of the eggs. This new ability facilitated the spread of species into colder regions relatively free from reptilian predators. The danger of predation on the eggs from various nocturnal enemies—especially from contemporary mammals, which were small and probably nocturnal—gave considerable value to the habit of staying with the eggs and defending them, if necessary, during the night. Total risk from predation on the eggs would diminish with a shortening of the developmental period. Herrick (1911) suggests that the origin of incubation by sitting on the eggs probably arose from the tendency of birds to conceal their eggs from potential predators with the body as a protection.

Cavity-nesting Birds

Cavity-nesting has evolved in birds at virtually every stage of evolution. Early use of natural cavities was followed by special modification of the cavity. About half the orders of birds contain some species that nest in cavities. Whole orders of cavity-nesters are represented by the kiwis, parrots, trogons, coraciiform birds (kingfishers and relatives), and piciform birds (woodpeckers and relatives).

Cavity-nesting provides shelter from the elements and conserves energy (Kendeigh 1961). In addition, much direct statistical evidence from various studies shows that it is safer for altricial birds of the North Temperate Zone to nest in holes than in open nests. Nice's (1957) summary shows that only about half of some 22,000 eggs of various species with open nests fledged young birds, whereas two-thirds of 94,400 eggs were successful in hole-nesting birds. Populations of small birds, like the House Wren (*Troglodytes aedon*) (Kendeigh 1941), have often been greatly increased by putting out a good supply of nest boxes. Lack (1966) shows that nestlings remain and develop in the safety of the nest longer in species having enclosed nests than in species with open nests.

The shelter and safety furnished by cavities result in intense competition for these cavities. Aggressive competition for tree holes have been a profound force in the evolution of different size-classes among such birds as woodpeckers, corresponding to the different size entrance holes typical of each species. Along with each species of woodpecker go a host of other species of birds of the same size that compete with the woodpecker for the corresponding size of nest cavity. The European Starling (*Sturnus vulgaris*) is notorious in this regard, and one of us (NC) has seen a starling in Ohio seize a flicker by the tail and cast it out of the flicker's freshly dug tree cavity, in which a pair of starlings subsequently nested and reared a brood. Sielmann (1959) described an interesting example in Germany, showing how a small bird can compete successfully with a larger one for a nest cavity in a tree. When the European Nuthatch (*Sitta europaea*) takes over a tree cavity, it forestalls its rival, the European Starling, by collecting mud from nearby puddles and plastering the mud around the entrance to the tree hole, making

Fig. 2.3. Red-billed Hornbill (*Tockus erythrorhynchus*) at a prospective nest site, Kenya. (Photo: Thomas R. Howell)

the entrance so small and narrow that while the nuthatch can slip through, the larger starling cannot.

In the classic case of the hornbills, the male was said to provide for the safety of his mate and young ones by imprisoning the female in her nest cavity in a tree and walling up the entrance with mud, leaving just enough room for her to put her beak out so that he could feed her during the prolonged period of incubation and care of the young, and releasing her at the end of that time. But Moreau (1937) points out that it is the

Fig. 2.4 Red-billed Hornbill nest entrance, narrowed by the female using mud and her own droppings, Senegal. (Gérard and Marie-Yvonne Morrel, *Alanda* 1962)

female who plasters herself in—using such materials as mud brought by the male and mixed with saliva as an adhesive—and when she is ready to leave, it is the female who pecks her way out. Female Red-billed Hornbills (*Tockus erythrorhynchus*) (fig. 2.3) use mud and their own droppings for sealing the nest hole (fig. 2.4). Kemp (1970) suggests that the sealing technique of hornbills evolved from a common hornbill activity, bill cleaning. After handling nest debris the birds may have cleaned the bill on the entrance, leaving the dirt adhering to the sides of the entrance. The Ground Hornbill (*Bucorvus*) nests in trees in large cavities such as those formed at the tip of a big broken branch, but it does not wall them up with mud.

Different stages in the evolution of birds' ability to excavate nest cavities in trees probably were (1) the use of natural cavities; (2) the modification of these cavities in various ways by the bird; (3) the excavation in decaying or very soft wood, as by some titmice (Hinde 1952) and the tiny Olivaceous Piculet (*Picumnus olivaceus*) of South America (Skutch 1948); and finally, (4) the chiseling of nest cavities in hard living trees, as by the Black Woodpecker (*Dryocopus martius*) of Europe (Sielmann 1959).

Many birds nest in holes in the ground. Several stages in the evolution of excavated burrows in the ground may be suggested: (1) a shallow

Fig. 2.5. Sacred Kingfisher (*Halcyon sancta*) at its nest entrance in an arboreal termite nest, Australia (K. A. Hindwood, *Emu* 1959)

scrape such as that made by many ground-nesting birds; (2) a relatively short burrow like that dug by the Rough-winged Swallow (*Stelgidopteryx serripennis*), a bird that often merely nests in crevices; and (3) a long burrow, which may reach a length of over six feet in a bank, as in the Bank Swallow (*Riparia riparia*) (Bent 1942).

The evolutionary climax of excavated nests is the construction of nesting cavities by certain birds inside the nests of social insects. The distribution of the Orange-fronted Parakeet (*Aratinga canicularis*) in Mexico and Central America closely approximates that of the colonial termite, *Eutermes (Nasutitermes) nigriceps*, in the nests of which the parakeet breeds, apparently using only nests still occupied by the termites (Hardy 1963). Hindwood (1959) pointed out forty-nine species of birds,

Fig. 2.6. Section through the nest cavity of the Sacred Kingfisher, showing the eggs inside an arboreal termite nest, Australia. (K. A. Hindwood, *Emu* 1959)

including kingfishers, parrots, trogons, puffbirds, jacamars, and a cotinga, that are known to breed in either terrestrial or arboreal nests of termites. In fact, some 25 percent of the world's kingfisher species nest in termite nests (figs. 2.5, 2.6). As the excavation by a bird progresses, the termites seal the exposed portion of their nest so that there is no actual contact between the birds and the insects.

Species that breed in nests of social insects all belong to orders of birds that characteristically nest in holes or cavities. Cavities in old and deserted termite nests are at times used by birds that normally breed in earth banks or tree holes—a phenomenon that shows how the habit of consistently breeding in nests of social insects might have evolved.

We can make two general conclusions concerning nests either in natural or modified cavities or in cavities excavated by the nesting birds themselves or by other birds. First, various specialized types of holenesting have evolved, and second, nesting in a cavity goes a long way toward meeting the essential functions of a nest for warmth and safety and thereby tends to block further evolution of elaborate nests that are built up from specific materials. In fact, such nests as those that are placed within cavities may undergo a regressive evolution. All degrees of increasing simplification and reduction of the nest to a mere pad are seen in the case of Old World sparrows (Ploceidae, Passerinae) that nest in tree holes (N. Collias and Collias 1964).

Evolution of Open Nests on the Ground

After direct parental incubation evolved, it was no longer necessary to dig a pit for the eggs. However, most birds that nest on the surface of the ground today still begin their nest by making a circular scrape with the feet while crouching low and rotating the body (C. Dixon 1902). This hollow may then be more or less lined with various materials, protecting the eggs from the cold, damp ground.

A rim of materials around the body of the incubating parent helps to provide insulation for the eggs, the materials being pushed to the periphery and built up into a circular form by much the same type of movements of the feet and body as those involved in making the initial scrape in the ground. Other nest-building behavior prevents the flattening down of the nest rim. Many ground-nesting birds repeatedly reach out with the bill and draw in materials toward the breast or pass them back along one side of the body before dropping them. The Canada Goose clearly shows all of these patterns in making a ground nest (N. Collias and Jahn 1959).

Open nests on the surface of the ground are more exposed to the elements than are enclosed nests. Eggs of the Horned Lark (*Eremophila alpestris*) laid early in the season in the northern United States sometimes freeze. Horned Larks nest in open country and place their nest in a shallow scrape protected from the chill of prevailing winds only by a clod or tussock of grass (Bent 1942).

Parental behavior may supplement or substitute for a nest under particularly severe conditions of exposure. In the Arctic, persistent, close incubation by the parent bird seems to be a major adaptation and occurs regardless of whether or not the nest is well insulated (Irving and Krog 1956). The Semipalmated Sandpiper (*Calidris pusillus*), with no nest, keeps its eggs as warm as do various other birds nesting in the Arctic with a substantial nest. The Emperor Penguin (*Aptenodytes forsteri*), which breeds in the antarctic winter, rests its single egg on the feet, covers it with a fold of belly skin, and incubates it against the body. Probably no other animal breeds under such trying conditions. The fury of recurrent severe storms is met by the birds' huddling together in a close mass (Rivolier 1956).

Eggs or nestlings exposed to strong, tropical or subtropical sun in open

Fig. 2.7. American Avocet (*Recurvirostra americana*) with nest and eggs. Nests vary from almost none on dry land to elevated piles of debris on flooded ground. (Photo: Willard Luce)

situations are customarily shaded by the body and wings of the parent bird, for example, the Sooty Tern (*Sterna fuscata*) of Midway Island whose nest is a mere scrape in the coral sand (Howell and Bartholomew 1962).

Nests on the surface of the ground are especially vulnerable to floods. Ground-nesting birds may place their nests on any slight elevation and may build their nests up during a flood. The Adélie Penguin (*Pygoscelis adeliae*) of the Antarctic builds its nest of small stones, lessening the danger of flooding during thaws or of being buried by snow during blizzards (Sladen 1958). During a thaw, Sladen noticed one nest with a stream of ice-cold water running through it. The incubating male, his eggs half submerged, kept reaching forward, collecting and arranging stones around him. Next day the eggs were above water, though the stream passed on either side of the nest. Eventually these eggs hatched. The Painted Snipe (*Rostratula benghalensis*) in Australia may lay its eggs on the bare ground when dry, but if water is lying on the ground,

Fig. 2.8. Western Grebes (*Aechmophorus occidentalis*) on nests of rushes over water, North Dakota.

a solid nest of rushes and herbage is made (Serventy and Whittell 1962). Similarly, avocets build up their nest when the waters rise at their nest sites (fig. 2.7).

There is evidence that it is safer for a bird to nest on a platform over water in a marsh (fig. 2.8) than to nest on the surface of dry land. Kiel (1955) found during a four-year period of study in Manitoba that 50 percent of 149 nests of dabbling ducks, which nest on dry land, were successful. In contrast, he found that 73 percent of 227 nests of diving ducks, which nest over water, were successful.

The high degree of exposure to predation to which birds nesting on the surface of the ground are often subject is no doubt the reason why those species provide some of the classic examples of concealing coloration, such as the incubating ptarmigan, or the eggs and young of many shore birds. In these instances concealment by coloration and behavior acts as a substitute for concealment by a nest and a safe nesting site. In fact, the nest may disappear in evolution, as for the Whip-poor-will (*Caprimulgus vociferus*) and the European Stone Curlew (*Burhinus oedicnemus*), presumably because the nest itself would be too conspicuous on the surface of the ground.

Fig. 2.9. Blue-footed Booby (*Sula nebouxii*) incubating its eggs on bare ground, Galapagos Islands.

Evolution of Open Nests in Trees and on Cliffs

On islands where there are no mammalian predators, many birds nest on the ground (fig. 2.9). However, the dangers of ground nesting and the intense competition for tree holes have provided a strong selection pressure leading to the building of nests in trees or bushes by many birds (fig. 2.10). The Tooth-billed Pigeon (*Didunculus strigirostris*) of Samoa is said to have abandoned its ground-nesting habits and taken to nesting in trees after cats were introduced by whaling ships (O. Austin and Singer 1961).

The nature of the materials used to help solve the problem of securely placing and attaching a nest in a tree varies with the body size of the bird and its lifting power. Large birds use twigs and branches that are not readily blown out of the tree by ordinary winds. Medium-sized birds use small twigs or grasses or both, sometimes adding mud to help attach the nest and bind the nest materials together. A great many small birds are known to use spider silk or insect silk both for the attachment of the nest and for fastening together various other materials. Practically all birds line their nests with finer and softer materials than are used for the foundation and outer shell of the nest.

Fig. 2.10. Red-footed Booby (*Sula sula*) on its crude nest of twigs in a bush, Galapagos Islands.

The platform-nests of some large birds, such as the American Bald Eagle (*Haliaeetus leucocephalus*) (fig. 2.11) or the European White Stork (*Ciconia ciconia*), are largely constructed of twigs and branches and are added to, year after year. Such nests may become very large and very old. Herrick (1932) gives an age of thirty-six years for a Bald Eagle nest, and Haverschmidt (1949) dates back to 1549 one White Stork nest which was still in use in 1930. The limiting factor to continued nest growth is often the weakening of the nest tree and its increased vulnerability to windfall. The particular nest described by Herrick, one of the largest eagle nests on record, was 12 feet (3.7 m) tall, 8½ feet (2.6 m) across the top, and its weight was estimated at over 2 tons. It was situated in a tall tree and in its thirty-sixth year this nest fell with the tree in a storm.

Cup-nests of the smallest species of birds, particularly when in cool or exposed environments, are often heavily insulated; nests of most species of hummingbirds have a thick lining of downy material (Ruschi 1949) (fig. 2.12). The tightly constructed cup provides effective insulation of the incubating female's ventral surface, that part of her body from which the greatest heat loss probably occurs as T. R. Howell and W. R. Dawson (1954) demonstrate for the Anna Hummingbird (*Calypte*

Fig. 2.11. Bald Eagle (*Haliaeetus leucocephalus*) at its large nest of branches and twigs in the top of a tall tree, Alaska. (Photo: Brina Kessel)

anna). Hummingbirds that nest in high mountains build nests with relatively thick walls, compared with lowland species (Wagner 1955), or seek the protection of caves (Pearson 1953).

Compared with platform-nests, the cup-nest built by small birds provides more adequate protection for the altricial young, being so constructed that it resists stresses that might cause the nest to collapse inward or outward. According to Nickell (1958), rootlets used as nest

Fig. 2.12. Female Black-chinned Hummingbird (*Archilochus alexandri*) on its nest of plant down bound with spider silk, southern California. (Photo: Ray Quigley)

linings are the most consistent feature of the nests of the Catbird (*Dumetella carolinensis*) and the Brown Thrasher (*Toxostoma rufum*). These rootlets are moist and flexible when placed in the nest and become like small wire springs when dry, serving as an inner bracework that preserves the shape of the nest basket.

Probably every type of material characteristic of the nest of a given species of bird has a definite function according to the physical properties of the material. The proportions of materials of different types that are used vary not only with availability but also with the requirements of particular substrate and habitat situations. Horvath (1963) finds that American Robin (*Turdus migratorius*) nests contain more mud when the birds have to use short materials, more tough flexible rootlets when the nest is in an especially windy spot, and more moss when in a relatively cold microclimate.

Under nesting conditions that are safe from predators, certain species of birds that normally nest in trees may return to ground-nesting, thereby conserving the energy that would be required to fly up constantly

Fig. 2.13. Mountain White-crowned Sparrow (*Zonotrichia leucophrys oriantha*) on its cup-nest in a bush, California. Cup-nests are typical of most passerine birds. (Photo: Martin L. Morton)

into a tree, carrying nest materials or food for nestlings. On Gardiner's Island in New York, in the absence of mammalian predators, such birds as the Osprey (*Pandion haliaetus*) and the American Robin often nest on the ground, although they nest in trees elsewhere in the United States (Preston and Norris 1947).

Species of birds with precocial young are generally ground-nesters; species with altricial and therefore relatively helpless young may nest either on the ground or, more often, in trees and bushes (fig. 2.13). It is probable that passerine birds, with their perching-foot structure and altricial young, evolved first in arboreal life, and then some species invaded ground habitats where they continued to construct well-rounded, cup-like nests (fig. 2.14).

Elevated nests attached to vertical faces of cliffs, buildings, or caves are safe from non-avian predators, but pose special problems of nest-attachment. Swifts have generally specialized in adhesive saliva (Lack 1956, Medway 1960), while the swallows have evolved toward a more general use of mud, probably with some admixture of saliva (Bent 1942). Different species of cave swiftlets can be arranged in a graded series

Fig. 2.14. Ground-nest of the White-crowned Sparrow (*Zonotrichia leucophrys*), with eggs, California. (Photo: Ray Quigley)

from those swiftlets making nests of pure saliva (source of the ideal "birds' nest soup" of the Orient), through species having nests of various admixtures of plant and other materials with saliva, to more conventional types of bird nests. The nest cement secreted by the cave swiftlet *Collocalia fuciphaga* is sparse and soft, and the nest, which is built up from moss and other plant materials, can only be placed on an irregularity in the cave wall that will take all or a good part of the nest's weight, unlike the nest of other cave swiftlets that can be glued to vertical walls in a cave (Medway 1960).

Evolution of Domed and Pensile Nests

Small birds in particular are benefited by the protection from cold, rain, and predation that enclosed nests furnish. Building a roofed increment-nest is very rare among nonpasserine birds, whereas half of some eighty-two families and distinctive subfamilies of passerine birds recognized by Mayr and Amadon (1951) in their classification of birds of the world build domed nests or contain representatives that do so. Roofed nests,

TABLE 2.1. Nest type of passerine bird species in north temperate regions compared with those in tropical and subtropical areas

	Number of species	Percent nest types			Reference
		Open	Domed	Hole	
Temperate Regions					
W. North America	245	82	7	11	Peterson 1961
E. North America	223	72	6	21	von Haartman 1957
Palearctic	279	61	11	28	von Haartman 1957
New World Tropics					
Guatemala	76	46	30	24	Smithe 1966
Trinidad	110	63	22	15	ffrench 1973
Surinam	93	61	28	11	Haverschmidt 1968
Old World Tropics					
Western Africa	496	48	38	14	Mackworth-Praed and Grant 1970
Ceylon	78	53	29	18	G. Henry 1971
Borneo	81	44	46	10	Smythies and Cranbrook 1981

aside from the use of natural cavities, are unusual among passerine birds of the North Temperate Zone, but such domed nests are typical of many tropical species of passerine birds (table 2.1) and are characteristic of some families and subfamilies, and particularly of many genera (N. Collias and Collias 1964).

The domed nest probably evolved from a nest that was open above, as is suggested by the fact that birds having nonpensile roofed nests usually start with a basal platform and then build the sides and roofs. The inability of most passerine birds to compete successfully for tree holes and other natural nest cavities with the generally larger nonpasserine altricial birds may well have been a selection pressure for the building of enclosed nests by many Passeriformes in the tropics. Tropical or semitropical conditions were widespread in the world during the first half of the Tertiary when many passerine families evolved (Brodkorb 1971).

Snakes are more numerous and varied in the tropics than in colder regions, and domed nests probably help protect birds from snakes as well as other enemies. Pitman (1958) summarizes many instances of snake and lizard predation on birds. However, the exact techniques used by snakes or any other predators of nesting birds do not seem to have been much investigated. Knowledge of these techniques would help explain many nest specializations. The true weaverbirds (Ploceinae) belong to an Old World family (Ploceidae) in which all of the species build a domed nest or, in a few cases, nest in holes. For most of the species that place their nests in herbaceous vegetation, the nest has a side entrance. Nests of weaverbirds placed in trees tend to evolve a bottom entrance often with a long entrance tube, presumably as a protection against snakes and certain other predators that would have to approach the nest from above (N. Collias and Collias 1959a, 1963, 1964; Crook 1963b). V.G.L. Van Someren (1956:458) made an interesting observation in Kenya: "I once watched a green tree-snake trying to get at the young in a spectacled weaver's nest. The brute negotiated the slender, pendant branch and reached the nest but could not manage the 12-inch tubular entrance and fell into the pond below the nest." The nest of the Yellow-breasted Flycatcher (*Tolmomyias flaviventris*) of Surinam is pensile with a ventral entrance tube (Haverschmidt 1950) that very likely serves the same function as does the entrance tube in weaverbirds' nests.

Placing nests in suitable cover helps protect them from predators. Many species of birds build their nests in thorn trees. The buffalo weavers also build a thorny covering or shell over the nest. In fact, the White-headed Buffalo Weaver (*Dinemellia dinemelli*) of East Africa even places thorny twigs along the boughs leading to its nest, over a distance of several feet or more (Friedmann 1950, Chapin 1954, N. Collias and Collias 1964).

In the warm tropics, regular incubation is not always so necessary nor so characteristic of birds as in colder climes, consequently nests and eggs may sometimes be left alone for prolonged periods. For example, Immelmann (1962, 1965) observed that Australian Grass-finches (Estrildidae) stopped incubation completely when the temperature of the nest chamber exceeded 100°F (37.8°C). It seems that the presence of a roof not only helps hide the eggs from predators, but probably decreases the rate of heat loss during prolonged absences of the parents.

One other function of the roof of a domed nest must be to shed rain. Most small birds in the tropics nest during the rainy season when insect food is abundant. Grasses are arranged over the side entrances of many weaverbird nests in such a way as to deflect the rain. Skutch (1954) observes that during the early part of the breeding season, before the rains begin, the nests of the Yellow-rumped Cacique (*Cacicus cela*) (Icteridae) in Central America are all open at the top. But as the rains begin, after the eggs have been laid and even after the young hatched, the top of the entrance is gradually roofed over and the nest entrance becomes a bent tube opening downward.

The roof of a domed nest also has an important effect as shade from solar radiation. For example, the Galapagos Finches have an equatorial and relatively exposed habitat. Unlike most other Emberizidae, members of this subfamily (Geospizinae) build roofed nests (Lack 1947). One function of the roof in these nests is probably to furnish protection from the tropical sun. The small, naked altricial nestlings are no doubt very sensitive to direct exposure to strong sun. The danger from ultraviolet radiation is greater in the tropics than in the temperate or colder regions, as is also the danger from the heating effect of the sun.

The roofs of domed nests may be composed of very different materials in different birds—mud in Cliff Swallows (*Hirundo pyrrhonota*) (figs. 2.15, 2.16), a leaf in the tailorbirds (fig. 2.17), a mass of short, heterogeneous plant materials bound together by spider silk in sunbirds (fig. 2.18), plant fibers matted together in some New World flycatchers (fig. 2.19), or woven together in the true weaverbirds, (figs. 2.20-2.22). The convergent evolution in these diverse instances emphasizes the great importance of a roof in the life of small nesting birds.

Cases of tropical families of small birds that build open cup-nests are not yet fully understood, but various devices seem to substitute for a roof. Many hummingbirds (Ruschi 1949) and the Old World Palm Swifts (*Cypsiurus parvus*) (Chapin 1939:467) fasten their nests to the underside of a leaf. In the bulbul (Pycnonotidae) and cuckoo-shrike (Campephagidae), both male and female incubate and keep the eggs covered (Van Tyne and Berger 1976).

The roofed nest reaches its evolutionary climax of specialization in the pensile or hanging nest and in the compound nest. Pensile nests are attached from their upper portion while the lower part hangs free (figs. 2.22, 2.23). Such nests have evolved independently in birds of different families and may exhibit very different materials and binding techniques.

Many sunbirds use spider silk, while certain other sunbirds and the African Broadbills (*Smithornis*) use black-fungus fibers (*Marasmius*) as a binding material (Chapin 1953). A woven construction also facilitates evolution of domed and pendulous nests by enhancing the coherence of the nest. According to Skutch (1960:544) "The pensile nests of the American Flycatchers are matted rather than woven." This statement points up the crudeness of these nests. However, both of these terms are difficult to apply in any precise or objective way: the dictionary defines a mat as a piece of coarse fabric made by weaving or plaiting materials; weaving is any regular pattern of interlocking loops of flexible materials, as applied to the fabric of a nest (N. Collias and Collias 1962,

Fig. 2.15. Cliff Swallows (*Hirundo pyrrhonota*) in gourd-shaped nests of mud, fastened to the side of a barn, Wisconsin. The pale forehead of the bird signals occupancy of a nest. (Photo: John T. Emlen, Jr.)

Fig. 2.16. Cliff Swallows gathering mud pellets with which they build their nests. (Photo: John T. Emlen, Jr.)

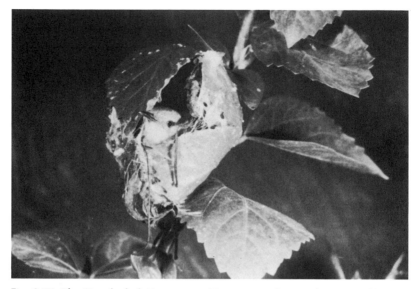

Fig. 2.17. The Grey-backed Camaroptera (*Camaroptera brevicaudata*), an Old World warbler, in its nest, Senegal. Like the Long-tailed Tailorbird (*Orthotomus sutorius*) of Asia, belonging to the same family (Sylviidae), it stitches together broad leaves with cobweb or plant down to form a frame that holds the nest. (Gérard and Marie-Yvonne Morel, *Alauda* 1962)

Fig. 2.18. (*left*). Roofed nest of Purple Sunbird (*Nectarinia asiatica*), bound together with spider silk and placed in a spider web, Ceylon.
Fig. 2.19. (*right*). Roofed nest of Sulphur-rumped Flycatcher (*Myiobius sulphureipygius*), built of matted plant fibers, Panama Canal Zone. The nest entrance opens downward. (Alexander F. Skutch, *Life Histories of Central American Birds* 1960)

Fig. 2.20. Male Reichenow's Weaver (*Ploceus baglafecht reichenowi*) at his crudely woven nest with a side entrance, Nairobi, Kenya.

Fig. 2.21. Male Village Weaver (*Ploceus cucullatus*) with his woven and pensile nests, Uganda. The nest entrance opens downward.

Fig. 2.22. Colony of Village Weavers (*Ploceus cucullatus*) with many domed nests suspended in an acacia tree, Senegal.

Fig. 2.23. Colony of Chestnut-headed Oropendolas (*Psarocolius wagleri*, Icteridae) with long, pouch-shaped nests hanging in a tall tree, Costa Rica. (Photo: Mildred Mathias)

Fig. 2.24. Nest of Cassin's Malimbe (*Malimbus cassini*), a weaverbird that builds one of the most finely constructed nests in the world, eastern Zaire. The egg chamber is the upper part of the nest, while the entrance opens at the bottom of the long, vertical tube. (N. E. and E. C. Collias, *Univ. Calif. Publ. Zool.* 1964)

Fig. 2.25. A Grey-capped Social Weaver (*Pseudonigrita arnaudi*) looks out the bottom entrance of its roofed nest, which is thatched of dry grass stems, Kenya.

Fig. 2.26. A Sociable Weaver (*Philetairus socius*) holds a long straw for building, southwestern Africa.

1964). The orioles and oropendolas (Icteridae) of the New World, like the true weaverbirds (Ploceidae) of the Old World, weave their pendulous nests with strips of flexible materials.

Only one of the four or five subfamilies of the weaverbirds (Ploceidae) can be said truly to weave. The true weavers (Ploceinae) normally use fresh green materials for their nests, while the rest of the "weavers" thatch rather than weave their nests, often using dry, stiff grass stems (fig. 2.25). A whole series of steps can be traced from loose, crude, irregular weaving (fig. 2.20) to the close, neat, regular pattern that is to be found especially among those species of weavers that build pendulous nests with long entrance tubes (N. Collias and Collias 1964, N. Collias 1980). Cassin's Malimbe (*Malimbus cassini*) of central Africa (fig. 2.24) constructs the most skillfully made nest we know of in any bird.

The Compound Nest

The compound nest refers to a common nest mass with more than one compartment. Different pairs of birds or different females of the same species occupy separate compartments. Strictly speaking, there should also be some common feature of the nest that benefits all the residents.

There are instances in which different pairs of birds build their nests in close physical contact with other nests. Such cases may illustrate early steps in the evolution of a compound nest. In colonies of the Grey-capped Social Weaver (*Pseudonigrita arnaudi*) (fig. 2.25) of East Africa, a number of separate nests may be contiguous (N. Collias and Collias 1964, 1977, 1980). Many of the nests found in ant-gall acacias and sometimes in other acacias are grouped into masses (fig. 14.5), and we have seen up to twenty nests in one mass.

Only a few species of birds are known to build compound nests. The main examples are the Palmchat (*Dulus dominicus*) of Haiti (Wetmore and Swales 1931), the Monk Parakeet (*Myopsitta monachus*) of Argentina (Gibson 1880, Hudson 1920), the Buffalo Weaver (*Bubalornis albirostris*) of sub-Saharan Africa (Chapin 1954, Crook 1958, N. Collias and Collias 1964), and the Sociable Weaver (*Philetairus socius*) of southwestern Africa (N. Collias and Collias 1964, Maclean 1973, E. Collias and Collias 1978).

The most spectacular and largest compound nest known is built by the small sparrowlike Sociable Weaver, whose giant nest mass has often been likened to a haystack in a tree (figs. 2.26, 2.27). These nest masses are not woven but are thatched of dry stems, with the addition of many fine twigs in the roof. Each nest mass, and there may be half a dozen

Fig. 2.27. The huge communal nest of the Sociable Weaver is often likened to a haystack in a tree. Records of the colony in this Camelthorn Acacia go back 100 years.

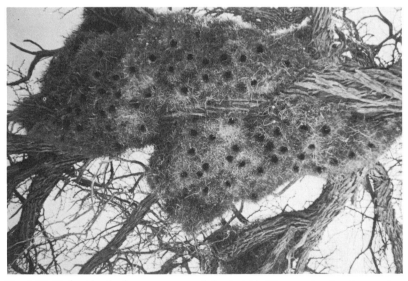

Fig. 2.28. Underside of a large nest mass of the Sociable Weaver, showing the openings of the many nest chambers in this bird "apartment-house." (N. E. and E. C. Collias, *Auk* 1977)

in one tree, is often several feet (1–2 m) thick, of irregular extent, and up to thirty feet (9 m) in the longest dimension. Each nest mass has a dome-shaped top and a relatively flat or irregularly shaped underside that is riddled with the openings of up to a hundred or more separate nest chambers (fig. 2.28). The common roof, on which many birds build together, may be one key to the evolution of the nest of this remarkable species, since it is a communal feature that enhances protection from predation for all—similar communal protection is provided by the outer, thorny shell in nests of the Buffalo Weaver, and by the projecting eaves in nests of the Monk Parakeet (N. Collias and Collias 1959a, 1963, 1964). Being domed, the roof also helps to shed the rain. The Sociable Weaver may breed in the Kalahari Desert at any time of year after suitable rains, even during the cold winter (Maclean 1973). The reduced temperature variations in larger nest masses compared with smaller ones, in conjunction with the social sleeping habits of the birds, give a selection pressure for the increased size of the nest mass in evolution (F. White et al. 1975).

Summary of More General Conclusions

The origin of bird nests can probably be traced back to the origin of the land egg in reptiles. The eggs of reptiles are often buried or concealed in pits in the ground, and generally take much longer to hatch than do those of most birds. Development of eggs in ancestral birds was speeded up with the beginning of direct parental incubation, which in turn was probably closely associated with the evolution of homeothermy and the ability to fly.

The primary function of a nest is to help the parent furnish warmth and safety to the developing eggs. By substituting in part for this function, nesting in cavities tends to block evolution of elaborate increment-nests, except as mere filling for the cavity. Small birds, being at a disadvantage in competing for most natural cavities as nest sites, were under greater selection pressure to construct their own nests.

Bird size influences the nature of the materials used in nests that are placed on the branches of trees and bushes. Large birds generally make twig platforms or bowls, while small birds, as a rule, make more compact and better enclosed cup-nests of finer materials, often binding these firmly together and to the substrate by use of spider or insect silk.

Domed nests are especially common among small, tropical passerine birds. Pensile nests with side or bottom entrances are often placed near tips of branches in trees, and presumably offer enhanced protection from predators. In turn, evolution of pensile or penduline nests was facilitated by a tough, woven construction—as seen among New World icterids and Old World weavers—or by firm binding with spider or insect silk—as among sunbirds, penduline titmice, and a number of other small passerines.

Compound nests, in which a number of birds occupy separate compartments in a common mass, are rare. The evolution of compound nests is associated with the origin of some feature of the nest mass that enhanced protection for all, such as a communal roof.

CHAPTER THREE

Speciation and Nest Building

THE major steps in the evolution of bird nests were indicated in the preceding chapter. These important steps can be investigated further by comparing closely related species or populations of the same species whose nest-building behaviors differ from each other in some major way. At the same time, since evolution integrates all aspects of the biology of a species, one can study the interrelation of various factors in the evolution of nest building. Mayr (1970:12) defines *species* as genetically distinctive "groups of interbreeding natural populations that are reproductively isolated from other such groups."

SPECIATION AND THE EVOLUTION OF NEST DIFFERENCES

In analyzing the evolution of nest building at the level of the species, a number of subsidiary problems are involved: (1) the taxonomic status of the species may need to be reexamined; (2) the roles of genetic factors and of experience in determining differences in nests between different species need to be determined; (3) the ecological factors and selection pressures associated with important nest variations between species must be investigated; and (4) the role of isolating factors leading to the division of species must be related to nest-building behavior. These four points are discussed in sequence below.

1. *Relation of nest building to taxonomic status of the species.* Stuhlmann's Weaver (*Othyphantes baglafecht stuhlmanni*) and Reichenow's Weaver (*O. b. reichenowi*) (fig. 2.20) of Africa, formerly considered separate species, are now believed to be one (Chapin 1954). Their nests differ in some respects: Stuhlmann's Weaver builds the outer shell of pieces and strips of grass leaves, whereas Reichenow's Weaver, inhabiting more arid country, often uses grass stems with leaves still attached in constructing the crudely woven outer shell of its nest (N. Collias and Collias 1964). On the other hand, after considerable study, Stein (1963) showed that the two types of Traill's Flycatcher, distinguished by their different songs and formerly thought to be of different races of one species (*Empidonax traillii*), represent distinct species, now known as

the Alder Flycatcher (*E. alnorum*) and the Willow Flycatcher (*E. traillii*). The Alder Flycatcher builds a loose, bulky nest mainly of grass stems and leaves like that of the Song Sparrow (*Melospiza melodia*); the Willow Flycatcher, a compact, cottony nest similar to that of the American Goldfinch (*Carduelis tristis*).

In the families of passerine birds, differences in nest form and structure may prove to be of value in the diagnosis of genera, as in swallows (Mayr and Bond 1943), swifts (Lack 1956), weaverbirds (N. Collias and Collias 1964), ovenbirds (Vaurie 1980), and probably in the diagnosis of New World flycatchers (Skutch 1960, Lanyon 1978, Traylor and Fitzpatrick 1982), and the Old World warblers (C. Harrison 1975).

2. *Genetic and experiential basis of nest building.* Almost nothing seems to be known about the genetics of nest building in birds. Dilger (1962) showed the operation of both genetic and experiential factors on the development of the ability to gather nest materials in different species of African parrots of the genus *Agapornis* (lovebirds). The Peach-faced Lovebird (*A. roseicollis*) cuts strips of bark and leaves, tucks them among the feathers of the lower back, and flies with them to a tree cavity, which it lines with the materials. Fischer's Lovebird (*A. personata*) also cuts strips of nest materials and carries them not in the back feathers but in the beak, one piece at a time. Hybrids between the two species attempted to tuck strips in their feathers but were unsuccessful in carrying them until they began to carry strips in their bills. It was about three years before the hybrids learned to cease generally irrelevant and ineffective attempts to tuck materials in their plumage.

Sargent (1965) found that a Zebra Finch (*Poephila guttata*) can develop a preference for new nest materials or new types of nest site based on its initial experience. Such a shift in preference based on experience could theoretically develop increased heritability by natural selection in any species of bird, if the new preference proves advantageous.

The importance of experience to nest building varies with the complexity of the nest built. Canaries make a simple cup-nest, and Hinde (1958) found that females raised in the absence of nest materials readily build normal nests as adults. On the other hand, in a similar experiment, we found that young male Village Weaverbirds (*Ploceus cucullatus*) raised without nest materials need considerable practice before they can build their complex nests (E. Collias and Collias 1964, 1973).

3. *Selection pressures in nest-building behavior.* The course evolution has taken can be determined by looking at closely related species, but insight into the selection pressures involved comes from the study of

cases of convergent evolution. For example, weaving of the nest is obviously convergent between the New World icterids and the Old World weaverbirds. In both cases, a common nest site is found among reeds or other aquatic vegetation over water, or else in trees towards the tips of branches. In either case, weaving helps bind the nest to a difficult substrate and makes possible the use of a nest site relatively safe from predators.

The principle of preadaptation is related to the modification of selection pressures. The Sacred Kingfisher (*Halcyon sancta*) of Australia drills a hole for its nest in a tree or in an arboreal termite nest. Nesting in tree holes preadapted it for nesting in arboreal termite nests. Another kingfisher, the Laughing Kookaburra (*Dacelo novaeguineae*), nests in tree holes throughout most of Australia, but in the northern half of Australia it often drills into an arboreal termite nest (Beruldsen 1980).

An example of a major step in the evolution of nest building is that between ground- and tree-nesting. There are examples of both types within the same species. The Brown Pelican (*Pelecanus occidentalis*) and the Double-crested Cormorant (*Phalacrocorax auritus*) may make practically no nest at all when nesting on the ground, but these same species will build elaborate nests in trees (Van Tets 1965). In Australia, the Royal Spoonbill (*Platalea regia*) builds a nest of twigs in a tree—usually one growing in water—or it may trample down reeds to make a nest platform in a reed bed (Beruldsen 1980).

In species of birds that nest either on the ground or in trees, the direction of subsequent evolution will probably depend on ecological conditions. Nests on islands devoid of predators are likely to be placed on the ground; on the mainland, nests in trees are often safer. Measurement of the amount of predation or of nest losses in different situations shows which nest sites are safest. In the prairie country of northwestern Oklahoma where there are few trees, Downing (1959) found in a Mourning Dove (*Zenaida macroura*) population 49 percent success in 167 tree nests but only 29 percent success in 130 ground nests. Specific sites in the tree may be more or less favorable. Nice (1922) found that 39 Mourning Dove nests in crotches were almost twice as successful in producing young large enough to fly as were 59 nests on branches.

Another major step in nest evolution was the development of the domed nest. Nonpasserine birds generally build open nests, and open nests probably preceded the evolution of domed nests. Some nonpasserine birds—including rails, button quails, and coucals (relatives of cuckoos)—build a canopy over their nest, which is usually on or near the ground. The Lesser Coucal (*Centropus toulou*) of India builds a domed nest on or near the ground, often among tussocks of grass, with the living grass blades of the substrate worked into a dome. The Common Coucal (*C. sinensis*) of India places its domed nest within a thick bush or bamboo clump, or among the branches of a tree at moderate heights, usually well concealed among tangled vines. The dome may be formed by intertwining living foliage and creeper stems over the nest cup (Ali and Ripley 1969).

It is not certain whether or not the ancestral passerine had a domed nest. Several primitive passerine families contain species that build domed nests on or near the ground (tapaculos, pittas, ovenbirds, New Zealand wrens, lyrebirds, and scrub-birds). The tapaculos (Rhinocryptidae) of Central and South America, an ancient suboscine group, is known from the Eocene (Brodkorb 1971), and some species build a cup-nest or a domed nest in a hole that they dig in the ground (C. Harrison 1978). Possibly, the ancestors of passerine birds dug a nest tunnel, but if early passerines began placing their nests at or near the surface of the ground, natural selection might have favored the building of a roofed nest of plant materials to replace the shelter of the tunnel. Among nonpasserines, the groundrollers (Coraciidae, Brachypteraciinae) of Madagascar may well resemble the ancestors of passerine birds (Feduccia 1980:157). Many Coraciiformes do not line their nest tunnels, but the Long-tailed Groundroller (*Uratelornis chimaera*) digs a nest hole in soil and lines the nest chamber with plant materials (Appert 1968).

The Magpie (*Pica pica*) often builds a roofed nest, but where it has the protection of dense thorny bushes, it builds an open nest (Linsdale 1937). Similarly, the Great Kiskadee (*Pitangus sulphuratus*), a Neotropical flycatcher, builds a roofed nest in exposed situations, but may build an open nest in concealed places (W. Smith 1962), as do several species of babblers and Old World warblers in southern Asia (Ali and Ripley 1971–1973). It would seem that a tendency to build a roof over a nest in an exposed situation is a very ancient trait among small land birds.

4. *Isolation of species and nest building.* Isolation and separation of different populations of a species, generally by geographic barriers, may lead to the division of a species into two or more species, particularly if the habitats in the separate areas differ. Geographic isolation may be associated with differences in nest-building behavior. Fodies (*Foudia*) are weaverbirds restricted to various islands of the Indian Ocean. The Madagascar Fody (*F. madagascariensis*) of open cultivated country builds a rather crude domed nest of heterogeneous materials, often placed in low bushes (Rand 1936). The Forest Fody (*F. eminentissima*) in the evergreen forest of the Comoro Islands builds its nest largely of thin

strong tendrils, and it covers the upper half with moss (Benson 1960). The Seychelles Fody (*F. seychellarum*) nests in low trees on three small islands in the Seychelles, and its bulky nest of heterogeneous materials is even more crude than that of the Madagascar Fody (Crook 1961).

An example of an important continental geographic barrier to bird distribution is the immense expanse of lowland rain forest and moist woodland that covers much of central Africa, separating wide areas of acacia savanna to the north from similar areas to the south. Many savanna birds, especially weaverbirds, are represented by different sub-species or by different, though closely related, species north and south of the rain forest (Hall and Moreau 1970). The Masked Weaver (*Ploceus velatus*) is the common weaver of thorn savanna and scrub in Africa. The nest of its northern subspecies, the Vitelline Masked Weaver (*P.v. vitellinus*), is peculiar in that the grass strips on the outside of the domed nest run parallel to each other from the bottom entrance to the top of the nest without being crossed by other strips. This striking parallel arrangement is not found in the nest of the Southern Masked Weaver (*P.v. velatus*).

In general, living species of birds arose in the Quarternary period (Brodkorb 1971), during times of tremendous worldwide climatic fluc-tuations accompanying successive glacial and interglacial periods. Dif-ferences in the expansion or restriction of rain forest, montane vege-tation, woodlands, savanna, grasslands, or deserts correspondingly influenced bird distribution and speciation. In Africa vegetational barriers were repeatedly formed and broken, particularly in East Africa during the Pleistocene epoch, and speciation was thereby accelerated. Kenya, in East Africa, has more species of weaverbirds (Ploceinae) than do all of western or southern Africa, despite its much smaller area (Moreau 1960).

Speciation is a more rapid process than used to be thought. Populations of the House Sparrow (*Passer domesticus*), introduced into North Amer-ica in the middle of the last century, have already—within only about a hundred generations—differentiated morphological and color differ-ences to a degree usually characterizing subspecies (Johnston and Se-lander 1964). It is probable that some differences in the nest-building behavior of related species of birds have evolved in historic times.

IMPLICATION OF THE NEST SITE FOR EVOLUTION

An excellent example of how the nature of the nest site may influence the evolution of many other aspects of the life history of birds is the adaptation of the Black-legged Kittiwake (*Rissa tridactyla*) to cliff-nesting, studied by Cullen (1957) on the Farne Islands off the coast of England. The great majority of gulls, such as the Herring Gull (*Larus argentatus*) and the Common Black-head Gull (*L. ridibundus*), nest on more or less level ground, presumably the ancestral breeding habitat. But Kittiwakes fasten their nests to very narrow ledges on steep cliffs by building a mud platform that helps make a level base for the nest on the often-slanting ledges. To begin the nest the Kittiwakes bring mud or soil, often mixed with roots or grass tufts. Sometimes they alternate the trips for mud with trips for grass, seaweed, or other fibrous material. The bird shakes the sticky mud loose from the open bill, bit by bit, onto the nesting platform with jerky movements of the head. It then tramples the material down with rhythmic movements of the feet until the mud and fibers are stamped into a firm platform. Ground-nesting gulls do not use mud and often gather materials near the nest; when building they show few jerking movements and only traces of trampling. Kittiwakes must often collect nest materials well away from the nesting cliff. For this reason stealing nest materials from a neighboring nest is much more common among Kittiwakes than among ground-nesting gulls, and nests are more closely guarded by the former. Partly finished nests left unguarded may be dismantled completely by other Kittiwakes. Normally, both mates take turns guarding the nest.

Cliff-nesting reduces predation not only from ground predators such as foxes, but also from large gulls. Cullen never saw a single Kittiwake egg taken from the nest by Herring Gulls or Lesser Black-backed Gulls (*L. fuscus*), which frequently preyed on the eggs and young of ducks and terns nesting on the ground nearby. Unlike ground-nesting gulls, Kittiwakes rarely attack predators. Whereas the alarm call of ground-nesting gulls against predators is often heard, the Kittiwake rarely gives the alarm call. As losses from predators are relatively slight, a clutch of two eggs suffices to replace the population of the Kittiwake, compared with a normal clutch size of three eggs in ground-nesting gulls. During incubation, ground-nesting gulls leave the nest in order to defecate, and when the young hatch, the parents carry away the conspicuous eggshells that might attract predators. But a Kittiwake simply defecates over the rim of the nest causing a conspicuous white stain to form on the side of the cliff below. The eggshells lie on the nest until they are accidentally knocked off. Young ground-nesting gulls are cryptically colored and when a predator approaches they run to hide under cover. But downy young Kittiwakes are conspicuously white and light gray and stay in the nest.

The number of potential nest sites is more limited on a cliff than on the ground, and there seems to be more competition for nest sites on cliffs. In threatening an opponent, ground-nesting gulls stretch the neck upward, preparing to peck downward, but such an upright threat-posture is not suitable for the different levels on which cliff nests are placed. Instead, a Kittiwake attempts to seize the bill of an opponent and force it off the cliff with a twisting motion.

Male Kittiwakes occupy and defend their nesting ledges on the cliff as soon as they arrive from the winter quarters. Pair formation takes place on the nesting ledges, whereas in ground-nesting gulls the pairs often form on neutral ground and only later occupy the nest sites. The male Kittiwake advertises himself to prospective mates by a special "choking" display in which he jerks his head, neck, and open bill rhythmically up and down. The male goes to the nest or a prospective nest site and chokes there; this behavior at once attracts the female, who may approach and join in. There is some question whether choking evolved from the regurgitation movements used in feeding chicks, or from displacement nest-building activity; both elements may be involved (Tinbergen 1969). Choking is closely associated with the nest site and is the normal advertisement display of the unmated male in Kittiwakes, but not ground-nesting gulls.

Kittiwakes are adapted in various ways to keep from falling off the cliff. They have sharp claws and strong feet. Unlike the female ground-nesting gull who stands during copulation and may shift about a little, the female Kittiwake sits, bracing herself firmly against the weight of the male on her back. The deep nest cup better safeguards the eggs from being accidentally kicked out, which would likely result in falling and breaking, than does the shallow nest of ground-nesting gulls. Kittiwake chicks generally face toward the wall of the cliff. If attacked by other chicks in the nest when competing to be fed by the parent, the chick has a special appeasement ceremony: it turns its head away from the opponent and hides its beak in its plumage. This action is made more conspicuous by a black band across the back of the neck in young Kittiwakes that is found in no other gulls.

Young ground-nesting gulls leave the nest a few days after hatching and hide in nearby cover. Young Kittiwakes are confined to the cliff nest and have to be fed at the nest site until about six weeks of age when they can fly. When a ground-nesting gull comes with food, it may give a feeding call that attracts the young, which are then fed by regurgitation at any place in the territory. The Kittiwake parent has no feeding call. All gulls feed the young by regurgitation, but whereas the food is often dropped on the ground by the parent ground-nesting gull, the Kittiwake feeds its young directly from its throat, maintaining nest sanitation. Both young and adults will pick up and throw out strange objects falling into the cliff nest, but such nest cleaning is absent or rare in ground-nesting gulls. Sometimes the whole Kittiwake nest collapses, precipitating the young off the cliff, so it appears that cliff-nesting is still being perfected in this gull through natural selection.

The many ways in which nesting on steep cliffs affects general behavior and life history justify the conclusion that "the Kittiwake stands as a beautiful example of the general rule that adaptation involves the whole animal" (Tinbergen 1969:217).

Speciation and Evolution of Nest Building in the Weaverbirds (Ploceinae)

The object of this section is to illustrate how different taxonomic categories may show different levels of adaptation and different stages in the evolution of nest building and related behavior. The members of the family Ploceidae build domed nests, a characteristic of many tropical passerine birds. The subfamily Ploceinae is the only one of four subfamilies in the family Ploceidae (Mayr and Greenway 1962) that truly weaves the nest. There is a current tendency by some taxonomists to raise all these subfamilies to family rank, but regardless of the level of taxonomic category recognized, these four groups together with the Estrildidae (grass finches and allies), form a cluster of closely related groups (Sibley and Ahlquist 1980).

Subfamily Level: Origin of Nest Weaving

The Ploceinae, or true weavers, probably originated in open country where most species are still found, particularly in the acacia savanna of Africa. The ability to weave was a primary adaptation, enabling the birds to fasten their nests in places relatively safe from predators—such as from the tips of hanging branches, or between reeds over waters. The true weavers were then able to spread and to occupy a variety of diverse habitats, with concomitant speciation.

Unlike other subfamilies of Ploceidae—such as the Passerinae (sparrows and allies), which merely thatch their nest of dry straws or other materials—the Ploceinae weave their nests of interlocking loops of flexible green materials. Inexperienced young male Village Weavers (*Ploceus cucullatus*) show an increasing preference for green over other colors of nest materials, a preference that guides them to flexible materials suitable for weaving.

Another characteristic of the Ploceinae is the great importance of the nest in courtship (J. Emlen 1957, N. Collias and Collias 1959b). The male weaves all or most of the nest and then attempts to attract an unmated female to the nest with special displays and call-notes. The unmated female will not choose a male without a nest, nor a nest without a male (J. Emlen 1957, Victoria 1969). In choosing among males, the female Village Weaver is influenced by the frequency of male displays of the species-typical colors, and she prefers a fresh green nest to old, weak nests that have turned brown (N. Collias and Victoria 1978, Jacobs et al. 1978). Painting the wings of males black to look like those of the closely related Black Weaver (*Ploceus nigerrimus*) significantly reduced their success in attracting mates (E. Collias et al. 1979).

In the Ploceinae, the high intensity of sexual selection, or the different effects of natural selection on the two sexes, must account for the prevalence of sex dichromatism and the high rate of speciation. The females of different species frequently appear very similar while the males often differ greatly. The relatively large number of species (92) in the Ploceinae is correlated with a high percentage of species having strong sex dichromatism, three times as many as in the related subfamily Passerinae, which has only thirty-seven species. The important use of the nest in courtship has probably facilitated sexual selection and speciation in the Ploceinae.

Adaptive Radiation of Nests among Different Genera or Species Groups of Weavers

Detailed descriptions of different weaverbird nests are available in our monograph (N. Collias and Collias 1964) and in reviews by Crook (1963) and by Schnell (1973). In general, our account of the nests confirms and agrees with Chapin's (1954) classification of the weaverbirds. Chapin also helped arrange the sequence of Ploceidae genera for *Peters' Checklist of Birds of the World* (Mayr and Greenway 1962). Moreau, who decided the grouping of species into genera for this checklist, lumped together many genera into *Ploceus* that Chapin (1954) had placed in separate genera. There is an endless argument among taxonomists between "lumpers" who emphasize similarities and "splitters" who emphasize differences. Mayr (1969:238) suggests that, rather than trying to name formally all shades of taxonomic difference or similarity among species, one use the informal category *species group*. Chapin's genera can be considered subgenera or species groups in Moreau's classification, but in either case they are useful as guides to real differences in the birds and their nests. Morlion (1980) finds that the distribution of feather tracts on the body corresponds with several of Chapin's genera.

Figure 3.1 illustrates the evolution of nest form and structure in the

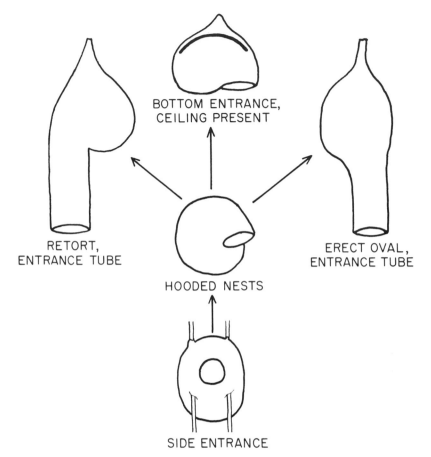

Fig. 3.1. Evolution of nest form in the true weaverbirds (Ploceinae). (N. E. and E. C. Collias, *Univ. Calif. Publ. Zool.* 1964)

Ploceinae. There are two main types of nest, one with the long axis of the brood chamber vertical, the second with the long axis horizontal. The first type generally has a side entrance, is often placed in herbaceous vegetation, and is found in the genera *Amblyospiza, Foudia, Quelea* and *Euplectes*, as well as among Asiatic species of *Ploceus*. The second type of nest generally has a bottom entrance, is often placed in trees, and is found in almost all African *Ploceus* and in *Malimbus*. Long entrance tubes giving some protection against predators such as snakes have evolved convergently in nests of certain Asiatic weavers (erect oval, fig. 3.1 *right*) and African weavers (retort, fig. 3.1 *left*).

Each type of nest has probably evolved convergently more than once. All the variations shown in figure 3.1 are also found *within* Moreau's broad genus *Ploceus*, which includes forty-eight African, five Asiatic, and two Madagascar species. This genus could be compared with an average of about five species per genus of birds in general (Mayr 1969). Nest variations and species groups equivalent to Chapin's genera (in parentheses) representing each nest type within *Ploceus* are: side entrance (*Ploceëlla*), hooded side entrance (*Othyphantes*), bottom entrance with ceiling (*Textor*), retort with entrance tube but no ceiling (*Hyphanturgus*), and erect oval with entrance tube (*Ploceus* of Asia). Another good species group within *Ploceus* is that of the nuthatch weavers (*Phormoplectes*), the different species of which line their nests with *Usnea* lichens. They inhabit montane and lowland forests and moist woodlands in Africa, and creep about trees and branches in the manner of nuthatches.

The other main genus of Ploceinae, *Euplectes*, has sixteen species and illustrates regressive evolution in weaving. In this genus, one species group (bishop birds) have short tails and often nest in emergent vegetation over water. The other species group (widowbirds) have long tails and usually place their nests in grassland on or near the ground; the male's weaving may be little more than a green canopy over the thick lining of grassheads put in by the females. Weaving is of little use in a nest placed on the ground like that of the Long-tailed Widowbird (*E. progne*). Male *Euplectes* are often brilliantly and distinctively colored, while the females appear dull and sparrowlike and often resemble each other closely in the different species. Comparing different species of *Euplectes*, Craig (1980) finds that elaboration of the flight display accompanies a decline in nest building by the male. The male Jackson's Widowbird (*E. jacksoni*), by dancing and calling, attracts unmated females to a tuft of grass, which is apparently a "symbolic nest," in the center of his cleared display area. The female builds the brood nest elsewhere (Van Someren 1958).

Nest Evolution within Genera or within Species Groups

The genus *Malimbus* consists of red and black weavers of the African lowland rainforest. Its species are very similar to those in *Ploceus*, but males of the latter genus are usually yellow or yellow and black. Different species of *Malimbus* use different nest materials, and they show particularly well the evolutionary trend from loose, coarse, irregular stitches to tight, fine, regular weaving—the climax being the nest of *M. cassini* (fig. 2.24). In *Malimbus*, Brosset (1978) observed communal construction of large and elaborate nests by more than two birds in the species *cassini* and *coronatus*, but only one pair bred in the nest after it was

Fig. 3.2. Nests of Giant Weaver (*Ploceus grandis*) and Village Weaver (*P. cucullatus*). Nest of *P. grandis* (left) collected by René de Naurois, Saõ Tomé Island, western Africa.

completed. In species with smaller and simpler nests only the male (*nitens*) or the pair (*malimbicus*) builds the nest.

Hall and Moreau (1970) recognize five species in the *Ploceus cucullatus* species group. These species differ in their nesting habitats. The nests of this group have special ceilings and short or no entrance tubes. The Village Weaver (*P. cucullatus*) is one of the most common and widespread weavers of Africa, being found in forest clearings, in open cultivated country, in villages, or near water. The male is about 6½ inches (16.5 cm) long. The Giant Weaver (*P. grandis*) is a related species, endemic to the island of São Thomé off western Africa in the Gulf of Guinea, and is the largest, known true weaver. The males are about 8½ inches long (21.5 cm) and weave a correspondingly large nest (fig. 3.2) compared with that of the Village Weaver. The nest of the Giant Weaver is less pensile, being supported by twigs laced into the outer layer, but it also has a special ceiling and in other ways resembles the nest of the Village Weaver. But whereas the Village Weaver nests in colonies in open country with many nests in one tree, the nests of the Giant Weaver occur singly in forests (de Naurois and Wolters 1975).

The three other species of this group are *spekei, spekeoides,* and *nigerrimus.* Speke's Weaver (*P. spekei*) of East Africa rather closely resembles the Village Weaver in its nest, body size, and coloration, but is more of a highland bird, and usually nests away from water. Fox's Weaver (*P. spekeoides*), restricted to a small area in Uganda, is almost identical in plumage to Speke's Weaver but has a short tail; being confined to large swamps, it always builds over water. The Black Weaver (*P. n. nigerrimus*)and its other subspecies, the Chestnut-and-Black Weaver (*P. n. castaneofuscus*), are found especially in clearings in the rain forest of western and central Africa.

When courting unmated females, males of this species group hang from the bottom entrance of the nest, flap their wings, and call. The different species illustrate at least three different ways in which the male facilitates the entrance of the female to inspect his nest: (1) the male Village Weaver stops beating his wings just before and as the female enters; (2) the male Chestnut-and-Black Weaver, whose nest is placed in denser foliage, beats or flutters his wings rapidly through a short arc well below the horizontal and away from the nest entrance; and (3) the male Speke's Weaver hangs his head and body downward from the entrance while he flaps his wings (N. Collias and Collias 1970). The nests of these three species are very similar.

Nest Evolution within a Species

Within a species, such as the Village Weaver, the different functions of a nest may be of different relative importance in different parts of the geographic range, and different parts of the nest may differ accordingly. The bottom lining gives insulation for the eggs and young, the ceiling helps shed the rain, the nest form and structure may be adapted for protection from predation, and the nest itself is used by the male to attract a mate. The different races of the Village Weaver have been described by Chapin (1954).

In a brood nest of the race *P.c. graueri* from a cool mountainous area in central Africa, we counted twice as many pieces of nest material in the lining as in nests of two other subspecies from warmer climates in western (*P.c. cucullatus*) and in southern (*P.c. spilonotus*) Africa. The increased insulation must help keep the eggs and young warmer in the colder climate (N. Collias and Collias 1971a, 1971b).

The South African subspecies of the Village Weaver (*P.c. spilonotus*), also known as the Spotted-backed Weaver, differs from the other subspecies in that the male has a yellow crown, whereas most or all of the crown is black in the other races. The proportion of brood-nests that fledged any young in a colony of *spilonotus* in South Africa was less than half of that from another colony of *P.c. cucullatus* we watched in western Africa (Senegal). There are usually three eggs to a clutch of *spilonotus*, two of *cucullatus*. This difference probably reflects a difference in average nest mortality, much of which must be caused by predation.

Most of the differences in behavior between these two races that we observed were small and quantitative and could be accounted for by greater predation pressure on the South African colony (N. Collias and Collias 1971c). A strong tendency of *spilonotus* to nest in reeds over water rather than in trees gives added protection from some predators. The Banded Harrier Hawk (*Polyboroides typus*) often attacks weaverbird colonies removing nestlings from the nests, but when a hawk of this species tried to seize a nest of *spilonotus* suspended from a reed while we were observing the nest, the reed swung down and about to such an extent that the hawk gave up its predatory efforts. When nesting in trees, the male *spilonotus*, instead of spending most of his time in his territory in the peripheral branches as the male *cucullatus* does, often rests near the center of the tree where there is more foliage and he is better hidden. But if a female or rival male visits his territory, he speedily returns. The male *spilonotus* in the course of a territorial dispute bows his head much less frequently than does a male *cucullatus*, probably permitting more effective monitoring of the surroundings in case of the sudden appearance of a hawk. Also, male *spilonotus* engage in severe fights less often than do male *cucullatus*. Male *spilonotus* weave their nests much faster and build fewer nests, reducing the length of time they are exposed to danger. They also use split strips in nest construction more often, weaving the ends in different directions, making a tighter nest that is more resistant to being torn open by a predator.

When copulating, birds may not be very attentive to danger from enemies. This vulnerability is reduced in *spilonotus*, which unlike *cucullatus* often mate outside the territory, well away from the nest. The incubating female *spilonotus*, like the female *cucullatus*, leaves her nest at frequent intervals to feed, but on returning, the former is more likely to fly directly into her nest and less likely to perch in the open nearby.

The Village Weaver is polygynous but the degree of polygyny varied in the colonies from different subspecies that we studied in western, central, and southern Africa (table 3.1) (N. Collias and Collias 1971a, 1971b; N. Collias 1980). During a two-week period in the main part of the breeding season, males of the western race (*cucullatus*) averaged

TABLE 3.1. Nests, polygyny, and nestling care in three races of *Ploceus cucullatus*

	Western Africa *cucullatus*	Central Africa *graueri*	Southern Africa *spilonotus*
Aver. min. temp. when breeding	24°C	11°C	14°C
Number of males	9	18	11
Nests per male at start	5.1	2.4	3.5
Nests built in two weeks	3.3	1.4	1.9
Mates per male	3.1	1.8	2.0
Feeding rate per hour per nest:			
By male	0.1	2.3	1.4
By female	4.1	4.7	4.2
Number of nests	15	11	39
Nest-hours observed	52	95	86

three mates each, whereas in a comparable period males of the central race (*graueri*) and those of the southern race (*spilonotus*) averaged only two mates each. During this same time the west African males built on the average significantly more nests than did the males from the other two areas. In the west African race the male almost never helped the female feed the nestlings, whereas males from the other two races took a very substantial share in this task.

As the climate in western Africa, in the area of our study in northwest Senegal, was much warmer than in the other localities, the nestlings there needed less food, and in fact the feeding rate by the parents was less than in the other two races. The female of the west African race was able to rear the young alone, enabling the male to devote more of his time to building nests to attract additional mates.

SUMMARY

Before considering speciation and the evolution of nest-building behavior in any taxonomic group of birds, it may be necessary to review the taxonomic status and classification of the species concerned. Species are generally assumed to differ genetically, but when considering behavior both genetic and experiential contributions to the difference in behavior need to be related to each other. The heritability contribution can be increased by natural selection.

It is profitable to consider groups of related species in order to discern the direction of evolution, whereas convergent evolution among unrelated species gives clues to the nature of the selection pressures. Instances of major variations in nest construction within a species are of particular value in the study of the selection pressures that have led to important stages in nest evolution. Differences in nest building among species can be related to isolating factors in the same way as can other characteristics of the species.

The nature of the site used by a species for nesting may profoundly influence many other aspects of its behavior and life history, emphasizing the principle that adaptation involves the whole animal. This principle is illustrated by a cliff-nesting gull, the Kittiwake (*Rissa tridactyla*).

Different taxonomic levels illustrate different degrees of adaptation in nest-building behavior, as is exemplified by the weaverbird family (Ploceidae). In this family, the domed nest, typical of many tropical passerines, characterizes the entire family. At the subfamily level, only the Ploceinae weave their nests, a primary adaptation the evolution of which was accelerated by increased use of the nest in courtship. Adaptive radiation of nest form at the level of genera or of species groups is related to the occupation of diverse habitats and nest sites, and particularly to predation pressure. Among species we find evolution of differences in habitat and nest sites, in nature of nest materials, in closeness of weave, in size of the nest, in number of birds building the nest, and in courtship related to the nest. At the level of subspecies there is evolution of quantitative differences, as in the amount of nest insulation, number of nests built by each male, and differences relating to predation pressure in the rate at which the male builds his nests, in the amount of time he spends in his territory, and in how quickly the female enters her nest after a period of absence.

CHAPTER FOUR

Mate Selection and Nest Building

PAIR formation in birds is closely related to nest-building behavior as seen in the selection of the nest site and in the use of nest materials by many birds during the courtship and pair-formation process. To attract a mate the male often advertises a potential nest site, nest cavity, or a more complete nest that he has constructed. In some birds manipulation of symbolic nest materials by the male helps attract the female.

Darwin (1871) advanced the theory of sexual selection to account particularly for the secondary sexual characteristics of animals. Unlike natural selection, sexual selection, he says, "depends on the advantage which certain individuals have over individuals of the same sex and species, in exclusive relation to reproduction" (I:256). But "in a multitude of cases the males which conquer other males, do not obtain possession of the females, independently of choice on the part of the latter. . . . The females are most excited by, or prefer pairing with, the more ornamented males, or those which are the best songsters, or play the best antics" (I:262).

Darwin, however, had very little to say about the role of nest-building behavior in courtship and mate selection, the importance of which we attempt to develop as a broad generalization in this chapter. Our object is to focus on mate selection in relation to nest-site selection and nest-building behavior, and not to drift into a general discussion of sexual selection theory. That theory has been reviewed in recent years in a book edited by Campbell (1972: see especially chaps. by Mayr, Trivers, and Selander), and in other reviews by Wilson (1975), S. T. Emlen and Oring (1977), Searcy (1982), and Bateson (1983). The most important and relevant principle here is that the female can generally be expected to be the more discriminating sex because she usually invests more in the care of the young. Many studies indicate that it is indeed the female bird who usually makes the final choice of a nest site.

SELECTION OF THE NEST SITE

Either the male or female bird, or both, may select the nest site depending on the species. There is often a subtle interplay between the two sexes, and competition with other birds may also be involved. In the Greater Rhea (*Rhea americana*), a large, flightless, running bird of the vast pampas grasslands of Argentina, the male builds the nest (Bruning 1974). After driving off other males and taking over a harem, usually of six to eight hens, the male induces the females to follow him by a special display, spreading and drooping his wings, and bobbing and swaying his head. He tramples down and scrapes out a circular place in the grass and builds a rim of grass, sticks, and dirt at the edge of the nest. He then leads a female to this nest, in or next to which she lays an egg. The male rolls the egg into the nest, and he alone incubates the eggs, which may be contributed by up to fifteen hens. Eventually the nest may contain two dozen or more eggs. Many male rheas build several nests, but until the females begin laying eggs, the male does not remain at any one nest location. After a male starts incubating, the females may move on to lay eggs for another male.

In the monogamous Canada Goose (*Branta canadensis*) the female selects the nest site. After the birds pair, she leads the male on exploratory jaunts, poking about with her beak at promising sites, such as small islets heaped with twigs and grass, or spots along the shore with a good supply of dry weed stalks for building. If a desirable nest site is already occupied by another pair of geese, the male, who is larger and more aggressive than the female, will forge ahead to take the lead in driving away the other birds. The search for a suitable nest site might take one or many days, depending on the dominance status of the male relative to competitors for specific sites. Once a nest site has been chosen, the female Canada Goose alone builds the nest and incubates the eggs, while the male stands guard nearby (N. Collias and Jahn 1959).

In many species of birds the two sexes hunt for and inspect potential sites together, but usually the female makes the final decision. In many shore birds the male and female each make a number of nest scrapes in the ground before the female lays eggs in one. Among Greenshanks (*Tringa nebularia*), a sandpiper studied for many years in Scotland by the Nethersole-Thompsons (1944), "while the pair normally together seek a nest-site the hen generally peremptorily disposes of the cock's proposals."

Most Australian grass-finches (Estrildidae) nest in bushes or small trees. In the search for a nest site the male leads his mate and indicates potential nesting places. As soon as he has found a suitable fork of a branch he attracts the female's attention to it by hopping back and forth, uttering special calls. "The final choice is then made by the female. If she refuses she flies away and the male has to look for another nesting-site. Sometimes the male proposes up to more than one hundred sites before the female finally accepts one." The female does not look for a nest site by herself but waits for the proposals of the male. She indicates acceptance by staying at the fork, and the male then brings materials to her that she builds into a nest (Immelmann 1965).

When selecting a nest site, a female bird—besides responding to the male's invitation—is influenced by the following factors:

1. *Local food availability.* Male Red-winged Blackbirds (*Agelaius phoeniceus*) are often monogamous, bigamous, or polygynous (Orians 1972), and the variance in breeding success may be greater for males than for females (Payne 1979). The female may prefer to mate with a territorial male having a rich supply of food in his territory, even though he already has another mate, rather than to pair with a bachelor male having a food-poor territory (Orians 1971, 1972, 1980). Lenington (1980) found that Red-winged Blackbirds on a marsh near Princeton fed almost entirely on the marsh itself. The males arrived first in the spring and set up territories. The order in which females chose male territories reflected differences in food quality of the territory. Ten territorial aspects presumed important to female choice were measured, and those that gave the highest positive correlations with the number of young fledged from successful nests were just those that reflected better food quality in the territory—for example, the amount of cattail edge. Insect emergence within a lake or marsh is greatest at the edge of vegetation, and Redwing nestlings are fed on insects.

2. *Presence of suitable nest materials.* Female Canada Geese searching for a nest site ignored islets heaped with branches and twigs until some marsh hay, suitable for nest building, was placed on them. They then promptly showed interest (N. Collias and Jahn 1959).

3. *Shelter from the physical environment.* In Argentina, Greater Rheas usually build in a shaded area or in tall grass. Nests in very sunny, short-grass areas often failed as the weather got hotter toward the end of the breeding season (Bruning 1974).

4. *Security from predators.* In its native home in Australia the Zebra Finch (*Poephila guttata*) prefers to nest in thorny shrubs, but it sometimes nests in the large stick nests of birds of prey, where it is well protected from predators (Immelmann 1965:141).

NEST-BUILDING BEHAVIOR IN COURTSHIP

Many species of birds from many families incorporate some elements of nest-building behavior into the male's courtship of the female, both in pair-formation displays and in precoitional displays. The degree to which nest-building behavior is used in courtship varies from mere manipulation of a piece of nest material, or display of a potential nest site, to the building of an entire nest by the male—except for the lining which is ordinarily put in by the female after she has accepted the nest. Symbolic holding of nest materials in the beak during courtship displays is characteristic of birds as different as grebes, boobies, and finches.

The male Blue-footed Booby (*Sula nebouxii*) picks up a scrap of material and presents it to the female with a high sweep of his head before placing it in the nest, where the pair bend their heads together and busily "build" in this fragment (B. Nelson 1968:191). Nelson has called this "symbolic nest-building" because it has nothing to do with producing a real nest for holding the egg or young. This species nests on the ground in the Galapagos Islands, and the nest may contain little or no useful nesting material (fig. 2.9). By observing a color-ringed pair the Nelsons discovered that the blue-foots may defend and use in turn two or three different nest sites before the female lays her eggs in one. According to Van Tets (1965:44) several types of courtship bowing displays in the Pelecaniformes (pelicans, boobies, and cormorants) probably evolved independently from nest-building movements.

The male Song Sparrow (*Melospiza melodia*) normally does not assist the female in building the nest, yet early in the breeding cycle he may pick up and carry nesting material in his bill. Both male and female indulge in this symbolic nesting—the male more often than his mate— and this activity is most frequent at the time that copulations begin (Nice 1943:177–178).

During pair formation among the grass-finches of Australia, the male first directs his singing and courtship to a number of different females in succession. His courtship dance is a vertical up-and-down bob achieved by alternate stretching and bending of the legs. The final stage of courtship is the female's invitation for copulation. "In some species the male holds a piece of grass during courtship, which is clearly to be understood as a nesting symbol. In other species this symbol has disappeared, and other activities (beak-wiping, bowing, body-shaking, etc.) have been taken over into courtship as a substitute" (Immelmann 1965:5). During courtship, the male African Waxbill (*Estrilda astrild*), another estrilidid finch, holds a feather in his beak (fig. 4.1), clearly a nesting symbol (Steiner 1955, Immelman 1980:187).

Use of nest-building movements as a part of courtship is well exemplified by the scrape-ceremony of shore birds, in which both sexes participate. The male Mountain Plover (*Charadrius montanus*) of the short-grass prairies of the western United States, when courting the female, presses his breast against the ground and scrapes back each foot

Fig. 4.1. Male Waxbill (*Estrilda astrild*) holds a feather in his beak while courting the female. (After Steiner 1955.)

alternately while he moves his spread tail up and down, frequently pivoting about ninety degrees. Then he stands and throws nest material with his beak along one side of his body. Many nest scrapes are scattered throughout the male's territory. After the male scrapes, the female either replaces the male in his scrape, or else she scrapes nearby. When she moves off, the male follows, goes through further courtship posturing, and if she stops he mounts and copulates. The scraping ceremony is both a precoital and a pair-formation type of courtship. A female initially visits the territories of several males, but she soon develops a preference for certain males (Graul 1974).

In many birds that nest in holes or cavities, the male first establishes ownership of a particular nest site and then he endeavors to attract an unmated female by special invitation displays (Nethersole-Thompson 1944, von Haartman 1957, Skutch 1976). Common examples among passerine birds of the United States include the House Wren, and in Europe the House Sparrow, Starling, Great Tit, Blue Tit, Redstart, and Pied Flycatcher. In the common European Swift (*Apus apus*), the male and the female of a pair migrate independently to the wintering grounds in southern Africa and back again. A previously mated pair may be reunited by returning to the same nest cavity in which they had previously bred (Lack 1956).

In some species of birds the unmated male arrives at the nesting grounds well before the female, and takes over and repairs an old nest, or builds a new one more or less complete except for the lining. After the females arrive, with special courtship displays he induces a female to accept his nest and to pair with him. If a female accepts she may help complete the nest, and often she lines it. Some examples are given to bring out the close and varied relationship between courtship behavior and nest building.

Male Green-backed (formerly Green) Herons (*Butorides striatus*) arrive before the females in the spring and each takes up a territory centering about an old twig nest, which he repairs, or else he constructs the foundation of a new nest. The male attracts the attention of other herons by loud calls and a "snap" display identifying his sex, in which he extends his neck forward and down and snaps his mandibles together to produce an audible click. The "snap" display resembles movements of nest building, and Meyerriecks (1960) considers it to be ritualized twig-grasping. When the female approaches near the nest, the male at first pursues her aggressively, but she keeps circling back, and his behavior gradually changes from aggression to courtship display expressing sexual interest. When he permits her to enter the nest she at once manipulates the nest twigs. This action inhibits the aggression of the male who begins to pass twigs to the female. The male now gathers and brings most of the twigs, while the female does most of the actual building. Copulation, frequent during the period of nest building, is initiated by the female, and the vast majority of copulations take place on the nest. Other species of North American herons show a basic pattern of pair formation very similar to that of the Green-backed Heron (Palmer 1962).

The male European Wren (*Troglodytes troglodytes*), known as the Winter Wren in the United States, is often polygynous, builds many nests each season, and leads unmated females to one of his unoccupied nests. Females prefer the male with the largest number of complete but unoccupied nests (Garson 1980). The male House Wren (*Troglodytes aedon*) of North America, usually monogamous, places twigs in several nest boxes, but the female accepts only a complete nest, which she then lines with feathers (McCabe 1965).

Unlike the vast majority of species in their family (Emberizidae), which build open or cup-nests, the Galapagos or Darwin's Finches build roofed nests with a side entrance. All the fourteen species are monogamous, are closely related taxonomically, have similar nesting requirements, and build rather similar nests. Lack (1947) describes their remarkable breeding behavior. The unmated cock not only builds several nests, but he also builds and displays regularly to passing females at nests that have been started by, or are still being used by, other birds—even of other species. "Indeed," Lack writes (p. 32), "there are no other birds in which the nests of other species are taken over so frequently and so cavalierly, since often they are just 'borrowed' for a particular occasion." Display building is carried out primarily by the cock, but the final nest is usually built partly or mainly by the hen, who puts in most of the lining of the nest. For their final nest a pair often takes over a nest built largely by members of another species. During two days, one courting male of the Small Ground Finch (*Geospiza fuliginosa*) visited, built on, and displayed regularly at eight nests, some of which were also visited by males, or pairs, of four other species. Indeed, one wonders how reproductive isolation among species is maintained in the Galapagos Finches, long a showcase group for evolution in action. Interbreeding between species, according to Lack, is extremely rare. He believed that Darwin's Finches recognize their own kind primarily by a marked beak difference from other species. He found song characteristics of the different species ill-defined. However, Bowman (1979) finds that larger species sing at a lower frequency and more loudly than similar but smaller species.

Flower decorations are frequently used in India to court the female by male Black-throated Weavers (*Ploceus benghalensis*) and Striated Weavers (*P. manyar*). At a certain stage of nest construction the male dabs wet mud onto part of the nest chamber into which he implants brightly colored flowers or flower petals—red, orange, yellow, blue, or white. He then tries to attract unmated females to his nest with special displays and vocalizations (V. C. Ambedkar, personal communication; Ali and Ripley 1974).

Why should nest-building behavior be so widely incorporated into the courtship of birds? It is as if nest-building behavior were projected forward in the life cycle because of its value as a signal of reproductive condition and in stimulating the partner (Collias 1964). All that is required to produce courtship behavior from nest building is to change the timing of gene action a little, activating sooner a behavior pattern, nest building, for which the genetic basis already exists.

NEST AND MATE SELECTION IN THE VILLAGE WEAVER

Pair formation is closely related to nest building in the Village Weaver (*Ploceus cucullatus*), and enough information is available for this species to give some insight into the complexities of the whole process. This bird breeds in colonies with many nests in one tree (fig. 2.22) and is a common species in much of sub-Saharan Africa. The adult male is black and yellow with a black head and red eyes. The adult female is olive-green above and yellow below.

The birds breed in the rainy season when there is plenty of green grass available for weaving the nest and abundant insect food for the nestlings. The males arrive first at the nesting tree. They prefer acacia trees for their nests but also use several other tree species, particularly when the trees are at the edge of streams or lakes. Each male defends a territory consisting of a few branches in the tree, where he weaves the outer shell of his roofed and pensile nest, using long (25–35 cm) green strips that he tears from the leaves of tall grasses or palm fronds. He makes the initial selection of the nest site, preferring the tips of branches directed downward to those directed horizontally. The entrance of the nest opens downward, and is separated by a ridge from the bottom of the egg chamber.

When unmated females visit the tree each male gives an invitation display, calling repeatedly—while hanging upside down beneath the bottom entrance of his nest with his feet—and flapping his wings, an action made more conspicuous by the bright yellow inner lining of the wings. This nest display attracts the female who will not usually enter a nest until the male invites her to do so with this special display (fig. 4.2). When a female enters, the male at once sings to her (fig. 4.3). She inspects the interior thoroughly, taking from a few minutes to twenty or more, while she pulls and tugs with her beak at the materials within the nest as if testing them. The female often visits different nests and males before making her choice. She signals her acceptance by bringing soft grass tops or other lining materials into the nest, continues to line the nest, and usually within a day, she copulates with the male of her choice (fig. 4.4).

After laying her clutch of two or three eggs the female does all the incubating, and when the eggs hatch she does all or most of the feeding of the nestlings. Meanwhile the male builds another nest and tries to attract more females. This species is polygynous and a male may have up to five mates simultaneously in his different nests (N. Collias and Collias 1959b, 1970).

If a female rejects a nest she simply flies away and does not return. If a particular nest is rejected repeatedly, when it fades from a bright green and turns brown, the male tears it down and builds a fresh nest in its place. When fresh green nests were painted brown, the male tore them down three times as often as he tore down nests of similar age

Fig. 4.2. Male Village Weaver (*Ploceus cucullatus*) shows the entrance at the bottom of his nest to a visiting, unmated female. (Photo: Catherine H. Jacobs)

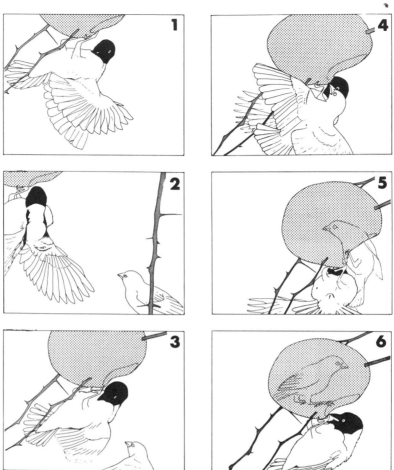

Fig. 4.3. Sequence, selected from a motion picture taken at 64 frames per second, depicting the nest-invitation, inverted wing-flapping display of a male Village Weaver to an unmated female: (1) male flaps his wings and utters attraction calls; (2 to 5) female comes and enters the nest, while male continues his display; (6) male sings to the female right after she enters his nest. (N. E. and E. C. Collias 1970)

that had been sprayed with green paint; so brown color is one cue that stimulates the male to tear down old nests (Jacobs et al. 1978). However, he sometimes tears down green nests that have been rejected.

What determines the female's choice among different males and their nests? Both male and nest are essential: at least in an aviary, females will not lay eggs in fresh green nests if the males are removed, nor will the females lay eggs in an aviary that lacks nests, even though males in breeding condition to whom they have previously been mated are

Pair formation

Repetitions of above sequence stimulate ovaries of female and lead to:

Copulatory sequence

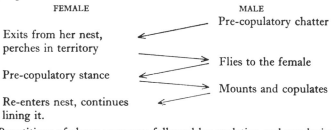

Repetitions of above sequence followed by ovulation and egg-laying.

Fig. 4.4. Diagram of male-female interactions in the Village Weaver, leading to pair formation and to mating. (N. E. and E. C. Collias 1970)

present (Victoria 1969). Nevertheless, a female's choice will vary with differences among males and among nests.

Factors in the female's choice associated with properties of the *male* include the following:

1. *Number of males in the tree.* In Senegal, we found that colonies with fewer than ten males were significantly less successful in attracting females than were larger colonies (N. Collias and Collias 1969a).

2. *Frequency with which a male gives the wing-flapping, nest-invitation display.* In experiments in aviaries, we found that the males who gave this display more frequently were more likely to have their nests accepted by a female (N. Collias and Victoria 1978). In part, this difference was due to the fact that males owning more nests displayed more frequently (N. Collias and Victoria 1978). However, we also found it to be true that nests that were subsequently accepted were displayed more than twice as frequently on the day of acceptance as nests that were rejected (Jacobs et al. 1978).

3. *Conspicuousness of the male's nest-invitation display.* When male Village Weavers' wings were painted all black, obliterating the bright yellow color of the wing linings, those males were significantly less successful in securing mates than were control males with normally colored wings (E. Collias et al. 1979).

4. *Previous mating.* Whether the female has been previously mated to a given male that season also helps determine her choice. In one series of aviary experiments six of twelve adult females repeatedly chose the same male with whom they had paired for a preceding clutch (N. Collias and Victoria 1978). Yearling females are more fickle and, although capable of laying eggs by the time they are one year of age are more likely to change mates between successive clutches than are adult females.

Factors in the female's choice associated with properties of the *nest* woven by the male may include the following:

1. *Color of the nest.* As a nest ages it fades from a bright green to a dull brown over a period of little more than week. At the same time the materials of the nest become weaker and more brittle. In a series of aviary experiments, the females showed a significant preference for fresh green nests over faded green nests, and of the latter over old brown nests (N. Collias and Victoria 1978). Painting old brown nests green does not restore their attractiveness, and there was no significant preference between 9 such painted nests (0.5 percent chosen) and 77 old brown nests (1 percent chosen). One difficulty with this experiment is that males display old nests very little if at all, whether or not one paints them green. To avoid this difficulty we tried painting fresh green nests, brown or green. The males displayed these fresh nests often and at about the same frequency regardless of color. Under these conditions, the females tended to prefer fresh nests painted green over fresh nests painted brown (P = .07). Fresh nests painted green were just as attractive as were fresh unpainted green nests, eliminating paint *per se* as a basis of choice (Jacobs et al. 1978).

2. *Strength of nest materials.* Fragmented materials from discarded and demolished nests come to litter the ground under colonies of Village Weavers. If the birds are given no fresh materials to build with, eventually they will pick up and build nests of this old fragmented material. These recycled or trash nests have normal form and appearance (fig. 4.5) but are built of abnormally short and rather brittle materials. When it is his most recently built nest, the male displays to females the nest built of litter more often than he does his older nests built of normal materials. In one aviary experiment, females actually accepted 12 percent of 15 such trash nests, but only 3 percent of 19 older normal nests, a significant difference (P = .01) (N. Collias and Victoria 1978). However, the females' decision was often tentative, since they remained to lay eggs in only 4 of 23 (13 percent) trash nests accepted, whereas they remained to lay eggs in 9 of 20 (45 percent) older nests that had been built of normal materials and accepted (N. Collias 1979). More recent experiments (by N. E. Collias, C. H. Jacobs, and C. R. Cox; unpubl.)

Fig. 4.5. Male Village Weaver in his territory with two nests, in an aviary. The nest on the left is normal, the one on the right was built of the discarded litter from nests built and demolished previously by the males. (N. E. Collias and J. K. Victoria, *Animal Behaviour* 1978)

Fig. 4.6. Village Weaver nest, very loosely constructed from abnormally long and unmanageable strips of palm leaf. The entrance is at the lower left. (N. E. Collias and J. K. Victoria, *Animal Behaviour* 1978)

have extended and confirmed these results. Females laid eggs in only 10 of 37 trash nests, but in fully 19 of 38 old normal nests (χ^2 = 3.26, P = .037, one-tailed test). It appears that a female is swayed to a considerable degree in her decision to accept a nest by the importunities of the male and his nest-invitation display, but if the nest is very weak and unsatisfactory she may "change her mind."

3. *Neatness of external weave.* By giving aviary-housed males very long (75–90 cm) and therefore unmanageable strips of palm leaf to weave, we induced them to build nests covered externally with many loose loops, lacking altogether the neat, closely woven appearance of a normal nest (fig. 4.6). Nevertheless, and rather surprisingly, there was no significant difference between the percentage of 20 loosely woven nests that were chosen by the females and that of 27 closely woven normal nests (N. Collias and Victoria 1978). It appears that tidy external appearance of a nest is of no great moment to the female weaver, who seems to base her decision primarily on her close and active inspection of the interior of the nest. The interior surface of the loosely woven nests was much smoother and more tightly woven than was their exterior surface.

Up to this point we have considered mate selection in the Village Weaver to be solely a matter of female choice. However, there is some evidence that the male too exercises some preference among females. Occasionally two females will simultaneously compete for a male's nest, each one of them trying to enter the nest before the other. On some such occasions the male may enter the nest and repeatedly evict one of the two females, always the same one, whereas he allows the other to remain. In recent observations in our aviaries, Dr. Cathleen Cox found that a male discriminates between different females in that he gives the nest-invitation display more frequently to one female than to the other.

MALE AND FEMALE ROLES IN NEST BUILDING

Information on sex roles in nest building is summarized by Van Tyne and Berger (1976), by C.J.O. Harrison (1978), and by many other authors; we have summarized this information for each family of birds in Appendix One. The following discussion presents the kinds of variations found among different species.

Both Sexes Build the Nest

Both sexes build the nest, with each doing a substantial part of the work. This seems to be the primitive pattern among birds (Skutch 1976).

In over half the families, both sexes incubate the eggs (Van Tyne and Berger 1976:494), and in general if the male helps incubate, he also helps build the nest. Participation by both sexes in nest building is more common among the nonpasserine birds than among the passerines. According to Skutch (1976:157) "Among passerines, incubation and brooding are the nesting activities least frequently undertaken by males, who as a rule do not incubate unless they also build the nest and feed the young." Presumably helping to build the nest strengthens the pair bond, and possibly helps insure that the male will also help incubate. There are of course many exceptions to these general rules.

Both sexes build, the female doing the greater share. Often the male merely indicates a potential nest site and brings nest materials to the female at the site; she does all or most of the actual building. Examples include grass-finches (Estrildidae), doves and pigeons (Columbidae), the Roseate Spoonbill (*Ajaia ajaja*), and the Magnificent Frigatebird (*Fregata magnificens*).

Both sexes build, the male doing the greater share. The male may build the outer shell of the nest, while the female puts in the lining. The male may use a partially completed nest to attract a mate who, if she accepts, completes the nest and puts in the lining. Examples include many true weaverbirds (Ploceinae), the Yellow-faced Grassquit (*Tiaris olivacea*; Fringillidae), the Phainopepla (*Phainopepla nitens*; Ptilogonatidae), the Marsh Wren (*Cistothorus palustris*; Troglodytidae), and the White-throat (*Sylvia communis*; Sylviidae). Some hole-nesting species, such as the House Sparrow, fit in this classification.

The Female Does All the Building and Gathers the Nest Materials

In these instances, the female usually builds an open or cup-nest and does all the incubating. Aside from a few exceptional species, this is the characteristic pattern of nest building for the vast majority of the finches (Fringillidae), troupials (Icteridae), Old World orioles (Oriolidae), many American wood warblers (Parulidae), manakins (Pipridae), birds of paradise (Paradisaeidae), hummingbirds (Trochilidae), many gallinaceous birds, and many ducks. In general, in these species the male makes little or no use of a nest in courting the female.

In many of these birds the males have brilliant plumage while the females are drab in color. Such sex differences in plumage are particularly marked in species with communal display areas, such as the Ruff (*Philomachus pugnax*), manakins, and many birds of paradise. A brilliantly colored male would be a liability near the nest to which he might attract predators. A number of these species are polygynous and the female raises the young alone, in addition to taking over all other nesting duties.

In monogamous species, the male often accompanies the female as she builds and gathers materials. In the Willow Flycatcher (*Empidonax traillii*), Ettinger and King (1980) found that the male's total daily energy expenditure was at a seasonal maximum during the nest-site selection and construction phase, mainly because of longer flights and increased flight time that resulted when he accompanied the female during her nest-building activities. At this time the female is approaching ovulation, and it is important for the male to protect his "genetic investment" from other males.

The Male Builds Alone

Building by the male alone, unaided by the female, is usually correlated with incubation only by the male. In about 6 percent of bird families only the male incubates (Appendix One). The example of the Greater Rhea in Argentina has been described. Polyandry is common in those families where the male alone builds the nest and incubates, the classic example being the jacanas (Jacanidae). A low raft of water weeds, usually on floating vegetation, is built by the males of the Northern Jacana (*Jacana spinosa*) of Central America, the African Jacana (*Actophilornis africanus*), and the Pheasant-tailed Jacana (*Hydrophasianus chirurgus*) of the Orient. Jenni (1974) suggests that the evolution of polyandry may have been due to an erratic food supply combined with a high rate of egg predation. The female tends to be larger and brighter than the male in polyandrous species, and if the female were to build and incubate, her frequent presence near the nest might endanger the eggs.

The Red Phalarope (*Phalaropus fulicarius*), a shore bird that nests on arctic islands, is polyandrous. Both male and female make numerous nest scrapes while searching for a nest site. Once the female starts laying eggs in one of these scrapes the dull-colored male puts in the nest lining and does all the incubation (Mayfield 1979). In the Wilson's Phalarope (*Phalaropus tricolor*), the male alone prepares several nest scrapes in one of which the female lays (Howe 1975).

SUMMARY

Either the male or the female bird may select the nest site, or more commonly, both sexes participate, with the female making the final decision. Factors that help decide the location of a nest site, and probably the choice of a mate as well, include local food availability, presence of suitable nest materials, shelter from the physical environment, and protection from predators.

Symbolic use of nest materials during courtship is common among many birds, and some courtship displays have evolved from nest building; the mechanism seems to involve earlier activation in the breeding cycle of the genetic basis for nest building. The male may display a nest site or a nest to the female during the process of pair formation. For example, the male Village Weaver (*Ploceus cucullatus*) of sub-Saharan Africa weaves the outer shell of the nest that he displays to unmated females. If a female accepts the nest she mates with the male and lines the nest. She bases her selection both on properties of the male and of his nest, which must be strong enough to endure until a brood has fledged.

The relative roles of male and female in nest building vary greatly in different species. In general, if the male helps incubate he also helps build the nest. The male may take a very active role in building if he uses the nest in his courtship. In many species he brings nest materials to the female who builds the nest. The female builds the nest alone in many passerine birds. Participation of both sexes in nest building is more common among nonpasserine birds than among passerines.

In many of the species where the female does all or most of the building, sex dichromatism and sex dimorphism is marked—the males being brilliantly colored while the females are duller or more modest in coloration. Building by the male alone is rare among birds, and may be associated with reversed sex dimorphism, polyandry, and incubation solely by the male, as in the jacanas (Jacanidae) of the New World and Old World tropics.

CHAPTER FIVE

Bowerbirds, Bowers, and Nests

WE define a bower as a construction adapted to facilitate the mating relationship, independently of care of eggs or young, and providing some screening from possible interference.

RELATION BETWEEN BOWERS AND NESTS

The relationship between nest-building behavior and the elaborate bowers that male bowerbirds (Ptilonorhynchidae) build and use in courting visiting females has long been a puzzle. In relating this behavior and the evolution of bowers we discuss the theories of the origin of bowers, and we examine the evidence for the sexually stimulating effects of nest and bower materials. We consider the effects of the emancipation of males from nesting duties and the origins of special courtship and mating places in bowerbirds. We then discuss the implications of these phenomena for the evolution of different types of bowers.

Origin of the Bower in Evolution

A. J. Marshall (1954:171) advances the theory that "bower-building may have originated as a displacement activity that is fundamentally allied to nest-building." In most birds, both sexes have an inherent urge to build nests, but today only female bowerbirds, so far as is known, make nests. According to Marshall, nest building by females and bower building by males is controlled essentially by the seasonal liberation of hormones. When the female visits the male's bower the male seems to exhibit conflict between sexual attraction and a tendency to attack any bird coming near his bower as an intruder. A female may visit the male's display grounds many times before copulating. Marshall suggests that the male finds some relief from his tension by manipulating twigs and other objects, that is, in displacement, or "symbolic" nest building. Since this behavior presumably attracts the female, who makes her own nest entirely, or to a large degree, of twigs, a selection pressure for the origin of bower building is set up.

It is characteristic of a chain of instinctive reactions that when blocked before consummation, the preliminary behavior patterns are often repeated. This would lead to a progressive accumulation of twigs at the male's display ground. We can also apply Tinbergen's (1951) concept of the "supernormal stimulus," and speculate that the larger the accumulation of twigs the more stimulating the situation for the female, particularly when the male manipulates or holds the twigs. Bowers may greatly exceed in size the nest that the female builds herself. Davies (in Cooper and Forshaw 1977:27) and Diamond (1982a) have expressed somewhat similar ideas on bower evolution. We also wish to suggest the importance of the screening function of the bower, shielding the participants to some degree from the eyes of potential rivals, and even from each other, since bowerbirds often interfere with the courtship of other individuals (Villenga 1970). Male birds of many species will interfere with a copulation in progress by conspecifics. Should stimulation become too intense, or the male become too aggressive, the female might depart, as she often does, unless the male disappears momentarily behind the screen. This phenomenon is an example of the "stimulus cut-off" principle in ethology (Chance 1962) and may have been of key importance in the evolution of the bower form.

Sexually Stimulating Effects of Nest Materials

There is some evidence that nest materials, or the manipulation of nest materials in building a nest (or bower) is sexually stimulating (chaps. 4, 13). For many birds there is a correlation between nest building and copulation, and in many species copulation takes place in the nest. Ovulation may be delayed or inhibited by removing the nest. In cases where the male takes no part in building the nest, he may nevertheless manipulate nest materials during the copulation period, as does the male Song Sparrow (Nice 1943). It is probable that manipulation of nest materials is sexually stimulating to both males and females.

Emancipation of Males from Nesting Duties and the Origin of Special Courtship and Mating Areas in Bowerbirds

Not all members of the bowerbird family build bowers (depending on definition), but in most species the male does have a special area within which courtship and copulation take place and which is not used for feeding or nesting. These areas in some species may be clustered in the same neighborhood. Some eighty-five species, about one percent of living species of the world's birds, have display arenas (Gilliard 1969:49). Gilliard believed that arena display preceded evolution of well-developed bowers, and that the bowers are the pinnacle of arena evolution. The degree of crowding that results in what should be termed an "arena" is rather arbitrary. Males can probably hear each other calling near their bowers, but bowers placed close together are more liable to theft of materials or to destruction by neighboring males.

The nest built by the female is well removed from the male's display area, about two hundred meters or more in the Satin Bowerbird (Villenga 1980). The problem is to identify the selection pressures that have emancipated the male from nesting duties. The male helps feed the nestlings in the Spotted Catbird (*Ailuroedus melanotis*). Little is known of the nest-building behavior of the catbirds but, from what is known, in bowerbirds that build bowers only the female builds the nest, incubates and cares for the young. A large part of the diet of the bowerbirds consists of fruits, and Snow has suggested that frugivory favors the evolution of arena behavior in altricial birds, as it allows the adults to feed themselves in a small fraction of the daylight hours. This in turn enables females to tend the nest alone, and males to devote most of their time to competing with each other for mates (Snow 1971, Snow and Snow 1979).

Birds with special display and mating areas that are independent of nesting sites include some bowerbird species that do not really build bowers. The next problem then is what channeled the evolution of the more advanced bowerbirds into building bowers for display, rather than merely clearing a ground court. Possibly, the determining factor was the male's symbolic use of nest materials to help attract the female. Natural selection would reinforce the use and manipulation of any objects that the females found attractive. Shortly after the male was freed of nesting duties, one would expect that he would retain to a considerable degree the capacity and motivation to play with materials resembling those that the female used in building her nest; but as he further evolved, he would perhaps gradually include materials which did not necessarily closely resemble the actual materials used in nest building—that is, the use of nest materials in courtship would become "symbolic" and ritualized.

The Green Catbird (*Ailuroedus crassirostris*) of southeastern Australia is monogamous and builds a bulky cup-shaped nest from dried vines, tendrils, and twigs with which numerous broad leaves are interwoven. The nest is lined with tendrils and fine rootlets. A pair in a planted aviary maintained a rudimentary display area decorated with lemon leaves placed face down in a rough circle on the ground. As the leaves withered they were thrown to one side and replaced with fresh ones (Cooper and Forshaw 1977). One can see a resemblance between the

Fig. 5.1. A male Satin Bowerbird (*Ptilonorhynchus violaceus*) copulating with a female in his avenue-type bower, Australia. (Photo: Norman Chaffer)

leaves used in the nest and in the display area, respectively. The male Archbold's Bowerbird (*Archboldia papuensis*) has a display site which is little more than a disorderly mat of brown dried ferns, grasses, and sticks, decorated with berries. While courting a nearby female he often holds a piece of vine or grass stem in his beak (Gilliard 1969). The nest is undescribed.

EVOLUTION OF DIFFERENT TYPES OF BOWERS

There are two main types of true bowers, avenue bowers and maypole bowers. The avenue bower consists of two parallel rows of more or less vertical twigs thrust into a basal platform of irregularly arranged twigs. Copulation, which has rarely been observed, generally takes place within the bower (fig. 5.1). In maypole bowers, the male courts the female around a central structure.

The Satin Bowerbird (*Ptilinorhynchus violaceus*) is an avenue builder of eastern Australia. During one year Villenga (1970, 1980) saw one color-banded male mate with five different females, all of which were banded with individually distinctive colored rings. The male of this species decorates his bower especially with blue objects—blue feathers, blue flowers, blue marbles, various blue plastic items, blue strands of wool. It takes up to seven years for the male Satin Bowerbird to acquire his dark blue plumage (Villenga 1972), and in the meantime the immature males build more or less rudimentary practice bowers (Villenga 1970), which seem to be reminiscent of nests. Their first attempt at building is confined to making a platform. They gather a few sticks and place them in a circular arrangement in the ground. Gradually, the platform gets thicker as the season progresses, and sometimes the older immature male birds place a few sticks upright into the platform in a crossed interlocking arrangement, the foundation of every avenue. Early bowers are smaller than those built by mature males. Perhaps the various stages a young bower bird goes through in making his practice bowers reflect the evolutionary stages of the bower.

The Regent Bowerbird (*Sericulus chrysocephalus*) builds a smaller avenue bower than do other genera of avenue builders and with fewer decorative objects. Building of the bower has been studied in birds captive in zoos. Whereas the adult male builds a typical, walled avenue on a rudimentary platform of twigs with an entrance at either end of the avenue, a young male may build a crude structure in the shape of a horseshoe having only one entrance, and with all twigs laid flat (Gilliard 1969). This bower ontogeny suggests a possible stage in the evolution of the two-walled type of bower.

In the avenue builders, the male when courting a female keeps one wall between himself and the female, or stations himself near one entrance of the avenue. The very shy female therefore has an escape route available to her from the aggressive male, and it seems this encourages her to approach the male and his bower.

A. J. Marshall (1954) was of the opinion that bowers do not in the least resemble nests. They obviously are very different structures. However, some definite resemblances between bowers and nests do exist. Both nests and bowers, as Marshall noted, are largely made of twigs. In the bower of the Spotted Bowerbird (*Chlamydera maculata*) the walls of the avenue are made of fine twigs and are lined on the inside with grass stems, just as the nest is made of twigs and lined with grass stems (Cooper and Forshaw 1977). The walls of the bower of the Great Grey Bowerbird (*C. nuchalis*) are built of twigs, only rarely with grass stems, and its nest is made of twigs; there is no mention of grass stems in the nest (Cooper and Forshaw 1977). The bower of the Fawn-breasted Bowerbird (*C. cerviniventris*) has avenue walls made of twigs (fig. 5.2), but a few bowers have an extra finish—numerous fine rootlets are inter-woven horizontally along the tops of each wall. Peckover (1969), who describes this, also states that nests are built with twigs and have fine rootlets lining the nest. Here again, we see a fragmentary but definite resemblance between bower structure and nest structure.

The male Lauterbach's Bowerbird (*C. lauterbachi*) of New Guinea, builds the most complex avenue bowers. He erects a screen of twigs near and at right angles to the ends of the central avenue, but not closing it off (fig. 5.3). The female enters the central avenue while the male displays at the far end (Cooper and Forshaw 1977), both birds being screened from the view of ground predators and possibly from competing males by the cross walls near each end of the central avenue.

In the maypole builders, such as Macgregor's Gardener Bowerbird (*Amblyornis macgregoriae*) the male arranges a mass of twigs in a crisscross and interlocking fashion around and up a small sapling. He also clears an area on the ground with this sapling in the center. This central column is the "maypole" about which the birds dance in a series of hops, the male and female keeping for the most part to opposite sides of the maypole during the courtship dance (fig. 5.4). During the ex-citement of the dance the male raises and fans out a brilliant orange, circular crest on his head. Some maypole builders, such as the Striped Gardener Bowerbird (*A. subalaris*) and the Brown Gardener Bowerbird (*A. inornatus*), build around the central column a circular hut of twigs with a domed roof leaving a large opening at one side. The region of the opening is the "forecourt," which the male decorates with colorful fruits, fresh flowers and a variety of other objects (fig. 5.5). These hut bowers are the most elaborately decorated structures built by birds.

BOWER DECORATIONS AND BOWER PAINTING

Bowerbirds decorate their courts and bowers with often highly colored fruits and flowers, shiny objects such as insect exoskeletons, bits of glass or plastic, and a great variety of other materials—leaves, moss, feathers, lichens, stones, bones, snail shells, and bits of charcoal. Some objects are edible—many are not—most are conspicuous and may be sorted and piled in heaps. It is difficult to find a common element. Among the avenue builders, blue objects are preferred by *Ptilonorhynchus*; white, green, or blue by *Chlamydera*; while the maypole builders (*Amblyornis*) seem to favor objects predominantly red ranging to yellow (Schodde 1976).

Diamond (1982a) suggests that the decoration of bowers with colored objects may have evolved from courtship feeding. The male often picks

Fig. 5.2. Bower of the Fawn-breasted Bowerbird (*Chlamydera cerviniventris*) with a prominent west display platform, New Guinea. The bower is decorated with oval green berries, which the male uses in his courtship display. (Photo: N. E. Collias)

Fig. 5.3. A male Lauterbach's Bowerbird (*Chlamydera lauterbachi*) holds a fruit in his bill while courting a female. He is between the avenue (side view) and one of the screens he builds at each end of the avenue. (Photo: Sigmund Diczbalis)

Fig. 5.4. Macgregor's Gardener Bowerbird (*Amblyornus macgregoriae*); male and female on opposite sides of maypole bower during courtship. (Photo: Sigmund Diczbalis)

Fig. 5.5. Hutlike bower of the Brown, or Vogelkop, Gardener Bowerbird (*Amblyornus inornatus*), western New Guinea. The structure, built of twigs around a central sapling, is over one meter high. The front court is decorated with piles of different colored fruits, and with fresh flowers. (Photo: E. Thomas Gilliard; courtesy of the American Museum of Natural History)

up an object during courtship, and may extend it toward the female. In the Yellow-fronted Bowerbird (*Amblyornis flavifrons*), a species recently rediscovered by Diamond in western New Guinea, the male holds a blue fruit in his beak, which contrasts maximally with his golden crest, when courting the female (Diamond 1982b). The male Fawn-breasted Bowerbird, while courting the female, sometimes picks up a bunch of green berries from his bower and holds it in his bill (Peckover 1969). The many shiny blue objects that the male Satin Bowerbird uses for decoration and in courtship, resemble the lilac-blue color of his eyes and the sheen of his glossy blue-black plumage. One gains the impression that any object that serves to attract the female's attention, even a blue pebble, may be used. Such decorations are often stolen by a neighboring male and used to decorate his own bower (A. J. Marshall 1954).

Flower decorations suggest something in bowerbirds akin to the human aesthetic sense. A Brown Gardener Bowerbird will replace flowers in his bower with fresh ones daily for months on end, carefully inspecting each blossom as he puts it in place, shifting its position if he is not satisfied (Galliard 1969).

Bowers of the Fawn-breasted Bowerbird are consistently oriented in an east-west direction, and are decorated with green berries on the west platform, in the central avenue, and along the tops of both walls (fig. 5.2). This arrangement allows the male to display to best advantage from the west end to females at the east end of the bower during his main display period, the first three hours after sunrise (Peckover 1969). However, Peckover points out that certain other bowerbird species may orient their avenues on a north-south axis and he suggests that the problem of bower orientation needs more study.

The avenue builders often paint their bowers and, so far as is known, only the avenue-building bowerbirds do so (Peckover 1969). The male—taking a bit of fruit pulp, bark, chewed green vegetable material, or charcoal in his bill—stimulates the flow of saliva and applies the secretion with his beak to the inner walls of the avenue, staining them a different color. The function of bower painting is unknown. A. J. Marshall (1954) suggests that it may be a substitute for courtship feeding, while Villenga (1970) suggests bower painting may provide identification, visual or olfactory, of the individual male owning the bower.

GILLIARD'S THEORY OF TRANSFERRAL EFFECT IN EVOLUTION

E. Thomas Gilliard (1969) points out that in bowerbirds there is an inverse relationship between the complexity of the bower and the colorfulness of the male bird. Species with sexual dichromatism and colorful males, build relatively simple bowers, while the males of the plain-colored species in which the sexes are colored alike build larger, more elaborate, and highly decorated bowers.

Among the avenue builders the simplest and smallest bowers are built by the bright, yellow and black, male Regent Bowerbird. In the relatively dull-colored Lauterbach's Bowerbird, in which male and female resemble one another, the male builds an elaborate avenue bower having four walls and much decorated with stones and fruits.

The males of the Spotted Bowerbird and the Great Grey Bowerbird build simple avenue bowers and have a vivid rose or pink-lilac patch of feathers on the hind neck, which is erected during courtship when the male turns the back of the neck toward the female. The male Fawn-breasted Bowerbird has a more complex bower. During courtship he turns the back of his crestless neck toward the female while holding a bunch of green berries in his bill. Similarly, the male Lauterbach's Bowerbird turns his crestless hind neck toward the female as he picks up a red berry in his bill (Cooper and Forshaw 1977). Gilliard postulates that with the use of fruits as sexual ornaments, the crest was eclipsed in importance and was lost through natural selection.

Gilliard (1969:54) also notices an inverse ratio in the three then known *Amblyornis* species between the complexity of the bower and the plumage of the male (the three females are virtually indistinguishable). The male Macgregor's Bowerbird builds a simple maypole bower, scarcely decorated, and he wears a long golden-orange crest. The male of the recently rediscovered Yellow-fronted Bowerbird (*A. flavifrons*) also builds a simple maypole bower, decorates his court with a few piles of blue, green, and yellow fruit, and has a long golden crest (Diamond 1982b). The male Striped Gardener Bowerbird builds a hut of three walls around the maypole, and he wears a short crest. The male Brown Gardener Bowerbird builds the most elaborate bower, a hut around and over the central column with a broad roof overhanging a court richly decorated with piles of berries, shells, and flowers (fig. 5.5); he has no crest and appears indistinguishable from the drab-colored female. Gilliard writes (1969:55) "I believe that the forces of sexual selection in these birds have been transferred from morphological characteristics—the male plumage—to external objects and that this 'tranferral effect'—may be the key factor in the evolution of the more complex bower birds." The transfer of colorful display from the male himself to his display objects means that "natural selection operates in the direction of protective coloration and the male tends more and more to resemble the females."

One problem that remains is the direction of evolution, as this is often difficult to determine by attempts to deduce appearance of ancestors from present-day forms. What we see is correlations of appearance with habitat and behavior in living species. Did the ancestor of gardener bowerbirds (*Amblyornis*) have a crest or not? In birds there is some evidence that in a specific behavioral display the motor patterns may sometimes evolve before plumage features that enhance the movement (Lorenz 1935). However, some argument for Gilliard's view that the transferral effect has resulted in reduction or loss of conspicuous crests in the bowerbirds comes from the great variability of crest length in the species of *Amblyornis* with elaborate bowers, indicating lessened selection pressure on the crest. The crest of the hut-building Striped Gardner Bowerbird varies from 34 millimeters to 74 millimeters in length, while within various subspecies of the Macgregor's Bowerbird, which builds a simple maypole bower, the variation in crest length is only half as great (cf. Gilliard 1969; Schodde and McKean 1973).

SUMMARY

Courtship and copulation take place in or next to the bower built by the male bowerbird. Bowers are a special class of structures facilitating courtship and mating, as do the special courts cleared by males in a number of families besides the bowerbirds. Some of the materials used in bowers resemble nesting materials, and there is some evidence that nest materials or the handling of nest materials is sexually stimulating to birds. A. J. Marshall suggested the theory that bower building may have originated in evolution as a displacement activity that is fundamentally allied to nest building. The concept of the supernormal stimulus helps explain the large size of bowers. We suggest that bowers may facilitate mating not only by stimulating the female but also by screening the male and female from rival males and at times even from each other.

Not all the eighteen species of bowerbirds (Ptilonorhynchidae) build bowers, but generally the male has a special cleared ground area in which courtship takes place. Such display behavior is associated with frugivorous habits, which according to Snow may have freed the male from nesting duties.

The two main types of bowers are avenue bowers (two walls of parallel upright twigs) and maypole bowers (twigs placed around a central sapling in the court). The male and female during much of the courtship are separated by a wall or the maypole. Bowers are decorated with a great variety of objects, including flowers, fruits, pebbles, bones, etc., the prevalent color of which varies with the species of bowerbird. Decoration of the bower may have evolved from courtship feeding. Some species of avenue builders "paint" their bowers; the function of this act is unknown.

E. T. Gilliard pointed out an inverse relationship between the complexity of the bower and the colorfulness of the plumage in different species of bowerbirds. He suggested that the forces of sexual selection in the bowerbirds have been transferred from the male plumage to external objects, and that this transferral may be the key factor in the evolution of the most complex bowerbirds and their bowers.

CHAPTER SIX

Nest-site Selection and the Physical Environment

THE purpose of this chapter and the next is to describe the relationship of nest sites and of nests to the physical environment, including changes in temperature and humidity, strong winds, heavy rainfall, and different types of substrate. The energy demands of nest building in a species will vary with the physical environment. The apportionment of energy among needs for temperature regulation, nest-building activities, and other activities will vary accordingly.

Time and energy budgets for the various activities of a species give an overall perspective on its life history (Pearson 1954, Orians 1961). One can also compare the relative energy demands of selected activities of a species without attempting to construct a complete energy budget. The measurement of the energy requirements for different behavioral acts and of energy income, in terms of metabolic measures such as the amount of oxygen consumed, can be translated into calories or other units of energy. Using these units of energy one can compare the energy demands of nest building with those of other behavioral activities (N. Collias and Collias 1965, 1967, 1971b). Unfortunately there is still no precise method available for measuring continuously and accurately the metabolic rate for all types of activities in free-ranging, unrestrained wild animals. The methods available give only approximations of the actual amounts of energy expended, although the relative expenditures may be fairly reliable. The whole topic of animal energetics in relation to behavioral and physiological ecology has been reviewed recently by Bartholomew (1982) and by Schmidt-Nielsen (1979), while avian energetics has been reviewed by various specialists in a book edited by Paynter (1974) and in reviews by Kendeigh et al. (1977) and by Wolf and Hainsworth (1978).

Competition for nest sites has led to the evolution of a great diversity of specialized nesting sites for different species. The need for security from predators has often led to the location of nests in relatively inaccessible places or in harsh climates. In turn, the nature of the nest site helps determine other aspects of the life cycle and behavior of a species. All nest sites must meet the basic needs of eggs and young for security, regulation of temperature, and moisture, and at the same time the nest site must be close to good food sources. We shall discuss adaptations, first, in choice of the nest site (this chap.) and, second, in nest building to extreme environments, such as high mountains, polar regions, hot dry deserts, and tropical rain forests (chap. 7).

ADAPTATION TO COLD IN CHOICE OF NEST SITE

The altiplano is a grassy high-altitude plateau generally above 4000 meters in the Andes Mountains. The climate is severe with an annual rainfall of about 1000 millimeters, most of it falling during roughly five months of the "warm season" when rain or hail storms occur daily. The minimum night temperature in summer is about −2°C, and in winter it often drops to −15°C. In Peru, the altiplano is inhabited by a large hummingbird, the Andean Hillstar (*Oreotrochilus estella*), weighing about 8 grams, which nests during the warm season. The Andean Hillstar is the only species of hummingbird resident the year round, compared with about a hundred species of hummingbirds found at lower levels in corresponding latitudes.

F. Lynn Carpenter (1976) studied thermal adaptations of the Andean Hillstar to its stressful environment, measured its metabolic demands in laboratory and field, and made a time and energy budget for this species. The three adaptations that reduce its energy costs the most are feeding while perched (unlike the hovering method usually practiced by most other hummingbirds), roosting in caves or rocky gorges where minimum temperatures remain as much as 15°C higher than outside, and nocturnal torpor. In torpor the body temperature of a bird falls and remains at temperatures too low for coordinated muscular activity. Spontaneous arousal of Hillstars normally occurs about two hours before dawn in the field. Incubating females and those feeding nestlings do not undergo torpor.

The female builds her nest in the summer roost sites, fastening it to the rocky wall by a sticky solution. She defends a feeding territory consisting of orange flowers of *Cajophora* (Loasaceae) on the adjacent mountain slope. The male visits the female's territory only for courtship and copulation and dwells elsewhere. Carpenter (1976) calculated the total energy expended by an incubating or brooding female at the nest site, where minimum ambient temperatures were about 5°C to 8°C above the outside temperature, at 18.4 kilocalories per day. At outside temperatures the same female would have had to expend 19.3 kilocalories per day, a 5 percent greater metabolic cost, representing the energy savings resulting from the warmer thermal environment of the nest site. The shelter provided by the cave or the rocky ledge over the nest also protects the female from rain and hail. Carpenter's study was concerned primarily with evaluating the thermal environment of nest sites and roost sites, and did not attempt to evaluate the energy savings to the female of the large and heavily insulated nest itself (cf. Dorst 1962). During the winter the thermal advantage of roosting deeper in rocky crevices and caves where the birds are protected from the colder air outside the cave results in greater metabolic savings. The safe nesting and roosting sites give the Andean Hillstar virtual immunity from predation, and it seems the population is limited by competition for nest sites and by winter stress.

In a study of the Broad-tailed Hummingbird (*Selasphorus platycercus*) nesting in the chilly climate of the Rocky Mountains in Colorado, Calder (1974) found that overhead shelter can cut in half metabolic, radiative heat losses to the cold night sky. Radiation temperatures of the sky, rocks, ground, and surrounding vegetation were obtained with an infrared radiometric-thermometer. The temperature of the night sky reached $-20°C$ or even colder. Rocks, ridges, and vegetation were important shelters to the extent that they blocked exposure of the nest to the cold night sky.

The Pinyon Jay (*Gymnorhinus cyanocephalus*) builds a bulky cup-nest in coniferous trees of the southwestern United States. In Arizona, 85 percent of 153 nests were built in the southern half of the tree, where foliage temperatures averaged 2.3°C to 2.8°C warmer than in the northern half during the early part of the nesting season, resulting in metabolic savings to the birds (Balda and Bateman, 1972).

Breeding of Mountain White-crowned Sparrows (*Zonotrichia leucophrys oriantha*) is delayed in years of deep snow. Many females then nest in small pines or willows, although they normally prefer to nest in dense grass on the ground (Morton 1978) (figs. 2.13, 2.14). Walsberg and King (1978) took hemispherical photographs with a "fish-eye lens" from the nest at 18 nest sites in Oregon, and found that the vegetative canopy over the nest on the average occluded 62 percent of the sky. These nests were exposed to the sun as it traveled across the sky 1.7 times longer before noon than after noon, and they were therefore exposed longer to the warming rays of the sun during the relatively cool hours of the morning. On the other hand, Zerba and Morton (1983) found that eggs in nests of Mountain White-crowned Sparrows in California exposed to the warm afternoon sun quickly became overheated unless shaded by the parent.

Penguins spend long hours hunting for food in cold waters, and their subcutaneous fat and dense plumage give them efficient body insulation. Of the eighteen species of penguins, temperate zone and polar species breed in dense colonies on open ground where there is more sun, and the hazards of snowdrift formation are reduced. Species of penguins that live in tropical, subtropical, and warm temperate regions nest in caverns or in burrows under dense vegetation, sheltered from the sun (Stonehouse 1970).

Among antarctic petrels the nature of the nest site and the timing of the breeding season in different species is determined by their relative immunity to snow conditions and to predation. In turn, the nest site helps determine other aspects of the life cycle. This point can be illustrated by five species of small antarctic petrels (Beck, 1970).

The Snow Petrel (*Pagodroma nivea*) and the Cape Petrel (*Daption capensis*), relatively robust birds with powerful bills and claws, are able to clear quickly the exposed sites in which they nest, in cliff recesses and on open cliff ledges, respectively. They also have the ability to eject stomach oil, a strong defense mechanism that makes them almost immune to predation by the large, gull-like skuas (*Catharacta skua*). They therefore are able to breed early in the summer in exposed situations and to begin laying eggs with the first increase of the zooplankton food, leaving time for a complete moult near the breeding grounds.

Smaller and more delicate antarctic petrels, including the Dove Prion (*Pachyptila desolata*) and two storm-petrels (*Fregetta tropica* and *Oceanites oceanicus*), must breed in deep crevices or in burrows in cliffs and slopes in order to survive skua predation. They can clear small amounts of loose snow, but are unable to deal with ice and hard-packed snow blocking their sheltered sites. They depend on the melting of snow and ice to make their nest holes available, necessitating late and extended breeding, which in turn forces them to moult in winter quarters.

Nest Sites in Hot and Dry Habitats

Examples of species with nest sites in very hot and dry habitats are the Egyptian Plover or Black-backed Courser (*Pluvianus aegyptius*), which breeds along rivers in tropical Africa, and the Gray Gull (*Larus modestus*), which nests in the driest desert of the world in the interior of northern Chile.

T. R. Howell (1979) studied the nesting behavior of the Egyptian Plover in southwestern Ethiopia. He points out that the bird is no longer found in Egypt, nor is it a plover, but a courser (Glareolidae). It nests on sand-bar islands exposed by low water during the dry season. The birds begin by making a great many nest scrapes in the sand-gravel substrate and the island becomes pockmarked with them. Both birds of a pair participate in scrape making, which may be continued for thirty days or more before egg laying. In making a scrape the bird tilts forward raising the hind parts, scrapes backward with its feet, and, lowering its breast, excavates a hollow by pushing backward with the feet while rotating slowly and sporadically. There may be some lateral sand tossing by the bill near the edge of the scrape, but most of the excavating is done with the feet. In Howell's study the scrape chosen as the final nest site could not be identified until after the laying of the first egg of the two- or three-egg clutch; no bits of vegetation, shells, pebbles or any other materials were ever placed around the nest.

Sand-bar islands in the tropics provide nesting places safe from most terrestrial predators but not from aerial predators. These islands are very hot and dry places to which the Egyptian Plover adapts in ingenious ways. The multiple nest scrapes may help to distract predators from the actual nest site. The parents take turns sitting on the eggs most of the day. Whenever the incubating bird leaves, it quickly throws sand over the eggs with the bill, concealing the eggs. In Howell's study, during the six hottest hours of the day, each parent frequently soaked its ventral feathers in the river nearby (river temperature 27°C) and returned to settle on the buried eggs, keeping them surrounded by wet sand and preventing them from overheating (fig. 6.1). At night the eggs were about two-thirds uncovered and were incubated continuously.

Incubation temperatures were measured by using a fresh egg implanted with a thermocouple as a replacement for one of a pair's own eggs, and simultaneously, relevant ambient temperatures were recorded. Air temperatures in the shade rose during the day to peaks of 45°C to 46°C (over 50°C in the sun). The bird often poked its bill in the sand around the eggs, presumably testing the temperature of the sand. As shaded air temperatures and surface dry sand temperatures often exceed 45°C, mere shading of the buried eggs would not prevent overheating. A balanced combination of body heat, solar heat, heat retained by the sand, and cooling with water at appropriate times kept egg temperatures within appropriate limits, averaging 37.5°C over the twenty-four hour period.

The soaking of the eggs for about six hours each day greatly reduces daily water loss from the egg and permits a long incubation period (30 days) without excessive dehydration, despite the relatively small size of the eggs in this species and in other coursers. Daily weight loss of eggs, resulting from loss of water vapor, was measured in natural nests and in a silica gel desiccator. Howell hypothesizes that the long incubation period is adaptive "by allowing enough time for prehatching maturation to produce a highly precocial chick, necessary for survival in an open sandbar island." At any approach of danger the chicks crouch down and

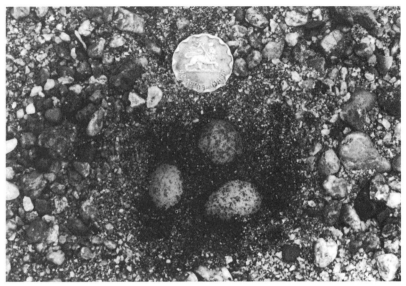

Fig. 6.1. Clutch of Egyptian Plover (*Pluvianus aegyptius*) eggs partly uncovered for photographing, southwestern Ethiopia. Dark area shows sand wetted by the parent bird; diameter of coin is 23 mm. (Thomas R. Howell, *Univ. Calif. Publ. Zool.* 1979)

Fig. 6.2. Egyptian Plover, parent bird with soaked ventral feathers settling on newly hatched chicks. (Thomas R. Howell, *Univ. Calif. Publ. Zool.* 1979)

Fig. 6.3. Nest scrape of Gray Gull (*Larus modestus*) with full clutch of two eggs, in a desert colony, northern Chile. (T. R. Howell, B. Araya, and W. R. Millie, *Univ. Calif. Publ. Zool.* 1974)

are quickly and completely covered with sand by a parent in the same way that the eggs are covered. Newly hatched chicks are also wetted by the parent with its soaked ventral feathers (fig. 6.2). Chicks can swim not long after hatching, and can fly in about thirty-five days.

In the interior deserts of northern Chile where the Gray Gull nests, rain has fallen at irregular intervals of many years or not at all in some places, within recorded history. T. R. Howell, Araya, and Millie (1974) observed a nesting colony of Gray Gulls in places where air temperatures ranged from a low of about 2.5°C at night to a high of about 38°C at midday. Surface temperatures in the sun often exceeded 50°C at midday. The surface of the soil was sandy with much rock rubble.

The birds fed along the coast and at sunset left for the interior. Many returned again to the coast at dawn. The nesting colony of some 10,000 pairs was about 30 kilometers from the coast, and security from predation was apparently the key reason for location of the colony in this hot desert.

Most of the territorial and courtship behavior before the eggs were laid took place at night. In the day birds not attending nests stood on rocks, which were cooler than the ground, and the birds cooled off by keeping their feet in their own shade. There was no vegetation in the

Fig. 6.4. Gray Gull shading chick in hot, dry desert, northern Chile. (T. R. Howell, B. Araya, and W. R. Millie, *Univ. Calif. Publ. Zool.* 1974)

area, and the nest was a simple scrape in the substrate with no materials gathered for it (fig. 6.3). Eggs were attended at all times, and during the hottest midday periods one parent stood over and shaded the eggs, as it does the chicks after they hatch (fig. 6.4). The authors suggest that the dark plumage of these gulls "may aid in avoiding excessive heat loading from solar radiation by allowing the outer surface to absorb heat and then lose it by convection, thus preventing deep penetration of heat to the body proper." Strong winds invariably started in the early afternoon, and then chicks of all ages could lose enough heat to avoid fatal heat stress, even if unshaded. Chicks were fed primarily at night by parents coming from the coast.

Originally the Gray Gull may have nested about now extinct lakes, the former existence of which is indicated by the presence of wave-cut benches of probable Pleistocene age in the surrounding area. The gulls probably flew inland from the coast to nest around lake borders, and this habit persisted as the lakes gradually disappeared and gave place to dry desert. This phenomenon necessitated daily feeding flights to the coast but, in compensation, there was a scarcity of predators in the desert nesting grounds.

The Phainopepla (*Phainopepla nitens*), a Silky Flycatcher (*Ptilogonatidae*), has another mode of adaptation to hot dry conditions in southern California. It breeds in March and April in the Colorado River desert area early in the season before conditions become severe. Then, as the desert heat and dryness and the food situation become worse, the Phainopeplas move west to the coastal oak and riparian woodlands of California where the population breeds again in late May through July (Walsberg 1977). Hence, the adaptation consists of shifting the nest sites from a hot dry habitat to a different, more mesic habitat when conditions in the desert become too severe. Woodland Phainopeplas expended about two to six times as much energy for flight as did desert birds, mainly because of the separation of food and nest sites. The large trees preferred for nesting in the woodlands are concentrated in canyon bottoms, usually at least 100 meters from fruiting shrubs. In the desert, food, mostly mistletoe berries, and nest sites were close together. Time and energy budgets revealed that the daily energy expenditure of Phainopeplas was 19 to 28 percent higher in woodland than in desert, primarily due to the increased time spent in flight.

The hot desert sun stimulates the cooling mechanisms of the birds and imposes an additional energy demand. When Weathers and Nagy (1980) measured the metabolism of free-ranging Phainopeplas more directly by physiological techniques, the results indicated energy needs about 40 percent greater than estimates derived from time-budget data. It pays the birds to move out of the desert as the weather gets hotter.

Nest-site Selection in Relation to Rain and Wind

Some of the rainiest places on earth are in the Hawaiian Islands and in the Malayan rain forests. Many of the Hawaiian honeycreepers (Drepanididae) inhabit high-elevation rain forests. About 40 percent of the 22 known species are extinct, but many still exist in the Kokee and Alakai swamp regions on the island of Kauai where over 600 inches (50 feet!) of rainfall have been recorded in a single year on Mt. Waialeale, only a few miles from the Kokee Swamp.

The Anianiau (*Hemignathus parvus*), a small yellowish honeycreeper, is common in the Kokee, and inhabits the rain forest where Ohia (*Metrosideros polymorpha*) is the dominant tree. All the nests of the Anianiau found there have been built in Ohia trees. Berger's (1972:133) photograph shows a nest well protected from the heavy rains by a dense cluster of Ohia leaves over the nest. The nest is built largely of mosses with the outer surface often covered by a layer of lichens. The Iiwi (*Vestiaria coccinea*), a brilliant orange-red honeycreeper with mostly black wings and tail, also hides its nest among Ohia leaves. Only the female incubates, and the male feeds her, calling her off the nest to be fed, so she can keep the eggs covered most of the time. The nest is built largely of Ohia twigs and lined with lichens and mosses (Berger 1972).

Most of the drepanidids build open cup-nests hidden in vegetation, but a few species may nest in cavities. The Apapane (*Himatione sanguinea*) may nest in lava tubes or in lava caves (Van Riper 1973). The first Akepa (*Loxops coccineus*) nest discovered in Hawaii was in a cavity in an Ohia tree and was built primarily of fern rhizomes and bryophytes with a lining of shredded grass and sedge leaves. Two other drepanidids, the Hawaiian Creeper (*Oreomystis mana*) and the Kauai Oo (*Moho braccatus*) may also nest in tree cavities (Sincock and Scott 1980). These species must derive greater protection from the rain by nesting in cavities than by nesting in the open, and it seems surprising that more Hawaiian honeycreepers do not do so.

The Elepaio (*Chasiempis sandwichensis*) is a native Hawaiian species belonging to the Old World flycatcher family (Muscicapidae). It builds a small cup-shaped nest. The Elepaio is fairly common in the Ohia rain forests, but in some places it also nests in introduced forests where one study by S. C. Frings (cf. Berger 1972) found that only 13 percent of 27 nests fledged at least one young. The high mortality was attributed to the fact that the birds built their nests in slender-stemmed trees in an area of high winds and extremely heavy rain. More than half of the 53 eggs were destroyed by heavy wind.

The spider hunters, members of the sunbird family (Nectariniidae), in the rain forests of southeast Asia fix their nests to the underside of a broad leaf that gives shelter from the frequent heavy rains. With their sharp pointed bills spider hunters force the ends of plant fibers or cobwebs, which support the nest, through the leaf from below and the cut surfaces then close together gripping the material (C. Harrison 1978). The Streaked Spider Hunter (*Arachnothera magna*) suspends its cup-nest just beneath the shelter of a large leaf. A nest of the Long-billed Spider Hunter (*A. robusta*) found at Selangor, Malaya, was trough-shaped, constructed of grass stems woven together and held closely against the underside of a banana leaf by a series of cobweb slings, with a long entrance tunnel opening towards the tip of the leaf (Medway and Wells 1976).

A problem similar to that met by birds nesting in high-rainfall areas is faced by the dippers (Cinclidae) that place their domed nests on rocky ledges next to rushing mountain streams where spray keeps the nest moist or even wet. The American Dipper (*Cinclus mexicanus*) may even build its nest behind the safety of a waterfall, diving through the falls to reach it. The exterior of the nest is made largely of living mosses, the interior lined with dry grasses and a few leaves (H. Harrison 1979).

An interesting convergence is that between the nest sites of dippers and those of certain swifts, birds belonging to different orders. The White-collared Swift (*Streptoprocne zonaris*), found from Mexico to Argentina, often nests in rock walls behind waterfalls, flying through gaps in the waterfall to reach the nest. Nests are shallow, mossy cups placed on narrow ledges in grottos behind the falls (J. Rowley and Orr 1965, Whitacre and Ukrain 1982).

A ten-year survey of Bald Eagle (*Haliaeetus leucocephalus*) nests, in the Sitka Spruce and Western Hemlock coastal forest of southeastern Alaska, found that nest loss from natural causes averaged 5 percent of the 73 to 91 nests surveyed per year. Nests were usually in the tops of tall trees near the shoreline. Of 33 nests destroyed in the ten-year period, 2 were in trees that were blown down, while the remaining 31 nests were blown out of their trees. The loss rate implied an average life expectancy of 20 years per nest. The average number of new nests built per year about equaled the loss rate, and that fact, in conjunction with continued low breeding success, suggests that the Bald Eagles in this area have reached a static population level relative to the available food supply (Hodges 1982).

During the mid-1960s, Ospreys (*Pandion haliaetus*) in Michigan reproduced very poorly and declined in numbers. The limiting factor was a shortage of natural nest sites, large dead trees killed by flooding. Such trees deteriorate faster than the capacity of a pond to supply the fish that the Ospreys eat. When artificial nest platforms were provided in appropriate places the population decline was reversed and the Ospreys increased in numbers. The platforms were plywood discs or octagons, 0.9 meter across, equipped with concentric rows of dowels to keep sticks and other nesting material in place. Most platforms were mounted on three steel legs, others were placed on existing dead, but still sturdy, trees.

Platforms were placed in what was believed to be a prime habitat for ospreys, and the number of young fledged per nest over a ten-year period was twice as great in 234 platform-nests as in 126 natural nests. While nest blow-downs during wind storms caused 57 percent of the nestling mortality in natural nests, only 6 percent of the nestling mortality was caused by blow-downs of platform-nests. In the Lower Peninsula (of Michigan) approximately two-thirds of the breeding population of ospreys were using the platforms in 1977, accounting for 80 percent of the reproduction (Postupalsky 1978).

Many birds place their nests on the protected side of a tree, to the lee of prevailing storms. The White-browed Sparrow Weaver (*Plocepasser mahali*) of East Africa and South Africa nests in small colonies with many nests in one tree. We noticed that nests of these species were often placed on the side of the tree away from the direction of approaching storms. Near Isiolo in north central Kenya, in 29 of 30 successive colonies along the roadside, the nests were on the west side of the tree (N. Collias and Collias 1964:14); storms here generally come from the east. In western India near the vicinity of Bombay, the Baya Weaver (*Ploceus philippinus*), which breeds in colonies at the time of the southwest monsoon, "almost invariably selects the eastern side of the tree to build upon" (Ambedkar 1964:18).

In north central Colorado, White-breasted Nuthatches (*Sitta carolinensis*) nest in cavities in living ponderosa pines, while Pygmy Nuthatches (*S. pygmaea*) nest in cavities in dead pines. Both species avoid cavities with openings facing north or west. In that region of the Rocky Mountains, the prevailing winds and rains come from the west and north, and during the breeding season of the nuthatches, temperatures below freezing are not uncommon. The selection of cavities facing away from the cold wind and rain results in energy conservation for parents and young (McEllin 1979).

In the Sierra Nevada mountains of California the American Kestrel (*Falco sparverius*) breeds mainly in nest cavities excavated by Northern Flickers (*Colaptes auratus*). It prefers nest trees on east-facing slopes or a nest entrance facing east as an eastern exposure gives protection from prevailing storms and facilitates warming of the nest in the morning (Balgooyen 1973).

Conner (1975) located seventy-eight nest holes of five species of woodpeckers in Virginia. More than twice as many of the nest entrances faced in a general northeasterly direction and away from the prevailing southwest winds. All but one of the nest openings faced downward, and Conner suggests that slope of the tree trunk is the most important factor in nest orientation. A nest opening that points moderately downward gives better protection from rain.

Predation and wind can be opposing factors in determining the placement of nests in trees. An isolated tree gives security from some predators, but such a tree is more exposed to wind forces. The neotropical Brown Jay (*Cyanocorax morio*) nests in small communal groups. In thirty nesting attempts at Monteverde, Costa Rica, these jays most commonly (86 percent) built in isolated trees, well away from windbreaks or patches of woods (Lawton and Lawton 1980). All five nests built in trees whose crowns touched other trees were destroyed by nocturnal predators, whereas only one of twenty-five nests built in isolated trees failed because of predation. However, at Monteverde, isolated trees are subject to strong prevailing winds. During a four-day storm, there were very strong winds (70 kph), and ten of the twelve broods under study were destroyed. The young were blown out of six nests, eggs fell out of three, and the entire nest with eggs was blown out of another tree.

Twenty test trees were chosen at random from all isolated trees without nests in the study area and compared with thirteen nest trees for degree of wind disturbance during a four-day windy spell. The Beaufort Scale was used, so that the relative wind speeds could be objectively judged from the movement of tree trunks, branches, or leaves. The average wind disturbance of the thirteen nest trees was significantly lower than that of the twenty other isolated trees. Flocks building in the more wind-protected sites fledged more young than flocks building in more exposed sites. Various investigators have shown that lack of suitable nest sites may limit populations of hole-nesting birds, but as the Lawtons point out, the possibility that suitable nest trees may be limiting to some tree-nesting species has received scant attention.

Building a Suitable Substrate for the Nest

Most ground-nesting birds merely modify and prepare the substrate by the usual nest scrape, but some birds prepare a more elaborate substrate for their nest. The Black Wheatear (*Oenanthe leucura*), a member of the thrush family (Turdidae), places its nest of plant fibers in holes or cracks in caves or on cliffs in arid, rocky, canyon regions, and builds a foundation of rocks for the nest. First the male, and later both male and female, carry rocks for the nest site. In twenty-two of thirty-seven nests examined in southeastern Spain, the rocks clearly prevented the nest from sliding off a sloping surface or formed a depression in which the nest rested. The number of rocks carried to a nest site varied from three or four to several hundred, each rock often weighing more than half the weight of the bird (Richardson 1965). The Rock Wren (*Salpinctes obsoletus*) of the western United States and Mexico, which lives in an arid, rocky habitat rather similar to that of the Black Wheatear in Spain, also commonly nests in rocky holes or cracks and regularly collects rocks to serve as a foundation for its nest, and as an approach to it (P. Smith 1904).

In the Kalahari Desert of southwestern Africa the nest of the Grey-backed Finch-lark (*Eremopterix verticalis*) is a simple cup, set in a foundation that varies with the substrate. In soft sand the foundation consists of perhaps a dozen pieces of stone or earth. On hard calcrete where it is difficult to make any sort of excavation at all, the finch-lark builds a substantial foundation of small stones surrounding the grassy nest cup. Of 194 nests, 153 were on calcrete and 33 in sand dunes. Most of the nests were sheltered by being placed against a grass tuft or shrub on one side. Like nests of other species of larks in the Kalahari Desert, the nests were oriented to face east or south so as to obtain maximal shade, especially in the summer (Maclean 1970).

In the Central Negev desert of Israel, Orr (1970) measured temperature and wind movements at two nests of the Desert Lark (*Ammomanes deserti*). Each nest faced north and was shaded against the midday sun by a bush or an overhanging stone. A semicircle of small stones forming a wall up to 4 centimeters high was built on the open side of the nest, enclosing the nest to its full height. This wall of pebbles contributed to the heat balance of the nest, which was apparently self-incubating for several hours of the day. The most rapid rise in air temperature at the nests began right after sunrise, helping to keep the eggs warm after the females left the nest to feed (the desert seeds contain a great deal more absorbed moisture early in the morning than later in the day). The females also periodically left their nests to forage at times of day when the nest were protected from overheating by being shaded or cooled by air movements.

In the shallow water of Andean lakes, where there is a great paucity of vegetation, the Horned Coot (*Fulica cornuta*) builds an islet of small stones on which it places a thin cover of water vegetation (*Myriophyllum*) for its nest. The supporting mound may contain one and a half tons of rocks. In contrast, in a lake at a lower elevation in northern Chile, where vegetation was more abundant, nests of this species were constructed entirely of vegetation, apparently *Myriophyllum* (Ripley 1957a, 1957b).

SUMMARY

Natural selection and competitive exclusion have forced many species of birds to select a nest site in difficult locations or in harsh climatic regions. Special microhabitats, behavioral adaptations, or modifications of nest sites, are then necessary for protection from cold, heat, drought, wind, and rain, or for adjustment to unstable subtrates.

In recent years there has been increasing emphasis on measurement of the microclimatic conditions at nest sites. Birds nesting in cold climates or on high mountains, seek shelter from the cold night sky and from cold winds and storms, in rocky crevices or in caves, or under sheltering vegetation. Nests may be situated to receive the warming rays of the early morning sun. In south polar regions, antarctic penguins nest out in the open where the birds get more sun and the danger of being covered by snow drifts is less.

In hot dry climates, where little or no nest insulation is needed, some birds dispense with the nest entirely. Nests of many desert birds are placed on the ground next to a sheltering bush or rock and receive the warming rays of the early morning sun, while being shaded in the hot afternoon when cooling breezes often prevail. Where shade is not available, nest sites may receive strong breezes during the hottest parts of the day, as in the case of the Gray Gull in deserts of Chile. The Egyptian Plover, which nests on sand bars, buries its eggs and even small young under the sand, and cools them off by water carried to the nest site in its belly feathers.

Many birds derive protection from wind and rain by placing their nests in trees on the side opposite to the direction of prevailing storms, or by placing the nest under or among leaves, in a large strong tree, or in a cavity that opens away from prevailing winds and storms.

Birds nesting on sloping ground in hilly areas may use small stones to build up and level the substrate supporting the nest, as do some wheatears, rock wrens, finch-larks, and desert larks. The Horned Coot in the Andean lakes builds a small island of stones on which it places its nest.

CHAPTER SEVEN

Adaptations of Nest Building to the Physical Environment

NEST-BUILDING behavior is adapted to extremes of cold, heat, wind, and rain. The nest may also be adapted to seasonal changes in conditions.

NEST-BUILDING ADAPTATIONS TO COLD

Keeping the Eggs and Nestlings Warm

Ancestral birds may have kept their eggs warm, as the megapodes or mound builders do today, by utilizing heat from decomposing vegetation, or from soil warmed by the sun, hot springs or volcanic action (H. Frith 1962). On New Britain, the Scrub-fowl (*Megapodius freycinet*) digs a burrow for its eggs, selecting soil of optimum temperature near creeks heated by volcanoes (Bishop 1979–1980).

The open cup-nest is typical of most passerine birds, especially in the North Temperate Zone (table 2.1). The size of the inner cup is automatically molded to the body size of the species because of the typical movements used in building, pushing in the nest with the breast while rotating and pushing back with the feet. The close fit of nest to bird helps make something of a seal, holding in warmth when the incubating bird is sitting closely. The tightly constructed cup-nest of the Anna Hummingbird (*Calypte anna*) provides effective insulation for the ventral surface of the body of the incubating female, including those body parts that produce the most heat—the large pectoral muscles and the viscera. The nest insulation and the reduced activity of the incubating female conserve considerable energy. A nest in Los Angeles was generally maintained about 10°C warmer than the surrounding air (T. Howell and Dawson 1954).

One reason for the prevalence of open nests among small birds of temperate and cool climates may be the need of the bird on the nest and its nestlings for the warming rays of the morning sun. One would expect enclosed nests to be warmer than open nests because they impede heat loss by trapping inside the roof the warm air rising from the birds within the nest. However, domed nests are typical of many tropical passerines and are relatively uncommon in birds of north temperate and colder regions (table 2.1). The primary function of a roof, therefore, is probably not protection from the cold, although a roof may be important for some very small birds especially vulnerable to cold weather—including titmice of which all species nest in holes or build enclosed nests. In winter titmice do not migrate but roost in holes, in clumps of dense foliage, or in tunnels in the snow (Perrins 1979).

Recent direct measurement of thermal conductivity for various nests marks the beginning of a quantitative study of the effectiveness of nest insulation (Whittow and Berger 1977, Walsberg and King 1978, Skowron and Kern 1980). Skowron and Kern found that measurement of the nest density by the degree of light penetration through the nest gives a good index of nest insulation. In general, the inner layer of the bird nest seems to provide most of the insulation, and is built of finer, more closely packed materials than is the outer layer.

Many species of birds line their nests with feathers, plant down, or hair. Special materials used for lining vary greatly with climate and availability. In open country many birds use fine grasses, in mountain forests birds often use mosses and lichens, while in lowland, tropical rain forests many species line their nests with fine filaments of *Marasmius*, the "horsehair fungus" (Sick 1957, N. Collias and Collias 1964).

Small birds in cold regions generally line their nests heavily. The tiny Long-tailed Tit (*Aegithalos caudatus*) of Eurasia (5–6 gm body weight) places from one thousand to over two thousand feathers inside its domed nest. The globular nest is built largely of moss, beautifully decorated with lichens on the outside, and bound together with spider silk. Another tiny resident species and the smallest bird of Europe, the Goldcrest (*Regulus regulus*) (3.8 gm), builds a deep cup-nest with a narrow upper opening. The nest is suspended in spruce trees, consists mainly of lichens, moss and cobwebs, and is lined with feathers and hair. In a single nest 2,672 feathers have been counted (von Haartman 1969).

The Calliope Hummingbird (*Stellula calliope*), the smallest bird of temperate North America, weighing only 2.6 grams to 3.4 grams, nests in the high mountains of western North America. The female incubates her eggs when exposed to nocturnal temperatures that approach freezing. She does not become torpid at night while incubating, nor does she show more reduction of activity while nesting than do other hummingbirds. Temperatures were recorded continuously from thermocouples imbedded in synthetic eggs placed in two Calliope nests in northwestern Wyoming. The average egg temperature in one nest was maintained at 34.6°C, in the other at 30.8°C. These temperatures are very similar to the average egg temperatures maintained during incubation by much larger birds in warmer climates. A protected nest site and the thick insulation of the nest seem to be the major factors in successful thermal adaptation of the nesting Calliope Hummingbird (Calder 1971). Like other hummingbirds this species builds a deep cup-shaped nest. The nest is made of thin strips of bark held together with spider webbing and is heavily lined with plant down. It is generally placed on a small branch or twig directly under a larger branch or under a canopy of foliage. The outside diameter of the nest is only 1¼ inches (3.2 cm), the inside diameter ¾ inch (1.8 cm) (Headstrom 1951).

The depth of the nest cup and incubation behavior are important in conserving energy. A female Broad-tailed Hummingbird (*Selasphorus platycercus*), which nests in the Rocky Mountains, who incubates with one-half her body exposed above the nest rim expends about 50 percent more energy than does a female who incubates with only one-fourth of her body exposed (Calder 1973).

Because of their large body size and their habit of lining their nests with down feathers plucked by the incubating female from her breast—ducks, geese and swans are preadapted to invasion of arctic regions and are among the common birds in those areas. The female covers the eggs with a blanket of down that keeps them from cooling rapidly whenever she leaves her nest, which is rather seldom. Eggs of a Mallard (*Anas platyrynchos*) in an uncovered nest cool about twice as fast as eggs under a covering of down (Caldwell and Cornwell 1975). Eider ducks breed on the northern coasts of North America and Eurasia, and the down of the Common Eider (*Somateria mollissima*), also used by man for eiderdowns and padded clothing, is a classic example of insulating material. Its insulating properties are said to be unsurpassed by man-made fibers (C. Harrison 1978).

Experiments in our captive colony of Village Weavers (*Ploceus cucullatus*) at Los Angeles showed that removal or reduction of the nest lining increases the percentage of time the female spends incubating, and so reduces the time she has available for foraging. The temperature of the egg is sensed through the brood patch and if the latter is treated with local anesthetic, the female allows her eggs to reach an abnormally high temperature before leaving her nest to forage, preen or bathe (F. White annd Kinney 1974). In Finland the hole-nesting Pied Flycatcher (*Ficedula hypoleuca*) shortens its sitting spells when the nest box is artificially warmed (von Haartman 1956). In cool climates, birds like the Barn Swallow (*Hirundo rustica*) (Kendeigh 1952) incubate more on colder days.

An incubating bird may conserve energy merely by sitting in the nest.

Walsberg and King (1978) measured the heat budget of White-crowned Sparrows in Oregon, and calculated that the heat expenditure of the incubating female while resting was 15 percent lower than in a bird perched outside the nest.

Properties of Some Nest-lining Materials

The physical properties of some materials that are used by birds in lining their nests, such as fine grasses, plant down, and feathers, have been summarized by Wainwright et al. (1976). The fine grass with which a great many birds line their nest entraps a lot of air which serves as good insulation. Heat moves faster through the material than through the still air, and the high proportion of dead air space per unit volume is responsible for the good insulating properties of the fine grasses lining the nest. Grasses have a high proportion of cellulose, and cellulose fibers have high tensile strength that serves to resist the stress and strain of growing nestlings pushing against the nest walls. Cellulose also has the advantage of being light in weight, reducing the labor of the bird in gathering fine grasses to line its nest.

The things that make fine grasses good nest-lining materials are present to an even greater degree in plant down and in feathers. A good example of the kind of plant down for which precise information on physical properties is available is kapok fiber from the seeds of the Kapok tree (Ceiba pentandra), which grows in many tropical regions. The hollow fibers of kapok down are very light, waterproof, and do not mat down but retain their elasticity. Kapok is used by people as filling for mattresses, sleeping bags, and life preservers, as well as for general insulation. Many tropical birds line their nests with kapok. The tiny Cape Penduline Tit (Anthoscopus minutus) of southern Africa often builds much of its nest of kapok and is sometimes called the "Kapok Bird."

Feathers, which are made of keratin, are the ideal nest lining material. According to Wainwright et al. (1976:188) "Down is one of the best known insulating materials because a small mass of keratin can trap an enormous volume of air." This high volume to mass ratio, so important to a flying animal, is possible only because the keratin, a helical protein, itself is very rigid. This means that the barbules on the down feather can be extremely thin and yet stiff enough so that the down will not collapse under its own weight or under reasonable compressive loads such as the weight of small nestlings. A similar argument applies to mammalian hair, which is also made of keratin. Some birds line their nests with hair, although not so many as use feathers.

Feathers lose much of their insulating value if they get wet. Stead's Bush Wren (*Xenicus longipes*) of New Zealand nests in holes in the ground or in logs, often in musty or wet conditions, and the parent birds frequently replace the feathers with which they line the nest (C. Harrison 1978).

ADAPTATIONS OF NEST BUILDING AND NESTING BEHAVIOR TO HEAT

Birds prevent very high temperatures from developing inside their nests in various ways: (1) by nesting in burrows, (2) by reducing the size and insulation of the nest or even by dispensing with the nest completely, the parent reducing its own body temperature by evaporative cooling while covering or shading the eggs and young with its body, (3) by bringing water or moist vegetation to cool the nest, eggs, or nestlings, and (4) by building a thick roof over the nest.

1. *Nesting in burrows* is widespread among birds, especially in non-passerine tropical land birds. The European Bee-eater (*Merops apiaster*) is a good example. It breeds in colonies in southern Europe, and nests at the ends of tunnels in bluffs, river banks, or road cuts. It digs a tunnel, six to seven centimeters in diameter, into the vertical face of a bank to a depth of one or two meters and usually one or more meters below the top of the bank (fig. 7.1). Both sexes dig, loosening the soil with the beak and kicking it backward with the feet. F. N. White, G. A. Bartholomew, and J. L. Kinney (1978) studied the physiological and ecological correlates of tunnel nesting in the European Bee-eater in two breeding colonies near Cordoba, Spain. They watched the behavior of the birds inside the nest holes through a fiberscope, a highly flexible, fiber-optics light-tube two meters long that piped light from an external light source to the area being viewed in the nest chamber at the end of the tunnel (fig. 7.2). No nest was built in the chamber and the nestlings, which were fed on insects, rested on the floor of the chamber on a bed of discarded insect remains—the small naked young often buried to their necks in insect debris. Temperatures inside the nest chamber were measured by a thermocouple attached to the flexible tip of the fiberscope. Nest-chamber and tunnel humidities were measured with a hygrometer.

The birds breed in the hot dry season. The surface temperature of the soil ranged from 13°C to 51°C, but in the cool depths of the tunnel, temperature fluctuations were effectively damped and the temperature in the nest chamber remained within or near the thermoneutral zone of the birds, requiring no increase in metabolic work for the birds to maintain normal body temperature. The mean of 24 nest-chamber tem-

Fig. 7.1. European Bee-eater (*Merops apiaster*) colony with nest holes in an earthen bank, Spain. (Reprinted from F. N. White, G. A. Bartholomew, and J. L. Kinney, *Physiological Zoology* 1978 by permission of the University of Chicago Press, © by The University of Chicago.)

peratures was 25.1°C ± 2.1°C, only about 3.5°C above that of the surrounding soil. The moisture given off by the breathing of nestlings and adults helped keep the humidity in the nest chamber at or near saturation. High chamber humidity, minimal thermal stress, and succulent insect food all combined to keep the nestlings in water balance.

The absence of nest sanitation combined with decomposition by microorganisms caused significant periodic elevations of ammonia and carbon dioxide and decreases in oxygen in the nest chamber particularly when there was little or no wind, as at dawn. Gas samples were obtained from nest chambers and tunnels by syringe through a 2-meter long polyethylene tube. On two occasions when the CO_2 concentration rose to about 6 percent from the average 3.3 percent, the breathing of the feathered nestlings observed through the fiberscope was conspicuously labored and rapid. However, gusts of wind across the mouth of the tunnel rapidly ventilated the nest chamber. By blowing tobacco smoke directly into the nest chamber through a polyethylene tube down the tunnel, it was demonstrated that air entered the tunnel along its walls while air from the nest chamber moved out along the central axis of the tunnel in a series of pulsating spirals. Other factors helping to ventilate the nest chamber were diffusion of gases into the soil from the nest chamber and tunnel walls—convection and diffusion resulting from the temperature difference between nest chamber and outside air—and fi-

Fig. 7.2. Fiberscope photograph of a European Bee-eater (*Merops apiaster*) inside its nest tunnel, the adult nestled in litter of insect parts while brooding its young. (Reprinted from F. N. White, G. A. Bartholomew, and J. L. Kinney, *Physiological Zoology* 1978 by permission of the University of Chicago Press, © by The University of Chicago.)

nally, the piston effect of adult birds moving rapidly along the close fitting tunnel. After the young were about half-feathered neither adult remained at the nest for more than a few minutes at a time but spent the night perched in trees in the vicinity of the breeding colonies, thereby reducing O_2 intake and CO_2 output in the nest chamber.

2. *A very thin nest or the complete lack of a nest* is typical of some birds that nest in very hot, dry places. The parent reduces its own body temperature by evaporative cooling. The White-winged Dove (*Zenaida asiatica*), which nests in the deserts of the southwestern United States, often places its nest in the top of a cholla cactus (*Opuntia* sp.) where the nest receives little or no shade during the day. The nest is a flimsy platform of about one hundred to one hundred fifty twigs with little or

no lining materials, and the two eggs can be seen from beneath through the nest material.

In Arizona, Russell (1969) discovered that at high ambient temperatures of 42°C to 45°C the incubation patch temperature of the incubating White-winged Dove did not exceed 39.5°C, and egg temperatures were generally maintained only slightly higher (less than 1°C) than the temperature of the incubation patch. On the six hottest days of the study the maximum egg temperature recorded each day ranged from 37.9°C to 40.5°C. He suggested that the egg may be cooled on very hot days by heat transfer from the egg to the brood patch. In effect, the bird sits on its eggs to keep them cool.

Unlike birds that stand over the eggs and shade them to keep them cool, the White-winged Doves in hot weather settled even more closely on the eggs, and they did not appear to pant or gular flutter in order to increase their rate of evaporative cooling under the conditions of Russell's field study. However, it has been found that birds may lose more than half of their evaporative water through the skin (Bernstein 1971). The brood patch—being bare of feathers, highly vascularized, and edematous—may be important to increase cutaneous water loss. Since the dove sits closely over the eggs, it seems that the very loose and open construction of the flimsy nest facilitates evaporative cooling and the escape of moisture from the incubation patch.

Heerman's Gulls (*Larus heermanni*), which breed on Mexican desert islands, sit closely on their eggs and maintain continuous contact between brood patches and eggs at least during the hours of daylight. They do not stand in the nest to shade their eggs as does the Gray Gull (*L. modestus*) in north Chilean deserts, but keep their eggs from overheating by behavioral thermoregulation of their own body temperature (Bartholomew and Dawson 1979). Under severe heat loading during calm, clear days they cool off by elevating the scapular, head and nape feathers, drooping their wings, and panting heavily. Although ground temperatures may be critical and often exceed 50°C (measured 3 to 5 mm below the surface), the gulls keep the temperature of their eggs nearly 20°C below that of the adjacent bare ground, as well as 5°C above that of the air. The wind is normally much cooler than ground temperatures during the day because of the cold water surrounding the island. In the open valleys of the island (in this study), the nests of the Heermann's Gulls were shallow depressions scraped in the loose soil. Nests on surrounding rocky ridges were often more exposed to cool winds, and many of these nests were well-formed bowls of twigs and scraps of dry vegetation.

Some species of birds in very hot regions have dispensed with nest material completely. In the Salton Sea area of southeastern California, the Lesser Nighthawk (*Chordeiles acutipennis*) lays and incubates its eggs directly on the ground during the hot summer. This area is one of the hottest, driest parts of the world, where summer ground temperatures in the sun exceed 50°C almost daily. Grant (1982) studied the temperature and water relations of several birds in this region. Nighthawks can maintain their body temperatures well below ambient temperatures in very hot weather by evaporative water loss resulting from more or less continuous gular flutter. Grant suggests that the temperature of the abdominal air sacs near the incubation patch may be lowered even more than core body temperature. The incubating, female Lesser Nighthawk can keep her eggs at a temperature of 41°C when the surrounding shaded ground temperature is 2°C higher, and she keeps her eggs covered throughout the day. Of 11 nighthawk nests found during this study only four sites were fully exposed to the sun. Three females incubating near shade moved their eggs several centimeters during the day to take advantage of the available shade.

3. *Bringing water or wet vegetation to the nest* is another way in which birds cool their eggs and nests in hot dry places and prevent excessive water loss from the eggs—for example, some shorebirds, sand grouse (Maclean 1968), and several kinds of storks (Kahl 1971). By cooling the eggs with water or moist materials instead of eliminating the nest, the advantages of a nest are retained. Several species of storks in tropical areas carry water in their bills to their nests; even though they nest in very exposed sites, they prevent their eggs from overheating by dripping the water over their nest and eggs.

By soaking its belly feathers in the water at frequent intervals the Black-necked Stilt (*Himantopus mexicanus*) keeps its eggs cool and can nest in some very hot places near water, such as the Salton Sea region (Grant 1982). Like other shore birds generally, it nests on the ground in the open, exposed to the full power of the sun. Carrying water to cool its nest helps make this possible, the advantage of an exposed site presumably being a better lookout for approaching predators. Grant measured temperatures at the surface of the egg (incubation patch temperature) and inside the egg and could detect no consistent differences. It appears, therefore, that the Black-necked Stilt relics on carrying water in its belly feathers for keeping the eggs cool.

4. *A thick roof protects the nest contents from the sun* in many species of tropical and subtropical passerine birds. The Village Weaver, like a number of related species of weaverbirds, makes the roof of its nest thick with a special lining or ceiling just inside the roof. In an aviary colony

of Village Weavers at Los Angeles the shade provided by the roof in twelve unlined nests gave summer temperatures that were 5°C to 8°C cooler on a hot day than outside black-bulb temperatures in the sun (35.0°C–37.8°C). Brood nests are lined below, and were somewhat cooler than unlined nests because of the generally thicker roof and walls of the brood nests (N. Collias and Collias 1964).

Within certain large families of widely distributed passerine birds, some species build open nests while others build domed nests, including in the latter case a larger proportion of those species found in the tropics. Of 27 species of New World flycatchers (Tyrannidae) in the western United States and Canada, only 2 build domed nests (Peterson 1961), whereas of 29 species of this family in tropical Surinam, 14 build domed nests (Haverschmidt 1968). Similarly, among Old World flycatchers (Sylviidae) in Europe, 41 species have open nests and only 11 have domed nests (C. Harrison 1975); whereas in West Africa, 33 species have open nests while fully 37 species build domed nests (Mackworth-Praed and Grant 1970).

Nest-building Adaptations to Daily Changes in Temperature

Nesting in cavities helps stabilize temperatures for many birds, sheltering them from extremes of cold and heat. A good example is the hornbill nests studied in South Africa by F. N. White et al. (in press). These nests were instrumented with remote temperature sensors (thermistors) placed in drill holes at appropriate locations in the tree cavities in which the hornbills nested. A fiberoptic scope was used to observe the nest interior.

Temperatures during one day inside the nest chamber of a Grey Hornbill (*Tockus nasutus*) varied only between 21°C and 31°C, whereas the tree surface varied from 15°C to 44°C. Temperatures within the nest chamber were stable throughout the cool night, and 5°C to 7°C higher than the external air temperature. This was important since a large proportion of the dark hours were characterized by outside air temperatures below the lower critical temperature (about 20°C) for the birds. During the daylight hours shaded air temperatures were always within the presumptive thermoneutral zone of the birds, the temperature range over which metabolism is minimal.

There are two reasons for the relative stability of temperatures within the nest cavity of hornbills. First, the thick walls of the tree trunk have sufficient insulative quality and low thermal conductivity to cause a pronounced lag in temperature changes between the air outside and inside the walls. Thermal lag during the hot period of the day prevents excessive overheating of the nest chamber. During the cool night, heat stored within the wall flows into the nest chamber while the outer part of the wall cools.

Secondly, the hornbills use the same principle as do humans in ventilating a room by opening a window at top and bottom, allowing warm air to escape at the top while cool air enters at the bottom. The nest chamber is situated below the vertical entrance slit and heat from the bird's body rises by convection and flows out the top part of the entrance while cool air enters at the bottom of the slit. Measurements of temperatures at the entrance slit showed that a gradient of about 0.5°C exists from the upper to the lower parts of the slit.

The same system powers the ventilation of the nest cavity. Measures of gas composition revealed that O_2 levels in the chamber were seldom more than 5 percent lower than in ambient air, and the CO_2 levels reached were not sufficient to be of physiological concern. As a matter of fact, there was additional venting in most of the many hornbill nests examined through heart-rot channels in the wood next to the nest cavity.

ADAPTIVE SEASONAL VARIATIONS IN NEST BUILDING

Nest-building behavior may be adapted to withstand marked seasonal changes in temperature, particularly in dry and desert regions. The Mallee-fowl (*Leipoa ocellata*, Megapodidae) of the dry dwarf eucalypt scrub ("mallee scrub") of southern Australia, instead of sitting on its eggs, builds a mound of sand, digs a hole in the mound, scratches leaf and twig litter into the sand, makes a depression to a depth of one or two feet within which the eggs are laid, and then covers the eggs with leaf litter and soil. The eggs are incubated by a combination of heat produced by decomposing vegetation and the sun. By scratching soil on or off the mound the attending bird, mostly the male, closely regulates the temperature within the mound about the eggs, keeping the eggs at a temperature of 32°C to 35°C, despite marked seasonal variations in conditions (H. Frith 1962). At the same time, by turning over the soil of the mound, the male improves oxygen conditions for the developing eggs and facilitates decomposition of vegetation within the mound. Oxygen consumption of embryos is higher than predicted on the basis of egg mass (Vleck et al. 1980).

During much of the long breeding season the Mallee-fowl keeps the eggs from becoming overheated from decomposing leaf litter in the early morning by opening the mound to permit excess heat to escape, or later in the day by piling sand high over the mound to protect the eggs from the sun's heat. But late in the season, with no organic matter left in the mound and a weaker sun, the problem becomes one of keeping the eggs warm. This the bird does by thinning the soil covering them thereby exposing them to the sun's heat, or by scratching sand warmed by the sun over the eggs (H. Frith 1962).

During one breeding season the hen lays some twenty to thirty eggs, which hatch, depending on conditions, in about fifty to ninety days. The great variation in the incubation period suggests that mound incubation is not as efficient as the normal style of incubation by birds. But since the eggs are laid at intervals of four to eight days and chicks hatch and depart individually, there is less risk of losing the whole brood to a predator.

The Cactus Wren (*Campylorhynchus brunneicapillus*) nests in the deserts of Arizona where the weather is often very cool early in the breeding season and very hot in the latter part of breeding season. The roofed nest is usually placed in a cholla cactus and the side entrance faces outward. The nest is built of short pieces of small tufted grasses in a framework of long grass stems or dried stiff stems of buckwheat (*Eriogonum trichopes*), and is lined with finer grasses, small feathers, and some plant down. The resident birds build winter roosting nests in which they sleep singly, and build breeding nests in the springtime. There is no essential difference between the two kinds of nests and they are sometimes interchangeable. Both sexes build the first breeding nest. While the female is incubating the first brood, the male builds another nest for the second brood. When the young fledge, the adult wrens lead them to a roosting nest in the evening (Anderson and Anderson 1973).

During cold weather the breeding nest of the Cactus Wren helps retain heat. Temperatures in nests containing small young incapable of thermogenesis were elevated as much as 10°C above ambient temperatures, most of this heat probably contributed by the brooding adult. During hot weather with ambient temperatures above 33°C the nests were often cooler than the surrounding air. As the ambient temperature increased, the difference between nest and outside temperature decreased (Ricklefs and Hainsworth 1969).

Orientation of nests may vary with season in an adaptive way. The Verdin, or Yellow-headed Tit (*Auriparus flaviceps*), a small bird inhabiting the deserts of the southwestern United States and neighboring Mexico, builds a roofed nest of twigs and grasses, lined with feathers, and having a side entrance. Early in the breeding season, nests are placed on the east side of trees with the entrance usually facing east. Later nests used for the second brood are placed on the southwest side of the tree and with the entrance usually facing southwest. Based on 182 early brood nests and 206 later brood nests, G. T. Austin (1976) found differences in placement and orientations significantly different from uniform distribution.

In the area under study, the direction of strong winds is from the southwest and remains roughly the same throughout the breeding season. The entrance of early nests faces away from the wind during the cool part of the season and also receives the warmth of the early morning sun. The entrance of later breeding nests is oriented into the prevailing winds during the hottest part of the breeding season and presumably derives some cooling effect from this air movement. The percentage of eggs laid that fledged young was significantly greater in both early and late breeding nests with the preferred orientation than in nests having other orientations. Small roost nests, with smaller and thinner walls than breeding nests and no linings, are generally built in summer by both adult and young Verdins. They are used at a time when temperatures reach their highest levels and little insulation is needed.

The nest of the Sociable Weaver (*Philetairus socius*) of southwestern Africa, a gigantic communal structure, was described and illustrated in chapter 2. F. White, Bartholomew, and Howell (1975) have studied temperature regulation in the nest of this species. They placed temperature-measuring devices in some nest chambers and in various parts of the nest matrix in a large, and also in a very small, nest mass in the Kalahari Desert. Temperatures compared with the outside air were very stable inside the nest chambers, and temperature fluctuations were much less in the large nest mass than in the small one. In the nest chambers of the large nest mass the temperature was maintained at or near the thermoneutral zone of the birds, permitting them to maintain a stable body temperature with little or no increase in energy requirements. During the winter nights temperatures fell below freezing in the Kalahari Desert, but temperatures in the chambers were maintained as much as 18°C to 23°C above external air temperature. Extra warmth was provided by the huddling activity of birds sleeping together, and heat was retained by the insulating qualities of the nest mass. The more birds that slept together the more heat produced, and the larger the nest mass the better the heat retention. Natural selection has therefore favored increase in size of the compound nest in this species. A nest mass may occupy most of the crown of the supporting tree and grow to be 5 meters to 6 meters long and 1 meter to 2 meters or more thick.

The energy savings provided by the compound nest permits year-round breeding of the birds as long as the erratic rainfall results in adequate grain and insect food. Under suitable conditions of food supply the Sociable Weaver can breed in the winter time when its arch enemy the Cape Cobra (*Naja nivea*) is inactive. F. White et al. (1975) calculated that birds the size of Sociable Weavers needed 43 percent less oxygen for temperature regulation if they huddled together in the nest chambers than if they roosted in the open. The reduced metabolic costs in effect means that the birds require less food and less foraging time, increasing the effective carrying capacity of the environment. As many as five hundred Sociable Weavers have been known to live in a single tree (Maclean 1973). Since the nest is built by and lasts through successive generations of birds, a given generation contributes to the energetic costs of thermoregulation over many decades (F. White et al. 1975). A colony of Sociable Weavers has been known to occupy the same tree for over one hundred years (N. Collias and Collias 1964).

The same three investigators returned to study the same Sociable Weaver nest in the following summer (Bartholomew, White, and Howell 1976). They found about the same number of birds (142) sleeping in the nest mass at night during the summer as they had previously counted in the winter (150). But whereas in the winter they had found usually four or five birds roosting in the same chamber with many chambers unoccupied at night, during the hot summer there were no more than two adults per chamber with 94 percent of the chambers occupied. Air temperatures during the summer outside the nest ranged from 16°C to 33.5°C but temperatures in occupied chambers varied only 7 or 8°C. Temperatures remained well within the zone of thermal neutrality for the Sociable Weaver. Thus their large compound nest enables the birds to conserve considerable energy in both winter and summer.

ADAPTATIONS OF NEST BUILDING TO FLOODS, WIND, AND RAIN

The Adélie Penguins, which build their nests of small stones above water from melting snow, have been mentioned in chapter 2. Analogous cases are those of the Black-browed Albatross (*Diomedea melanophrys*) and the Grey-headed Albatross (*D. chrysostoma*), both of which nest on South Georgia Island in the South Atlantic (lat. 54°S). The nests of both species are short, thick columns of packed soil and grass with a depression at the top, and are about 30 centimeters in diameter and 10 to 45 centimeters high. The ground between the nesting columns is often very wet and muddy, but the columnar nests provide effective protection for the eggs and nestlings. In bad weather the sitting adult drapes its wings over the edge of the column and keeps the nest depression perfectly dry. Most nests last for many years, and the occupants renovate the upper portion before and during incubation. Where there is grass within reach, older nestlings sometimes line the cup with it (Tickell and Pinder 1975).

Several species of gulls nest in colonies in tidal marshes that flood daily. Spring tides, onshore winds, or prolonged rain may cause even higher flooding and create additional hazards. Laughing Gulls (*Larus atricilla*) nest in grassy (*Spartina*) salt marshes of the eastern United States and build substantial nests. They continue adding material throughout incubation. Under normal conditions nest size increases until the chicks are five days old and able to swim well. Nests are built highest during incubation and widest when they contain young chicks. A heavy rain that fell for twenty-four hours during the egg-laying period was followed by increased nest building. When two liters of water was poured over each of fifteen nest at various stages of the reproductive cycle, the gulls increased the nest depth, whereas all control nests remained the same size over the twenty-four hour experimental period. Laughing Gulls establish pairing territories at least three weeks before egg laying, and these areas subsequently become their nesting territories. Selection of nest territories well in advance of egg laying allows the birds to ascertain that the selected location is free from normal flooding (Burger 1978).

Herring Gulls (*Larus argentatus*) also nest in salt marshes, often alongside Laughing Gulls but in higher, drier places. The fate of 124 nests of Herring Gulls in different marsh areas was followed. In the dry areas at least one egg hatched in 95 percent of the 15 nests, in wet-dry areas hatching success in 84 nests varied from 40 to 75 percent, while in the wettest areas none of the eggs hatched. The gulls abandoned their nests only after a very high tide raised the water over the top of the eggs. Herring Gulls constructed larger and deeper nests in wet areas than in dry areas, and experimental reduction of the nest depth by removing part of the nest materials resulted in immediate repair only in the wet areas (Burger 1977, 1978).

Birds may vary the nest site or nest to adapt to strong wind conditions. Schaeffer (1977) measured the thickness of supporting twigs and of nest-attachments for 285 nests of the Northern Oriole (*Icterus galbula*) in Canada and the United States. Nests in the windy Great Plains are built on thicker, more stable branches and are more securely attached to the tree than are nests in the Ontario-Quebec area of Canada. The Great Plains nests also have a smaller diameter at the top opening of the nest, giving more protection from wind, rain and sun—despite the larger average body size of the orioles there.

In the African Village Weaver, when the pensile nests are tossed about by strong winds, the females sit closely and do not leave to feed at the short intervals they normally do (N. Collias and Collias 1970). Davis (1971) observed that the nests of the Baya Weaver (*Ploceus philippinus*) in India are attached to the tree so that the side of the nest

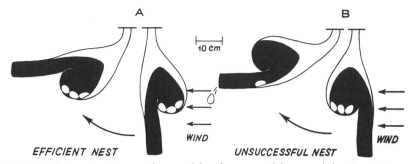

Fig. 7.3. Orientation in tree of successful and unsuccessful nests of the Baya Weaver (*Ploceus philippinus*), in relation to prevailing winds, India. The eggs are tossed out of improperly oriented nests. (T. A. Davis, *Forma et Functio* 1971)

containing the eggs faces the prevailing wind. The entrance is at the bottom of a long tube attached to the opposite side of the nest from the egg chamber. When a nest with the normal attachment to the tree is tilted by the wind, the egg chamber is lowermost and the eggs are safe within. But if a nest built with the egg-chamber side facing away from the wind is strongly tilted by the wind, the eggs would roll into the entrance tube and be ejected (fig. 7.3).

Nests of some birds are counterbalanced against gravity and wind by pellets of soil or small stones placed in the nest. The cup-nest of the Sooty-capped Hermit (*Phaethornis augusti*), a hummingbird of Venezuela, hangs from some overhead support by a single stout cable of spiders' silk attached to one side of the rim of the nest. This eccentric attachment would permit the nest to tilt when the female sits in it, except that directly below the point of attachment she fastens, also by cobwebs, little lumps of dry clay or pebbles in a streamer that dangles from the bottom of the nest. The added weight acts as a counterpoise to keep the nest level (Skutch 1973:73). Skutch notes that frequently among species of hummingbirds the rim of the cup-nest is incurved, reducing the danger that the eggs will be shaken out by the wind.

Birds with cup-nests in the tropical rain forest adapt to heavy rain in various ways other than just sitting on the nest protecting its contents. In Trinidad, Snow (1976:117) found that the Black-and-White Manakin (*Manacus manacus*) almost always used for its nest lining the fine branching panicles of a forest-edge plant *Nepsera aquatica*, which forms a tenacious interlocking cup and "probably has the further advantage that it dries out quickly so that the nest cup does not become sodden after heavy downpours of rain." He quotes (p. 120) Yoshika Willis, that many species of birds near Belem, at the mouth of the Amazon, use

Nepsera panicles in their nests. Snow also points out that hummingbird nests are often covered on the outside with lichens and cobwebs, forming a more or less waterproof coat. The Bronzy Hermit (*Glaucis aenea*) uses thin, rather stiff rootlets and leafless stems of mosses and liverworts for its nest, making loose, open walls that dry rapidly after a rain (Skutch 1973). The nest is so thin-walled that the eggs can be seen through the sides of the nest (Greenwalt 1960:23). The relatively poor insulation of such a nest is no great handicap in the warm lowlands where these hummingbirds live. Furthermore, hermit hummingbirds fasten their cup-nests beneath a living leaf providing some shelter from the rain.

The roof of domed nests has many functions, but one must be protection from the rain, since most passerine birds of the tropics either nest in rain forest, or else during the rainy season in more open country. Skead (1947) made a direct test of the rain-shedding ability of the nest of the Cape Weaver (*Ploceus capensis*) of South Africa. When he poured five gallons (3.8 l) of water from a watering can over a nest, not a drop penetrated. The male Cape Weaver puts in a special lining or ceiling just under the woven roof of the nest, and this ceiling is thatched rather than woven.

Roofed Nests and Possible Protection from Ultraviolet

We have suggested that danger from the ultraviolet radiation of the sun to young altricial nestlings might be a factor of importance in the evolution of the roofed nest of small birds in the tropics (N. Collias and Collias 1964:129). However, this still seems to be an open question.

The amount of ultraviolet radiation in sunlight that reaches the earth's surface depends mainly on the amount of ozone in the atmosphere. This ozone is responsible for the fact that radiations below 2,900 A are absorbed before reaching the surface of the earth. The amount of ozone in the North Temperate Zone is practically double that at the equator, and the absorption coefficients indicate some five to ten times more absorption of ultraviolet in the North Temperate Zone than at the equator during the spring and early summer (Goody, 1954). These are the characteristic breeding times for most birds in the northern hemisphere.

From the preceding considerations we concluded that an important function of the roof or domed nest in the tropics might be protection from solar radiation. The danger from ultraviolet radiation could be relatively greater in the tropics, when compared with temperate or arctic geographic regions, than the difference in the relative heating effects of the sun. Present evidence is insufficient to decide which of these two hazards has been the more important evolutionary force. Both might well have been of considerable importance. Indeed, solar radiation might be of primary importance only in such exposed habitats as savanna and desert, whereas predation pressure and rainfall might exercise relatively greater influence on the evolution of domed nests in the tropical rain forest.

Some Parallels between Bird Nests and Primitive Human Houses

The earliest known human dwellings were in the Stone Age and were natural caves or shallow pits dug in the ground and roofed over with animal skins or other materials (F. Howell 1965). Some of the earliest bird nests were probably in burrows or among rocky crevices, as is the case in most present-day shearwaters and petrels. Burrows and rock crevices, like caves, provide protection not only from wind and precipitation, but also from wide temperature fluctuations, because of the high heat capacity of soil and rock. Early man probably also built roofed shelters of sticks and grasses, just as hunter-gatherers, such as Australian aborigines and African bushmen, still do. Similarly, a number of birds build simple domed nests of twigs and grasses on the ground.

J. M. Fitch and D. P. Branch (1960) review primitive human architecture in relation to climate. There are some interesting parallels with bird nests. The adobe hut is admirably adapted to a hot dry climate. The high heat capacity of the thick mud-masonary walls stabilizes internal temperatures by absorbing the sun's heat during the day and releasing it gradually during the night. The Hornero, or Rufous Ovenbird (*Furnarius rufus*) of the Argentine pampas builds a nest with a side doorway, and thick walls and roof of mud with some straw, hair, and dung (Fraga 1980); essentially a little adobe hut, comparable to those built for withstanding the heat of the sun by the human inhabitants of tropical and warm temperate America. The quality of the mud is important. The mud nests in some colonies of Cliff Swallows contain much sandy silt and are clearly more friable than nests in other colonies. It has been found that adding sand to adobe reduces its compressive and tensile strength in direct proportion to the amount of sand added. Inclusion of organic matter (straw and manure) in adobe also decreases its strength (Kilgore and Knudsen 1977), so Cliff Swallows seem to have compensated for this by building their nest shell of pure mud.

Many African natives cover their huts with a thick roof thatched of palm, reeds, or other plant materials. The heavy domed roof of the huge nest of the Sociable Weaver of the arid savanna and deserts of southwestern Africa is also thatched of dry grass stems and fine twigs, and the thick walls and roof of the nest similarly protect the birds from the strong sun and reduce temperature fluctuations within the nest chambers.

In tropical rain forest, the heavy rainfall, the intense solar radiation, and the high humidity are problems. In primitive human dwellings the roof becomes the dominant structural element, steeply sloping to shed torrential rains, opaque to solar radiation, and of minimal mass to avoid heat buildup and subsequent irradiation into the living space. Walls are thin or even lacking. Bird nests in lowland rain forest frequently have a domed roof or are placed under a leaf, and the walls and floor of the nest are often very thin compared with nests of related species in cooler, drier climates.

It would seem difficult to find a parallel between anything constructed by a bird and the snow igloo of the Eskimo, which is so ingeniously adapted to the arctic climate. The intense and steady cold of the Arctic winter requires a wall material of the lowest possible heat capacity, and dry snow meets this criterion admirably. Then too, the Eskimo drapes the interior of his snow shell with furs, thereby preventing the chilling of his body by either radiant or conductive heat loss to the cold floor and walls. The ptarmigans (*Lagopus*), of the Arctic regions and the high Rocky Mountains above timberline, may dig little hollows in the snow where they sit sheltered from the cold wind whistling overhead. To sleep they may even fly into banks of snow, sometimes going out of sight (Grosvenor and Wetmore 1937). Insulation in the interior of their snow chambers is furnished by their own thick coats of body feathers.

The parallels one can draw between bird nests and human houses are somewhat limited, because the functions of the two are not exactly the same. The bird's nest is not only an abode, but also an incubator in which the bird and its nest together act as a functional unit.

SUMMARY

Nest-building behavior is adapted in different species of birds to help them withstand cold, heat, rain, wind, or flood. In recent years there has been an emphasis on actual measurement of the increased energy demands of stressful microenvironments in relation to the type of nest built, and new techniques for direct measurement of thermal conductivity of nests have been developed.

Nests of megapodes or mound builders provide warmth to incubating eggs from heat sources such as decomposing vegetation, solar radiation, or volcanic activity. Frequent moving of the materials in the mound by the birds facilitates decomposition and helps meet the oxygen needs of the developing embryo eggs.

Almost all birds provide heat from their bodies to their eggs or nestlings by sitting on them. Many birds line their nests with feathers and plant down, which are the best insulating materials because they are very light, firm enough not to compress excessively under the weight of the incubating bird or the nestlings, and their fine structure entraps a great deal of still air. Different species of birds line their nests with a great variety of materials according to availability, for example, fine grasses in open country, mosses and lichens in wet mountain forests, and filaments of *Marasmius*, the "horsehair fungus," in tropical rain forests.

In general, nest linings are thicker in cold localities, and may be thin or even absent in very hot localities, although small birds generally put in some form of nest lining regardless of geographic location. The outer layer is generally of relatively coarse supporting materials that help prevent the lighter, finer lining materials from being blown away. Nest insulation, by facilitating the warming of eggs and nestlings, saves energy and allows the parent to spend more time foraging.

In very hot regions the nests of some species of birds are reduced or disappear in evolution, and various heat-dissipating measures, including shading by the parents, keep the eggs and nestlings cool. Some desert birds actually sit on their eggs to keep them from overheating in very hot weather, and incubation patch temperature in these species is lower than ambient temperatures. Other means of keeping the nest and its contents cool in hot climates include digging of burrows or use of tree cavities (many nonpasserine land birds), and building of roofed nests (many tropical passerines). Some birds (sandgrouse, stilts, and storks), which have open nests exposed to the hot sun, cool their eggs by bringing water to the nest at suitable intervals.

Nest-building behavior in a variety of species may change with seasonal conditions so as to stabilize temperatures in the nest. Nests or nest cavities with thick walls stabilize wide daily fluctuations in temperature.

In wintertime, the Sociable Weaver of the Kalahari Desert of southwestern Africa keeps warm at night by sleeping in groups of up to five birds per nest chamber in their huge compound nest, and many chambers are left unoccupied. In the hot summer the birds generally sleep in pairs, with most of the chambers occupied. This behavior, combined with the large size and heat capacity of the nest mass, keeps temperatures relatively stable with minimum energy expenditure.

Birds adapt their nests to rain, wind, and flood in various ways, in addition to placing the nest in a sheltered or dry place. For protection from rain, various species of birds use waterproof materials, build a cup-nest with an open, porous structure that drains readily, or build a roofed nest, sometimes adding a special ceiling. For protection from wind, some species of birds build a deep cup with strong attachments to the support, other species build roofed nests with the entrance oriented away from the wind. For protection from floods, water birds may build the nest higher in wet places, especially after it rains.

There are some parallels between bird nests and primitive human houses in different climates, but such parallels are limited because the nest is not only an abode, but also an incubator in which the bird and its nest function as a unit.

CHAPTER EIGHT

Nest Competitors and Parasites

COMPETITION for nest sites, or for nests, has had a profound influence on the evolution of nest diversity, as well as on the general life history of birds. There is much evidence of direct competition for nest sites among birds, and competition as a cause of nest diversity follows by implication. Adaptations of nest-building behavior against avian and invertebrate nest parasites have also evolved.

COMPETITION FOR NEST SITES

During the present century the Herring Gull (*Larus argentatus*), with improved feeding conditions, has been expanding its breeding range southward along the Atlantic coast of the United States, displacing the smaller Laughing Gull (*L. atricilla*) from the grassy (*Spartina*) salt marshes. Although the Herring Gull normally nests on higher ground, the preferred nesting areas of the two species overlap, and where they do, the larger and more dominant Herring Gull evicts the Laughing Gull from the higher parts of its nesting grounds. Eggs and chicks of Laughing Gulls are also eaten by Herring Gulls nesting nearby. The Herring Gulls arrive earlier in the spring and preempt much of the nesting grounds well before the Laughing Gulls arrive. Laughing Gulls are forced to nest in lower parts of the salt marsh, in places relatively free from Herring Gull predation and where their nests become more subject to tidal floods, particularly in years of high flooding. At Clam Island, New Jersey, over a three-year period from 1976 to 1978, numbers of Herring Gulls increased from eight hundred to twelve hundred pairs, while Laughing Gulls decreased from five thousand to five hundred pairs (Burger and Shishler 1978, Burger 1979).

Nest-site competition between species of penguins has increased recently in the Antarctic in mixed colonies of the Adélie Penguins (*Pygoscelis adeliae*) and Chinstrap Penguins (*P. antarctica*) (Trivelpiece and Volkman 1979). Adélie Penguins arrive on the nesting grounds first and become weakened by prolonged fasting during incubation; the Chinstraps then arrive and aggressively usurp their nests, and as a result the Adélies have a high egg loss. Competition for nest sites has increased with recent dramatic population growth among pygoscelid penguins in response to increased availability of the krill food supply in areas of past whaling activities.

The raptors provide many good examples of competition for nest sites (Newton 1979). Their numbers and nest success are in some regions clearly limited by the availability of nesting places. The breeding density of cliff-nesting raptors is limited by the number of cliffs with suitable ledges, and their breeding success by the accessibility of these ledges to predators. Other raptors may be limited in their nest building by short-age of suitable nesting trees. The Mississippi Kite (*Ictinia mississipiensis*) extended its original breeding distribution in the Great Plains of America to places where trees were extensively planted by man. Pairs of Prairie Falcons (*F. mexicanus*) increased locally after suitable nest holes were dug for them in banks along rivers. European Kestrels (*Falco tinnunculus*) increased in one Dutch area from fewer than twenty to more than a hundred pairs when nesting boxes were provided, and similar results have been obtained with Kestrels (*F. sparverius*) in America. On the other hand destruction of nesting areas may sometimes reduce breeding density, as in the case of Peregrines where breeding cliffs were destroyed by mining.

Good nest sites are often traditional, serving as "ecological magnets" over many years, or even centuries, and regularly continue to attract individuals of the same species. This is especially true for the larger species of raptors. Particular cliffs are known to have been used by successive pairs of Golden Eagles (*Aquila chrysaetos*), White-tailed Eagles (*Haliaeetus albicilla*), Peregrine Falcons (*Falco peregrinus*), and Gyrfalcons (*F. rusticolus*) for periods of seventy to one hundred years. Of British Peregrine cliffs in use from 1930 to 1939, at least forty-two were known to falconers between the sixteenth and nineteenth centuries. Certain eagle nests have been used for longer than a man's lifetime. Some nest sites remain in use by raptors even when both occupants are shot every year. The type of acceptable nest site may vary geographically. The Gyrfalcon uses trees regularly in much of its Asiatic range, but only very rarely in Europe and North America.

In the competition for nest sites among raptors there is a general precedence of larger species over smaller ones. At cliffs in Britain, Golden Eagles take precedence over Peregrines, and Peregrines over Kestrels. When numbers of Peregrines were reduced by pesticides, Kestrels took over many of the nesting cliffs, only to be displaced when the Peregrines returned. An 18-year study involving 80 cliffs on the Colville River, Alaska, found that Gyrfalcons and Common Ravens (*Corvus corax*) began nesting early in the year and used only the best sites such as vertical cliffs that were sheltered by overhangs. The later-nesting Per-egrines occupied a wider range of generally more exposed sites to which a person could easily walk, and the Rough-legged Hawks (*Buteo lagopus*) occupied an even wider range including very exposed ledges and steep talus slopes or boulder tops on hillsides (C. White and Cade 1971). Aerial surveys of a bay in Florida over several years showed fewer Osprey nests on islets following establishment of a pair of Bald Eagles (*Hali-aeetus leucocephalus*), and more Osprey nests on islets that had lost an eagle pair. On one islet the establishment of an eagle pair was followed by relocation of nest sites by eight of thirteen Osprey pairs and a re-duction of Osprey breeding success that year (Ogden 1975).

Raptors defend the vicinity of their nest sites, especially against their own species, and fights are sometimes fatal. Territorial displays consist of aerial maneuvers visible over long distances and conspicuous calling or perching near the nest site. Many eagles and hawks bring fresh, green, leafy sprigs to their nests, and Newton (1979:90) suggests that the green leaves (which fade quickly) may denote an occupied territory as opposed to an unoccupied one. In continuously suitable habitat, the nests of different pairs of raptors are often separated from one another by approximately equal distances, as for the Sparrow Hawk (*Accipiter nisus*) in Scotland. Such regular spacing accords with the idea that the breeding density is limited by the territorial behavior of the birds.

Individual behavior during competition for nest sites can be observed within the species by use of color-marked individuals. Early in the breeding season different pairs of Canada Geese (*Branta canadensis*) competing for the same nest site may be successively displaced by more dominant pairs (fig. 8.1). The larger, more aggressive male drives off a more subordinate pair from a nest site in which his mate is interested. Breeding success was strongly correlated with differences in relative dominance status of the different males (N. Collias and Jahn 1959).

In central Africa, we watched color-banded Village Weavers (*Ploceus cucullatus*), a polygynous species, over the nine-month breeding season (N. Collias and Collias 1959). Violent fights between males seeking to establish territory were common early in the season. One banded male, AW, was the first male to build in the colony tree in October and the last to leave in June. In contrast, a second male, BA, who began to build almost as early as AW did, was evicted from his territory after a few months and thereafter led a shifting existence. During the next six months he built nests in succession on three other sides of the tree, and even in an adjoining colony. During all this time he secured only one mate, whereas some other color-banded males had up to seven mates in the breeding season, and as many as five at one time. The territory of

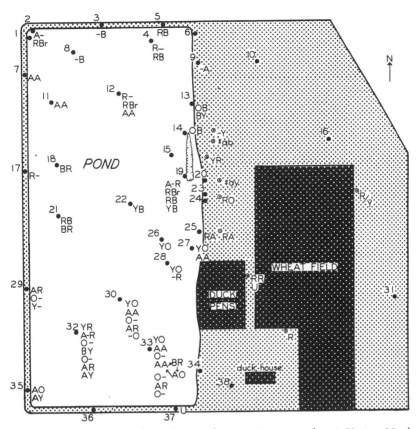

Fig. 8.1. Map of 11-acre enclosure for Canada Geese (*Branta canadensis*), Horicon Marsh Wildlife Refuge, Wisconsin, showing successive territorial occupants (indicated by letters) of specific nest sites during one season (March–May, 1952). Artificially provided nest sites (black dots) are numbered; a nest built by a female in some other locality is shown by a dot in a circle. Letter designations refer only to the male of a pair, unless otherwise indicated. Stippled area is land. (N. E. Collias and L. R. Jahn, *Auk* 1959)

another male who was captured by a hawk was promptly taken over by a neighboring male.

During most of the season there were generally about fifteen males and from thirty to forty nests in the tree. When most of the suitable twigs were occupied by brood nests, many of the males invaded other colonies nearby *en masse*, just as they might themselves be invaded by strange males coming in a group. Invaders frequently gang up on one male and so fight their way into the tree. However, most of the invaders did not stay permanently.

COMPETITION FOR NEST HOLES AND NESTS

Competition for nest holes in trees by birds is likely to be intense, because such sites are often in limited supply. Species of birds that use tree holes will often use nest boxes put out by man, and populations of such species as House Wrens (*Troglodytes aedon*) (Kendeigh 1934) and Pied Fly-catchers (*Ficedula hypoleuca*) (von Haartman 1971), may be increased dramatically by putting up many nest boxes. According to Perrins (1979), with the provision of nest boxes in British woods, the number of tits starts to grow immediately. However, above a certain level, an increase of nest boxes seems to have no noticeable effect on the number of tits.

Competition for nest boxes takes place between species as well as between individuals of the same species. The Prothonotary Warbler (*Protonotaria citrea*) is one of the few American warblers that build their nests within natural tree cavities or birdhouses. The House Wren destroys the warbler's eggs by puncturing them with its bill when the warbler is absent. The same observer found a fledging rate for the Prothonotary Warbler of only 26 percent (of 413 eggs) in Michigan at a place with many House Wrens, whereas at a locality in Tennessee where House Wrens were absent, the fledging rate for the warbler was much higher, 61 percent (of 163 eggs) (Walkinshaw 1941).

Different sizes of entrance holes result in competition for tree cavities or nest boxes by species according to body size. The greatest single cause of the drastic decline in populations of the Eastern Bluebird (*Sialia sialis*) is thought to be the competition for nesting sites in cavities between the Bluebirds and the introduced House Sparrow (*Passer domesticus*) and Starling (*Sturnus vulgaris*) (Zeleny 1978). The European Starling is the most serious enemy of nesting bluebirds, but with an entrance hole of the right size—"not less than 36 mm and not more than 40 mm in diameter"—lines of from several to thousands of nesting boxes put up by concerned individuals and organizations in recent years, have been highly effective as a means of restoring and increasing bluebird popu-lations.

Success in competition between species for nest holes may vary with circumstances in different parts of the geographic range. In Britain, the House Sparrow nests most frequently under the eaves of houses and in other suitable holes and crevices in buildings, while the Eurasian Tree Sparrow (*Passer montanus*) nests most commonly in tree holes. The two species may compete for tree holes near buildings, and the House Sparrow is usually successful over its slightly smaller relative. In the Far East, where the House Sparrow is absent, the Tree Sparrow breeds in typical House Sparrow sites in buildings. In Russian Turkestan, Afghanistan, and North Pakistan, where the House Sparrow is a summer visitor while the Tree Sparrow is resident, the normal roles are reversed, the Tree Sparrow breeding in the houses, the House Sparrow in holes in banks and cliffs, as well as in trees (Summers-Smith 1963).

Some species that nest in tree cavities may depend on tree holes dug by woodpeckers where other tree cavities are scarce. The Northern Flicker (*Colaptes auratus*) may be critical to the maintenance of some populations of the American Kestrel, which takes over nesting-cavities from Flickers (Balgooyen 1973). Other species of birds that are so dependent on woodpecker holes for nest sites that their abundance and distribution is affected by that of the woodpeckers include many different species of starlings, the Tree Swallow (*Tachycineta bicolor*) of North America, Elf Owls (*Micrathene whitneyi*) and Pygmy-Owls (*Glaucidium gnoma*) in the western United States, New World flycatchers (*Myiarchus*), and Old World flycatchers (*Ficedula*) (Short 1979).

Birds and other animals that find the nesting-cavities built in trees by different woodpeckers ideal as nest sites compete actively for these nest holes, as do the woodpeckers themselves (Short 1979). Jackson (1978) lists nineteen different species of animals using the highly preferred nest site excavated by the Red-cockaded Woodpecker (*Picoides borealis*) of the pine forests of the southeastern United States. This woodpecker digs its nest cavity in a living pine, often taking months to a year to complete the cavity. European Starlings are not able to enter Red-cockaded Woodpecker cavities of normal size, but can enter cavities that have been enlarged by Red-bellied (*Melanerpes carolinus*) or Red-headed (*M. erythrocephalus*) Woodpeckers. In some areas Acorn Woodpeckers (*M. formicivorus*) lose almost all of the nests that they excavate early in the season to Starlings (Short 1979).

Tropical woodpeckers often lose nest sites to competitors. Short (1979) saw Nubian Woodpeckers (*Campethera nubica*) and Bearded Woodpeckers (*Dendropicos namaquus*) lose nest holes to various African starlings. The tityras (Tyrannidae) of the New World tropics successfully usurp the nest holes of several species of melanerpine woodpeckers by filling the nest holes with leaves and debris whenever the owners are absent, until the woodpeckers eventually give up removing the leaves and abandon the nest. Other tropical birds that may usurp woodpecker holes include toucans, barbets, parrots, hornbills, some ovenbirds (*Xenops*), and some wood creepers (Dendrocolaptidae).

Many woodpeckers excavate their nest holes in live trees and most competitors larger than woodpeckers are physically unable to enlarge the hole in live or very hard dead wood. Woodpeckers compete with each other for holes, one species simply driving away another, usually smaller, woodpecker. The Hairy Woodpecker (*Picoides villosus*) may take over the nest hole of a Downy Woodpecker (*P. pubescens*), which it then enlarges for its own use. This may explain the tendency of smaller woodpeckers to select branches that barely permit the dimensions of their nest or roost cavity.

Virtually all woodpeckers require individual roost cavities, and most species excavate a new nest cavity yearly. Almost every adult woodpecker has one to several roost cavities or evasion holes to which it can retire at night, and it may switch to an alternate hole if a cavity is lost. During the initial period of nest excavation, a woodpecker may start several holes before finally deciding on the one to be used for nesting. The availability of other partly completed or completed holes facilitates rapid renesting in case of eviction. There are many known cases of woodpeckers excavating two, three, or even more cavities and losing them to competitors just at the completion of excavation. Woodpeckers become very attached to a nest site as its excavation nears completion, and when the adult is within the cavity, the chances of a nest competitor dislodging it are slim.

Most woodpeckers nest at that time of year when insect food is most readily available for the young, and any loss of a nest hole delays and reduces chances of successful breeding. The availability of several alternate holes is especially advantageous after the young fledge, for recently fledged young are particularly vulnerable until the time when they can excavate their own cavities.

Woodpeckers are highly territorial. Red-bellied Woodpeckers may harass Red-cockaded Woodpeckers, which are somewhat smaller, and sometimes take over the latters' nest cavities for their own use. Red-cockaded Woodpeckers are unusual in that they live in social groups which defend one to over thirty trees with cavities. These trees are usually clustered in a small part of the clan's large home-range, facilitating their defense by the group as a whole against other species of woodpeckers, which more often occur as widely dispersed pairs or individuals (Short 1979).

Competition for burrows is common among birds, and sometimes involves competition with mammals. The distribution of Burrowing Owls (*Athene cunicularia*) coincides with the occurrence of colonial burrowing rodents (*Spermophilus* and *Cynomys*) whose burrows the owls use for nest sites. In fact, availability of burrow sites appeared to be the critical factor in the prediction of Burrowing Owl numbers in one study in southern California (Coulombe 1971). Near San Francisco, Thomsen (1971) found that California Ground Squirrels (*Spermophilus beecheyi*) provided most of the burrows used by Burrowing Owls. On several occasions the owls apparently evicted the squirrels. Sometimes the owls dig their own burrow.

The breeding population of the Bermuda Petrel (*Pterodroma cahow*) was reduced to only eighteen pairs in 1962 by a combination of rat predation, which forced the petrels to nest only on offshore islets free of rats, and killing of petrel nestlings by White-tailed Tropicbirds (*Phaethon lepturus*). The tropicbirds preempted burrows occupied by the petrels. The conservation division of the Bermuda Government installed a partition or "buffer" at the mouth of the burrows occupied by petrels with an entrance hole so designed that the petrels (25 gm body weight) could enter easily while the larger tropicbirds (400 gm body weight) were excluded. By this means the production of petrel young tripled and the breeding population increased to twenty-six pairs between 1961 and 1977 (Wingate 1978). In effect, the same principle, which had been shown to be effective in excluding starlings from bluebird nest boxes, was applied to a burrow-nesting species.

Birds compete with each other for nest materials. An unguarded nest in a Village Weaver colony is subject to theft of fresh nest materials by neighboring males (N. Collias and Collias 1959b, 1970). Rufous-tailed Hummingbirds (*Amazilia tzacatl*) of Central America in locally concentrated populations may have nesting failures up to 50 percent as a result of nest materials stolen by other hummingbirds, apparently because of poor territorial defense by the female which builds the nest (Skutch 1931).

The Great Horned Owl (*Bubo virginianus*) of North America, does not build its own nest, but breeds very early in the year and preempts the old nest of some other bird, such as a hawk or a heron. Owls and falcons often use the old nests of other species of birds—such as crows, ravens, or hawks—in which to lay their eggs. The Prairie Falcon may use an old nest of a Common Raven (fig. 8.2), or lay its eggs on a bare cliff site (fig. 8.3).

Use of old nests might lead in evolution to competition by some species for freshly built or occupied nests. Strong, enclosed nests of some passerine birds are in special demand by some other bird species that do not build their own nests. The White-rumped Swift (*Apus caffer*) of Africa almost invariably uses the retort-shaped, mud nests of certain swallows, either old nests or a new nest appropriated from the owner. It rarely builds its own shallow, saucer-shaped nest (MacWorth-Praed and Grant 1960). Several species of birds in Argentina may use the adobe, oven-shaped nest of the Hornero or Rufous Ovenbird (*Furnarius rufus*) for breeding or roosting. House Sparrows (*Passer domesticus*) will sometimes usurp the nest. Horneros build a new nest each season;

Fig. 8.2. Prairie Falcon (*Falco mexicanus*) with its young in an old Common Raven (*Corvus corax*) nest on the side of a cliff, Mojave Desert, California. (Photo: Thomas J. Kaiser)

Fig. 8.3. Prairie Falcon young on a bare cliff ledge, no nest having been built, Mojave Desert, California. (Photo: Thomas J. Kaiser)

the nest may be started two or three months before egg laying, may weigh four kilograms, and may last up to eight years. The Hornero tends to avoid nest and brood parasites by laying early, compared with other local passerines (Fraga 1980).

The Large-billed Scrub Wren (*Sericornis magnirostris*) may construct its own small nest, oval with a side entrance, in parts of Australia where no other wren warblers (Sylviidae) occur. But in south Queensland and New South Wales it lays its eggs in the large (up to 1 m long) domed nest of the Yellow-throated Scrub Wren (*S. citreogularis*), using old and disused nests, or sometimes usurping freshly built nests (H. Frith 1979). In Africa, the Cut-throat Finch (*Amadina fasciata*), an estrildid finch, will use old or new nests of the Grey-capped Social Weaver (*Pseudonigrita arnaudi*) (Cunningham-van Someren 1971). A pair of Piratic Flycatchers (*Legatus leucophaius*) will persistently harass a female Chestnut-headed Oropendola (*Psarocolius wagleri*), which is about twice the size of the flycatcher, until she abandons her large elaborate nest to them (Chapman 1929). These flycatchers typically appropriate domed or closed nests of various species of birds, and virtually every oropendola or cacique colony in Panama includes a pair of Piratic Flycatchers (Ridgely 1976).

Avian Brood Parasites and Competition for Nests

The ecology of brood parasitism by birds has recently been reviewed by Payne (1977). About one percent of all bird species are brood parasites, laying their eggs in other birds' nests, leaving their young to be reared by other species. Brood parasites usually find the nests of their hosts by watching the owners build. Brood parasites with altricial young include cuckoos (Cuculidae), honey-guides (Indicatoridae), cowbirds (Icteridae), widowbirds and indigobirds (Ploceidae, Viduinae), and the Cuckoo Finch (*Anomalospiza imberbis*) whose taxonomic relations are uncertain; it is usually placed in the Ploceidae. Among birds, the only obligate parasite with precocial young is the Black-headed Duck (*Heteronetta atricapilla*, Anatidae) of Argentina.

Four steps in the evolution of brood parasitism in birds can be recognized (Friedmann 1929, 1960, Payne 1977):

1. Many species of birds appropriate old nests of other species for breeding. In Africa alone more than a hundred species of birds frequently use the old nest of other birds but rear their own young (Payne 1977:19). Friedmann (1960:18) lists nine species of estrildid finches that often use old, abandoned nests of other kinds of birds.

2. Active take-over of the nest of another species, particularly at the time of nest building and egg laying, may have been a precursor of

brood parasitism. Chestnut Sparrows (*Passer eminibey*) of Africa may occasionally build a nest, but usually take over a nest of some other finch, such as the Grey-capped Social Weaver (*Pseudonigrita arnaudi*). The sparrows then rear their own young in the usurped nests, sometimes adding a lining (Payne 1969).

3. Occasionally, a bird that normally rears its own young lays an egg in a nest occupied by another bird, either of its own or of a different species. Use of a fresh nest would help insure that the reproductive cycle of the bird laying this egg was synchronized with that of the nest owner, as might use of a nest of the same or of closely related species. In North America, the Yellow-billed Cuckoo (*Coccyzus americanus*) and the Black-billed Cuckoo (*C. erythropthalmus*) occasionally lay in nests of other species, and often in each other's nests (Harrison 1979). The female Redhead Duck (*Aythya americana*) often lays in the nests of other ducks, both of the same and different species (Weller 1959).

4. Obligate brood parasitism, in which one species must lay its eggs in the nest of another because it has lost the tendency and ability to incubate its own eggs, is the last and critical step in the evolutionary origin of interspecific brood parasitism (Friedmann 1960:21). At the same time the fact that most parasites lay only a single egg in a host nest, would help spread the risks of predation (Payne 1977:22). Total number of eggs laid in a breeding season by parasitic birds is generally higher than the number laid by related species that rear their own young. Freed of the need to incubate their eggs and raise their young, brood parasites can devote more energy to producing eggs.

In 1909, Carlo Emery formulated a principle that parasitic ants "generally originate from the closely related forms that serve them as hosts" (Wilson 1971:30), and this principle, later known as Emery's rule, was shown to apply to parasitic social Hymenoptera in general by E. O. Wilson (1971:383–84). Emery's rule also applies to avian brood parasites, but for the most part only in a broad, general way. The following give instances of this general phenomenon. The viduine finches have as hosts the estrildine or estrildid finches belonging to the same or closely related family; there has been a parallel evolution of parasitic species and their specific hosts (Nicolai 1964, 1967; Payne 1982). The primitively parasitic cowbirds parasitize members of the same genus. The honey-guides lay their eggs in nest holes of barbets and woodpeckers, which belong to families in the same order (Piciformes) as the honey-guides. The Black-headed duck may lay its eggs in nests of the Rosybill Duck (*Netta peposaca*) of the same subfamily (Anatinae), but it also parasitizes nests of the unrelated coots and ibis (Weller 1968). The cuckoos (Cuculidae) seem to be most out of line with Emery's rule, since they parasitize a wide range of small birds from another order, the Passeriformes. However, as mentioned above, two species of North American cuckoos that normally build their own nests and raise their own young, often lay in each other's nests.

The classic sequence in evolution of brood parasitism in birds is that of the cowbirds (Friedmann 1929). The Bay-winged Cowbird (*Molothrus badius*) of South America sometimes makes its own nest but usually lays its eggs in other birds' nests. However, it incubates its own eggs and raises its own young. It will fight vigorously for the nest of other birds, for example, various species of ovenbirds including the Rufous Ovenbird (Friedmann 1929). The Screaming Cowbird (*Molothrus rufoaxillaris*) lives in the same geographic range as the Bay-winged Cowbird (*M. badius*) and lays its eggs in nests used by the latter, which then rears the young of the former. The eggs and young of the two species appear similar. The Shiny Cowbird (*M. bonariensis*), another South American cowbird, may parasitize various small birds, for example, the Rufous Ovenbird. The Brown-headed Cowbird (*M. ater*) of North America has been known to lay its eggs in the nests of more than a hundred species of birds, which have then reared the young cowbirds to fledging (Friedmann 1963).

Friedmann (1963) has listed 29 species that have been known to avoid parasitism by burying the eggs of the cowbird beneath new nest linings. Berger (Van Tyne and Berger 1976:528) found a six-storied nest of a Yellow Warbler that held 11 cowbird eggs. A Hooded Oriole (*Icterus cucullatus*) has been known to avoid parasitism by a cowbird by building a second adjoining compartment in its nest, in which it reared its brood, leaving the cowbird egg unhatched in the original compartment (Hardy 1970).

Several species of waxbills (*Estrilda*) of Africa are frequently parasitized by viduine finches. A pair of waxbills often builds an open false nest on top of their domed nest; the latter contains their eggs (Chapin 1954). A remarkable evolutionary convergence is the similar open false nest built on top of its domed nest by an Australian warbler, the Yellow-rumped Thornbill (*Acanthiza chrysorrhoea*), which is frequently parasitized by a cuckoo (Beruldson 1980). Presumably, the false nest tends to deceive or divert brood parasites, but evidence is needed to support this supposition.

Some host species are less adaptable. Expansion of Brown-headed Cowbirds into the range of Kirtland's Warbler (*Dendroica kirtlandii*) in Michigan was followed by a marked decrease in the total population of the warbler. When cowbirds were removed by human observers, breeding success of the warblers increased greatly (Walkinshaw and Faust 1974).

The Didric Cuckoo (*Chrysococcyx caprius*) in Africa often parasitizes weaverbird hosts having the same color and pattern of eggs as the cuckoo (Payne 1967, Friedmann 1968). It has a wide range of color and pattern in its eggs, which may or may not match those of a given host. The Village Weaverbird (*Ploceus cucullatus*), as a species, has a wide range of color and pattern of eggs, but each female consistently lays one type of egg throughout her lifetime (E. Collias 1984) and will throw out eggs that do not match hers (Victoria 1972).

Arthropod Ectoparasites in Nests

The object of this section is to show how arthropod nest ectoparasites influence the nest-building behavior of birds. The main arthropod ectoparasites of birds include members of the Class Arachnida—such as mites and ticks—and of the Class Insecta—such as bird fleas, cimicid bugs, various flies and their larvae, and feather lice.

The book by Miriam Rothschild and Theresa Clay (1957) is a classic and an authoritative and readable introduction to the study of bird parasites. Recent literature on the ecology of ectoparasitic insects is summarized by A. G. Marshall (1981), and the literature on mites is reviewed in the proceedings of an international congress of acarology edited by Rodriguez (1979). Much of the extensive literature on the insect fauna of birds' nests has been listed by Hicks (1953, 1962, 1971).

It is important to understand the arthropod fauna found in birds' nests to understand the origin of arthropod ectoparasites of birds. In turn, these parasites have influenced the evolution of building behavior in birds. Marshall (1981:21–22) notes that "the radiation of the mammals and the birds marked the beginning of the nest or burrow microhabitat with its stable environment and abundance of potential food for insects and it is from the nest communities associated with this habitat that many ectoparasitic insects are thought to have evolved."

The fauna of a bird's nest is a biotic community, the species composition of which varies with the nature of the food base provided. Decomposers feed on plant matter in the nest, scavengers on the birds' excrement and on remains of insect and vertebrate prey, predators and parasites attack the other invertebrate nest inhabitants, while other ectoparasites feed on the blood, skin, and feathers of the bird host. Arthropod ectoparasites of birds also serve as vectors of many diseases. There is a definite succession of invertebrates at each stage in the history of a bird's nest from its inception, during its use, and after final desertion (Phillips and Dindal, 1977).

The Main Arthropod Nest Parasites

The inhabitants of birds' nests are chiefly arthropods. Norberg (1936) analyzed the fauna in the nests of 56 species of birds in Finland, from which he recorded no less than 529 different kinds of arthropods, including 228 species of mites and 118 species of beetles, while the rest consisted of various species of bugs, flies, ticks, feather lice, moths, springtails, earwigs, book-lice, spiders, and a few parasitic Hymenoptera. From the nest of one species of swallow, the Sand Martin (*Riparia riparia*) of Switzerland, Büttiker (1969) recorded 42 species of arthropods, including 23 parasitic species.

Many niches for invertebrates exist in bird nests. Certain mites and fly larvae and a few moth larvae feed on birds feces. The larva of a clothes moth, *Tinea pellionella*, common in swallow and sparrow nests, feeds on the nest lining. Rove beetles (Staphylinidae) are regular inhabitants of bird nests and prey on other insects and mites, while histerid beetles (Histeridae) have been observed in nests devouring fleas. A group of predaceous mites (Chelytidae) lives permanently on the bodies of birds and preys on feather mites (Analgesidae). Pseudoscorpions (Arachnida) also hunt and eat mites.

The woodroach (*Parcoblatta pennsylvania*) lives in and near the damp and rather unsanitary nest cavities of the Red-bellied Woodpecker (*Melanerpes carolinus*) of the southeastern United States and illustrates some of the complex relations of commensals and parasites to the nesting habits of birds. This woodpecker often selects for its nest site tree stubs or branches covered with a lot of loose bark where it forages for the woodroaches concealed underneath. But the Red-headed Woodpecker (*M. erythrocephalus*), in the same general areas, selected limbs without bark for its nest hole and did not feed on woodroaches. It also keeps its nest cavity cleaner. The woodroach serves as an intermediate host for an intestinal parasite, a spiny-headed worm (*Mediorhynchus centurorum*; Phylum Acanthocephala) that appears to be restricted to Red-bellied Woodpeckers (Jackson and Nickol 1979).

Blood-sucking arthropod ectoparasites that live in the nest and attack the host bird intermittently include ticks, fleas, cimicid bugs, flies, and fly larvae. They can go a long time between meals and may overwinter in or near the nest during the nonbreeding season when the bird host is absent.

Over half the species of described bird fleas are from birds that return to the same nesting sites year after year (Rothschild and Clay 1957:90). Fleas often lay their eggs in the nest, where the flea larvae live and later pupate. Most bird fleas are found on birds that breed in burrows, on the ground, in banks, or that use mud in constructing their nests. Most species of fleas inhabit rodent burrows, and bird fleas may have evolved several times from mammalian fleas (A. G. Marshall, 1981). Different species of fleas may prefer different kinds of bird nests. The hen flea (*Ceratophyllus gallinae*), with 75 different bird hosts in Britain, prefers relatively dry nests in elevated situations; the duck flea (*C. garei*) prefers wet nests of bird species nesting on the ground and in swampy situations.

Ticks (Order Acarina) often infest birds that nest on the ground or in low bushes, or predatory birds that feed on tick-infested rodents. The *Ornithodoros capensis* (Ixoidea; Argasidae) remains in the abandoned nest of the White-capped Noddy tern (*Anous minutus*) during the non-nesting season, and reuse of the nests in the breeding season by the birds allows the ticks to reinfest the terns (Humphrey-Smith and Moorhouse 1981). Baerg (1944) observed that low nests of the Cliff Swallow (*Hirundo pyrrhonota*) appeared to be more susceptible to attacks by the tick *Ixodes baergi* than did higher nests. Heavy tick infestation resulting in blindness and death of prefledging Prairie Falcons (*Falco mexicanus*) is a recurring problem in northeastern Colorado, where in 1979 postmortem examination indicated that the primary cause of death was massive infestation of *Ornithodoros concanesis* (Bodner 1980).

"Ticks are the great exponents of the gentle art of waiting," and an adult can wait for four to seven years for a meal (Rothschild and Clay 1957:230). Such persistence in these and other parasites that infest bird nests could help explain why some birds, such as Cliff Swallows, shift their colony nest sites from time to time.

The swallow bug (*Oeciacus viarius*), a nocturnal, blood-sucking hemipteran parasite related to the bedbug (Cimicidae), has been observed to survive for two years in Cliff Swallow nests during the absence of the swallows (Smith and Eads 1978). Myers (1928) saw Cliff Swallows sitting at the openings of their nests, picking at the bugs without eating them, and he suspected that the offensive odor the bugs give off when irritated protects them. Spiders, commonly found in and around the nests, were seen eating the bugs.

Most of the flies (Diptera) parasitic on birds are blood-suckers, including louse-flies (Hippoboscidae), mosquitoes, midges, blackflies, bluebottle flies (Calliphoridae), nest-flies (Carnidae) and botflies (Muscidae). The louse-flies are viviparous and produce only one young at a time, which is deposited as a full-grown larva in the nest. The larva immediately pupates, passes the winter in the nest, and emerges the following spring as an adult, which then lives among the bird's feathers and sucks blood from the skin. Some louse-flies have well-developed wings, other mere vestiges of wings, as, for example, the swift louse-fly (*Crataerina pallida*) and the swallow louse-fly (*Stenepteryx hirundinis*). Since swifts and swallows often return year after year to an old nest, the difficulty of finding a host is reduced. The common louse-fly (*Ornithomyia avicularia*) found on a wide variety of birds has more difficulty finding a host, and wings are fully developed in this species.

Mason (1944) made a ten-year study of nest parasitism by the fly, *Protocalliphora splendida* (Calliphoridae), on birds in Massachusetts. In 162 broods of cavity-nesting birds he found infestations in 94 percent of bluebird (*Sialia sialis*) nests, 82 percent of tree swallow (*Tachycineta bicolor*) nests, and 47 percent of house wren (*Troglodytes aedon*) nests. The three species averaged 113, 90, and 19 *Protocalliphora* larvae, respectively, per brood of birds hatched. Most of the fly larvae are found in the nest material just below the inner lining, and feed primarily at night, when the maggots attack especially the feet and legs, and also the abdomen and base of the primary flight feathers of the host. Mason also gathered data indicating that seven species of passerine birds that build open nests had only light infestations, compared with bluebirds and tree swallows. A hymenopterous secondary parasite, *Nasonia vitripennis*, helped keep the *Protocalliphora* in check.

According to N. G. Smith (1980), the chief source of mortality among the colonial icterids (oropendolas and caciques) that he observed in Central America were botflies of the genus *Philornis*. These flies deposit eggs or living larvae on nestling birds. The larvae burrow under the skin of the nestlings where they feed; when grown they emerge and pupate in the nest. Many icterids place their long baglike nests directly around a bee or wasp nest, and Smith found that the nearer the bird's nest was to the entr..nce of a wasp or bee nest, the less likely were the nestlings to suffer parasitism by *Philornis*, since the wasps and bees repel the adult flies. If the wasp or bee nest was destroyed, the birds abandoned their nesting site. *Philornis* infestation of a falcon has also been described by Hector (1982) who found up to 35 larvae on one nestling Aploplomado Falcon (*Falco femoralis*).

In contrast to the ectoparasites that live in the nest and attack the host intermittently are those ectoparasites—such as the feather mites (Order Acarina; Analgesidae) and the feather lice (Order Phthiraptera; Amblycera and Ischnocera)—that live permanently on the body of the host, thereby occupying a more stable and favorable environment and being less affected by differences in nests. They feed on feathers and horny layers of the skin, and some feather lice also feed on blood and serum.

The mites are minute in size, and most of the species are probably still undescribed. Of the known species the free-living mites outnumber the parasitic ones by about three to one, and it is believed that parasitism has evolved more than once in this group from forms living free at first in the nest of the host (Rodriguez 1979). The feather lice seem to have evolved from free-living ancestors similar to the Psocida or book-lice (Rothschild and Clay 1957) which occur in bird nests and feed on organic debris.

For transfer from one host to another, the feather mites and feather lice generally depend on bodily contact between hosts. Since such contact normally does not occur between species, the feather mites and feather lice are often host-specific, evolve along with their hosts, and give clues to phylogenetic relationships of birds. Sometimes, however, transfer of a parasite from one individual to another may occur by means other than direct contact of conspecifics. In the phenomenon known as "phoresy" an immature feather mite or feather louse attaches to some other larger parasite, such as a flea or a hippoboscid fly, which then serves as an intermediate agent, transporting the small hitchhiker to its host-bird.

A given species of feather mite is frequently restricted to a single species, genus, or family of host-bird, and frequently a genus of mite is restricted to one bird-family or to one order of birds (Cerny, 1973). Among feather lice, in a great many cases, there is a genus that is found on one order of birds and no other (Rothschild and Clay, 1957:130), although other genera are found on more than one order. Inspection of tables of host-birds and their feather lice as given by Clay (1957) and Turner (1971) for the Mallophaga in general, by Emerson (1972) for North America (north of Mexico), and by Ledger (1980) for Africa south of the Sahara, indicates that the Order Passeriformes shares more genera of feather lice with the coraciiform and piciform orders than with any other orders of bird. The list of ectoparasites on birds of Asia given by McClure and Ratanaworabhan and their collaborators (1972) indicates the same conclusion for both feather lice and feather mites in Asia. In turn, this conclusion suggests that ancestral and early passerine birds, like the coraciiform and piciform birds today, may have nested in holes in the ground or in holes in trees.

Adaptations against Arthropod Nest Parasites

Besides preening themselves and each other, birds have adapted in various ways to the presence of parasitic and disease-carrying organisms infesting their nests. One way is by keeping the nest clean (although some species seem to get along with little or no nest sanitation despite fouling of the nest). The parents and the young themselves may help keep the nest clean by ejecting their feces over the side of the nest.

Many small birds carry out a form of nest sanitation by promptly removing the fecal sacs of their young.

Nests heavily infested with ectoparasites may be abandoned for later broods. As early as the first day after a brood is fledged the male Blue-Gray Gnatcatcher (*Polioptila caerulea*) starts a new nest for the next brood. Pairs usually move the materials from their own abandoned nests to new building sites as much as five hundred feet away. But materials are not moved from nests overrun by the mite *Ornithonyssus sylviarum*, which may cause the death of entire broods of nestlings (Root 1969).

The commonest parasite found in nest boxes of tits in Britain is the flea, *Ceratophyllus gallinae*. The fleas develop in the nest during the summer and cluster around the entrance hole the following spring, waiting for the birds to enter with the advent of a new breeding season. Large number of fleas may cause such discomfort that the birds desert their nest. Second broods sometimes fail as a result of the flea infestation, and the birds may choose a different nest site for their second brood if one is available (Perrins 1979).

Houston (1979) suggests that the reason Fairy (White) Terns (*Gygis alba*) do not build nests but lay their eggs on a bare branch is to avoid infestation of parasites. On Cousin Island in the Seychelles he found many feather lice of three species on Black Noddy tern chicks (*Anous tenuirostris*) that lived in nests of leaves, but none were found on seventeen White Tern chicks examined.

Old woodpecker holes develop a microfauna of parasites and other vermin and become less attractive to hole-nesting birds. Newly excavated holes lack pests and are preferred. Woodpecker holes are most subject to take-over, or to take-over attempts, by competitors when the holes are just at the point of completion (Short 1979).

Nests of predatory birds often contain many invertebrates, including ectoparasites, decomposers of carrion and excretory pellets, and invertebrates associated with decaying nest material (Phillips and Dindal 1977). Raptors may pluck their prey at some place other than the nest, and the adults often feed themselves away from the nest containing the young, keeping the nest relatively clean.

The smaller *Accipiter* hawks and kites can build their small nests in a few weeks or less. Large hawks and eagles often make huge nests, spend months on the job, and seldom build a completely new nest in a year in which they breed (Newton 1979:88). Each pair in most species has several nests in its territory, and may use different nests in different years (e.g., *Aquila, Pandion, Buteo*). If the breeding attempt fails, they may switch to another nest for a repeat attempt, or they may build on another nest for use in future years.

The Swallow-tailed Kite (*Elanoides forficatus*) of tropical America is one of the few known raptors in which the chicks do not eject their feces clear of the nest. Instead the feces accumulate on the nest rim, rather than on the ground where they might attract such climbing predators as raccoons, and they are continually covered by fresh nest material (*Usnea*) brought by the adults (Snyder 1975).

Many species of hawks and eagles bring fresh green leafy sprays to their completed nests. This habit has been the subject of much conjecture, and one idea is that it adds to nest sanitation by covering rotten meat and excreta. Newton (1979:89) points out that this does not explain why the birds use green sprays rather than other materials or bring the greenery long before the eggs are laid and the nest is soiled. Green sprays often continue to be added for the whole season, whether eggs are laid or not, and are placed around the chicks, usually with no attempt to incorporate them into the nest structure. A novel suggestion is that green leaves placed in the nest of birds might function as an arthropod repellent or insecticide by releasing hydrocyanic acid as they wilt and dry (Johnston and Hardy 1962), but this idea seems not to have been tested.

When all else fails, birds can always deal with heavy infestation of ectoparasites by deserting their nest. In a large breeding colony of Sooty Terns (*Sterna fuscata*) on Bird Island in the Seychelles, Feare (1976) estimated that five thousand pairs deserted well-incubated eggs or newly hatched chicks because of a heavy infestation by virus-infected ticks. During the day there was no indication of the cause of the desertion, but a night visit showed that the ground of the deserted area was covered with ticks (*Ornithodoros capensis*; Argasidae). After ten to fifteen days significantly more infested chicks died than did chicks with no signs of ticks on them. As the ticks were carrying a virus, disease may have hastened death after desertion by the parents. The terns avoided the infested area when nesting the following year; ticks were still present in large numbers hidden in and under rotting wood and among roots. A heavy infestation by the same species of tick has also been found to cause desertion and nest failure in a colony of Brown Pelicans (*Pelicanus occidentalis*) on the Texas coast (King et al. 1977).

Summary

Competition for nest sites may result in displacement of one species from part of its breeding range by another species. Aggressive competition between individuals or pairs of the same species for a desirable nest site early in the breeding season may result in successive replacement of different individuals or pairs, according to relative dominance. Birds defend their nest sites, and defense of territory probably originated in evolution by extension from defense of a nest site. The nature of the nest site and success in interspecific competition may vary in different parts of the geographic range.

Tree holes are often limited in supply, and populations of hole-nesting birds have often been dramatically increased by supplying them with nest boxes. Woodpeckers may make possible the occupation of otherwise suitable habitat by birds unable to dig their own holes. Aggressive encounters between different species of woodpeckers and other birds, competing for the same hole, may be frequent. Different-size entrances result in competition for tree holes or burrows by different species of birds according to body size. Sometimes a species will take over a nesting hole from a smaller species and enlarge the hole for its own use.

Birds also compete for nest materials and for more or less completed nests, well-constructed or elaborate nests being especially in demand. While some birds breed in old nests of other species, some aggressively take over fresh nests of other species. Use of the nest of another species for breeding may have been a precursor, or initial step, in the evolution of brood parasitism, particularly between closely related species with generally similar life histories. Obligate brood parasitism, in which one species must lay its eggs in the nest of another because it has lost the ability not only to make its own nest but to incubate its own eggs, is the last and crucial step in the evolution of interspecific brood parasitism.

Some host-species, such as the Yellow Warbler, avoid being parasitized by burying the parasite's egg under a new nest lining. Other host-species, such as Kirtland's Warbler, are less adaptable; its population was seriously reduced by cowbird parasitism. Some African weaverbirds lay eggs that differ consistently in color and pattern for different individual females. The Didric Cuckoo, a common parasite of weavers, lays eggs with a series of variations parallel to those of the Village Weaver, but a female weaver will throw out of her nest an egg that differs greatly from her own eggs in appearance.

Many invertebrate parasites and disease organisms infest nests of birds. Nests and nest sites heavily infested with parasites may be abandoned by the birds for later broods. Some sanitation is effected in many species of birds by keeping the nest clear of feces.

CHAPTER NINE

Predators and Nests

THE major evolutionary force determining the form and structure of nests has probably been predation. Lack (1954:77) thought it likely that predation causes over three-fourths of the losses of eggs, and young of open-nesting song birds. Also, much of the variation in location of birds' nest sites is related to avoidance of predation. Birds have evolved a variety of anti-predator adaptations in their nest-building behavior (Koepcke 1972, Skutch 1976). The following classification gives an overview, with examples, of these different adaptations. After the classification is presented, each category will be discussed and exemplified in greater detail with evidence that the adaptations really function in the way indicated. We do not exclude the possibility of additional functions, not related to predation, for some of these nest features.

A CLASSIFICATION OF NEST DEFENSES AGAINST PREDATORS

A. Concealment of the nest and its contents
   1. Nest hidden in vegetation. Most small birds.
   2. Eggs hidden by their concealing coloration (Stone Curlew), by parent sitting on them or covering them on leaving the nest (ducks and geese).
   3. Eggs hidden within an enclosed nest, as a burrow, tree cavity, or domed nest. Many altricial birds.
   4. Very small nest hidden under the incubating parent. Some cotingas (Cotingidae) and tree swifts (Hemiprocnidae).
   5. No nest. Whip-poor-will, nighthawk.
B. Confusing or deceiving predators
   1. Camouflaged nest, covered with lichens (Wood-Pewee) or bits of bark (Orange-winged Sitella, Sittidae), or resembling a mass of natural vegetation (Northern Parula Warbler) or debris.
   2. Multiple nests in the same tree, with many nests empty (Scaly-feathered Finch, White-browed Sparrow Weaver).
   3. Nest with two entrance or exit holes. East African Social Weavers (*Pseudonigrita*) and a South American ovenbird (*Certhiaxis pyrrophia*).
   4. Nest with false entrance resembling the true (closed) entrance. Cape Penduline Tit of South Africa.

C. Nests in inaccessible or relatively safe places
    1. Site inaccessible to many predators. Islands (many sea birds), sand bars (Egyptian Plover), emergent vegetation over water (Marsh Wren), cliffs (Cliff Swallow), banks (Bank Swallow), trees (Tree Swallow), tips of long branches (orioles, sunbirds, many weaverbirds).
    2. Relatively safe place. Burrows (Burrowing Owl), tree holes (woodpeckers, most parrots), cactus (Cactus Wren), thorny acacia trees (Red-billed Weaver), caves (Oilbird, cave swiftlets).
    3. Protective barricade is built by the bird at the nest entrance, of thorny twigs (White-headed Buffalo Weaver), of mud or excrement (most hornbills), or of pine resin (Red-cockaded Woodpecker).
    4. Long, vertical tube with bottom entrance to a nest suspended in a tree. Certain weaverbirds of Africa, Madagascar, and Asia.
D. Protective nesting association with formidable species
    1. Nest placed by small bird in or near the nest of a large bird of prey. Spanish Sparrows in nests of eagles.
    2. Nest placed on or near human habitation. House Sparrow, House Martin, Village Weaverbird, White Stork.
    3. Nest placed close to the nest of wasps, bees, ants, or termites. Bronze Mannikin (Africa), Double-barred Finch (Australia), Banded Wren (tropical America).
    4. Nest cavity dug by the bird inside the nest of a colony of wasps (Violaceous Trogon), ants (Rufous Woodpecker), or termites (many kingfishers).
E. Multiple nesting attempts
    1. Exceeding capacity of predators to destroy population, by synchronized nesting of huge numbers of individuals. Red-billed Weaver (*Quelea*).
    2. Repeated nesting attempts with many small clutches each season. Antbirds and many other tropical forest passerines.
F. Relatively impregnable nests with thick, strong walls
    1. Tree cavities. Many altricial birds.
    2. Nest with thick, strong walls of earthen material. Rufous Ovenbird.
    3. Large-roofed nest built of twigs. Castlebuilders (*Synallaxis*) and House Builders (*Pseudoseiura*) of the ovenbird family.
    4. Large compound nests with a thick communal roof built of twigs (Monk Parakeet, Palmchat, Buffalo Weaver), or of straw and twigs (Sociable Weaver).
G. Various combinations of preceding categories

CONCEALMENT OF THE NEST

Many birds, particularly small birds, conceal their nests in vegetation. In the North Temperate Zone early in the breeding season, when there still are few or no leaves on bushes and trees, some species, such as the Song Sparrow (*Melospiza melodia*) in Ohio (Nice 1937) and the Prairie Warbler (*Dendroica discolor*) in Indiana (Nolan 1978), place their nests amidst vegetation on or near the ground. Later in the season they place their nests at higher levels, when plant growth provides more adequate concealment at these higher levels. Success among 268 nests in fledging at least one young Prairie Warbler varied with nest height. In early May low nests succeeded more than twice as often as did high nests; by late June or July the relationship of success to height was reversed (Nolan 1978:400).

Some authors have made subjective assessments of the correlation of the degree of nest concealment with nesting success. Mrs. Nice (1937:93–94) found that of 135 Song Sparrow nests whose concealment she considered excellent, 55 percent produced young, while of 64 other nests she thought less well concealed, only 36 percent were productive. She seldom could get evidence of nest destruction by any particular predator, but predators in the area included seven species of birds, eight species of mammals, and one snake. Similarly, Nolan (1978:401) evaluated the concealment of Prairie Warbler nests on the basis of the difficulty he had in finding them. Of 33 nests, one to two meters high, whose concealment he rated below average, none succeeded, of 42 nests at the same height but better concealed, 21 percent succeeded. This difference was statistically significant. Predators were rarely observed in the act of predation, but likely nest predators included racers and rat snakes, Blue Jays, chipmunks, opossums, raccoons, and Striped Skunks.

In Illinois, of 262 nests of the Eastern Meadowlark (*Sturnella magna*), 60 percent of those nests open above were lost to predation, as against only 51 percent of nests fully roofed with a grassy canopy built by the birds and serving to hide the eggs (Roseberry and Klimstra 1970). In a study of the Field Sparrow (*Spizella pusilla*) in Illinois, Best (1978) found 76 percent of 112 nests suffered predation, which he attributed mostly to snakes. The principal predator was the Blue Racer (*Coluber constrictor*), which hunts both by visual and chemical cues (H. Fitch 1963). Nest vulnerability to snake predation was independent of relative nest concealment.

It seems that the importance of nest concealment varies with ecological circumstances and with the type of predators at a given time and place. Because of the difficulty of distinguishing among predation by birds, by small mammals, or by snakes without direct observation, it is often difficult to evaluate the meaning and validity of observations on the degree of nest concealment as related to predation. More precise information of the nature of the predators is needed.

We need to learn more about the techniques used by each species of predator when hunting for specific types of nest. Successful acts of nest predation are rarely observed directly, even by persons who have spent hundreds of hours in the field studying a given species, although unsuccessful attempts are seen fairly often. Predators might conceivably look for the nest itself, watch the parents building, cruise a promising area and flush the incubating parent off the nest, smell the parent on the nest or its eggs or the nestlings, see the eggs or eggshells from hatched eggs, or see the movements and hear the sounds made by the nestlings.

In southern Sweden, Hooded Crows (*Corvus corone cornix*) preferred spruce and pine trees to deciduous trees for nesting, as indicated by a sample of 356 nests. Nests in conifers suffered significantly less nonhuman predation than did those in deciduous trees. Nests were best concealed in the dense foliage of spruce, the preferred tree. The most likely predator of crows' eggs were other crows. No eggs were lost from nests in spruce trees, while 11 nests (7 percent) with eggs were lost in deciduous trees. Buzzards (*Buteo buteo*) were considered the main predators of nestlings; in spruce trees only 3 nests (15 percent) with nestlings were preyed upon, compared with 40 (25 percent) in deciduous trees (Loman 1979).

Rufous Hummingbirds (*Selasphorus rufus*) in Canada nest low in conifers in the spring, but higher in deciduous trees in summer after the latter have leafed out (Horvath 1964). Besides the favorable microclimatic changes involved, such a shift would be of advantage in frustrating any search-image of the nest site that predators might have learned early in the breeding season.

Some caprimulgids famed for their concealing coloration, such as the Whip-poor-will (*Caprimulgus vociferus*), lay their eggs on the ground and have no nest that might attract the attention of a predator. Some birds build such a small nest that it is largely or entirely hidden by the body of the incubating parent, as do several cotingas (Cotingidae) in the Neotropics (Snow 1976, 1981) and the crested tree swifts (Hemiprocnidae) in the Oriental and Australasian tropics. Tree swifts lay a single egg in a very tiny nest that is invisible when the parent is sitting on it. Snow (1981) interprets diminution in nest size as an adapation to intense predation in tropical forests, and he also suggests that small nest size imposes a selection pressure for limitation of clutch size. In any event, it seems that, because of the small clutch size so characteristic of tropical birds, reduction in nest size as an anti-predator adaptation would be more possible among tropical birds than among species of colder regions where small birds generally lay larger clutches.

Predators probably often find nests by watching the parent birds building, just as human bird-watchers do. Cowbirds apparently find and select nests to parasitize by watching the building activities of prospective hosts (Hann 1941, Mayfield 1960, Thompson and Gottfried 1976), since cowbirds seem to spend much time watching other birds build and usually synchronize their laying with the egg-laying period of the host. If cowbirds can locate nests by watching other birds build, it is reasonable to expect that some predators can do the same, but more information is needed.

When a predator is detected many birds give alarm cries and stop building. The Prairie Warbler often builds in brief sessions, and for a limited part of the day—for example, during the early morning—and so is less likely to attract predators. It may desert its nest if it is discovered building (Nolan 1978:142).

Exposed eggs in open nests may attract predators when the incubating parent is away. Ducks and geese cover their eggs whenever the female leaves the nest without having been flushed off her eggs. Ducks frequently defecate upon sudden flushing from nests, and there is a possibility that odor of the feces may attract predators. But an experiment with hens' eggs set out in duck habitats found no significant difference in predation rate when half the eggs were scented with duck feces and half were not (Hammond and Foreward 1956). In the southern Appalachians, V. G. Henry (1969) found that Ruffed Grouse (*Bonasa umbellus*) and Wild Turkeys (*Meleagris gallopavo*) cover their eggs when leaving the nest. Dummy nests were established, each consisting of a small depression in leaves with five chicken eggs covered lightly with leaves. Total predation was significantly higher when eggs were not replaced by fresh eggs. Apparently predators were attracted by the odor of deteriorating eggs. The highest percentage of eggs was destroyed by animals with a good olfactory sense—snakes, raccoons, foxes, and opossums. This experiment has implications for normal nests where one or more eggs in the clutch fail to hatch.

When eggs hatch, the discarded eggshells provide conspicuous visual cues aiding predators to locate the nest. Many birds will remove shells from the nest, although some species do not. The Black-headed Gull (*Larus ridibundus*) of Europe removes and carries away the empty shell shortly after the chick has hatched. Field experiments showed that an empty shell placed ten to fifteen centimeters from normal eggs renders such eggs more vulnerable to predation by Carrion Crows and Herring Gulls. Removal of eggshells from the nest by the parents helps to reduce predation (Tinbergen et al. 1963).

Enclosed nests conceal the eggs from the eyes of predators. Magpies (*Pica pica*) usually roof their twig nests, and one study in the Netherlands found that 91 percent of 61 roofed nests fledged young, but only 17 percent of 18 open nests did so. Chicken eggs placed in open magpie nests were taken by Carrion Crows (*Corvus corone corone*) significantly sooner than eggs placed in domed nests (Baeyens 1981).

In many species of birds, enclosed nests provide more protection and success than open nests (Nice 1957, Skutch 1966, von Haartman 1971, Oniki 1979). In central and eastern Brazil, Oniki found that among 552 nests of 80 species of birds at Belem (lat. 1°28′S) in eastern Brazil, enclosed nests were twice as successful as open nests. Predation caused most nest failures. In tropical forest areas of Central America, particularly in Costa Rica, Skutch found that among sixteen species of hole-nesting birds 60 percent of the nests were successful in fledging at least one young. They were almost three times as successful as birds with open nests in the same tropical forest. Skutch also summarized studies from six different localities in Central America showing that nesting success increased with altitude. He interprets the differences as mainly due to the number of snakes decreasing with altitude, and he considers snakes to be the main predators of small birds in tropical areas.

Darwin (1871) discussed at some length the sex differences in plumage color between birds that build open nests and those that build enclosed nests, particularly with regard to a theory of Alfred Russell Wallace. The generalization that Wallace (1891:124) advanced was that "When both sexes are of strikingly gay and conspicuous colours the nest . . . is such as to conceal the sitting birds; while, whenever the male is gay and conspicuous and the nest is open so as to expose the setting bird to view, the female is of dull or obscure colours." Darwin was somewhat perturbed by the numerous exceptions, but he concluded (II:170-71) "Notwithstanding the foregoing objections, I cannot doubt after reading Mr. Wallace's excellent essay, that looking to the birds of the world, a large majority of the species in which the females are conspicuously coloured (and in this case the males with rare exception are equally conspicuous), build concealed nests for the sake of protection. Mr. Wallace enumerates a long series of groups in which this rule holds good; but it will suffice here to give as instances, the more familiar groups of kingfishers, toucans, trogons, puff-birds (Capitonidae), plantain-eaters (Musophagidae), woodpeckers, and parrots."

CONFUSING OR DECEIVING PREDATORS

The nest building of some species of birds illustrates defense by deception against predators, but there is often no information available about the specific nest predators. One common feature is camouflage of the exterior of the nest to resemble the immediate environment. A covering of lichens over the nest in unrelated species of birds must have been due to convergent evolution, and the convergence is evidence that natural selection has produced this particular nest adaptation.

Examples of birds from different families that cover the outside of their cup-nests with lichens are the Ruby-throated Hummingbird (*Archilochus colubris*), Blue-Gray Gnatcatcher (*Polioptila caerulea*), and Eastern Wood-Pewee (*Contopus virens*), all of North America, and the Chaffinch (*Fringilla coelebs*) of Europe. The Yellow-bellied Elaenia (*Elaenia flavogaster*) is a tropical New World flycatcher, the open cup-nest of which is "plastered on its outer surface with lichens, resembling a large hummingbird's nest" (Haverschmidt 1968: plate 24). Several species of tropical hummingbirds cover the outside of the nest with lichens (Skutch 1973). Often lichen-covered nests of various birds are saddled on a branch and look like a knot on the branch.

Some birds disguise the outside of the nest with bark. The Orange-winged Sitella (*Neositta chrysoptera*), a nuthatch-like bird (Sittidae) of Australia, fastens small pieces of barklike shingles on the outside of its nest, "often forming a perfect imitation of the bark of the tree in which the nest is built" (Cayley 1959:130).

Nests of some species resemble bits of vegetative materials or rubble in the normal habitat. The nest of the Northern Parula Warbler (*Parula americana*) may be completely hidden in festoons of *Usnea* hanging from tree branches, or in pendant tufts or "beards" of the Spanish Moss (*Tillandsia*, an epiphyte of the Bromeleaceae), which covers many trees in the southeastern United States (H. Harrison 1975). The Bearded Greenbul (*Criniger barbatus*) of African rain forests works into the rim of its nest an epiphytic fern that remains green until after the young fledge (Brosset 1974). Nests of the Royal Flycatcher (*Onychorhynchus coronatus*) of Central America (Skutch 1976) and of the Blue-throated Brown Sunbird (*Nectarinia cyanolaema*) of the Afrotropical region (Chapin 1954) are each an elongated mass of plant rubble, about a meter long, suspended over a small shady stream in tropical rain forest, with the eggs in a small chamber near the center of the nest mass. The nest of an ovenbird (*Certhiaxis vulpina*) of the Amazon basin is merely a crude nest cavity within a nondescript mass of drift, including grass, small sticks, and other vegetation caught in some obstruction near receding waters (Vaurie 1980).

Some birds nest gregariously in the open where the nests are conspicuous. The tiny Scaly-feathered Finch (*Sporopipes squamifrons*, Ploceidae) of southern Africa nests in small trees, often with several domed nests in one tree and with others in several neighboring trees. Over a dozen birds may sleep in one nest of a colony leaving the other nests vacant. These extra nests can confuse a predator as to the location of the birds, and also provide additional sleeping places in case a predator, such as the Fiscal Shrike (*Lanius collaris*), frightens the birds from a nest (N. Collias and Collias 1964).

White-browed Sparrow Weavers (*Plocepasser mahali*) nest gregariously in acacia trees in Africa, and sleep in their domed nests, one bird to a nest. In north central Kenya at the Samburu Game Reserve, we found seventeen colonies had an average of four or five birds and ten to twelve nests per colony. All the nests of a colony were generally in one tree and only about half of them were occupied at night. In addition, the nest has two side entrances so that if a predator started to enter one, the occupant could fly out the other. Shortly before eggs were laid, one hole was plugged up by the birds, and it was unplugged as soon as the young fledged (N. Collias and Collias 1978).

The Grey-capped Social Weaver (*Pseudonigrita arnaudi*) (fig. 9.1) and the Black-capped Social Weaver (*P. cabanisi*) of East Africa live in colonies in dry savanna areas, and also have two holes in the domed sleeping nests, which are built of dry grass stems, but the nest holes open directly downward. These birds usually sleep in small groups, often with four or five birds to a nest. A pair will plug one hole in breeding nests (N. Collias and Collias 1980). An interesting example of convergent evolution is the nest of an ovenbird (*Certhiaxis pyrrhophia*) in South America that constructs two different types of domed nests. One nest is used as a dormitory, the other for breeding; the former is provided with two round entrances opening directly from underneath the nest through its floor, whereas the breeding nest has only a single entrance. Both types of nests are otherwise similar, and built of dry twigs and strands of vegetable fiber as well as other materials (Vaurie 1980).

The most remarkable case of deception is the false entrance in the nest of the Cape Penduline Tit (*Anthoscopus minutus*) (fig. 9.2) of South Africa; Skead (1959) described the nest. This tiny bird builds an oval domed nest felted of cobwebs and other soft materials, such as wool or the cottony fibers of the seeds of the Kapok tree (*Ceiba pentandra*). The nest hangs from a twig in a bush, and the entrance opens through a short tube at one side near the top. The entrance can be closed along its horizontal axis by the birds. Directly beneath and adjacent to the true entrance is a deep, rounded depression or false "entrance." The lips, floor, and roof of the true entrance are overlaid with coarse cobweb

Fig. 9.1. Nest of a Grey-capped Social Weaver (*Pseudonigrita arnaudi*), showing the two entrance (and exit) holes opening on the bottom side of the roofed nest. The nest is thatched of dry grass stems.

Fig. 9.2. Nest of Cape Penduline Tit (*Anthoscopus minutus*) with the true entrance opened (left) and closed (right), Cape Province, South Africa. A blind, false entrance is just below the true entrance. (C. J. Skead, *Ostrich Suppl.* 1959)

and readily cling together when manipulated by the bird, and the entrance tube can be closed along its full length. When coming out the bird opens the entrance and parts the lips by the forward pressure of its body inside. After the breeding season, the birds continue to sleep in the nest for some months, and as many as eighteen of these little birds have been observed to sleep in one nest.

It is a reasonable assumption that the false entrance deceives snakes and other predators seeking to get into the nest, although no direct study of the effect on predators seems to have been made. Skead observed that a tit will repeatedly prod with its beak into the bottom and sides of the false entrance. Perhaps such a behavior serves to further confuse any predator that might happen to be watching as to the exact location of the true entrance. The Mouse-colored Penduline Tit (*Anthoscopus musculus*) of eastern Africa, builds a similar, felted, oval domed nest, which not only has a false entrance just under the true one but is covered over much of its outer surface with numerous deep depressions that could be considered supernumerary "false entrances" that presumably confuse some predators.

Birds attempting to lead predators away from their nests often feign injury, a distraction-display sometimes called the "broken-wing trick." Skutch (1976:412) lists thirty-five avian families in which injury simulation or other distraction-displays occur with some frequency. Most of these are birds that commonly nest on or near the ground in an open nest. Skutch notes that birds that nest in burrows or in tree holes and similar cavities, or birds that seldom build their open nests on the ground, do not simulate injury when a predator is near the nest, with rare exceptions.

NESTS IN INACCESSIBLE OR RELATIVELY SAFE PLACES

Many birds nest in places inaccessible to many predators. Cliff Swallows (*Hirundo pyrrhonota*) and Bank Swallows (*Riparia riparia*) are named for their inaccessible nesting places. Most sea birds breed in colonies on islands, the Egyptian Plover (*Pluvianus aegyptius*) and African River Martin (*Pseudochelidon eurystomina*) breed on sand bars in large rivers in Africa, Marsh Wrens (*Cistothorus palustris*) in America and Reed Warblers (*Acrocephalus scripaceus*) in Europe nest in emergent vegetation over water. Birds that nest in relatively inaccessible places may have better breeding success. A study in Manitoba found 73 percent success of 227 nests of diving ducks, which nest over water, and only 50 percent success of 149 nests of dabbling ducks, which nest on land (Nice 1957).

When a formerly protected nesting site becomes accessible to predators—for example, an island becomes connected with the mainland by lowered water levels, or terrestrial predators are introduced to an area—the predators can destroy the nests. Brown Noddy terns (*Anous stoldius*) may nest on the ground on oceanic islands free of ground predators (fig. 9.3), but where rats have been introduced they often nest in trees or bushes (fig. 9.4). On the island of Aldabra in the Indian Ocean, a weaverbird, the Aldabran Fody (*Foudia eminentissima aldabrana*) prefers to nest in the introduced Coconut Palm and Casuarina trees, instead of in the native mixed scrub, and these trees are safer from the introduced rats (*Rattus rattus*) which are nest predators of the weaverbird (C. B. Frith 1976).

Canada Geese (*Branta canadensis*) typically nest on the ground, but sometimes nest in trees, taking over nests from herons, hawks, or eagles. Craighead and Stockstad (1961) in the Flathead Valley of Montana observed 1,267 nesting pairs of Canada Geese, over a six-year period, mostly with ground nests on islands, but including 58 nests in natural sites in trees or cliffs and 49 nests in wooden platforms (containing soil and chaff) placed high in trees by the investigators. Predation was the major cause of nest failure, and accounted for 61 percent of the 404 failures in the study population, but only one of the 14 failures of platform-nests was caused by predators. Mortality of goslings leaving platform-nests was negligible; three goslings were seen to launch themselves safely off an Osprey nest 80 feet high. The percentage of nesting geese using aerial platforms increased each year from one percent the first year to 9 percent the fifth year; the geese preferred platforms more than 20 feet high in the trees.

Bald Eagles generally nest in trees, but on those Aleutian islands where Arctic Foxes are not found, the eagles may nest on the ground (Sherrod et al. 1977). Ospreys over most of their range nest in trees; they may nest on the ground on islands where there are no mammalian predators, but they disappeared from a treeless island off California following its colonization by Coyotes (Newton 1979:85).

A number of birds, especially tropical birds, hang their nests from the tips of long branches, including New World orioles and oropendolas, and many weaverbirds and sunbirds in Africa. In Senegal, West African Village Weavers prefer to fasten their nest to the tips of branches that hang down rather than to more horizontal branches. For some years we maintained a breeding colony of West African Village Weaverbirds in Los Angeles, providing suitable nest sites for these gregarious breeders merely by hanging branches from the roof of large outdoor aviaries. When a male was given a choice between a vertical and a horizontal

Fig. 9.3. Brown Noddy tern (*Anous stolidus*) on its nest on the ground, on an island free of terrestrial predators, Tern Island, French Frigate Shoals, central Pacific Ocean. (Photo: Elizabeth N. Flint)

Fig. 9.4. Brown Noddy tern (*Anous stolidus*) on its nest in a tree, on an island infested with rats, Dry Tortugas, Florida. (Photo: Diane E. Riska)

branch in his territory, he almost invariably wove his nests on the vertical branch, provided it was not too near to the side walls of the aviary (C. H. Jacobs, C. R. Cox, and N. E. Collias, MS in preparation).

The quality of the nest site may make the difference between success and failure in breeding. The Puerto Rican Parrot (*Amazona vittata*), an endangered species that nests in tree holes, is limited by a scarcity of nest sites and suffers from the depredations of the Pearly-eyed Thrasher (*Margarops fuscatus*), which enters the nest cavities of the parrot and destroys its eggs. But the thrasher is reluctant to descend into deep cavities, and by putting out nest boxes of sufficient depth, the parrot's eggs are protected from the thrasher (Temple 1978). The Mauritius Kestrel (*Falco punctatus*), one of the rarest birds in the world, until recently nested in tree cavities where it was vulnerable to introduced monkeys (*Macaca irus*). In 1974 one pair of the birds nested on a sheer cliff, a nesting site safe from the monkeys. This pair raised young that apparently became imprinted on cliff-nesting sites, resulting in a tradition shift. Reproductive success increased, and by 1977 the population had tripled (Temple 1978).

Some birds protect their nests from predators by constructing a barricade at the entrance. Female hornbills plaster mud or excrement about the entrance to the tree cavity in which they nest until this entrance is so narrowed that only the formidible bill of the female can be protruded, making the nest cavity more defensible (Kemp 1970). Red-cockaded Woodpeckers (*Picoides borealis*) of the pine forests of the southeastern United States, by pecking at the tree, keep pine resin flowing about their nesting and roosting holes. The sticky resin probably helps prevent intrusion by snakes and other enemies (Dennis 1971). The White-headed Buffalo Weaver (*Dinamellia dinemelli*) of East Africa covers its grassy domed nest with thorny twigs, but in addition it places many thorny twigs along the boughs supporting and leading to the nest, discouraging climbing mammals from approaching.

Several weaverbirds weave a long vertical tube about the entrance of their nests, and this entrance tube with the nest opening at the bottom of the tube may extend downward for two feet or more in some species, such as Cassin's Malimbe (*Malimbus cassini*) of the tropical forests of Africa (fig. 2.24) and the Baya Weaver (*Ploceus philippinus*) of India, Sri Lanka, and southeast Asia (fig. 9.5). Long entrance tubes have arisen separately by convergent evolution in nests of African and Asiatic species of weaver, and of the Nelicourvi Weaver (*Ploceus nelicourvi*) of the humid forest of eastern Madagascar (N. Collias and Collias 1964). In each case, the nest is suspended by its roof from palm leaflets, or from a long, hanging twig or vine stem, so that the entrance may be one or

Fig. 9.5. For the Baya Weaver (*Ploceus philippinus*) of India and Ceylon, the long nest suspension and the long entrance tube, with the nest opening at the bottom, help protect the nest contents from predators. New nests are often suspended from old ones, enhancing security from enemies.

two meters directly below a place where a snake might be able to find any convenient support. V. C. Ambedkar (in Crook 1960:4) made an interesting observation of a snake that tried to prey on a Baya's nest hanging over water in a well. The snake had difficulty in gripping the nest, which contracted under pressure, as it crawled down and tried to enter the tube. At this point, the serpent slipped and fell into the water.

In addition to increasing the difficulty of entering the nest, an entrance tube enables a more effective, active defense of the nest by the birds. In South Africa, in the Kruger National Park, we saw a poisonous tree snake, the Boomslang (*Dispholidus typus*), attack a colony of Spotted-backed Weavers (*Ploceus cucullatus spilonotus*). The snake, about two meters long, suddenly appeared in the colony tree and was at once surrounded by a fluttering, excited mob of weavers. Some birds dove at the snake and a few even struck it on the body whenever it put its head into a nest. They managed to drive the snake back into the dense foliage around the lower part of the tree, but it soon crawled back out toward the nests. This time it seized and swallowed two small nestlings, even though the mother bird and one male struck it on the body while its head was hidden from view in the short entrance tube of the nest. The snake then retreated. It appears that the entrance tube, although only about eight to fifteen centimeters long in this species, does permit the birds to counterattack with greater safety to themselves, than if there were no entrance tube (N. Collias and Collias 1971a).

Spotted-backed Weavers, like the Baya and many other species of weavers, also remove all or most of the leaves from twigs near their nests. This behavior probably makes it more difficult for a snake to support itself while approaching the nest, particularly when the nest hangs from a long vertical twig or vine, or from palm leaflets.

PROTECTION BY NESTING WITH OR NEAR FORMIDABLE SPECIES

Many species of birds, particularly in tropical regions, build their nests with impunity close to the nests of aggressive or formidable animals—such as large birds of prey, ants, bees, wasps, and termites—or in the vicinity of human habitations. The protection furnished to birds by this proximity may enable them to rear their young in safety.

Protection by Nesting near Large or Aggressive Species of Birds

On Scandinavian coasts, Tufted Ducks (*Aythya fuligula*) habitually nest in colonies of terns and Black-headed Gulls, which by their mobbing activities help protect the area from the larger species of gulls (Durango 1949).

Some species of weaverbirds in Africa and Madagascar may nest in the same tree and close to the nest of various large birds of prey (Chapin 1932, Rand 1936, Moreau 1942, Walsh and Walsh 1976). The Red-bellied Malimbe (*Malimbus erythrogaster*), a weaverbird of tropical rain forests in central Africa, often nests singly, but it may also nest in colonies of 20 to 120 nests in the same tree with a pair of Crowned Eagles (*Stephanoaetus coronatus*). Since this eagle is primarily a monkey-eater in central African forests, the weavers are effectively protected from marauding monkeys and doubtless from many other predators as well (Chapin 1932).

Heuglin's Weaver (*Ploceus heuglini*) of west and central Africa may nest close to nesting pairs of Red-necked Buzzards (*Buteo auguralis*), vultures, or marabous. Unlike other weavers which generally breed during the rains, Heuglin's Weaver tends to nest in the dry season when many birds of prey are nesting. Chapin (1932:614) observed that 12 to 15 nests of Heuglin's Weaver in a tree near a nest of a Red-necked Buzzard had been built after the buzzards' nest. Since this omnivorous hawk also feeds on snakes, it probably furnishes some protection to the weavers from these great enemies of small tropical birds.

Protection by Nesting near Human Habitations

Some birds seem deliberately to seek the vicinity of man for nesting, and it is likely that many of their natural enemies are either absent or scarce because of human activities. In the Netherlands, magpies often nest near houses where they have improved nesting success, probably because of protection from the main predator on their eggs, the Hooded Crow (Baeyens 1981).

In both the tropics and the North Temperate Zone it appears to be generally safer for birds to nest in man-made habitats rather than in forests; evidently because there are more predators in the forest (Skutch 1966). Of 756 nests of 23 species of altricial birds in clearings and second-growth areas of the Central American tropical lowlands, Skutch found 37 percent were successful. But in the neighboring forests nesting success was much lower and only 23 percent of 136 nests built by 30 species (28 altricial) produced at least one fledgling. These data were gathered over a period of more than 30 years. Skutch also notes that many forest birds increase their chances of success by entering neighboring clearings to breed, but few open-country birds build their nests in the forest.

The Village Weaver (*Ploceus cucullatus*) of tropical Africa often establishes its nesting colonies near human dwellings. In northwest Senegal, along 150 kilometers of road where the road passed through moist savanna, rural and urban country, 20 of 25 colonies we counted were near houses (N. Collias and Collias 1969b). This species will not nest inside forests away from clearings and also avoids nesting in very dry places since it needs green leaves of tall grasses or of palms for nest material. The presence of man tends to diminish the numbers of many predators, such as snakes and monkeys. However, in our experience, tropical accipitrine hawks, which are secretive and important weaverbird predators, are not much deterred by human presence (N. Collias and Collias 1959b, 1978).

Nesting in Association with Dangerous Social Insects

Some tropical birds, particularly passerine species with roofed nests, frequently build their nests in trees near the nests of ants, bees, or wasps, in Africa, Asia, Australia, and Central and South America. In Africa, weaverbirds, estrildid finches, and sunbirds often build near arboreal nests of wasps or ants (Moreau 1936, 1942, MacLaren 1950). We have seen two pairs of Bronze Mannikins (*Lonchura cucullata*) in central Africa building their nest within a meter of an occupied polistine wasp nest.

In Ghana, L. G. Grimes (1973) found a statistically significant association of Heuglin's Weaver nesting colonies in trees with nests of red weaver ants (*Oecophylla longinoda*). The ants were never seen to attack nestlings in the tree, but did in nests that fell to the ground. Tweedie and Harrison (1954:73) state that colonies of the Baya Weaver in Malaya are frequently found in trees infested by red weaver ants (*Oecophylla smaragdena*). These ants have no sting but bite with their jaws and eject an acrid fluid over the wound, savagely attacking anyone who touches or brushes against the branches bearing their nest.

In Australia, the Double-barred Finch (*Poephila bichenovii*) nests close to the nests of paper wasps (Hindwood 1955), and several species of warblers of the genus *Gerygone* often place their domed nests in trees close to the nests of ants or wasps (Cayley 1959). In tropical America, several species of tyrant flycatchers, wrens and icterids place their nests close to occupied wasp nests (Skutch 1976). In Ecuador, of 20 nests of Sclater's Tyrannulet (*Camptostoma obsoletum*), 12 were within one meter of active wasp nests, and 2 of these were seen to be started alongside wasp nests (Marchant 1960). In Surinam, Haverschmidt (1968) found 52 nests of the Yellow-breasted Flycatcher (*Tolmomyias flaviventris*), of which 39 were near a wasp nest.

The frequency of association with social-insect nests varies even among closely related species of birds. In Surinam, the Yellow-rumped Cacique (*Cacicus cela*; Icteridae) builds its nests more often (43 percent of 82 nests), near wasp and bee nests than does the Red-rumped Cacique (*Cacicus haemorrhous*) (17 percent of 54 nests), according to Feekes (1981). Nest enemies included toucans, owls, hawks, bats, opossums, monkeys, and snakes, but it is not known, or it is difficult to say, against which of these the wasps and bees furnished protection.

Myrmecophytes are plants having a mutualistic relationship with the ants that live in them. Many birds nest in the protection of myrmecophytes. The Ant Gall Acacia or Whistling Thorn (*Acacia drepanolobium*) is often used as a nest site by Grey-capped Social Weavers (*Pseudonigrita arnaudi*) in Africa, particularly by the southern race *dorsalis* of Tanzania where 57 of 138 weaver colonies we saw were in Ant Gall Acacias (N. Collias and Collias 1977). Colonies of small aggressive ants live inside the numerous galls at the base of the thorns on these little acacia trees; the ants instantly swarmed out and attacked us when we tried to collect any weaverbird nests from these trees.

In Central America, various species of ants of the genus *Pseudomyrmex* live in the swollen thorns of several shrubs or trees, referred to collectively as swollen-thorn or bull's-horn acacias, and these acacia ants attack herbivores, primarily insects, by biting and stinging. Janzen (1969) observed that in areas swollen-thorn acacias occurred at low density (one or fewer per mile of roadside), over fifty percent of the acacias over three meters tall had at least one bird's nest in them. Eggs or young in these nests were never removed by any predator during many days of observation, involving at least eight species of birds, including a dove, tyrant flycatcher, antshrike, icterid, and wren. Each day the ants patrolled the branch near their home thorns; if a branch was shaken lightly or pulled down slightly to permit a look into a bird's nest the ants at once swarmed out and attacked. But a bird landing on the branch did not cause such a disturbance, and the ants also seemed to become accustomed to the nest material when the bird was building, perhaps because it acquired the odor of the ant colony. When Janzen placed arboreal snakes quietly in an acacia, they were severely bitten and stung by the ants and the snakes quickly departed.

The climax of a nesting relationship between birds and insects is seen where birds actually nest inside the nest of social insects, particularly in ant or termite colonies. The phenomenon is worldwide in tropical regions (Chapin 1932, Moreau 1942, Hindwood 1959, Skutch 1976, Short 1979), and is especially characteristic of certain species of nonpasserine land birds belonging to orders where the birds are generally hole-nesters, such as kingfishers, woodpeckers, jacamars, puffbirds, parrots, and trogons. Birds of these orders are preadapted to excavating holes in nests of social insects by their hole-nesting habits and their large, strong bills.

The Rufous Woodpecker (*Celeus brachyurus*) of oriental regions nests almost exclusively in the arboreal nests of Crematogaster ants, which can give a painful bite. The White-tailed Kingfisher (*Tanysiptera sylvia*) is limited in northeast Australia by scarcity of the termite mounds in which it breeds. Sacred Kingfishers (*Halcyon sancta*) in Australia have been known to nest for successive generations up to thirty years in the same termite mound (Breeden and Slater 1968). Some species of termites have soldiers with very large mandibles which can deliver a bite or pinch painful even to humans, while in many other species the soldiers are able to eject a sticky fluid at the enemy (Wilson 1971:186–189). A predator seeking the eggs or young of a bird nesting in a termite nest would quite likely damage the termite nest, and so draw an attack on itself from the termites.

MULTIPLE NESTING ATTEMPTS

Some birds nest together in such huge numbers over such a short period of time that local predators become satiated, and some broods reach independence before sufficient predators can gather to exterminate the colony. Other species of birds, in which the individual pairs are dispersed, especially in the tropics, may lay many small clutches over one season. Despite a high nest mortality, if one brood gets through occasionally, it may be enough to maintain a population of long-lived adults. In either case the adage followed, quite literally, seems to be "Don't put all your eggs in one basket."

Breeding colonies of the Red-billed Weaver or Quelea (*Quelea quelea*), widely distributed in dry, open, and cultivated country in Africa south of the Sahara, may contain half a million to ten million nests. The building of colonies harboring millions of birds does not take more than a week (Morel et al. 1957). Elgood and Ward (1963) suggest that the sheer numbers of these birds breeding in large synchronized colonies may exceed the capacity of local predators to consume more than a fraction of the young. Predators of Quelea other than man are numerous and include Tawny Eagles, Marabou Storks, Red-billed Hornbills, pythons and other snakes (Morel et al. 1957). The eagles and storks tear open the nests and eat the young, the hornbills pluck the young out of the entrance with their huge bills. Interestingly, the lower rim of the Quelea's nest entrance is prolonged inward as a broad shelf beneath which the young can hide and perhaps escape the probing bill of an enemy (N. Collias and Collias 1964).

Weaverbirds seem to be quite helpless against nocturnal aboreal snakes, such as the Egg-eating Snake (*Dasypeltis*), often found in weaverbird colonies (Pitman 1958). The only defense the birds seem to have is to build another nest and lay another clutch. Weaverbirds may have a considerable capacity to replace lost clutches. The normal clutch of the Village Weaver is two or three eggs. In a captive colony, when clutches were repeatedly removed during the five to six months breeding season, one female laid twenty-six eggs, another laid twenty-nine eggs, in successive clutches, generally shifting to a new nest for each clutch.

Predation on nests may be severe in tropical rain forests (Skutch 1966, Ricklefs 1969). E. O. Willis, who has made a special study of the antbirds (Formicariidae), says of them "As in all forest birds there is a high mortality of nests due to predators—reaching 90 or 95% loss in Panama, where up to 10 or 13 nestings may be attempted by a single pair in one year and only one or two succeed" (in C. Harrison 1978:71). High nest mortality was also found in a wide variety of species near Belem in Eastern equatorial Brazil, but nest mortality in forests near Manaus in central equatorial Brazil was not especially high (Oniki 1979).

NESTS WITH VERY THICK, STRONG WALLS

Few if any nests are absolutely impregnable to large natural enemies, but the walled-up tree holes of hornbills, where the narrow entrance is guarded by the formidable beak of the parent, seem impregnable to most enemies other than man. The thick, hard, earthen walls of the oven-shaped nest of the Rufous Ovenbird make the nest difficult for an enemy to break into.

Some birds build very strong nests of twigs. The Cachalotes or House Builders (*Pseudoseiura*) of South America are large, noisy birds that belong to the ovenbird family (Furnariidae) but more resemble jays in their habits and actions—eating eggs and robbing other birds' nests. The nest of *P. guttaralis* is the largest built by an ovenbird, a spherical mass of twigs, four to five feet in diameter, placed in a strong spreading bush. The large inside chamber is reached by side entrance through a narrow, arched gallery. So strong is the nest that a man was able to stand and stamp on one without injuring it in the least (Vaurie 1980).

All species of birds building compound nests (Monk Parakeet, Palm Chat, Buffalo Weaver, Sociable Weaver) strengthen the nest by using many twigs, particularly in the roof, and such twigs would seem to function particularly as a deterrent against bird and mammal predators

(N. Collias 1980). Enhanced security from predation may be a key feature in the evolution of the compound nest (N. Collias and Collias 1964, and see chap. 2).

SUMMARY

The nest and its contents may be *concealed* in various ways. Most small birds hide their nests in vegetation. Eggs may be concealed by their color and pattern, by being covered with nest materials when the parent leaves the nest, or by being laid in an enclosed nest. In some tropical birds with an open nest, such as several cotingas and tree swifts, the nest is very small and hidden beneath the incubating parent. Many caprimulgids such as the Whip-poor-will, birds noted for their concealing coloration, do not use a nest. To assess the effectiveness of nest concealment we need more specific information about the various techniques used to find nests by different predators. Birds with enclosed nests have better breeding success than birds with open nests.

Predators may be confused or deceived by nests camouflaged to resemble the surroundings, or by many nests built close together with only some of the nests occupied at any one time. The African Grey-capped Social Weaver (*Pseudonigrita arnaudi*) and a South American ovenbird *Certhiaxis pyrrhophia*) build nests with two entrances either one of which can serve as an emergency exit. Some penduline titmice (Remizidae) build a nest having a false entrance resembling the true entrance that is closed when the birds are in the nest. Many birds that nest on the ground simulate injury in an attempt to lead a predator away from the nest, but such distraction-displays are rare in birds that nest in trees or in burrows.

Many species of birds build their nests in various inaccessible or relatively safe places. Some birds construct a barricade near the nest entrance, making it difficult for a predator to enter the nest. Long, vertical entrance tubes with the nest entrance at the bottom of the tube have evolved independently in weaverbirds of Asia, Africa, and Madagascar. These entrances help protect the nest contents from snakes and other enemies.

Protective nesting associations with formidable species guard the nests of some small birds, particularly of species that build roofed nests in the tropics. They build their nests in or near the nests of large birds of prey, human habitations, or nests of ants, wasps, bees, or termites. The frequency of such protective associations varies greatly even among closely related species of birds.

Multiple nesting attempts help defend birds against predation in two general ways. Where very many birds nest gregariously over a short period of time, local nest predators may become satiated, and some broods manage to fledge, for example, the Red-billed Weaver (*Quelea quelea*). Many passerine species of tropical forests, such as the Neotropical antbirds, breed in dispersed pairs. Each female may attempt many small clutches each season, and despite a high nest mortality, enough broods succeed to maintain the species.

Some birds build nests with thick, strong walls that are relatively impregnable to many enemies. This type of nest is especially characteristic of some members of the ovenbird family of Central and South America, as well as the few species of birds in the world that build a compound, or apartment-style nest. Birds with compound nests build thich-walled nests of strong twigs (Monk Parakeet, Palmchat, Buffalo Weaver) or of straws and twigs (Sociable Weaver). The thick communal roof helps provide security to all, and may have been a key feature permitting evolution of the compound nest.

CHAPTER TEN

How Birds Build Their Nests

MECHANISMS of nest building involve problems of selecting suitable nest materials, fastening the nest to the substrate, binding nest materials together, and shaping the nest to a durable and species-specific pattern. Nest building often takes much work, involving problems in economy of effort.

SELECTION OF NEST MATERIALS

The significant cues whereby different species of birds recognize suitable nest materials need more investigation. Some birds have been known to build their nests of an artificial or atypical material—wire, glass, cotton, string, or cement. A pair of Rock Doves (*Columba livia*) near a factory in Michigan built a nest basically similar to normal Rock Dove nests, except that in place of twigs, 84 percent of the 1061 bits of nest material were pieces of iron wire. This nest contained a dead one to three-day-old squab and may have failed because the nest materials provided no insulation to retain the heat generated by the brooding parent (Paterson 1977). In Europe an Icterine Warbler (*Hippolais icterina*) built a nest from spun glass (Moenke 1978). Normally, its deep cup-nest is built of plant stems, fine grasses, and bark fibre, bound with plant down, fibre, hair, and spider webs (Van Dobben 1949, C. Harrison 1975). When cotton was placed near nesting American Goldfinches (*Carduelis tristis*), they readily adopted it in place of the thistle down that is normally a large component of their nests (Allen 1937:239). Similarly, when short lengths of string or light-colored yarn were placed near the nest site of a pair of Northern (Baltimore) Orioles (*Icterus galbula*) they wove their nest in good part of string and yarn, supplementing the milkweed fibers they normally use (Allen 1937:210,227). In Britain, what has been called one of the safest bird nests ever built, was constructed under the eaves of a house by House Martins (*Delichon urbica*) that, instead of the usual mud, inadvertently used wet cement put out by builders (Darlington 1962). What this use of various artificial nest materials shows is that birds may select man-made materials that in some way resemble those normally used. It takes controlled experimentation to determine the specific cues to which the birds are responding.

Availability no doubt plays an important role in the selection of nest materials. The female Village Weaver lines her nest with fine grass tops, but when chickens live nearby, she supplements this lining with many feathers. In the Antarctic where no plant material is available, the Adélie Penguins build nests of small stones. Flamingoes nest in shallow, muddy lakes where only mud is available and build their elevated nests of mud. The immensely abundant Peruvian Boobies (*Sula variegata*) have only their dried excreta and some molted feathers available for nest building on the arid guano islands of Peru (B. Nelson 1968).

The type of nest materials that young birds are raised with helps determine the type of nest materials the birds select later for nest building, as Sargent (1965) showed for the Zebra Finch (*Poephila guttata*).

Fastening the Nest to Difficult Substrates

Birds have various means for fastening their nests to more or less vertical substrates. Swifts generally use saliva to consolidate and to attach their nests (Lack 1956). The salivary glands in some species enlarge several times in size during the nesting season and diminish again after the breeding season. Nests of different species of cave swiftlets (*Collocalia*) have different relative amounts of plant material and adhesive saliva. Those nests with a large proportion of saliva can be attached to vertical faces in the cave, while nests with much vegetation may need to be partly supported by some irregularity in the cave wall (Medway 1960). The nest of the Palm Swifts (*Cypsiurus*) of the Old World is a simple strip of feathers or plant fibers with a shallow bowl for the eggs at the bottom and is fixed to a hanging palm leaf on the inner side. The leaf and the nest rock together with the wind, but since the eggs are glued to the nest with saliva they are safe from falling (Lack 1956). Perhaps the most difficult attachment sites of any bird's nest are those chosen by the Scissor-tailed Swifts (*Panyptila*) of tropical America, which fasten their nests to the underside of a branch or overhanging rock. The nest is a tube of dried plant down and bird feathers, worked with saliva into a close felt. The entrance is at the bottom, and a wider chamber at the top holds the eggs (Lack 1956).

Some birds use mud to help attach the nest to the substrate (Rowley 1971). Cliff Swallows (*Hirundo pyrrhonota*) attach their nests of pure mud to vertical faces of cliffs, or like House Martins to vertical sides of buildings under the eaves. Possibly some admixture of saliva increases the adhesive qualities of the mud. The Barn Swallow (*H. rustica*) uses mud, straw, and grass in building its nest on a horizontal or vertical surface, especially on rafters in barns.

In the western United States, the Black Phoebe (*Sayornis nigricans*) builds a nest of mud pellets and grass in natural sites on vertical or near-vertical surfaces protected from rain, whereas Say's Phoebe (*S. saya*) places its nest of grass, plant fibers, weed stems, and wool, in holes, crevices, and on the upper surface of cliff ledges or steep banks. Whereas the Black Phoebe chooses vertical surfaces of bridges for its nest, Say's Phoebe places its nest on the horizontal surfaces of pillars or beams under the bridge (Ohlendorf 1976).

Many small birds with pensile nests use cobwebs to help fasten their nests to the substrate, generally a twig. The Rock Warbler (*Origma solitaria*) of southeastern Australia builds a pensile domed nest with hooded side entrance, composed of bark fiber, rootlets, and grasses, and coated with moss and cobwebs. The upper portion of the nest, which is firmly attached to a minute rock cleft in the ceiling of a cave, is formed almost entirely of cobwebs (Cayley 1959, H. Frith 1979).

Nicator c. chloris, a bulbul (Pycnotidae) of the tropical rain forests of Africa, builds a tiny, loose, open nest of tendrils with rotten twigs for its base, within which a fungal mycelium (*Marasmius*) develops in a few days, firmly binding the nest to its support in a tree or bush (Brosset 1974).

In tropical America, some of the New World flycatchers, such as the Royal Flycatcher (*Onychorhychus coronatus*) and the Ochre-bellied Fly-catcher (*Pipromorpha oleagina*), attach the roof of their pensile nests to the end of a vertical twig or thin dangling vine by twisting long, thread-like plant materials round and round the slender support (Skutch 1960).

Most of the true weaverbirds (Ploceinae) of Africa and Asia attach their nests to emergent vegetation over water or to the tips of drooping branches. In general, most species weave with long strips torn from the green leaves of tall grasses or palm fronds. Such materials provide the necessary strength and flexibility. The Baya Weaver (*Ploceus philippinus*) in India often uses long strips torn from sugar cane leaves, and winds the strips round and round the supporting twig, interweaving them with each other. Repetition of the act forms first a wad and then a suspension cord or rope from which the nest chamber is subsequently built (Ambedkar 1964). The nest of the Nelicourvi Weaver (*Ploceus nelicourvi*) of Madagascar is suspended from a long, slender, vertical, hanging twig or vine by a rope 15 to 30 centimeters long woven of grass, sedge, and long palm fibers (Rand 1936, Collias 1980).

WHAT HOLDS A NEST TOGETHER

The materials of a nest are held together in different ways in different kinds of nests. Nests of twigs hold together because many of the twigs are pushed in by the birds toward a common center in the usually round or globular nest, and the twigs are held in place by the pressure of adjoining twigs, aided by slight irregularities, small side branches, or sometimes thorns on the twigs. Since the central part of the nest has a smaller diameter than the outer portion of the nest, the ends of those twigs pushed toward the center will be closer and more tightly packed together than the outer ends of the same twigs. When the supporting branch of a large globular nest mass of the Buffalo Weaver (*Bubalornis albirostris*) in Kenya was chopped down from a tree, the nest fell twenty-five feet (7.6 m), and so firmly were the component twigs united that scarcely a twig was dislodged when the nest crashed to the ground (N. Collias and Collias 1964).

In nests built of stiff grass stems and grass heads by sparrow weavers (*Plocepasser*) and by social weavers (*Pseudonigrita*), each stem or grass head is inserted base end first into the mass. Since most grass stems are inserted first to one side and then the other at one place on the bottom of the developing nests, their crisscrossing bases gradually form a tight and compact threshold that provides a firm support for the rest of the nest. The distal ends of the grass heads radiate out from the threshold to form the nest chamber (N. Collias and Collias 1964).

The nest of the White-capped Noddy (*Anous minutus*) on Australian coastal islands is placed in a small tree and is a shallow cup of soft leaves, seaweed, grass, and roots, cemented with the birds' own excreta and sticky Pisonia seed heads (H. Frith 1979). Seaweed contains a viscid protein-polysaccharide complex, and this mucilaginous substance probably also aids nest cohesion. The Black-legged Kittiwake (*Rissa tridactyla*), a gull that nests on cliff ledges, may use algae that dry to form a hard firm base for the foundation of its nest (Rowley 1971).

Swifts normally collect nest materials on the wing, often taking airborne materials. To bind together the feathers and small bits of plant material that many swifts use in their nests, the birds use sticky saliva, which owes its viscid nature to its mucoprotein content. Mucoproteins are a chemical complex of protein combined with relatively large amounts of polysaccharides, and are characterized by their ability to form a viscoelastic mucus in low concentrations and by their tendency to form rubbery gels in which the hydrated macromolecules are united by crossbridges to form a polymer network (Wainwright et al. 1976).

Birds in 16 families or subfamilies, close to 5 percent of the world's species, use mud in building their nests (Rowley 1971). Some genera and species of birds, particularly thrushes (Turdidae), use mud to cement together the grasses forming the bulk of their nests. The Australian Mud-nest Builders (Grallinidae) build predominantly mud nests, with plant fibers making up only 4 to 27 percent of the dry weight of the nest; however, since plant material is much lighter than mud, the total bulk of the fibre may approach that of the mud. The nests are mud bowls placed on a horizontal branch. Mud and mud-impregnated material is taken to the nest, "positioned and consolidated with much bill-wiping and shivering (Australian species) which appears to have a similar effect to a vibrator settling a concrete construction—the end result is that the fibre forms the framework and the mud oozes to the outside effectively masking the vegetable material" (Rowley 1971). Nests of the White-winged Chough (*Corcorax melanorhamphus*, Grallinidae) can last for years and be used again and again (H. Frith 1979).

Silk threads are one of the binding materials most often used by many small birds to hold together the plant materials of their nests. The Bushtit (*Psaltriparus minimus*) of the western United States concentrates the silk in the neck region of its gourd-shaped nest of heterogenous materials; the nest hangs among twigs in a tree or bush (Addicott 1938). The Cape Penduline Tit (*Anthoscopus minutus*, Remizidae) of South Africa will bring a lump of cobweb to its nest, draw out the threads of silk, and jab the ends with its beak into the mass of plant down or wool of which most of its nest consists (Skead 1959). Birds obtain silk from insect cocoons or spider constructions. There are many different kinds of silk but in general they are very light and elastic and have great tensile strength for their weight. Most silks are made of strands of the crystalline protein, fibroin, surrounded by an amorphous sheath of another protein, sericin. The sericin helps stick the extended chains of fibroin together, but is relatively unimportant in the tensile properties of silk. Some very extensible silks have the protein chains folded, or lack crystalline structure, as in the sticky spiral thread of *Meta reticulata*, a spider (Wainright et al. 1976). The strength of typical silks is increased by the way in which the protein chains are packed into sheets; movement between the different sheets results in a flexible fiber. The degree of extensibility of different silks is correlated with the extent of disordered regions between the crystalline regions of the silk (Vincent 1982).

Cellulose constitutes the chief part of the cell walls of plants, is the main component of woody fibers, and is the main load-bearing constituent in both woody and herbaceous plants; it is therefore the principal chemical component in most birds' nests. Cellulose has several properties that suit it for this important role: it is insoluble in water, so the nest does not dissolve away in rain; it is very light, lessening the work of building the nest; it is flexible but not very extensible, so the nest retains its shape; but its most outstanding property is its great tensile strength that, for equivalent weights, equals or exceeds that of silk or steel (Wainwright et al. 1976, Gordon 1978). Silk also has high tensile strength but its tensile strength decreases with increased humidity, whereas wet cellulose fibers appear to be stronger than dry ones, helping to make a nest built of plant materials resistant to rain.

Cellulose is a complex plant polysaccharide and polymer that yields only glucose on complete hydrolysis. The high tensile strength of cellulose results both from its extended chain structure and the numerous interchain hydrogen bonds. Its tensile strength increases with molecular weight up to a certain degree of polymerization. Cellulose molecules aggregated in parallel array form the microfibrils seen in electron micrographs (Wainwright et al. 1976).

Bast fibers are strong woody fibers associated with the phloem tissue of plants. Bast fibers from dicot stems are perhaps the best example of strong cellulose materials, and it is just this tensile strength that makes bast fibers so useful as textile fibers, such as those from flax (Wainwright et al. 1976). The Northern Oriole of the United States may weave its pendulous, pouchlike nest largely of bast fibers—from stems of milkweed (*Asclepias sp.*) or Indian Hemp (*Apocynum cannabinum*) (H. Harrison 1979). In general, birds that use long, flexible plant materials to bind their nests together will intertwine the materials in diverse orientations, distributing and equalizing stress and strains on the nest.

SHAPING THE NEST: BUILDING BY SOME REPRESENTATIVE SPECIES

The purpose of this section is to illustrate how some of the main types of complex nests are built—the cup-nest typical of most small birds; the deep pouch-nest of orioles and their allies, the climax of nest building in the New World; domed nests of various types, characteristic of many tropical passerine birds; and the compound nest, common among social insects but rare among birds.

Building a Cup-nest

Nolan (1978) describes the nest-building behavior of the Prairie Warbler (*Dendroica discolor*) in detail. This bird breeds in the eastern United States and generally places its nest in small trees. The nest has an outer shell, a middle layer of padding, and an inner lining. The outer shell is made of plant fibers, often bast fibers of milkweed or fleabane daisy, cemented together with spider or insect silk; the middle layer consists mainly of plant down, sometimes supplemented with feathers or hair; and the inner layer generally consists of soft grass tops.

The nest, built by the female in about a week, is held in place mainly by spider silk, although some long plant fibers are woven around supporting branches and twigs. The female first sticks silk threads to branch and leaf surfaces with her bill, thrusting forward, then sideways and backward along one side of her body, in quick shuttlelike movements. She begins the nest cup by making a shallow, saucer-shaped foundation of plant fibers; carrying fibers into the nest, she lays them across the site and presses them down with her breast and belly; she then seizes loose ends of fibers and fastens them to the prepared web-covered surfaces. She binds down new material in the developing walls by drawing fibers inward and over the material with her bill and jabbing them into position inside the nest. The female brings silk every few trips and fastens it to the nest exterior, whence she pulls the silk inward over the developing walls.

The cup shape and the proper size of the nest result from the fact that the female stays in one spot in the developing nest while she shapes it. She presses her breast against the wall in front of her, rapidly kicking first one foot, then the other, backwards, pivoting in the nest while doing so. At the same time, she presses the bend of her wings outwards, shaping the interior walls. Sometimes she stands and presses her throat down on the top of the wall, and she also helps shape the wall by pressing the lower side of the base of her tail downwards against the wall. While turning her body, the female smooths the top of the wall with throat and tail. Finally, she thickens and strengthens the walls with stiff short plant fibers that, like soft lining materials, she inserts while perched outside the nest or on its rim. The lining of plant down and soft grass tops is molded by the usual shaping movements, but the bill is used infrequently. All these techniques help to tighten the walls and mold the nest cup to the proper size for the species.

Building a Deep Pouch-nest

Some birds build a cup-nest suspended from twigs by its rim, as vireos and many antbirds do. This type of cup-nest has evolved into a deep pouch in the Northern Oriole. In a related Neotropical icterid, the Yellow-rumped Cacique (*Cacicus cela*), the hanging pouch may be 12 to 18 inches (30–40 cm) long, while in the largest icterid, Montezuma's Oropendola (Spanish for "oriole"), of Central America, the long pouch-nest is usually 2 to 4 feet (60–120 cm) and occasionally reaches a length of over 6 feet (180 cm).

Skutch (1954) has described the weaving of the nest of Montezuma's Oropendola (*Psarocolius montezuma*). The nests are built by the females in tall trees, in colonies where there are several females to each male. The males, much bigger than the females, serve as watchman but do no building, nor do they care for eggs or young.

The female weaves the nest of long, flexible fibers torn from the midribs of banana leaves or palm leaves; slender, green vines are also used. After making the initial attachment by wrapping many fibers around a twig or crotch high up in a tree, the female gradually pushes the materials apart to form a loop, which becomes the entrance of the nest; thereafter, she always stands in it as she works, invariably facing the center of the tree. She weaves more fibers into the loop which gradually lengthens into a vertical sleeve in which she hangs head downward. The sleeve soon becomes so long the bird is completely engulfed in it. Her orange-tipped bill can be seen at intervals as she pushes and pulls a fiber through the close-meshed network of the fabric. She invariably climbs back out the top of the sleeve, where she entered. Thus, the loop, just to one side of the top of the nest, remains the entrance of the nest. When the structure becomes sufficiently long the bird weaves the rounded bottom into the nest. The females then absent themselves for a day or two in the forest, during which time courtship and mating apparently take place. The females return and line the nest with pieces of dead leaves, which they pluck from trees growing at a distance. These leaves form a thick but loose and yielding litter in which the eggs rest, and probably serve to prevent the eggs from rolling together and breaking when a strong wind swings the pendulous nest. The average time for building a new nest from start to finish is ten days.

Building Roofed or Domed Nests

Roofed nests are constructed by different species from different materials—twigs, mud, short heterogenous materials bound with cobwebs, fine plant fibers matted together, or woven strips torn from monocot leaves. An example will be given of how the nest is built for each of these five general types of roofed or domed nest.

ROOFED TWIG NESTS. The Hamerkop or Hammerhead Stork (*Scopus umbretta*), widely distributed over sub-Saharan Africa, builds a massive domed nest with an entrance opening on one side in the lower half of the nest (fig. 10.1, 10.2). The nest is made of many different materials, but its basic framework is of twigs and branches. Other herons and storks build a large, open nest of twigs. The Hamerkop, which is the only species in its family (Scopidae), is one of the few nonpasserine birds known to build a domed nest in a tree. Nest building takes about six weeks (Cowles 1930). The huge nest, usually 3 to 5 feet (0.9–1.5 m) in height and breadth, is typically placed in the crotch or strong fork of a tree near water and is strong enough to support a man. Its roof is

Fig. 10.1. The large roofed nest of the Hamerkop, or Hammerhead Stork (*Scopus umbretta*) may be 1.5 m wide and 1 m high. The entrance opens low on one side. Malawi, Africa.

Fig. 10.2. A Hamerkop, or Hammerhead Stork, looking for food in a marsh.

impervious to moderate rain. The entrance leads by a short tunnel to an inner chamber.

Liversidge (1963) and Kahl (1967) have described how a pair of Hamerkops build their nest. The nest is started as a simple, bowl-shaped structure of twigs. The initial twigs for the roof frame are placed loosely across one back corner of the nest bowl, and the next group of twigs are put across the remaining corner at an angle of 120 degrees to the first roof-members. By this alternating patchwork, the roof is built forward from the back to the front until the whole roof is completed. Then the bulk of roofing materials is added to the top using a great variety of materials to cover the large twigs. While further roofing material is added by one bird, the other commences to plaster the floor and inside lower walls with mud gathered from a nearby pool. Finally, the entrance way is reduced to its normal dimensions and shape and lined inside with mud. Before the eggs are laid, the lining of the nest must dry sufficiently so that the final bed of dried grass will not stick to the floor.

ROOFED MUD NESTS. The Cliff Swallow (*Hirundo pyrrhonota*) builds a domed nest of pure mud, except that the inside may be lined with a little dried grass or feathers; the nest is described as gourd-shaped, or retort-shaped.

J. T. Emlen, Jr. (1954) has described the different stages by which the Cliff Swallow builds its nest (fig. 10.3). The preferred nest site is a vertical surface beneath a ledge or overhang with sufficient clearance below to be safe from terrestrial enemies. Pair formation takes place at the nest site. The nest is built by both sexes, and requires about a week. The male initiates the work, but the female soon joins him.

The birds collect pellets of mud in their beaks, taking turns, one remaining at the nest site while its mate is away collecting mud. (a) They place the first pellets on the vertical surface 4 to 4 ½ inches below the sheltering overhang, bringing more pellets to form a narrow line or crescent of mud, which (b) is gradually built up into a shallow crescent-shaped ledge, then (c) into a rounded half-cup projecting 2 to 4 inches. Copulation takes place within the nest, starting in the cup-stage. When building the birds consistently perch with their feet in the center of the nest, reaching laterally or forward to place their pellets on the rim. (d) The nest deepens as the sidewalls are built up. The cliff overhang provides much of the roof for the nest, but when an overhang is irregular or absent, the lateral walls of the nest are extended upward until they meet to form a mud roof. Egg laying is commonly started at this stage, and varying amounts of nest-lining material, generally of grasses, accumulate. (e) The nest is built out into a wide-mouthed retort; many nests

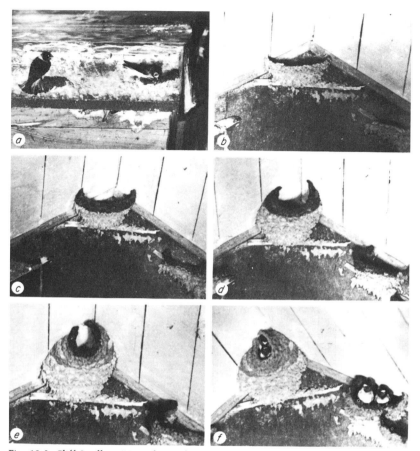

Fig. 10.3. Cliff Swallow (*Hirundo pyrrhonota*), stages of building a mud nest on the side of a barn, Wisconsin: (a) initial attachments to a vertical surface; (b) to (e) fresh mud (dark) placed on rim of the cup-stages must be allowed to dry and harden to form a firm base for new mud; (f) completed nest is roofed over with mud at the entrance. A pair of swallows is copulating just inside the entrance, while another pair nearby are building at the cup-stage. (After John T. Emlen, Jr., *Auk* 1954.)

extend no farther and retain a wide entrance. (f) In others, the birds crawl forward from within the nest to reach the rim and build it out and down to form a complete entrance tunnel, so the nest is a complete retort, projecting 6 to 10 inches (15–26 cm). The opening is narrowed to a circle about 1 ¼ to 1 ¾ inches (3.2–4.5 cm) in diameter. Almost invariably the tunnel is directed away from the nearest neighboring entrance, easing the amount of territorial quarreling with neighbors.

Nest building must proceed at a relatively slow rate so that each fresh addition of mud can dry and harden to form a firm base for further construction. Nests built too rapidly or in wet weather often collapse before they are completed.

DOMED NESTS BOUND WITH SILK. The domed nests of the sunbirds (Nectariniidae) of the Old World are generally built of short and heterogeneous plant materials bound together with spider silk. Skead (1967) describes the nests and building techniques of many African species. In general, they follow a quite similar pattern.

The nest of the Black Sunbird (*Nectarinia amesthystina*) is typical. The oval nest has a side entrance and hangs from a twig of a tree. It is built of a great mixture of materials—lichens, grassblades and other leaves, weed stems, vegetable down, fibres, bark, wool, and hair—all bound together with cobwebs.

Only the female builds; the male attends her closely, and he sings as she works. She begins the nest by winding cobwebs around the chosen twig, adding lichens and sundry bits of dead plant materials alternating with cobwebs. Gradually she forms a wad of material and into this thrusts her beak and head, opening a cavity—the beginning of the entrance hole. She adds more and more material to the lower half of the nest, and the nest cavity results from the regular entry of the bird into the nest, compressing the material within, apparently stamping it down with her feet in the way wool is stamped down into a wool-bag by a laborer. The elasticity and strength of the silk binding-threads permit the nest cavity to be formed in this way. The female thickens the nest further with more material, and then she adds a hood of long grass-tops over the entrance. She decorates the exterior of the nest with lichens and leaves and adds a soft lining of plant down within. One nest was lined with red flower petals. Three nests took from 33 to 36 days to complete.

MATTED DOMED NESTS. The hanging nests built by some Neotropical flycathers (Tyrannidae) are not woven, but are made by entangling a loose mass of fibrous material, which is then pushed apart to leave a cavity in its center (Skutch 1960).

The Sulphur-rumped Flycather (*Myiobius sulphureipygius*) is a small flycatcher, 5 inches (12.8 cm.) long, that inhabits the humid, lowland tropical forest and tall, second-growth woodland from Central America to Ecuador. Its pyriform or cone-shaped nest (fig. 2.19) often hangs from a dangling vine, slender twig, or bamboo stem over a shady stream. The nest is built in the dry season by the female, the male taking no part in any of the nesting duties. The nest fabric is too irregular to be called *woven*, and not compact enough to be called *felting*—the best

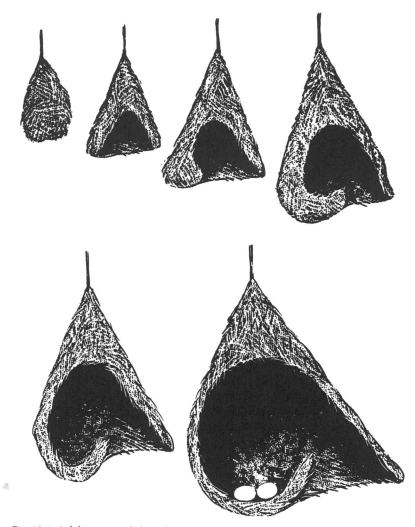

Fig. 10.4. Sulphur-rumped Flycatcher (*Myiobius sulphureipygius*), stages of nest building, Costa Rica. The pensile nest of plant fibers is matted together, and the bird hollows out the nest cavity from below. (Alexander F. Skutch, *Life Histories of Central American Birds* 1960)

term perhaps is *matting*. The nest is made of a variety of fiberlike materials, such as the long, pistillate inflorescences of a small tree (*Myriocarpa*) of the nettle family, much used by various tropical-forest flycatchers of the New World for building their nests.

Figure 10.4 illustrates the various stages of nest building in one nest observed by Skutch (1960). First, a small, irregular tuft of fibrous materials was attached to the end of a slender, hanging leafless twig of a small tree, 12 feet above the ground in a narrow opening in the forest undergrowth. The female, alighting on the tuft about the supporting twig, attached thin fibers with her bill to the tuft, making a quick revolution around the tuft with her whole body, ending each maneuver with her head down. The tuft of material slowly grew into a loose mass, and after several days the female began to push apart the matted fibers, working upward from the bottom and giving the mass roughly the form of a bell or hollow cone with the wall thicker on one side of the central hollow. She then brought fibrous material in her bill to the dangling nest, hovered below it an instant, rose upward into the cavity in the bottom of the cone, and attached what she had brought—always to the side where the wall was thickest. As a result this side grew in bulk, while the opposite wall of the hollow cone remained thin. Occasionally, she worked on the exterior, reinforcing the attachment with two or three turns around the supporting twig. Next, the female began to hollow out the egg chamber in the thickest part of the wall surrounding the central cavity, vigorously shaking the walls while arranging the fibers and shaping the fabric, stopping to rest just outside the nest at short intervals. When she could work in the nest in a less strained position, she sat in the egg chamber and devoted much longer periods to arranging the fibers and shaping the structure. The bottom of the egg chamber was lined with fine, light-colored fibers.

While the thick side of the nest developed into the egg chamber, the thin side became an antechamber or apron that shielded the bright yellow rump of the female from view when she sat upon her eggs. The female required three weeks to build this nest. Another nest was measured and was 9 inches (23 cm) high and 3 ½ inches (9 cm) in transverse diameter at the widest part, near the bottom.

WOVEN DOMED NESTS. Woven nests consist of intertwined flexible materials or interlocking loops of flexible materials but differ from matted nests in having some regularity of pattern in the fabric of the nest. In the next chapter we give a detailed description and analysis of how the African Village Weaver constructs its beautiful nest.

The Thick-billed or Grosbeak Weaver (*Amblyospiza albifrons*), pos-

Fig. 10.5. Thick-billed Weaver (*Amblyospiza albifrons*), stages of nest building, Kenya. The nest is built of fine plant fibers by the male, starting (a) as a thin bridge between upright supports, which is thickened (b) into a pad; a cup-stage (c) follows, the rear wall of which is extended upward (d) to form a roof (e); in a completed nest accepted by a female, the entrance to the nest is narrowed down considerably (f). (N. E. and E. C. Collias, *Univ. Calif. Publ. Zool.* 1964)

sibly the most primitive member of the subfamily Ploceinae or true weavers (Chapin 1954), uses long, very thin strips or fibers torn from leaves of cattails (*Typha latifolia*) and of sedges (*Cyperus papyrus*). Instead of weaving one strip in and out, like the Village Weaver (chap. 11), the Thick-billed Weaver works with the materials in a manner somewhat intermediate between weaving and matting.

Laycock (1979) describes how *Amblyospiza* builds its nest. It starts the nest as a bridge between upright supports of marsh plants, often over water. Standing on the bridge facing one way, the male, who does most of the building, bows down while weaving out a nest cup just in front of and below himself, then reaches across from his perch to build up the back and sidewalls, which he extends upward to form the domed roof.

The male brings a single strand or a bundle of strands, which he pushes into some part of the nest fabric and works in by a process of poking and pulling at loops and ends. Jabbing with his bill, he pokes loops of the material through the inner side of the nest wall, then reaches around to the outer side of the wall and pulls the loops of the thin strands around through the entrance hole, where he fastens them in place. The walls of the nest are lined from within with shorter strips of material. After the nest is accepted by a female, the male narrows the entrance hole.

A nest built by the Thick-billed Weaver (fig. 10.5) differs from those of most other true weavers in going through a cup-stage, whereas other weavers generally start the nest as a ring, on the bottom of which the bird perches while weaving (N. Collias and Collias 1964). The other Ploceinae also differ from *Amblyospiza* in usually building the roof before the bottom of the nest.

Some Old World warblers (*Sylviidae*) weave a domed nest of strips of green grass, as does the Karoo Prinia (*Prinia maculosa*) of South Africa, which is known to build a hammock and cup-stage before weaving the roof (Rowan and Broekhuysen 1962).

Building a Compound Nest

The gigantic apartment-style nest of the Sociable Weaver (*Philetairus socius*) is the most spectacular nest built by any bird, and therefore deserves some special attention (fig. 1.26–1.28). These small sparrow-size birds (14 cm, 27 gm) of arid southwestern Africa live and sleep in their huge nest the year round. They usually build the nest on strong horizontal branches of isolated Camelthorn (*Acacia giraffae*) trees, sometimes in other trees, such as the Kokerboom (*Aloe dichotoma*), and sometimes on the horizontal cross bar at the top of a telephone pole. The essential features of a nest site are strong support for the heavy nest and free access from below.

N. E. and E. C. Collias (1964, E. C. and N. E. Collias 1978), and G. L. Maclean (1973) have described nest building by the Sociable Weaver, based on observation of color-banded individual birds in nature and in aviaries. The following somewhat arbitrary stages may be recognized, but there is much overlap: (1) initiating the nest mass, (2) building the roof, (3) building the substructure and new chambers, and filling in or partially dismantling old chambers, and (4) extending the nest mass and repairing damage. Once the nest is established the birds may work on almost any part of it at any time throughout the long life of the nest.

1. *Initiating the nest mass.* The nest mass is begun with straws, usually wedged into the rough bark of an acacia tree or between twigs. The most commonly used building materials in the Kalahari Desert are the strong dry stems of the white desert grass, *Aristida celata.* The bird pushes a grass stem with its bill into the growing mass of straws with sideways movements of the head, shifting its hold up the stem repeatedly as it works the straw into the nest mass. The straw is merely pushed into place; at no time is there any pulling action, nor is the nest really woven.

The nest mass is initiated by several birds working together. The first chamber is built quickly since the birds, if they have no other home to return to, have urgent need of a safe sleeping place. Normally, a Sociable Weaver never sleeps outside a nest mass. In the Kalahari Gemsbok National Park, White et al. (1975) noted that most of the birds that they observed constructing small, new nests returned each night to the large nest mass of the parent colony.

2. *Building the roof.* The next urgent need is to increase the safety of the nest by strengthening the roof. The birds add twigs, as well as more straws and grass heads to the roof. The birds prefer twigs of moderate length (15–25 cm) to longer or shorter ones, and light twigs to heavy twigs of equal length. The roof gradually becomes dome-shaped as more materials are added to it.

Most of the work on the roof is done by the males. The birds work more on the roof when they are not breeding than when they are. For the roof they prefer twigs to straws, but when they are breeding they reverse this preference and then do more building on the nest chambers.

3. *Building the substructure and new chambers.* The substructure is built below the bough that supports the nest mass, from straws and

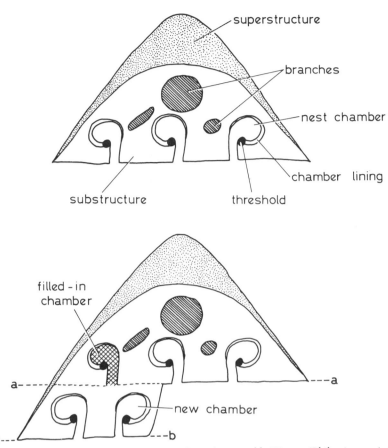

Fig. 10.6. (Above) diagrammatic section through a Sociable Weaver (*Philetairus socius*) nest mass at a mature stage of construction. (Below) diagrammatic section through an old nest mass, in which the chambers in the two levels (a and b) are occupied by birds of separate social units. (G. L. Maclean, *Ostrich* 1973)

grassheads, and contains the nest chambers. As the substructure extends downward, new chambers are built at a lower level and the initial chambers may be filled in with straws (fig. 10.6). A mature nest mass usually contains a single layer of chambers at one level, unless the site is irregular, in which case more than one structural level of chambers may result. Each bird seems to visit only those chambers within its own structural level (Maclean 1973), although all birds build on the roof.

We observed that when a chamber was started, many birds might build on it. As the chamber progressed, usually one dominant male prevented some or all of the other birds from building or roosting in this chamber, which would eventually be occupied by this dominant individual and his mate, if he had one, and perhaps by some other bird that he tolerated. The remaining birds had to seek or build other chambers. As more chambers become available, sleeping sites were less crowded, and building tended to slow down (E. Collias and Collias 1980). During the breeding period only the pair maintained the chamber (Maclean 1973).

New chambers, which are about 15 centimeters in diameter and globular or retort-shaped, are built in the following way: First, the birds begin spending a great deal of time at some particular spot, especially near the periphery of the substructure, where they repeatedly poke and push the straws that are already there deeper into the nest mass until a more or less vertical, compacted, depressed circular area is formed. The ends of straws that do not push in easily are bitten off and either inserted into the nest or dropped. The area becomes consolidated and firmly compacted as more and more straws are forced in. Second, the birds begin the chamber walls by building out the top, sides, and floor of the chamber with additional straws or grass heads. The chamber becomes gradually deeper and more compact by a process of pushing in, clipping off, and building out with straws and grass stems. A threshold is always added before eggs are laid and consists of short, crisscrossing straws or grass stems. The threshold forms a ridge, which keeps the eggs from rolling out, and is a good perch from which the birds continue building. Third, the first lining material is added while the chamber is being built. The entire chamber may be lined with an insulating layer of very short grass tops, mainly of *Aristida*, in which the short stem ends are thrust into the floor, walls, and roof of the chamber, so that the inwardly projecting, feathery tops form a soft lining, especially thick over the floor of the chamber. One often sees the birds coming with small feathery bits of grass heads in their bills. Finally, the birds construct an entrance tunnel to the chamber. They begin by adding straws and grass tops at the outer edge of the roof and to the sides of the chamber, gradually concealing the chamber and threshold from view. They then build a circlet of straws around the chamber entrance, adding more straws until an almost vertical tunnel some 12 to 25 centimeters long is formed, with its entrance opening downward. The birds also continue building out the substructure and the general undersurface of the nest mass within which the chambers become more deeply buried.

4. *Extending and repairing nest masses.* In very old colonies the different nest masses grow and fuse and may occupy most of the tree. The roof is first extended along the supporting boughs in different di-

rections, and new chambers are added beneath the roof as the nest mass grows. The birds also have a strong tendency to fill in spaces in the forks between twigs or branches and may start small, new nest masses in the same tree.

Maclean (1973) describes the reactions of Sociable Weavers to nest damage. Any cavities in the superstructure resulting from subsidence are filled in by the weavers. A partly damaged chamber is quickly repaired during a breeding period, but at other times it is seldom rebuilt. If damage to a nest mass is extensive, as when bad weather or a predator destroys almost all the chambers, the birds rapidly rebuild the whole structure, using the original materials as well as new ones. The birds are strongly attracted to fallen nest material, which they use to help repair a damaged nest.

AMOUNT OF WORK REQUIRED TO BUILD A NEST

A good nest in a good place is the key to breeding success for many birds. Birds often put in a great deal of time and energy building their nests. It is therefore important to work out methods to measure this energy investment and to relate it to other aspects of life history and behavior. Many passerine birds make over a thousand trips in constructing their nest.

It is theoretically possible to compare the energy used by a bird to build its nest with the energy used in performing other activities, by measuring the increase in metabolism—taken as the amount of oxygen consumed over that consumed while the bird is at rest—resulting from each of the various activities in the behavioral repertoire of the species (N. Collias and Collias 1965, 1967, 1971b). The methods now available are at least adequate to permit some rough estimates of the relative amounts of energy required by different activities. There are two methods in general use: the metabolic cost of transport over a given distance and time and energy budgets.

The first method is described by Bartholomew (1982), who defines the cost of transport as the total metabolic energy expended while moving one unit of body mass (grams or kilograms) over one unit of distance. The optimal speed is that at which the energy expended (oxygen consumption) per unit distance traveled is minimal. Tucker (1970) found experimentally the cost of transport for a 35-gram parrot, the Budgerigar (*Melopsittacus undulatus*), in flapping flight at 35 kilometers per hour, to be 2.9 kilocalories per kilogram for each kilometer traveled. The flight metabolism of the flying Budgerigar at 35 kilometers per hour is about 11 times basal metabolism and 6 or 7 times the resting metabolism measured under the same under the same conditions as the flight metabolism. If we apply this figure to the Village Weaver, a bird of about the same size (males, 40 gm; females, 32 gm) and with similar flapping flight, we can make some rough estimates of the energy costs of building nests in this species, relative to other behavior. Although the usual flight speed of the Village Weaver is unknown, a related species, the House Sparrow, with a similar mode of flight and body size (30 gm), has a cruising speed of 40 kilometers per hour (Summers–Smith 1963).

Since flying is one of the most energy-consuming activities of birds, we tried to estimate the amount of flying required by male and female Village Weavers (*Ploceus cucullatus graueri*) in central Africa to build nests and to feed their nestlings, taking into account all nests that were built in a colony and all breeding attempts, whether successful or not. A male Village Weaver had to build 9 or 10 nests for every one that succeeded. We found that an average pair of birds made 873 trips for the materials needed to construct a brood nest, 483 by the male, 390 by the female. Knowing the number of pieces in a nest, the number of trips required to build a nest, and the average distance of trips, we calculated that a male flew a total of 325 kilometers for gathering the materials for all his nests, while a female flew only 59 kilometers in order to line her brood nest. Knowing the number of feedings at the nest by each of the two sexes and the average distance of foraging, we calculated that the female had to fly 428 kilometers in searching for food to feed nestlings, while the male, who feeds the nestlings much less often, flew a total of only 185 kilometers (N. Collias and Collias 1967).

These figures may be put into more precise energy terms with a few reasonable assumptions. Assuming the same cost of transport as is known for the Budgerigar, knowing the average weight of a male Village Weaver, and knowing that the male had to fly an average of 325 kilometers to gather materials to build all of his nests, we can calculate the energy costs of building the nests as

$$2.9 \text{ k cal/kg km} \times .040 \text{ kg} \times 325 \text{ km} = 37.8 \text{ k cal}$$

By a similar mode of calculation, we estimated that the average female Village Weaver expended 5.5 kilocalories in gathering the materials she needed for lining her brood nest. Therefore, the average male of this colony used about 7 times more energy in building nests than did the average female. In contrast, the cost of transport in the course of feeding nestlings was only 21.5 kilocalories to the male and 39.9 kilocalories to the female, so the male did only about half as much work as the female in this aspect of breeding behavior.

The amount of energy devoted to nest building is reduced considerably when sources of nest materials are close to the colony tree. The Spotted-backed Weaver (*P.c. spilonotus*) of southern Africa is a race of the Village Weaver, similar in body size, that often nests in reeds (*Phragmites communis*) and is therefore surrounded by a convenient source of nest materials; the males weave their nests of strips torn from leaves of the reeds. They also obtain other nest materials they need nearby. The average round trip for the Spotted-backed Weaver males to obtain the long strips used in weaving the nest was only 20 meters, compared with 80 meters for Village Weaver males. In building one brood nest, the total kilometers flown by Spotted-backed Weaver males was only 20.3, while the males of the Village Weavers studied in central Africa had to fly a total of 34 kilometers for their work on a brood nest. Put into kilocalories, the male Spotted-backed Weavers needed 2.4 kilocalories to build to brood nest, instead of the 3.9 expended by Village Weaver males. They had to do 40 percent less work because of their location close to a good source of nest materials.

Differences were even greater between the females of the two races in the amount of energy expended for lining the nest, since the Spotted-backed females were not only much closer (10–20 m instead of 80–100 m) to the small grasses needed, but they also put in a much thinner lining (average of 233 pieces instead of 635), apparently sufficient for their warmer lowland climate. The female Spotted-backed Weaver in a colony located in reeds needed to put in only 6 percent of the energy expended by a female Village Weaver in the central African colony in order to gather materials to line her nest (N. Collias and Collias 1971b, N. Collias 1980).

The other method used to estimate the energy costs of nest building is the making of time and energy budgets for the various activities of the species (Orians 1961). One can compare the energy needs of any two activities by measuring the amount of time devoted to each, multiplied by the energy demands of each as estimated from the average increase in metabolism during the activity over the resting rate. For example, in the West African race of the Village Weaver (*P.c. cucullatus*) found in Senegal, four different males, observed for 15 hours, devoted 80 minutes to gathering nest materials and 213 minutes to actual building (N. Collias and Collias 1971b). But gathering involves much flying and if we make the reasonable assumption of a sixfold increase in oxygen intake over the resting level for flying time while gathering materials, versus only a doubling during actual nest building, the two activities turn out to be fairly similar in their energy demands in this case; gathering materials takes little time but much energy—the reverse is true of building.

These males had to fly only about 20 meters to obtain nest material, and it is evident that an increase in distance to the source of nest materials would quickly shift the energy demands of the male to flying and gathering materials, since the energy requirements for actual nest building tend to remain constant. Over its entire range, colonies of the Village Weaver are generally located close to patches of tall grasses or close to palms, sources of good materials for weaving.

Even when conditions are made optimal by furnishing the birds with plenty of nest materials close at hand and supplying them with plenty of food to solve their foraging problems, the daily energy expenditure may differ greatly, since the amount of building done by the males can vary greatly from day to day. We watched one male Village Weaver (*P.c. cucullatus*) in an outdoor aviary at Los Angeles all day for three warm days in summer. On two days he devoted his building time merely to refurbishing older nests, spending a total of only 90 minutes building on one day and 159 on the other, and he spent most of his time resting each day. But on the third day, he built a new nest from start to finish, taking eight hours to do so (N. Collias, Victoria, et al. 1971).

Energy expenditure needs to be balanced against energy intake. On the day he built a new nest, this male Village Weaver ate 100 mealworms and nothing else, although grain was available to him. Using Kale's (1965) measurement of 6.569 kilocalories per gram of mealworms, we found 100 of our mealworms, weighing 12 grams, equivalent to 4.26 grams ash-free dry weight, and assuming 70 percent assimilation, we estimated 19.6 kilocalories of energy received by this weaverbird from his food intake on the day he built a new nest. Energy expenditure was next considered. The standard resting metabolic rate for a bird of this weight (40 gm) is approximately 12 kilocalories per day (Lasiewski and Dawson 1967), leaving only about 8 kilocalories for everything else this male did, to be provided from his daily food intake and his stores of body fat. On each of his two inactive days he rested a great deal, and since he ate about the same amount (mealworms) as on his very active day, such quiet days very probably served to restore his energy balance (Collias, Victoria, et al. 1971).

The work required to build a nest can also be expressed in units of mechanical energy, since work is defined as force multiplied by distance. A joule is the work done over a distance of one meter by a force that accelerates a mass of one kilogram in the direction of the force, at a rate of one meter per second for every second it acts. Since this unit is small, kilojoules are usually used for convenience. In practice, it has proved easiest to measure oxygen consumption, which can then be transformed into kilocalories and kilojoules by conversion factors (Bartholomew 1982).

One calorie equals 4.187 joules. The production of energy at the rate of one joule per second is a watt. One watt equals 0.860 kilocalorie per hour.

The work done by a Cliff Swallow (*Hirundo pyrrhonota*) in building its mud retort-shaped nest has been calculated by Withers (1977) in terms of joules and watts. Swallows from about 10 nests were timed with a stopwatch as they collected mud from a creek bank 90 meters from the colony site. The effort required for each act was estimated as follows. The cost of resting metabolism for a bird of this size (24.6 gm) could be obtained from standard curves in terms of kilocalories per hour (Lasiewski and Dawson 1967) and converted into watts, giving 0.420 watt. The flight velocity over a 90-meter course was timed at 8.7 meters per second (ca. 38 kph), and the metabolic cost of flight at this velocity for a 24.6-gram bird can be predicted from a few wing measurements and aerodynamic theory to be 2.69 watts or 6.4 times the resting metabolism (Tucker 1973).

The metabolic cost of picking up the mud and also of packing it into the nest were assumed to be twice the resting metabolism. The average flight time for a round trip between the nest and the creek bank was about 20 seconds; it took 10 seconds to pick up the mud pellet and 30 seconds to pack it into the nest. The mean metabolic rate during such a 60-second cycle was therefore equal to ($\frac{1}{3} \times 6.4$) + ($\frac{1}{6} \times 2$) + ($\frac{1}{2} \times 2$) = 3.47 $\times$ the resting metabolism.

Knowing the average oven-dried weight of an average mud pellet and of one large nest, the latter was calculated to contain 1,400 pellets requiring 60 seconds each for placement in the construction of the nest. The total energy cost of nest construction was then calculated as 3.47 (mean cost) $\times$ 0.42 W (resting metabolism in joules/second) $\times$ 1,400 trips $\times$ 60 seconds = 122 kilojoules, which is the work done by Cliff Swallows in building one nest. By comparison, at the colony in central Africa, a male Village Weaver built 9 or 10 nests at a cost of 37.8 kilocalories, or 158 kilojoules.

There are several ways in which the Cliff Swallow economizes on this cost. Use of mud mixed with a little sand, rather than mud with a high silt content, makes the nest easier to work, although more fragile (Kilgore and Knudsen 1977). Since the birds work as a pair the labor is shared, and a considerable saving results from the fact that the nest is often used for more than one brood, whereas the African Village Weaver builds a fresh nest for every brood. The grassy nest of the latter soon deteriorates in the warm tropics, particularly in the rainy season when the weaverbird breeds.

SUMMARY

Birds select appropriate nest materials on the basis of availability, specific cues, and early experience. Nests are occasionally built of artificial materials—wire, spun glass, cotton, string, or cement—depending on availability and resemblance to the usual nest materials.

Various techniques are used by birds to fasten nests to difficult substrates. Nests may be attached to the vertical face of a cliff, or to the wall or roof of a cave by use of adhesive materials, such as mud (swallows), saliva (cave swiftlets), or spider silk (Rock Warbler). A great many small birds, particularly species with pensile nests, use cobwebs to fasten their nests to twigs or branches. Various flycatchers and oropendolas of the New World wrap fine plant fibers around hanging twigs or vines for the initial support of their pensile nests, and many weaverbirds in the Old World do the same with long strips torn from blades of grasses and leaves of palms.

The chief binding materials in the nests of most passerine birds are plant fibers (cellulose) and silk, which, because of their abundance in nature, great strength, and very light weight, are eminently suitable for their function as binding materials and are economical to gather. The high tensile strength of cellulose and most silks depends on their crystalline protein structure, consisting of extended protein chains with a high degree of polymerization. The adhesive properties of the sticky saliva used by swifts to hold together their nest materials result from mucoproteins with viscoelastic properties at low concentrations.

Observation of the procedures followed by specific birds in shaping their complex nests—cup-nests, deep pouch-nests, domed nests of various kinds, and compound nests—gives some indication of the range of nest-building techniques. The way in which the Sociable Weaver of southern Africa communally builds its huge apartment-style nest is of particular interest.

The roofs of domed nests are built in various ways: the walls of an initial basal platform or cup may be gradually built up to form the roof (Hammerhead Stork, Cliff Swallow, Thick-billed Weaver, some old World Warblers); the entrance and nest cavity may be hollowed out from an initial, solid mass of nest materials (some New World flycatchers, the Old World sunbirds); the roof, walls, and bottom of the nest may be built out from an initial loop or ring that is also the start of the nest entrance (oropendolas, most weaverbirds).

The relative amount of work required to build a nest can be measured, theoretically at least, by calculating the metabolic cost of transport of materials over a given distance, and by considering time and energy budgets in the various activities of a species. Units used to measure metabolic costs of building are customarily derived from rates of oxygen consumed and are expressed in kilocalories, kilojoules, and watts. At present, techniques of actual measurement of the energy demands of various activities in the field permit only rather rough estimates of the cost of building a nest relative to other activities of a species.

Many species of passerine birds make over a thousand trips to gather the materials used in constructing a nest, and the distance required to travel for materials is an important factor in deciding location of nest sites because of the relatively high energy demands of flying. There is often a division of labor between male and female in meeting the energy demands of nest building, relative to the demands of other aspects of the life cycle.

CHAPTER ELEVEN

The Analysis of Nest Building by Weaverbirds

THIS chapter attempts to illustrate the basic external forces that guide a bird at each stage of nest building. For this purpose, the analysis will be illustrated by the Village Weaver (*Ploceus cucullatus*) of sub-Saharan Africa, since no other species of bird seems to have been studied from this viewpoint to a comparable degree. After this analysis in one species, we compare weaving by birds and human beings. Tinbergen (in Thorpe 1963: 39–42) gave an interesting theoretical analysis of nest building by the Long-tailed Tit (*Aegithalos caudatus*) of Europe, but without any experimental verification.

DESCRIPTION OF NEST BUILDING BY THE VILLAGE WEAVER

The following description and illustrations of the nest and nest building apply equally well to nests built in nature or in aviaries (N. Collias and Collias 1959b, 1962, 1964). A male Village Weaver can build his complex, highly organized nest within a day.

The male weaves the outer shell of long strips he tears from the leaves of tall grasses or from palm fronds. The nest is ovoidal or kidney-shaped in form with a bottom entrance (fig. 11.1). Figure 11.2 shows a nest we made by imitating the weaving methods that a Village Weaver uses (N. Collias and Collias 1962). This artificial nest gave us some insight into the effective patterns of building.

Just beneath the woven roof of his nest the male inserts a ceiling of short, broad strips of grass or other leaves. This ceiling is thatched, rather than woven. Figure 11.3 illustrates a longitudinal section through a nest and shows the normal extent of the ceiling put in by the male, as well as of the lining which the female puts over the floor of the nest. The nest is usually about 15 centimeters long by 12 centimeters high. About the entrance in brood nests the male often weaves a short tube 5 to 10 centimeters long, with an entrance 5 centimeters in diameter at the bottom.

The male Village Weaver goes through seven stages in weaving the outer shell of the nest (see fig. 11.4): (1) initial attachment, (2) ring, (3) roof, (4) egg chamber, (5) antechamber, (6) entrance, and (7) entrance

Fig. 11.1. A male Village Weaver (*Ploceus cucullatus*) wove this nest in an outdoor aviary at Los Angeles. (N. E. and E. C. Collias, *Auk* 1962)

tube. The ceiling is part of the roof and the male often starts the ceiling before the egg chamber or the antechamber is completed. Figure 11.5 illustrates the principle stitches or fastenings used for the attachment and in the outer shell.

In weaving his nest the male typically uses certain basic movements: (1) he seizes a strip of nest material near one end, or mandibulates it along his beak until he has shifted his hold to one end; (2) with a vibratory motion he pokes this end of the strip into the nest mass or alongside some object such as a twig; (3) when the strip sticks he releases it, moves his head around to the other side of the twig or nest mass, again seizes the strip and pulls it through; (4) he then bends or winds the strip about a twig, the ring. or another piece of nest material and pokes the end of the strip back into the substrate; (5) at each stitch he reverses the direction in which he winds the strip, either between adjacent twigs or, alternately poking and pulling the strip, through the interstices of the nest.

The unit movements used in building are quite stereotyped. Alter-

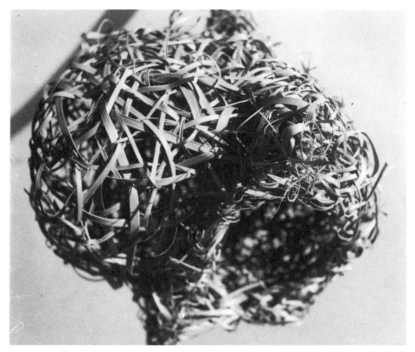

Fig. 11.2. The authors built this "Village Weaver" nest by imitating the bird's natural movements of building. (N. E. and E. C. Collias, *Auk* 1962)

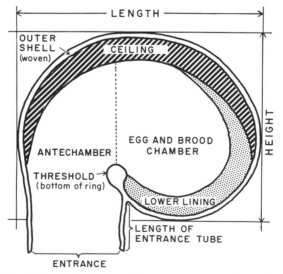

Fig. 11.3. Longitudinal and diagrammatic section through a Village Weaver nest, showing the inner construction. (N. E. and E. C. Collias, *Auk* 1962)

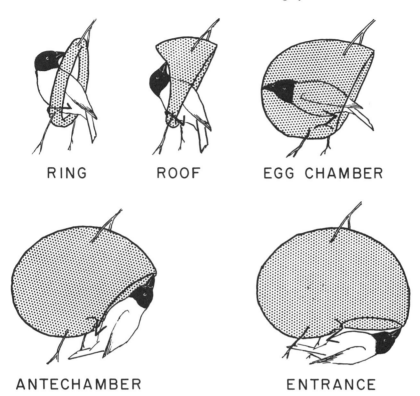

RING   ROOF   EGG CHAMBER

ANTECHAMBER   ENTRANCE

Fig. 11.4. The male Village Weaver follows this normal sequence of stages in weaving his nest. (N. E. and E. C. Collias, *Auk* 1962)

nately reversed winding of a strip between two twigs, two grasses, or a twig and a grass strip binds them firmly together and gives a strong suspension for the nest (fig. 11.5). In the egg or brood chamber many of the constituent strips are threaded over and under other grass strips (fig. 11.5), approaching the classic conception of human weaving, as in some simple forms of basketry or cloth making. If the basic movement is repeated more than once in the same direction, the strip is coiled about the twig, as seen in fig. 11.5 (upper right). At times, especially when strips are long, the male apparently loses sight of the ends and he then pokes and tucks loops in as much. The male frequently loops back the end of a strip on itself or on other strips in such a way that pulling on the strip tightens its attachment, a typical hitch-knot.

The female adds a soft, thick lining to the bottom of the egg chamber, beginning as soon as she accepts a nest. She first covers the bottom of the nest with a thin layer of strips that she tears from the leaves of tall

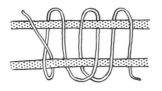

ALTERNATELY
REVERSED WINDING
BETWEEN TWIGS.

COILING ABOUT SINGLE
TWIG, ALTERNATELY REVERSED
WINDING, AND SPLIT STRIP.

DETAILS OF WEAVING
FROM EGG CHAMBER.

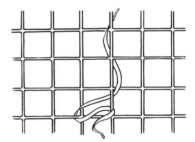

STRIP WOVEN INTO
A WIRE FRAME.

Fig. 11.5. (Above) details of attachment of the initial strip in a Village Weaver nest, and (below) nature of stitches in later stages of weaving. (N. E. and E. C. Collias, *Auk* 1962)

grasses or palm fronds. She perches on the threshold facing into the egg chamber and while holding a single strip near one end she inserts it into one side of the floor; she then inserts the other end of the strip into the opposite side of the nest floor, and pushes the center of the strip down into the bottom of the nest. She repeats this procedure with other strips until she has covered the coarse meshwork left by the male in weaving the bottom of the nest shell. She then inserts many soft grass tops, stem end first, into either side of the threshold, leaving their feathery tops extending over the bottom of the nest and forming a soft cup within the nest shell. If feathers are available the female gradually shifts from grass tops to feathers, until the nest has a thick layer of feathers on top of the grass heads and leaf strips.

When the female is incubating, the male no longer enters, but he often works on the outside of the nest. He strengthens the attachments of the nest, weaving in fresh green strips, their bright green color contrasting with the faded green or brown of the rest of the nest. He also tucks in loose ends here and there over the surface of the nest, so that egg or brood nests come to have a smooth, compact, and relatively neat appearance.

EXPERIMENTAL ANALYSIS OF THE STIMULUS SITUATION AT EACH STAGE OF NEST BUILDING

Only the male Village Weaver actually weaves; the soft lining put in by the female is not woven. The work of the male in building can be divided into different stages. Experiments have shown that each stage automatically provides the stimulus for its own termination and for the start of the next stage in construction (N. Collias and Collias 1962).

Gathering Nest Material

For weaving the outer shell the male requires some three hundred long, flexible strips of green grass or palm leaf, and he tears and transports each strip individually. That the green color serves as the signal to which the birds respond was shown by giving them materials of different colors. Green was selected far more frequently than were all the other five colors combined (table 11.1).

The possibility that birds were reacting to differences in intensity rather than in color was checked by testing preference for a given color from among various shades of gray (table 11.2). The birds easily selected green materials mixed with materials of eight different grays of various intensities. We concluded that green is definitely the color preferred by Village Weavers interested in nest materials, and that this color functions as a index to flexible materials suitable for weaving.

Initial Attachment of the Nest

In the initial stages of building, the male seems subject to some indecision as to where to attach his nest within his small territory in the colony tree. Often, he first attaches, then abandons, a few strips, especially where a particular substrate pattern is replicated several times. Forked twigs are preferred for nest attachment.

Analogy with human knots and stiches is a useful experimental approach to the problem of weaving by weaverbirds. When starting a new nest, the male Village Weaver holds the first strip underfoot against a twig, loops it back and alternately reverses the winding of it between

TABLE 11.1. Selection of green nest materials by weaverbirds when presented with various colors simultaneously

	Number of times chosen
Green	686
Black	146
Yellow	105
Red	80
White	70
Blue	33

Note: Half-hour test periods with 5 males for a total of 7½ hours.

TABLE 11.2. Selection of green nest materials by weaverbirds when presented with various grays simultaneously

	Number of times chosen
Green	299
White or whitish	45
Pale grays	18
Dark grays	12
Black or blackish	41

Note: Half-hour test periods with 5 males for a total of 2½ hours.

the twig and the strip itself (fig. 11.5). "Nippering", a knot used by people to lash two parallel ropes together (Hasluck 1942), is a very similar type of fastening.

In making the initial attachments for the nest, the male often passes the leading end of strips through the closed loops or meshwork produced by the weaving act itself. This tendency to poke the strip through any available hole can be demonstrated experimentally by providing the birds in an aviary with smooth, wooden perches through which many small holes have been drilled. Some birds poked and wove strips through these holes.

Constructing the Ring

The initial attachment is developed into a more or less vertical ring that provides the basic support for the whole nest. The adult male usually builds the ring and nest slung within and below the fork of a twig that inclines downward. He customarily straddles the two sides of the fork, one foot grasping a twig on either side. He weaves first along the adjacent twigs; if the nest is in a palm tree, he may follow the support afforded by palm leaflets and spines. Occasionally, slavish adherence to the substrate pattern leads to abnormalities such as incomplete rings lacking one entire side (fig. 11.6).

In closing the bottom of the ring beneath himself, the male faces special problems. Because of his general tendency to weave over his head and along the substrate, he often completes the top and sides of the ring first. Straddling the twig fork keeps the male from moving down with

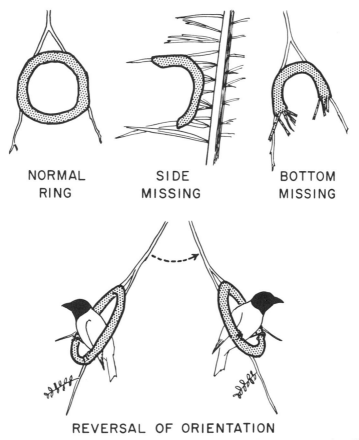

NORMAL
RING

SIDE
MISSING

BOTTOM
MISSING

REVERSAL OF ORIENTATION

Fig. 11.6. (Above) analysis of some factors in the construction of the ring-stage of a Village Weaver nest, and (below) in the determination of nest polarity. (N. E. and E. C. Collias, *Auk* 1962)

his work, and the dangling ends of strips gradually accumulate on either side. The tendency of the male to seize the ends of loose strips leads him to reach down and pick up these danglers one by one, and then either to weave them up on the same side or to cross them over and attach them to the other side, thereby bridging the gap beneath himself and gradually completing the ring. It is important that the strips be of sufficient length. When we supplied only abnormally short strips to the birds, one male succeeded in bridging the bottom of his ring but the other rings remained without bottoms (fig. 11.6). The one male that succeeded in closing his ring was able to do so because the twigs on either side converged below at the point where the bottom of the ring had to be closed.

The male always enters his ring from the same side and he faces in the same general direction while weaving, keeping one foot on each side of the bottom of the ring. We wondered what determined this consistent orientation. Observing the plane of the ring, we noticed that vertical rings are rare. Generally, the ring tilts from the vertical 10 to 40 degrees. When in his ring the male invariably faces so that the ring tilts toward him. When we tied back the twig containing the ring so that the tilt was reversed, the male upon his first subsequent visit immediately reversed the direction in which he faced (fig. 11.6). The significance of this consistent orientation is that it determines the longitudinal polarity of the nest. The male invariably builds the egg or brood chamber outside the ring in front of himself, and he leans over backward to build the antechamber and entrance on the opposite side of the ring, all the while keeping his feet on the bottom of the ring, which becomes the threshold of the nest (fig. 11.4).

When thickening his ring the male enters it with one end of a strip in his bill and the rest of the strip usually crossing his breast and trailing behind. Figure 11.7 illustrates a typical sequence of steps as the male weaves a strip into his ring. The male tends to insert successive strips first to his right, then to his left, so that the ring thickens uniformly.

Weaving the Roof and the Egg Chamber

What stimuli cause the male to stop building the ring and begin the roof and the egg chamber? One possibility is that once the male has done a certain amount of work on the ring, purely internal changes are set up leading him to begin the next stage of building, continuing through each successive stage in a gradual unfolding of internal processes. The alternative hypothesis is that each successive stage of the nest itself provides the necessary stimuli for its own termination and for the beginning of the next stage. Against the first hypothesis is the fact that destruction of one stage of the nest in most instances leads to prompt repair (fig. 11.8), regardless of its place in the normal sequence of building. If the egg chamber is removed from a fresh nest, the bird does not ignore the defect as if he had exhausted all of his building potential for that particular stage, nor does he continue merely building at the entrance side. Instead, he promptly builds a new egg chamber on the same nest. The one exception to this procedure is the destruction of the base of the ring. Whereas all other damages are repaired, a nest with the lower part of the ring cut out is usually abandoned. When a bird attempts

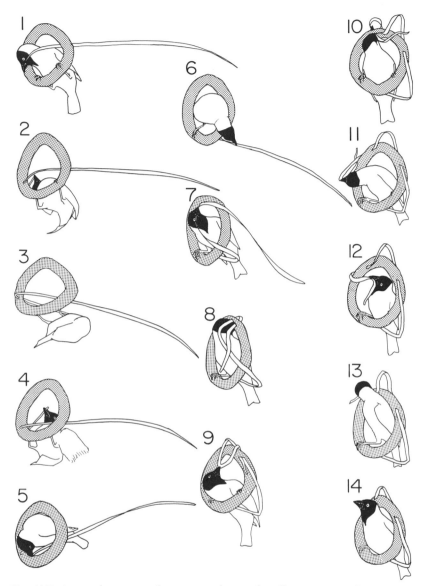

Fig. 11.7. A typical sequence of movements by a male Village Weaver as he weaves a single strip, torn from a leaf blade of elephant grass, into his ring (taken from motion picture frames). (N. E. and E. C. Collias, *Auk* 1962)

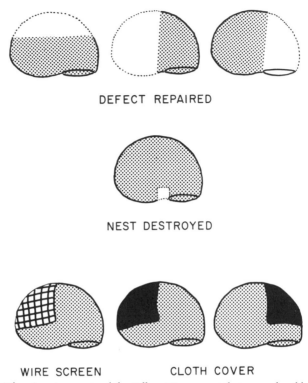

DEFECT REPAIRED

NEST DESTROYED

WIRE SCREEN   CLOTH COVER

Fig. 11.8. (Above) various parts of the Village Weaver nest that are replaced by the male when the experimenter cuts away that part, with the exception of the lower half of the ring (center). (Below) nature and location of various artificial covers fastened over the nest to analyze factors involved in building the egg chamber. (N. E. and E. C. Collias, *Auk* 1962)

to perch in such a nest, the two sides spread apart to such a degree that the bird finds it difficult to maintain position. An important function of the bottom of the ring is to provide a proper footrest from which to work. A nest with the bottom of the ring built around a twig was not abandoned when the strips around the twig were removed.

With the addition of each successive strip the ring becomes thicker and more compact, and it becomes more and more difficult for the male to push and pull a strip through the mass of the ring. It seems that increasing resistance leads him to weave in less of each end of the strip, resulting in the establishment of a system of loose loops extending out from the ring and providing a framework from which to weave out farther. When the male has woven in both ends of a particular strip and he can no longer see the ends but only the body of the strip, his pushing-out reaction is activated. Instead of weaving in the loose loop he pushes the body of the strip away from himself with his beak, keeping his feet on the threshold or bottom of the ring.

The egg chamber is often started from the roof of the ring, because of the stronger tendency of the male to weave over his head than to one side or beneath himself. A male Village Weaver placed in a small, wire cage often weaves strips of nest material into the roof; less often he weaves them into the sides of the cage, and almost never into the wire mesh of the floor.

The male continues to enter from the same side of the ring, facing into the developing egg chamber and perching in the bottom of his ring as he works. As he brings each strip, he holds it by one end in his bill, and as he lands he pokes that end into one side of the threshold. The size and globular shape of the egg chamber depend on the size of the bird and his tendency to keep his feet on the bottom of the ring, which becomes the threshold of the nest, while he pushes out with his beak in all directions as far as he can reach.

The pattern of weaving in the egg chamber results from the males's tendency to cross preexisting lines of the developing framework at right angles as he weaves in subsequent strips, and to alternate the direction of his winding with each stitch, which results in an in-and-out threading of the strip as he moves it along pushing and pulling it with his beak through the loose meshwork of the early stages of the egg chamber.

The tendency of the male weaver to regularly alternate the direction of his winding through the nest interstices is the essence of what we normally think of as "weaving." If the basic framework is very regular, as in a wire meshwork of squares, such threading in and out of strips of nest material by the bird often proceeds in perfect alternation (fig. 11.5).

The tendency of the male to weave above rather than below himself results in a much finer meshwork in the roof of the nest, compared with the floor (fig. 11.1). As the meshwork of the nest becomes smaller, the male tends to do less weaving. This tendency was shown by an experiment in which a large hole was cut in the roof of the egg chamber and then covered over with a green wire mesh (fig. 11.8). In experiments on different nests, frames with different-size meshes were used, and the bird did more weaving on frames where the meshes were larger.

Making the Ceiling

As the meshes of the nest become smaller and smaller, particularly in the roof, the male shifts abruptly from weaving long, narrow strips to thatching a ceiling with short, wide strips of grass or palm leaf just under the roof. This shift from weaving to thatching can be explained by the fact that after the meshwork of the roof becomes very fine, the male, who works inside the nest, finds it increasingly difficult to locate and pull back through the meshwork the ends of a strip that he has just pushed through. His tendency to push the main body of the strip away from himself is then activated, since he can no longer see the ends or pull them into place. When the male puts in a ceiling strip, he inserts first one end, then the other end, and then pushes the center of the strip well up into the arch of the roof. Evidently, the male is able to carry in his brain a picture or "set" of the best type of material for a given stage of the nest.

Work on the ceiling is greatly slowed and then discontinued by the male when the roof and ceiling become thoroughly opaque. We made an experimental test by sewing a piece of green cloth over the roof at an early stage of building the egg chamber (fig. 11.8), removing a few ceiling strips present. The male continued to work on the nest at places other than those covered by the cloth, putting in many ceiling strips under the roof on the entrance side, but almost none beneath the cloth. We also did the reciprocal experiment, hooding the entrance side (fig. 11.8), and this time the many ceiling strips subsequently put in by the male were almost entirely confined to the egg chamber. The finished ceiling itself provides the stimulus for its own termination. If one repeatedly removes the ceiling from a reasonably fresh nest, the male repeatedly replaces it.

We concluded that the ceiling of a Village Weaver's nest is started when the mesh size of the roof reaches the requisite smallness, and that work on the ceiling slows and stops as the ceiling becomes opaque.

Building the Antechamber and the Entrance

In general, the male does little work on the antechamber, aside from its roof, before the egg chamber is well-nigh complete. He gradually builds down the roof and sides of the antechamber until it reaches the horizontal at a level approximately even with the bottom of the nest (fig. 11.4). Throughout the process, the male as usual keeps his feet on the bottom of the ring or threshold, leaning over backward as he works. When the antechamber reaches the horizontal, he gradually narrows its opening and makes the bottom entrance of the nest, the narrowing probably being due to the shorter reach of the male as he hangs upside down beneath the threshold. If a nest is rotated backward about its transverse axis, bringing the entrance upward with its margins now vertical instead

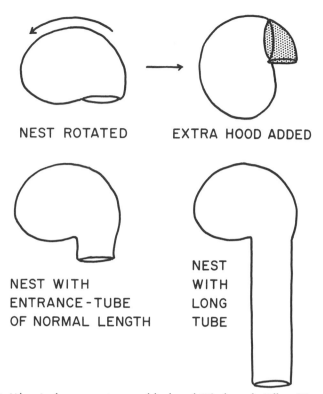

NEST ROTATED   EXTRA HOOD ADDED

NEST WITH
ENTRANCE-TUBE
OF NORMAL LENGTH

NEST
WITH
LONG
TUBE

Fig. 11.9. (Above) when a nest is rotated backward 90°, the male Village Weaver again builds the entrance down to the horizontal, adding an extra hood to the antechamber. (Below) a male Village Weaver was induced to build a nest with an abnormally long entrance tube by loosely attaching long strips of nest material to the rim of the entrance. (N. E. and E. C. Collias, *Auk* 1962)

of horizontal, the male promptly weaves the entrance back down to the horizontal level. In doing so, he builds an extra hood on the nest from top to bottom (fig. 11.9).

Building the Entrance Tube and Finishing the Brood Nests

When a female accepts a nest and settles down in it, she thenceforth excludes the male from the inside of the nest, although he often looks up into the entrance and sings to her. The male now generally adds a short tube about the entrance of the occupied nest, whereas he tears down his nests not accepted by any female without ever adding an entrance tube (N. Collias and Collias 1959b). If a female disappears or deserts a nest, the male owner soon tears it down.

In weaving the entrance tube, the male clings with his feet to almost any place on its rim as he adds to its length. The entrance tube is thin, with about one layer of woven material. The male abruptly shifts away from his previous orientation point on the bottom part of the ring because of the mechanical impossibility of weaving an entrance tube from that position.

The male can be caused experimentally to extend the entrance tube to several times the normal length (fig. 11.9). When he has smoothed and finished the rim, tucking loose ends in back away from the rim, he normally terminates work on the entrance tube. But if the experimenter repeatedly threads the ends of strips of nest material into the entrance tube, leaving the strips dangling, the male promptly weaves in the whole strip, instead of pulling it out and discarding it. With this technique, we induced a Village Weaver to add to his nest a tube 30 centimeters long, instead of the normal length of 5 to 10 centimeters.

NEST DESTRUCTION

The male ultimately destroys most of his own nests, those never accepted by females as well as brood nests from which the young have departed. The male attacks the nest vigorously with his beak from the outside, often demolishing it within a half hour. There is a balance between his tendency to tear a nest down and to build it up. Factors that stimulate building on a nest include fresh materials in the nest, position of the male inside the nest, and recent visits by inspecting females. Factors that favor destruction of his own nest by a male include aging of nest materials, position of the male on the outside of the nest, or abandonment of the nest by the female, which is normal after she leaves the nest with her young. As a nest ages it fades from green to brown; if a fresh green nest is painted brown the male is about three times more likely to tear it down than he is to tear down fresh nests painted green, so brown color must be one stimulus to destroy nests (Jacobs et al. 1978).

COMPARISON OF WEAVING BY BIRDS AND HUMANS

Weaving is essentially the intertwining of flexible materials in some regular pattern, as is seen in baskets and some human shelters, as well as in the nests of some birds. Like the human constructions, birds' nests also function as shelters and containers. Woven nests are more analogous to baskets than to cloth; no bird is known to simulate a loom, nor to spin thread or twist yarn. All weaverbirds weave their nests with their beaks, just as people wove their baskets and earliest textiles by hand. The history of human basketry (Crowfoot 1954) shows parallels with the evolution of nests woven by weaverbirds and other birds (N. Collias and Collias 1964), which suggests that rather similar and analogous forces may have operated to produce the end result. The earliest known human weaving dates to about 5000 B.C. during the Neolithic period. Weaving of fabrics and of baskets appear at about the same time, both already well developed.

While there are of course some important differences, weaving by birds and by people have some of the same general sequences in their historical development: (1) increased use of more suitable materials; (2) closer weaving, and a shift from the predominant use of coiling and wrapping to a plain weave with elements at right angles to each other; and (3) increased regularity of the weave.

1. *Increased use of more suitable materials for weaving.* Early man probably constructed primitive shelters, consisting of poles stuck in the ground, with flexible branches (wattles) interwoven between the poles (Bradford 1954). Such a technique might well have been preadapted to basket making. In wickerwork, or stake-frame basketry, strips are twined in and out of a frame consisting of parallel vertical stakes. Early humans wove their baskets with the same sorts of plant masterials that many birds use for their nests: reeds and other grasses (Gramineae), sedges (Cyperaceae), rushes (Juncaceae), and strips from palm fronds (Palmaceae). Basket makers sometimes soak dry, stiff plant materials in water to make them flexible for weaving, and some birds—such as the Great Reed Warbler (*Acrocephalus arundinaceus*) of Europe (Armstrong 1955) and the Yellow-headed Blackbird (*Xanthocephalus xanthocephalus*), a marsh inhabitant of the United States (H. Harrison 1979)—use dead plant materials soaked in water for weaving. All the chief natural-fiber groups—bast, cotton, silk, and wool—that people have used for weaving cloth from early times, as attested in textile remains from archaeological sites, are used by many birds in building their nests.

2. *Closer weaving and the shift from coiling to a plain weave.* In the earliest known type of human basketry a flexible strip is coiled or wrapped around bundles of materials, such as grass or fibers, holding them together. Plain weave in basketry refers to simple weaving in which, for example, two sets of rushes are interlaced at right angles to each other. In plain weave of textiles, a series of wefts passes over and under a series of warps, as in darning. The earliest textiles known are in plain weave.

In the evolution of weaving of weaverbirds, coiling or wrapping of strips about other strips preceded the origin of plain-weave techniques. Figure 11.10 illustrates the common stitches and fastenings used by various species of true weaverbirds (Ploceinae) to hold their nests together and to attach their nests to the substrate. A "stitch" in sewing or in darning means a single loop or turn of the thread or yarn, or one in-and-out pass of the needle that makes the loop. In birds the bill corresponds to the needle. The simpler type of stitches or fastenings— such as the simple loops used in overcasting strips around the edge of the nest entrance, loops tucked in as such, and interlocking loops— predominate in the relatively primitive nest of the Thick-billed Weaver (*Amblyospiza albifrons*). Spiral coiling is also much used in the crudely woven nests of the Red-billed Weaver (*Quelea quelea*) and of the Madagascar Fody (*Foudia madagascariensis*).

More sophisticated stitches are used by the Village Weaver, which fastens the roof of its nest to twigs with alternately reversed winding of strips while using a plain weave especially for the egg chamber. It also uses half hitches throughout the nest. More complicated, although still simple knots, such as overhand knots, and slipknots, are relatively rare in weaverbird nests.

3. *Regularity of woven patterns.* We do not know enough of the origin of human weaving to judge the degree of regularity in early basketry. The earliest known baskets already display beautiful symmetry and regularity in woven pattern. The climax of regular pattern in weaverbird nests is seen in the entrance tube of the nest of Cassin's Malimbe (*Malimbus cassini*) (N. Collias and Collias 1964). This tube is made of only one layer of palm strips. The bird first weaves in one end of each long strip diagonally upward from the inside of the rim of the entrance. It then shifts to the other end of the strip which it weaves diagonally upward and at right angles to the first limb of the strip. The regular crisscrossing of many such fibers gives a beautiful warp-and-woof pattern to the long entrance tube (figs. 2.24, 11.11). The entrance to the nest is at the bottom of the vertical tube, which may be over two feet long.

To explain the regularity of weaving in the entrance tube of the nest of Cassin's Malimbe, we need to consider the specialized function of this tube, particularly in relation to predation. The tube consists of two sets of long, thin strips woven in a pattern of opposing spirals, and resembling the bias-cut in dressmaking. This elegant construction, by analogy with engineering principles (J. Gordon 1978), may have several functions. Since the wall is composed of a single layer of palm strips, there is maximum economy of materials. Since the wind can blow through the

LOOP TUCK   SIMPLE LOOP   INTERLOCKING
                                            LOOPS

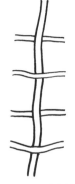
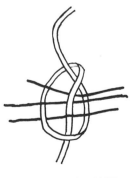

SPIRAL COIL   SIMPLE WEAVE   ALTERNATELY
                                      REVERSED WINDING

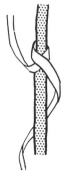

HALF HITCH   OVERHAND KNOT   SLIP KNOT

Fig. 11.10. Various common stitches and fastenings used by the true weaverbirds (Ploceinae) in weaving their nests. (N. E. and E. C. Collias, *Univ. Calif. Publ. Zool.* 1964)

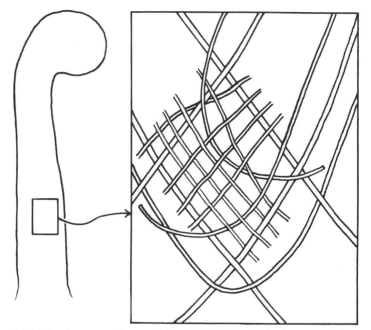

Fig. 11.11. Weaving pattern in nest of Cassin's Malimbe (*Malimbus cassini*). (N. E. and E. C. Collias, *Univ. Calif. Publ. Zool.* 1964)

network of the tube wall, movement of the tube during wind storms is reduced. The double-helical system of strips with the spirals at right angles to each other resists outward expansion of the tube and helps maintain its circular outline. The latticelike pattern of the two criss-crossing systems of strips and their orientation at 45 degrees to the long axis of the tube provide optimal resistance to the shear stress produced when the bird hangs from one side of the entrance at the bottom of the tube, as it does while building. If the two sets of strips were parallel to and at right angles to the long axis of the tube, only a small number of the strips would bear the weight of the bird and therefore be more liable to break or pull loose. The 45-degree orientation of the lattice-web also means that the tube as a whole will be extensible on its longitudinal axis and simultaneously will contract appreciably along the perpendicular radii, comparable to the clinging effect produced by the bias-cut in dress-making. If a tree snake attempts to crawl down the outside of the tube, the tube will compress under the weight of the snake and local buckling and distortions of the tube might shake the serpent off. Most snake predation on weaver nests probably occurs at night and is rarely wit-nessed, but Ambedkar's interesting observation of attempted snake predation on a Baya Weaver's nest in India (see chap. 9) indicates that the long entrance tube which contracts under the loading of the snake may actually protect a weaverbird's nest in the manner suggested above.

SUMMARY

The male Village Weaver (*Ploceus cucullatus*) of sub-Saharan Africa, weaves the outer shell of his nest in successive stages (fig. 11.4): initial attachment, ring, roof and egg chamber, antechamber, and entrance tube. The female puts a soft, nonwoven lining over the bottom of the nest. Each stage of the developing nest automatically provides the external stimuli for its own termination and for the starting of the next stage. There is experimental evidence for the following causal factors at each stage of nest building by the male:

1. Weaving requires the use of flexible materials. The selection of materials of a green color, the usual color of fresh herbaceous vegetation, helps insure this needed flexibility. For weaving his nest, the male tears long strips from the leaves of monocot plants, such as grasses and palms.

2. Initial attachment for the nest results from the tendency of the male to poke and vibrate ends of leaf strips alongside twigs, to wind such strips about twigs, to reverse the direction of winding a strip between adjacent twigs or other strips, and to poke and pull ends of a strip through the meshwork made by the act of weaving itself.

3. Construction of a ring results because the male weaves in all directions along and below a forked twig that opens downward while he perches facing in one direction inside the fork. He must bring strips of grass or palm leaf longer than about 15 centimeters to close the bottom of the ring beneath himself.

4. The polarity of the nest, with the egg chamber on one side and the antechamber on the other, is a consequence of the plane of tilt of the ring and the fact that the male in the ring consistently faces so that the ring tilts toward him. He builds out the egg chamber in front of himself, and its globular form and normal size result from the fact that the male always stands in the same place in the bottom of the ring while he weaves and pushes out the developing egg chamber with his bill as far as he can reach. The bottom of the ring becomes the threshold of the nest.

5. The male thatches a ceiling of short, wide leaf strips or of dicot leaves when the meshwork of the roof becomes too fine to permit easy weaving. The ceiling is finished when it becomes thoroughly opaque.

6. The entrance to the nest opens to the bottom of the antechamber. While keeping his feet in the usual place on the base of the ring, the male weaves over his head, gradually leaning over backward more and

more, until he has built the antechamber and the entrance down to the horizontal.

7. The male generally adds an entrance tube after a female has accepted his nest. She prevents the male from entering the nest, and he satisfies part of his building drive by weaving a tube about the entrance. One factor tending to terminate growth of the entrance tube is the smoothing and finishing of the rim when the male works in loose ends.

The history of human basketry shows parallels with the evolution of weaving by weaverbirds, indicating that rather similar and analagous forces have operated on each.

CHAPTER TWELVE

The Development of Nest-building Ability

THERE have been very few systematic and experimental studies of the development of nest-building ability in young birds. Nest building by weaverbirds has been considered a classical example of "instinct," but we found that a weaverbird must practice a great deal before it can build its complex nest. We carried out the experiments that are summarized below in a colony of captive Village Weavers of the West African race (Ploceus c. cucullatus) (E. Collias and Collias 1964, 1973). We have also described the breeding behavior of this West African subspecies in its natural habitat (N. Collias and Collias 1970).

SUBJECTS

The young Village Weavers used in the experiments were all hatched in large outdoor aviaries on the campus of the University of California at Los Angeles. The birds were taken from the nest at about one week of age, which is just before their eyes open. Normally, young Village Weavers leave the nest about three weeks after hatching. Birds that were to be reared without access to nest materials were kept in bowls lined with cloth until they were able to sit on a perch, at which time they were transferred to cages. These birds were never allowed to see anything that could be used as building material. Another group of young birds that were to be only partially deprived of nest materials were reared in Village Weaver nests with the tops of the nests cut off for convenience in feeding. These birds were kept in the nests until they started to take short flights and then were transferred to cages. Young birds reared as controls had normal access to nest materials.

DEVELOPMENT OF ABILITY TO MANIPULATE OBJECTS

The first use of the bill by young Village Weavers, other than in gaping to receive food from the parent, is to preen disintegrating sheaths off the feathers by biting and nibbling at the feather sheaths. Preening starts by two weeks of age. The mouthing of the feather sheaths seems to be the precursor of the ability to mandibulate strips of nest materials, and thus to adjust the position of a strip in the bill.

The development of pecking activities introduces new motor elements needed for nest building. In the third week after hatching, the young bird begins to lunge toward and tries to seize food offered by the parent. But not until its first week out of the nest does the young bird become able to pick up food from the ground for itself. Parental example facilitates development of this ability; young birds next to the parent, start to pick up food shortly after the parent does.

As it begins to feed itself, the young bird develops a strong exploratory urge. It now picks up and manipulates all sorts of objects with its beak, and spends a good part of its day in such activities. Nice (1962) mentions exploratory pecking in young birds of more than a dozen different species, including both altricial and precocial birds. Our general impression, after rearing and observing young birds of many species, is that few equaled and none exceeded these young weavers in the frequency with which they manipulated various objects. Although all Village Weavers seem fascinated with nest material and manipulate it for long periods of time, the female's interest wanes after about ten weeks, while that of the male increases.

SELECTION OF APPROPRIATE NEST MATERIALS

The key to the choice of flexible materials suitable for weaving is the green color of fresh vegetation. We tested the color preferences of young weaverbirds on their initial exposure to nest materials. Half of the newly hatched young were left in the aviaries to be reared by their parents and had access to fresh palm fronds and giant Mexican reed grass (*Arundo donax*), which were regularly placed in the aviary as a source of nest material. The rest of the young birds were removed from the nest before their eyes opened and were completely deprived of any normal nest materials. However, it is impossible completely to separate a young bird from everything resembling nest material, and these hand-reared young, in contrast to the controls, often manipulated their own feathers or those of cage-mates. It was not uncommon to see one of these deprived birds hold a protesting cage-mates's wing under one foot on a perch and attempt to "weave" the wing feathers. At times, a young bird would reach down and try to weave its own tail feathers. Since many of the feathers of young weavers are yellow, yellow-green, or olive-green, it is evident that we were far from having perfect control in this experiment. Nevertheless, relative to the controls, the hand-reared young had far less experience with anything that closely resembled normal nest materials.

TABLE 12.1. Selection of nest materials of different colors by four male weavers, reared without access to nest materials

	Number of times each color was selected						Percentage green
	Green	Yellow	Blue	Red	Black	White	
First two days	51	42	0	11	2	28	38
Second two days	163	16	6	13	1	29	71
Third two days	147	4	6	4	7	18	79

Note: Based on a total observation time of 6 hours, over 6 successive days when the birds were approximately 7 months old.

For a test of color preferences young male birds were exposed to equal numbers of materials, uniform in size and shape but differing in color. The colors tested were green, yellow, blue, red, black, and white. All the birds, whether or not they had been reared with nest materials, selected green over all other colors.

The preference for green by the relatively naive, deprived young quickly increased with experience (table 12.1). A statistical test of the relative preference for green over all other colors combined, in the first two days of testing compared with the second two days, showed a significant difference well beyond the one percent level ($\chi^2 > 50$). Five experienced young control weavers, under similar conditions of testing, had an immediate and consistent preference for green.

Four young males reared in the absence of normal nest materials preferred flexible over rigid nest materials when tested at approximately eight months of age. For these tests we used green, vinyl plastic strips of identical shape and weight, but differing in flexibility. The birds picked up flexible strips in 60 percent of 714 choices, but wove only 18 of these flexible strips. These young males also preferred long to short strips when offered equal numbers of grass and palm-leaf strips of various lengths from one to eight inches (2.5–20 cm) long.

Weaverbirds become more discriminating in their selection and use of nest materials with experience and soon come to reject such things as toothpicks, string, and even raffia when normal materials are available.

PREPARATION OF NEST MATERIALS

When an adult weaverbird tears a strip 10 to 15 inches long (ca. 25–38 cm) from a leaf of elephant grass (*Pennisetum purpureum*) in Africa, or from tall Mexican reed grass (*Arundo donax*) in our aviaries, it perches on the stalk or firm base of the leaf, bites through one edge of the leaf, and then tears a strip loose by flying with it in the general direction of the leaf tip. Young weaverbirds have to learn many things in order to carry out this process. While experienced adult males generally fly off with the strip toward the tip of the leaf, tearing the leaf in one smooth action, young birds often make mistakes such as perching on an unstable place, starting to tear too close to the tip of the leaf or at the very base, taking too broad or too narrow a bite, tearing in the wrong direction, tearing only part way and repeatedly starting again, or tearing strips that are too short to be woven.

Five young male weavers were deprived of nest materials from seven weeks of age, that is, they were allowed to handle nest materials only for one month after leaving the nest. They were then not exposed to fresh reed grass until they were about a year old, when they were unable to tear off any strips the first day. They seized the tip of a grass leaf and attempted to fly off with it on fifty-two separate occasions during their first week of exposure to reed grass. These efforts were ineffective because of the flexibility of the leaf. Five control yearling males in the same observation time tried to fly with the tip of a leaf only five times. All the young birds, both the deprived group and the controls, soon learned to tear off a strip lengthwise smoothly by flying off with it in the direction of the tip of the leaf.

After learning to tear strips, the partially deprived yearling males often tore strips that were shorter than the length of the bird, and therefore not so suitable for weaving as were the much longer strips torn by the controls. Here again, the partially-deprived young improved rather quickly with practice, although even after three weeks they had not quite equaled the controls. The partially-deprived young continued to increase the length of strips they tore off. The length of strips in the first nest built by a yearling were compared with those in a nest that he built in his second breeding season under similar conditions (table 12.2).

A male Village Weaver without early experience in preparing nest materials may never learn to tear strips for himself, although he may learn to weave if he is supplied with strips. Dr. Catherine H. Jacobs (personal communication) reared a young male Village Weaver, "Phineas," in isolation from other weavers for four years. Starting when Phineas was about six months old, she supplied him with many long strips that she tore for him from palm fronds at least once a week for a year, and more occasionally, thereafter. Phineas often wove the strips provided for him into the wire walls of his cage, and he wove a complete ring in his second year.

TABLE 12.2. A comparison of two nests built by a male weaver in his first and second years, showing the increase in length of all strips used in the nest

Year nest was built	Number of woven strips of different lengths (cm)			
	0-10	11-20	21-30	31-40
First year	77	183	139	81
Second year	6	76	138	177

Note: $\chi^2 = 88$, df $= 3$, P < 0.005.

When he was about four years old, he was put outdoors for the spring and summer breeding season in a large aviary along with other Village Weavers. A fresh palm frond (*Phoenix reclinata*) as a source of nest materials was placed daily in this aviary, and although the other weavers readily tore strips from the palm leaflets and wove nests, Phineas proved unable to tear a single strip for himself. He did manage to build a rather crude nest of strips that he stole from other birds. He also took over an incomplete nest from another male weaver and finished it.

DEVELOPMENT OF WEAVING ABILITY

In nature, first-year Village Weaver males build very crude nests, with many loose loops and loose ends projecting from the outer surface of the nests, in contrast to the neat compact nests of fully adult males (fig. 12.1). In India, Salim Ali (1931) observed that the nest of the young male Baya Weaver (*Ploceus philippinus*) is relatively crude compared with that of the adult male. This age-correlated difference in ability to construct a nest may turn out to be a general phenomenon among the true weaverbirds.

Weaving of the First Stitch

During the first month after fledging, young weaverbirds gradually become independent of their mother and able to feed themselves. Although they frequently manipulate all sorts of materials, they are generally unable to weave at all until at least seven weeks after hatching, or one month after fledging. At this time, a few of the young males may weave their first stitch. This ability grows out of their incessant manipulation of materials, combined with a genetic predisposition to poke and pull pieces of grass leaves and similar objects through holes. There is a certain amount of trial and error involved before they can weave their first

Fig. 12.1. Nest of an experienced adult male Village Weaver (left), with the crude nest of an immature male next to it (right). The nest entrance opens downward. (E. C. and N. E. Collias, *Auk* 1964)

stitch. Merely being able to play with and manipulate nest materials early in life probably facilitates development of the ability to weave.

The Need for Practice in Developing Weaving Ability

In the Village Weaver, the ability to weave improves with practice, and practice is required. Having picked up a strip the young male must learn what to do with it next, and he must learn places suitable for weaving. We demonstrated this need for practice experimentally (E. Collias and Collias 1964, 1973). When the same males employed in earlier experiments on color preference were about a year old, three control males and three males reared without any nest materials were tested for their ability to weave. These two groups of males were kept in two identical indoor aviaries, each aviary with a guava bush of the same size. Only the controls had been given regular access to normal nest materials before this experiment. An opaque, cloth partition between the two aviaries precluded the possibility of observational learning by the hand-reared young from the more experienced, aviary-reared young.

During the first week of testing, when the birds were given palm

TABLE 12.3. Retarded development of weaving ability in young male Village Weavers completely deprived of normal nest materials until about one year old

Age when tested (same individuals)	Strips carried	Percentage of strips woven	P (Controls vs deprived)*
One year:			
3 controls	73	62	
3 deprived	69	26	0.05
Two years:			
3 controls	104	39	
3 deprived	80	29	0.20

*Rank-sum test (Dixon and Massey 1969, p. 344) for percentage of strips woven.

strips, the deprived males did not weave a single stitch. In contrast, all the control males wove well. In the second week, when given reed grass, the deprived males wove a few stitches on the wire frame of the aviary only. In the third week, the experiments summarized in table 12.3 were started. The deprived males succeeded in weaving only a small percentage of strips compared with the controls. The difference was significant to the five percent level.

After the first experiment, a fresh supply of reed grass as a source of nest materials was maintained daily in both aviaries. After three months of practice, the deprived males improved considerably, doubled the percentage of strips woven over their initial performance, and the difference in percentages of strips woven by controls and by deprived birds was no longer significant. In the three-month practice period, two of the males that had been reared without access to nest materials managed to weave two nests. In the same period, the three control males built eleven nests. There was no obvious difference in the quality of nests.

We retested these same six birds during the next breeding season when they were two years old and sexually mature. They had been without nest materials for several months during the winter and had had no opportunity to practice weaving. We now found no significant difference between the males that had been deprived of nest materials their first year and the controls (table 12.3).

The most subordinate one of these deprived yearling males, male LL, after tearing a strip of nest material seldom had an opportunity to play with the strip for long before one of his more dominant cage-mates came and drove him away, stealing the strip for himself. This sort of thing went on repeatedly, and as a result male LL was generally deprived of nest materials during his second year. Apparently, as a result of this prolonged deprivation of educational opportunities in his first two years, male *LL* never learned to make a nest, and indeed he could not weave at all. After he became an adult, male *LL* continued to tear strips of nest material from the tall grass or palm fronds provided, but he could not weave these strips although he often tried to do so, playing ineffectively with a piece of nest material for many minutes at a time.

When we placed male *LL* in an outdoor aviary with other birds— including unmated females as well as other males—during the breeding season when he was in his third, fourth, and seventh years, he was completely unable to weave a nest, although each season he developed full breeding coloration of bill and plumage. The failure of male *LL* to build a nest did not, therefore, result from hormonal deficiency, since development of the black breeding coloration of the bill, together with nest building activity, can be stimulated in castrated male Village Weavers by injections of testosterone (chap. 13). Nor was male *LL*'s failure to build caused by his being suppressed by more dominant birds, since each year in the outdoor aviary he successfully defended a territory from other males. By the time he died in his ninth year he had never been able to start a nest despite having had numerous opportunities to do so.

We concluded that being completely deprived of nest materials and the opportunity to practice nest building during the first year will retard development of the ability to weave in a male Village Weaver. Such deprivation may also result in a persistent tendency to weave in abnormal and inadequate sites. If the deprivation continues for most of the second year, as in the case of male *LL*, the bird may become incapable of ever building a nest.

In another experiment, we also tested the responses of seven partially deprived young males to nest materials when they were about a year old. There was no significant difference between the partially deprived birds and seven control birds in the percentage of strips that they wove. Nor was there any difference when they were similarly tested again near the end of their second year.

However observations suggested that were some effects of deprivation during the first year, subsequent to the age of seven weeks—that is, one month after fledging. The partially deprived young males had a much stronger tendency than did the control birds to weave on the wire frame of the aviary rather than on twigs, and this difference persisted through their second year. It was also evident that the more dominant birds in an aviary often inhibited attempts of subordinate birds to weave, either by chasing them away from sources of nest materials or from good places to weave, or by taking strips of nest material from them. When the seven partially deprived young males and seven control birds were matched for similar rank in the dominance hierarchy in their respective aviaries, we found that there was a statistically significant effect of partial nest-

TABLE 12.4. Weaving ability in young male Village Weavers deprived of nest materials after their first month post-fledging.

Proportion of strips carried that were woven			
Seven control birds	Seven partially deprived birds	Difference*	Signed Rank
0.81	0.32	0.49	7
0.77	0.40	0.36	6
0.44	0.32	0.12	3
0.51	0.36	0.15	4
0.19	0.22	−0.03	−1
0.30	0.02	0.28	5
0.24	0.13	0.11	2

*P = 0.016 for all pairs. (One-tailed test, Wilcoxon matched-pairs, signed-rank test, Dixon and Massey 1969, p. 341.) Birds were tested toward the end of their first year and were matched for similar dominance level.

material deprivation on the proportion of carried strips that were woven (table. 12.4).

Other experiments confirmed the connection between the amount of practice in weaving that a bird has and its place in the dominance hierarchy. For seven different groups of yearling Village Weavers, the most dominant bird in each aviary carried more strips than did the most subordinate bird, and also wove more strips in all but one case.

How a Young Male Village Weaver Learns to Weave

It appears that some practice is important for successful weaving, and the next question that arises is just what do the birds learn? It is interesting to watch the initial reactions to nest materials of young male weavers that have been deprived of normal nest materials until an age where most males can weave. These deprived males already possess certain basic motor skills required for weaving. They can select suitable materials, hold a strip under one foot or in the beak, mandibulate to one end of the strip, and poke it toward or alongside the perch, or into the interstices of the wire meshwork of the cage. They also develop the normal ability to reach around to the other side of the twig while standing on a strip, seize the strip anew in the beak, and wind it around the twig.

In watching the numerous attempts of young male weavers to fasten initial strips of nest materials and their gradual improvement in weaving ability, it seemed to us that what every young male weaver has to learn is what in subjective terminology one would call "judgment." Frequently the young male attempts to weave with materials that are too short or too stiff. But the bird is channeled into the right direction by a normal preference for green, flexible, and long materials.

Before the male weaver can succeed in firmly fastening a stitch in place he must learn to carry out the basic movements in an effective sequence. Often the young bird starts to weave one end of a strip and, instead of following through, ineffectively shifts his point of attack. In contrast, the adult male is much more likely to *persist* systematically in his weaving at one end of the strip or at a given site. The young male may push a strip into a wire mesh and just as promptly pull it right out again, failing to let go in order to shift his hold and pull the strip through the next mesh. Learning when to let go of the strip is an important part of weaving. But even when released, the strip frequently falls out of place of its own weight or resilience, before the young bird can reach around to the other side of the twig or wire and seize it anew. The male apparently has to learn to push the strip through far enough so that it doesn't fall out or spring back when released. Unless the bird has also learned to hold a strip under foot, the strip may even fall to the ground when he shifts his beak-hold on the strip. Even when a young male weaver can effectively make several stitches, he still fails to make a nest. For one reason or another, he generally ends up removing each strip before he has thoroughly woven it into place (we have seen this repeatedly). He must learn to *leave in place* properly woven strips.

By the end of his second year a male Village Weaver normally establishes an exclusive nesting territory from which he rigorously and consistently excludes other males, but this exclusiveness is not true of yearling males, who often weave strips in each other's nests. Their nests are therefore often communal nests to a greater or lesser degree, and indeed some nests were worked on by every yearling male in the aviary.

Nest Form and the Development of Nest Building

Young male Village Weavers gradually develop the ability to produce the correct species-typical form of the nest. Yearlings establish small play-colonies in trees or bushes apart from adult colonies. In making play-nests, they frequently tear off pieces of grass so short that they are unable to close the bottom of the ring. Occasionally, young males produce a roofed nest without any bottom at all. The yearling male shows a gradually increasing tendency to build while standing in the lower half of the ring in a consistent orientation. This orientation ensures that he will build a brood chamber on one side and an entrance on the other side of the nest.

Yearling males may put a ceiling into their very first nest, although the initial ceiling is somewhat sparse and irregular, or thatched of narrower strips of materials than those characterizing the ceiling in the nest of an adult male.

Yearling males do build nests that have the normal bottom entrance— even in their first complete nest—but these nests lack an entrance tube. In nature, yearling males and their nests do not attract females, and it is usually only after a female has accepted his nest and has begun to incubate that the adult male adds an entrance tube to it.

We unintentionally gathered some evidence suggesting that the act of building a long, or a short, entrance tube may be self-reinforcing in determining the length of tube the male builds on future nests. We induced an adult male weaverbird to build an entrance tube some 30 centimeters long, instead of the more usual 5 to 10 centimeters, by threading the ends of long strips of nest material through the entrance of the nest (chap. 11). We later saw many subsequent nests of this particular male, built without our intervention, and much to our surprise, we found that the entrance tube in some nests was as long or even longer than the abnormally long tube we first induced him to build. It would seem that the male develops a mental picture of the sort of nest to build, based on his experience.

The bottom lining of the nest—consisting of strips of grass leaf, grass heads, and feathers—is put in by the female. Victoria (1969) observes that yearling females, although they carry many strips to their nests, fail to cover the floor of the egg chamber properly until they are ready to lay their first clutch of eggs. The young females first carry feathers into their nests during the copulatory period that precedes laying of their first egg.

In the case of the simple cup-nest of the domesticated canary, which is built by the female, Hinde (1958) finds that females reared without access to normal nest materials will, when they reach breeding age, go through all the movements of building in a nest pan and, when given suitable materials, build nests as neat in appearance as those built by normally experienced birds. It seems from this case, that some species of birds, particularly those building relatively simple nests, do not have so great a reliance on practice for building the nest as does the Village Weaver.

INFLUENCE OF THE EXAMPLE OF OTHER BIRDS

The role of instruction by example from other birds is a factor we have not quantitatively assessed. Probably, some social stimulation exists for nest building, just as for other activities, since different birds tend to gather materials and to build at about the same time.

Marais (1938), studying the South African "yellow weaverbird" (presumably *Ploceus subaureus*), took eggs from the nest and had them hatched under canaries. The nestlings were then reared out of sight of both adult weavers and normal nest materials. These young weaverbirds were able to weave nests, indicating that instruction by example of older weavers was not needed. However, Marais gives no information concerning possible improvement in nest building, nor does he indicate with certainty the species concerned.

We took a male Village Weaverbird from a nest in our colony before his eyes opened and reared him to an age of three years in complete visual isolation from all other weaverbirds. We supplied him with normal nest materials and raffia early in his life, and he gradually developed the ability to construct normal nests. The different acts involved in the nest building of this male developed in the following sequence: mandibulation, biting and pulling at various objects with the beak, poking of raffia into any nearby object with the beak, poking raffia into the wire meshwork of the cage, tearing of strips, and standing on strips with his feet. At five and a half months of age he wove his first stitch into the wire, but he at once pulled it loose. At six months he wove the first strip (with three stitches) that he left in place. At seven months he managed to fasten a strip onto a perch, at eleven months he made a ring, and by one year he built his first nest (of raffia). He subsequently wove several nests of reed grass or palm strips, which to us appeared no different from nests built by other males of comparable age.

We concluded, from this male reared in isolation from other weaverbirds, that instruction by example is not necessary for development of the ability in the Village Weaver to build a species-typical nest. However, example may have a facilitating role, since two control males, kept with other males in an outdoor aviary, could weave by four months, more than a month earlier than the age at which the isolated male wove his first strip.

EFFECTS OF PROLONGED DEPRIVATION OF NEST MATERIALS DURING ADULT LIFE

Having found that deprivation of nest materials in the first year of life retards the development of nest-building ability in male Village Weavers, we next wished to see if prolonged deprivation of nest materials and lack of practice in nest building during adult life would result in loss of the ability to build a nest. To this end, twelve adult males, all but one of which had previously built nests, were caged indoors without nest materials for about two and a half years. Seven of these males had had access to normal nest materials early in life, while five had been deprived completely for their first year. We then placed these males, together with seven females, in an outdoor aviary with fresh reed grass with which to build. All of the males were in full breeding plumage, although the darkness of the bill (an indicator of male hormone level) was generally intermediate between the nonbreeding and breeding condition. During the first day there were some fights and six of the males established territories—three nondeprived and three deprived males. These six males began to build or attempted to do so the very first day, although two of the deprived males fumbled a good deal and sometimes tried to use old materials unsuitable for weaving. By the end of the first month, as it was evident that some of the more subordinate males were being suppressed by the dominant males, we removed the dominant males that had already built nests. By the end of five weeks, eleven of the twelve males had built a total of twenty-eight nests. The one male (LL) that failed to build a nest was deemed incapable of weaving, because of prolonged deprivation during his first two years, as was described earlier.

This experiment shows that if a male Village Weaverbird has built nests during the first two years of his life, this ability is not lost despite lack of opportunity to practice.

SUMMARY

Development of the ability to build a well-formed nest of normal structure in young African Village Weavers (*Ploceus cucullatus*) depends on several factors: practice, appropriately directed by the growing structure of the nest itself; improvement in ability to select and prepare nest materials; a mental image of a properly built nest based on experience; and maturation of the endocrine system.

Young Village Weavers frequently manipulate all sorts of materials, starting almost as soon as they leave the nest. The males build practice-nests long before attaining sexual maturity. The crude appearance of the nests built by yearling males is caused by insufficient practice in selecting and preparing nest materials, and in weaving.

Of a group of young Village Weavers hatched in outdoor aviaries, half were reared without access to nest materials; of these some were completely deprived their first year, starting before their eyes opened, and others were deprived starting one month after leaving the nest before they began to weave (partially deprived). The young that had been completely deprived of nesting materials, unlike the controls, which had normal access to nest material, often manipulated or tried to "weave" their own feathers or those of cage-mates. In tests with differently colored artificial materials, they preferred green, the normal color of the nest material, to yellow, blue, red, black, or white; just as did the controls. These deprived young quickly developed a preference for green within the first few days of exposure to artificial nest materials. They also preferred long to short strips of grass or palm leaf, and flexible to stiff nest materials.

When about one year old, the survivors were given their first normal nest materials, and the males that had been reared without any nest materials wove a significantly smaller percentage of strips than did the control males. But this difference greatly diminished after three months' practice in handling strips, and two of three deprived males, like the controls, managed to weave nests. The third male, deprived through his first and second year, never learned to build a nest, although he reached nine years of age, developed normal adult breeding coloration, and held territory.

Deprivation of nest materials for the first year, after giving the birds a limited opportunity to manipulate nest materials for the first month after they left the nest, also had a retarding effect on development of the ability to weave. However, the difference from controls was significant only when the partially deprived birds were matched by dominance rank with controls. If a male has learned how to build nests during his first or second year, prolonged deprivation of nesting materials during adult life has no effect on his ability to weave a nest. One male, hand-reared and kept in complete visual isolation from other weavers for three years but supplied with nest materials from an early age, gradually developed the ability to construct the species-typical nest.

We conclude that practice, directed by specific response tendencies, but not instruction by example, is needed for development of the ability to build a normal nest in the male Village Weaver. The same could be true of many other species of birds in which the problem has not yet been investigated.

CHAPTER THIRTEEN

Internal Factors in the Control of Nest Building

FOR a more complete understanding of nest building, it is necessary to consider the role of the internal factors that control motivation to build. The role of brain mechanisms in nest building is not known; but, fortunately, there is information on the important role of the endocrine glands. Hormones, secreted by endocrine glands, play a major role in the control of two aspects of nest building: first, sex differences in nest building, and, second, the timing of the different phases of building—starting, stopping, and integration of nest building with other aspects of breeding behavior. Each of these two problems will be considered in turn. First, however, some background information may be useful.

BACKGROUND INFORMATION

Hormones are specific chemicals secreted by endocrine glands directly into the blood; they act as chemical messengers and exert specific effects on other organs and functions, including behavior. Hormones are effective in very minute amounts, and this has made their study difficult.

The first demonstration of a hormone was in relation to bird behavior. Many years ago, Berthold (1849) castrated a rooster and this bird ceased to crow, mate, or fight; but all these behavioral traits were restored when testes from another cock were implanted into the capon. Since the graft was in an abnormal location the evidence pointed to some substance transmitted in the blood as the active agent. The greater part of a century passed before this substance was chemically identified as testosterone. About the same time the corresponding sex hormone in the female was identified from ovarian follicles as estradiol. These two sex hormones are found in both mammals and birds, as well as in other vertebrates. Before the sex hormones were chemically identified, any substances that stimulated male characteristics were called androgens, and those that stimulated female characteristics were known as estrogens. Availability of the sex hormones in pure form stimulated an explosion of investigation into the relationship between these hormones and their specific effects.

Ovulation refers to the release of the egg from a mature ovarian follicle, a fluid-filled vesicle at the surface of the ovary. The follicle in mammals then transforms into a solid corpus luteum, which secretes still another hormone, isolated and identified from corpora lutea of pregnant mammals, and named progesterone. This hormone, like testosterone and estradiol, is a steroid hormone derived chemically from cholesterol. It has also been identified among birds in the mature follicles of hen ovaries.

Growth of testis and ovary and secretion of their respective hormones and gametes are stimulated by gonadotrophic hormones (FSH and LH) from the anterior pituitary gland, attached to the base of the brain at the hypothalamus. The follicle-stimulating hormone (FSH) stimulates ovarian follicles to grow and secrete estradiol. The luteinizing hormone (LH) stimulates ovulation and secretion of progesterone and testosterone. Another anterior pituitary hormone, prolactin, stimulates lactation in mammals. Its effects on behavior in birds will be discussed later. The gonadotrophic hormones and prolactin are protein hormones; all have been found in the different classes of vertebrates.

The measurement of hormone levels in the blood has always been an important objective of endocrinologists. Since hormones are present in the blood in nannogram (billionth of a gram) and picogram (trillionth of a gram) quantities, their measurement poses a difficult technical problem—a problem which was recently solved by the development of radioimmunoassay for which Rosalyn Yalow of New York received a Nobel Prize in 1977. This technique made possible a renewed attack on the physiology and behavioral effects of the hormones already known, and it also helped make possible the isolation and identification of the hypothalamic hormones, which control the activity of the pituitary gland. For the first syntheses of some of the hypothalamic hormones, Roger Guillemin and Andrew Schally also received a Nobel Prize in 1977.

It had been thought that two separate hormones existed in the hypothalamus, one stimulating FSH, the other LH, secretion from the anterior pituitary. But it was found that only one hypothalamic hormone was the gonadotrophic-releasing hormone (Gn–RH) for both FSH and LH from the pituitary. This meant that one type of molecule acting by way of the pituitary stimulates the gonads to produce gametes and to secrete sex hormones in both male and female. This hormone, Gn–RH, first isolated in mammals, stimulates the pituitary to secrete FSH and LH, and induces ovulation not only in various species of mammals but also in chickens and pigeons (Schally 1978, Reeves et al. 1973). It provides an important link between the brain, behavior, and the endocrine system. Current research on hormones and behavior is focusing special attention on the relationship between sensitivity to hormones, and specific hormone receptors, in specific regions of the brain.

The early literature on hormones and breeding behavior of birds was reviewed and synthesized by N. Collias (1950a) and by Lehrman (1961). More recent research on the hypothalamic-pituitary-gonadal system, as it regulates breeding behavior in birds, has been reviewed by Hutchison (1975, 1976), Barfield (1979), by Farner and Wingfield (1980), and by several authors in a book on avian endocrinology edited by Epple and Stetson (1980). The effect of hormones on breeding behavior of the Canary has been reviewed by Hinde (1965); of the Ring Dove by Lehrman (1964, 1965), Hutchison (1976), Silver (1978), and Cheng (1979).

CONTROL OF SEX DIFFERENCES IN NEST BUILDING

Investigations of the endocrine control of breeding behavior have very largely dealt with the Domestic Fowl, domesticated Ring Dove (*Streptopelia "risoria"*), and the domesticated Canary, for the obvious reason of convenience. These domestic forms still show much the same basic patterns of breeding behavior as do their principal wild ancestors, the Red Junglefowl (*Gallus gallus*), Rosy-grey Dove or African Collared Dove (*Streptopelia roseogrisea*), and the wild Canary (*Serinus canaria*) of the Canary Islands, respectively. They exemplify three of the main types of nest-building and breeding behavior among birds.

In the polygynous Domestic Fowl only the female builds the nest, which is little more than a simple scrape in the ground. In the monogamous Ring Dove, the female builds a shallow platform nest of such things as twigs or pine needles, while the male gathers and brings materials to her. In the Canary, which builds a cup-nest typical of most passerine birds, the female builds and lines the nest herself, and the male's contribution is negligible. Both male and female Ring Doves incubate, only the female of the Domestic Fowl and the Canary.

No other bird whose nest is largely built by the male and merely lined by the female has been as thoroughly investigated from the viewpoint of endocrine control of breeding behavior as the three preceding species. We have a little information on the hormonal control of building by the Village Weaver (*Ploceus cucullatus*) that will be mentioned later.

The standard procedure for investigating the role of gonadal differences and associated hormones in male and female birds has been to remove the testes or ovary, and then to see to what extent normal sex behavior can be restored by treatment with the appropriate hormones ("replacement therapy"). In the male bird the testes secrete the hormone testosterone. In the female bird the ovary secretes three hormones:

estradiol, progesterone, and testosterone (Domm 1927, Layne et al. 1957, Sharp 1980). Most of the original work concerning gonadal hormones in birds was done on the Domestic Fowl, as was the demonstration that *FSH* stimulates secretion of estradiol, *LH* of testosterone (Taber 1948, 1949) and progesterone (cf. Sharp 1980).

Most birds have only one developed ovary in the adult, that on the left side. However, the right ovary persists in a rudimentary state and, if the left one is removed, will regenerate and enlarge to a functional state. Therefore, in truly critical experiments on gonadal control of behavior in birds, both ovaries should be removed (Domm 1939). Because hormonal effects may sometimes last for a long time after removal of the gonads, particularly in the male, it is desirable to remove the gonads prepuberally when investigating effects on behavior.

Domestic Fowl

In the Red Junglefowl (*Gallus gallus*), the main if not the sole ancestor of domestic chickens, the cock in courting a hen may crouch low under the edge of a bush, and make a shallow nest scrape while calling the hen to him (Lill 1966). He does this repeatedly and at different places. Similar nest-invitation behavior has been observed in the domestic cock (Wood-Gush 1971:67). A castrated male domestic cock will only rarely court hens or copulate. Since the testes secrete only male hormone into the systemic circulation, his nest-scrape behavior, like his breeding behavior in general, probably depends normally on male hormone, but the matter should be specifically investigated.

The domestic hen makes a concealed nest scrape lined with dead leaves and a few feathers, as do her wild ancestors (Smythies 1953). In a pen, she may scrape a depression with her feet in the sawdust floor, scoop litter around herself with her beak, and pick up and toss materials along one side of herself or onto her back (Wood-Gush 1975). Unlike many other birds, a hen never carries nest material in her beak to a nest site.

Trap-nests, in which a hen is trapped inside the nest box when she enters to lay, are much used in the poultry industry. Wood-Gush (1954) has described the nesting behavior of hens in relation to trap-nests in detail. When about to lay a hen becomes restless, flaps her wings, and utters a special pre-laying call. She develops cautious, stealthy behavior, and usually inspects a number of nests before entering and sitting.

The presence of the oviduct is not necessary to produce nesting behavior in the hen since it can be removed and normal nesting still takes place provided ovulation has occurred—although in this case ovulation takes place into the body cavity. This observation suggests that the post-ovulatory follicle might be implicated in nesting, and when it is removed, normal nesting behavior in the hen largely disappears (Wood-Gush and Gilbert 1964, Wood-Gush 1971). But if the hen is subjected to the same operative procedure and the post-ovulatory follicle merely manipulated, or if only immature nonovulatory follicles are removed, the hen still shows normal nesting behavior.

The steroid hormones, estradiol and progesterone, are secreted by the maturing and post-ovulatory follicle (Sharp 1980). Injection of progesterone alone into ovariectomized hens fails to induce any aspect of nesting behavior (Wood-Gush and Gilbert 1964). Estradiol alone stimulates nest examination, but not nest entry and sitting. But injection of progesterone following long pretreatment (about six weeks) with estradiol stimulates both nest examination and entry (Wood-Gush and Gilbert 1973, Gilbert and Wood-Gush 1976).

With radioimmunoassay techniques, it has been possible to study more precisely the secretion patterns of estradiol and progesterone in the follicles of the ovary of the domestic hen (Sharp 1980). As a follicle enlarges it produces increasing quantities of estradiol while progesterone and testosterone synthesis in the follicle increases, but in the mature preovulatory follicle, estradiol synthesis diminishes and the main steroid synthesized is progesterone.

One Brown Leghorn hen that had been ovariectomized as an adult hen and that had often used trap-nests, constructed a normal nest of litter (wood shavings) and feathers on the floor of the pen, following long-term treatment with subcutaneous injections of estradiol and progesterone. Postmortem examination revealed no sign of original ovarian tissue. Also, the pre-laying call can be induced precociously in young immature females by injecting them with estradiol (Wood-Gush and Gilbert 1969).

In conclusion, interest in potential nest sites and nest-building behavior of domestic hens are stimulated by estradiol and progesterone secreted by the ovary, and these two hormones have a synergistic action. The relationship of testosterone to nesting behavior of hens has not been studied.

Ring Dove

Male and female Ring Doves look alike, and apparently the doves discriminate sex by differences in behavior. Experimenters sex the doves by laparotomy and direct inspection of the gonads.

When a pair of Ring Doves is put into a cage with a nest bowl and nesting material they do not begin at once to build a nest (Lehrman

1965). Instead, they first go through a period of sex identification, in which the male bows and coos to the female. After some hours, the male goes to the nest bowl and invites the female to enter with a special nest-solicitation display in which he holds his head low and the rear part of his body elevated while he flips or quivers his wings and gives a special nest-coo. This display attracts the female to the nest bowl. Only by the third or fourth day does nest building become a prominent feature in the birds' behavior (Erickson and Martinez-Vargas 1975).

Once the female accepts the nest site, she also gives the nest-solicitation display with lowered head, upended tail, wing-flips, and nest-coos. Her display stimulates the male to gather nest materials—such as twigs, bits of reed stems, straw, hay, or pine needles—and he brings them to the female, who builds a crude platform or saucer-shaped nest in the nest bowl. The doves build most actively in the late morning and early afternoon. Within four or five days after active nest building begins, the female lays her first egg in late afternoon (at 1700), followed next morning by a second egg (0900). Nest building declines at the time of egg laying, but some building continues well into the incubation period (White 1975). If a male or female dove is placed alone in a cage, it generally shows no interest in a nest bowl or nest materials, nor does a female kept alone ordinarily lay eggs.

Changes in weight and activity of the gonads and accessory sexual organs of doves during a breeding cycle (fig. 13.1, 13.2) correlate with changes in breeding behavior. When a male is castrated he gradually ceases to show any interest in the female, nest bowl, or nest materials, but if he is then injected with an oil solution of either testosterone or estradiol, his interest in a mate and his nesting behavior are restored and he performs extremely well in nest-solicitation and the gathering of nest materials (Martinez-Vargas 1974, Erickson and Martinez-Vargas 1975). Since the dove testis secretes testosterone, but not estradiol, the primary control of nest-soliciting and nest-building behavior in the male must be by the secretion of the male hormone. Using the sensitive radioimmunoassay technique, no estradiol could be detected in the blood of male Ring Doves at any time during the breeding cycle, nor was there any detectable level of estradiol in plasma of testosterone-treated or oil-treated castrate males (ibid).

In recent years it has been shown for a number of mammalian species that conversion from androgens to estrogens can be effected *in vitro* in the hypothalamus and certain other parts of the brain, and one theory of the way testosterone influences male behavior is conversion to estradiol. However, the bowing-coo of the male, a display the female rarely performs, can be restored in castrated males by injections of testosterone,

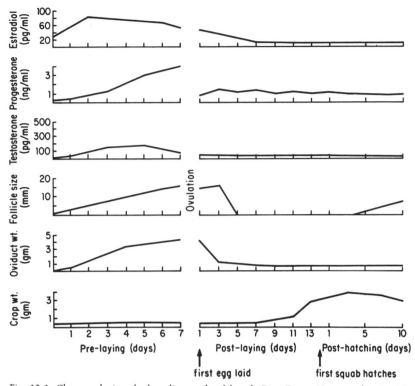

Fig. 13.1. Changes during the breeding cycle of female Ring Doves (*Streptopelia risoria*) in level of sexual steroid hormones (estradiol, progesterone, and testosterone) in the blood, as measured by radioimmunoassay. Relatively high hormone levels coincide with ovarian development, measured by follicle size, and with oviduct weight. All these measures are inversely related to crop weight, which is stimulated by prolactin from the anterior pituitary and which increases during the parental phase of the breeding cycle. (After Silver 1978; reprinted by permission of *American Scientist*, journal of Sigma Xi, the Scientific Research Society.)

but not by injections of estradiol. It appears, therefore, that androgen controls this aggressive courtship behavior pattern without intrabrain conversion to estrogen (Martinez-Vargas 1974).

Testosterone may normally induce nest-soliciting behavior in the male Ring Dove by conversion to estrodiol-17 in the brain. Conversion of testosterone to estradiol-17 is markedly increased in male doves injected with testosterone (Steimer and Hutchison 1980, 1981). Estradiol-17 has not been detected circulating in the blood, and its conversion from testosterone takes place by an aromatase system in a specific part of the brain, the preoptic area. Systemic injection or intrahypothalamic treat-

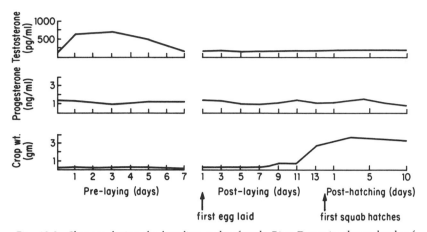

Fig. 13.2. Changes during the breeding cycle of male Ring Doves in plasma levels of testosterone, as measured by radioimmunoassay. There is an inverse relationship between testosterone, secreted by the testes, and crop weight stimulated by prolactin from the anterior pituitary. However, there are no significant differences in progesterone (possibly secreted by the adrenals) level in the blood at different times in the breeding cycle. (After Silver 1978; reprinted by permission of *American Scientist*, journal of Sigma Xi, the Scientific Research Society.)

ment with estradiol-17 is more effective for inducing nest-soliciting behavior by castrated males than is testosterone. Study of possible behavioral effects of such hormone metabolites is a new and expanding area of research.

An ovariectomized female Ring Dove avoids the male, never participates in courtship behavior, and rarely in nest building. In ovariectomized doves, nest building is not restored by injections of either estradiol alone or progesterone alone. Combined injections of estradiol and progesterone are necessary and effective in restoring nest building by females (Cheng and Silver 1975). Ten female doves that were pretreated with estradiol for four days before being given the combined hormones participated in nest building with their mates, tucking into their nests materials brought by the male. Females receiving combined injections stimulated significantly more gathering of nest materials by their untreated mates than was seen in other experimental groups.

In conclusion, in the male Ring Dove, testosterone stimulates nest-solicitation behavior and gathering of nest materials. In the female Ring Dove, nest-solicitation behavior is stimulated by estradiol, and its effect is enhanced by progesterone. Both estradiol and progesterone are required to stimulate nest building (working materials into the nest) in female Ring Doves. Possible influences of testosterone on the building behavior of female Ring Doves seem not to have been investigated, but there is evidence that testosterone may elicit nest-solicitation behavior in female doves.

Canary

Hinde (1958, 1965) and his associates in England have studied the nest-building behavior and its endocrine control in the Canary. Their Canaries were housed in male-female pairs in cages indoors, each cage being provided with a standard felt-lined, plastic nest pan and with nest materials.

The female appears to select the site, although the male often inspects it. He gathers and carries nest material, and occasionally places it in the nest pan, but his contribution to the actual building of the nest is negligible compared with that of the female. Female Canaries injected with testosterone frequently dangle a piece of nest material before other females, just as a male might do. Normally only the male Canary sings, but testosterone-treated females also sing (Shoemaker 1939).

Most female Canaries in Hinde's study began nest-building activity in March or in early April, gathering suitable nest materials, carrying them to the nest pan, and starting a nest while sitting in the nest cup. The female builds the nest of dried grass and lines it with feathers. She takes seven to eight days to build a nest before laying the first egg (White and Hinde 1968). Building and frequency of copulation reach their peak about two or three days before the first egg is laid. She lays one egg each day for up to four days. Nest building continues at a declining rate through the egg-laying period.

Various building activities appear in orderly sequence, perhaps in part because of their different thresholds of reponsiveness to hormones. As the female comes into reproductive condition she first gathers, then carries nest materials to the nest site. These actions are followed by pulling and tucking in with the beak loose strands projecting from the rim of the developing nest and pushing them down into the cup. The narrowing of the nest cup stimulates scrabbling, by which the female presses down into the cup and pushes back hard with each leg alternately. She shapes the cup by turning around while sitting in the nest and also by expanding her body feathers, pressing her body and wings into the cup.

All of these nest-building activities were stimulated in female Canaries outside the breeding season by injections of estradiol. Progesterone did not enhance nor inhibit the effect of estrogen, and progesterone alone did not maintain nest-building induced by estradiol (Warren and Hinde

1959). But the doses of estradiol required to produce nest building in winter were so high as to be almost toxic, and some additional factor seems probable. Addition of prolactin to estrodiol did not enhance the effect on nest building and, if anything, had a negative influence (Hinde and Steel 1962:166).

Nest building induced at various times of the year in ovariectomized Canaries with estradiol is more intense if the birds are exposed to long photoperiods rather than to short ones (Hinde et al. 1974). In ovariectomized females on long photoperiods in winter, testosterone treatment significantly increases the rate of gathering nest-building material, but not in ovariectomized females on normal day lengths. (Steel and Hinde 1972).

The changeover in nest building from collecting grass to feathers for the nest lining is controlled by both known external and unknown internal factors (Hinde 1958). Experiments reducing the size of the egg cup, or giving it a rough grassy texture, stimulate the female Canary to bring a lower proportion of grasses to the nest and a higher proportion of feathers. In recent experiments, Kern and Bushra (1980) found that female Canaries whose brood patches were denervated built a nest of normal size and composition and still lined their nests with feathers, as did control birds.

A week or two before egg laying the females lose the feathers from part of the ventral surface, and the bare skin becomes vascular, later edematous, and increasingly sensitive to touch around the time of egg laying. This bare incubation patch or brood patch, found in many species of birds, helps the bird to keep eggs and small young warm. In the Canary, nest building starts about the same time as defeathering of the brood patch begins and becomes intense at about the time defeathering is completed. In ovariectomized Canaries, defeathering and vascularity of the brood patch can be produced by estradiol alone. The effect of estradiol on defeathering, but not on vascularity, is augmented by either progesterone or prolactin (Hinde and Steel 1966). Bailey (1952) found that estrogen injections defeathered the brood patch in intact White-crowned Sparrows, but not in hypophysectomized ones, and he suggested that estrogen normally stimulates prolactin production.

In conclusion, nest-building behavior in the female Canary is stimulated by estradiol, according to present evidence; unknown hormonal factors are probably also involved. Estradiol also stimulates defeathering of the brood patch, its action being augmented by progesterone and prolactin. Gathering of nest materials by the male Canary, and perhaps by the female, is stimulated by testosterone.

Village Weaver

In this species, the male builds the outer shell of the nest before the arrival of a female who, if she accepts his nest, puts in a lining of soft grasses and, sometimes, feathers. Daily injections of testosterone propionate into a nonbreeding, intact male stimulated increased singing, a rise in the dominance hierarchy, the establishment of territory, and an increase in nest-building activities (N. Collias et al. 1961).

Castrated male Village Weavers develop a whitish bill, which treatment with testosterone, but not with gonadotrophins, turns to the normal black breeding coloration. One male that had been castrated completely (by T. R. Howell), as judged from bill coloration and post-mortem examination, built a complete and normal nest. He displayed this nest to females, one of whom accepted the nest and copulated with him (N. E. Collias and E. S. Tarvyd, unpubl.). This bird was castrated as an experienced adult, and it is possible that males castrated at an early age might not be able to build nests.

Another castrated male Village Weaver, who was at the bottom of the pecking order in a group of ten males in an outdoor aviary, was treated with testosterone propionate for about three months, starting in late August near the close of the normal breeding season for our birds. He showed little response until four males, including the most dominant males, were removed. The treated castrated male then rose to the top of the dominance hierarchy of the six remaining birds, sang much more often, built one nest in November and two more after the middle of December (N. E. Collias and R. J. Barfield, unpubl.). These were the only nests built by any of our Village Weavers in December in several years of observation. Since completely castrated males are able to build nests, it seems that, in the Village Weaver, testosterone stimulates nest building by lowering the threshold of responsiveness to building tendencies.

In male Red-billed Weavers (*Quelea quelea*) changes in the amount of nest building among caged birds were correlated with changes in testes size over a year (Butterfield and Crook 1968). Injection of testosterone propionate into the three poorest builders in a group of six *Quelea* improved their building scores to a level above that of the three previously best nest builders (Crook and Butterfield 1968).

To conclude, in two species of weaverbirds (Ploceidae), building by the male depends to some degree on male hormone; but more study is needed. The endocrine control of nest-lining activity by female weavers is not yet understood, but may turn out to be similar to that known for the female Canary.

INTEGRATION OF NEST BUILDING INTO THE BREEDING CYCLE

In the integration of nest building into the breeding cycle the relevant questions are: (1) What starts nest building? (2) Why does nest building largely precede egg laying? (3) What causes the birds to start incubating and then to continue sitting on their eggs? (4) What causes nest building to slow down and stop?

What starts nest building?

With regard to seasonal breeders, the most general principle is the well-known rule that the time of breeding in animals is so adjusted by natural selection that the young are usually hatched or born at the season most favorable for their development and survival. An endogenous, circannual (about one year long) rhythm of development of the gonads has now been shown for several species of birds (Assenmacher and Jallageas 1980). This endogenous rhythm is synchronized with suitable nesting conditions by various key external factors that vary with the species. One important synchronizing factor in birds of the North Temperate Zone is the seasonal change in day-length (Farner and Gwinner 1980, Farner and Wingfield 1980).

Gonadal development under artificially increased photoperiods during the nonbreeding season has been demonstrated for Domestic Fowl, Ring Doves, Canaries, House Sparrows, and numerous other species. Degree of response to the photoperiod as such varies genetically with the species. When a Mourning Dove (*Zenaida macroura*), a seasonal breeder of North America, was mated in the laboratory with a domestic Ring Dove, a nonseasonal breeder with tropical ancestors from Africa, seasonal periodicity in egg laying and fertility of the Mourning Dove was maintained (Cole 1933). McDonald (1982) finds among both normal male Ring Doves and castrated, testosterone-implanted male Ring Doves, that the amount of nest-building activity is significantly greater when the doves are on long days than when they are on short days. However, this difference is eliminated by removal of the pineal gland, and McDonald suggests that in doves the pineal mediates the effects of long days in stimulating increased nest-building activity; apparently the pineal gland does not act in this way by enhancing the secretion of testosterone.

Whereas full testicular development can often be initiated in the male bird by suitable photoperiods, ovarian development, begun in the female under similar photoperiods, is often incomplete and requires additional input from male courtship and suitable nesting conditions (Bartholomew 1949, Lehrman 1961). The male Ring Dove by his courtship behavior stimulates gonadotrophin secretion from the female's anterior pituitary (Barfield 1971), causing her ovaries to develop and to secrete estradiol and progesterone (fig. 13.1), which in turn stimulate her nest-building behavior. The effect is reciprocal and exposure to a female almost immediately increases the level of testosterone (fig. 13.2) in the blood of the male Ring Dove (Cheng 1979), stimulating him to court the female and to gather nest materials.

In tropical areas small birds generally breed during the rainy season. White-browed Sparrow Weavers that breed in arid African savanna and use dry grass stems for their nests promptly begin building nests on the day the rains begin (N. Collias and Collias 1964, 1978). A. J. Marshall and Disney (1957) stimulated breeding during the dry season by Red-billed Weavers (*Quelea quelea*), which normally breed in dry savanna country in the rainy season, by giving them suitable green grasses with which to build their nests.

The Village Weaver, which also weaves its nest of strips torn from the leaves of green grasses, is not so closely tied to the rains. Although Village Weavers in Africa normally breed during the rainy season (Morel and Morel 1962), they may anticipate the rains and begin weaving their nests before the rains begin. In our aviaries at Los Angeles the Village Weavers bred well in the long dry season of late spring and summer when no rain falls, so long as we provided them with suitable food and green nest materials. Normally, they breed here from April to September, but we could not prolong breeding into the autumn by giving the birds plenty of insect food and plenty of green nest materials, even with the aid of occasional rains. Seasonal changes of bill and plumage coloration of male Village Weavers kept in outdoor aviaries at Los Angeles, a land of winter rains, closely paralleled seasonal changes in day-length and not changes in rainfall (N. Collias and Collias 1969b).

Why does nest building precede egg laying?

For Ring Doves and Canaries an active period of nest building precedes egg laying, but there is a marked decline in nest-building activities about a day or two before the first egg is laid. Ovarian development and the frequency of ovulation, as well as the level of estradiol in the blood of the female Ring Dove, increase with the amount of normal courtship activity by the male, and the effect is augmented by nest building (Lehrman 1965, Cheng 1974). The initial approach of the male Ring Dove consists of aggressive courtship (chasing and bowing, apparently for sex identification) and nest-oriented courtship (nest soliciting). In one experiment, females, paired with males who engaged only in aggressive courtship, showed almost no nest soliciting to the males, and the males gathered few nest materials. Females, paired with males who also courted with nest-soliciting behavior, themselves nest solicited during the first day of parting, constructed elaborate nests, and laid eggs much sooner (Hutchinson and Lavori 1976).

Nest building and male courtship lead to ovulation presumably by stimulating the brain of the female to produce a hormone (*Gn-RH*) that stimulates the release of gonadotrophin (*LH* + *FSH*) from her anterior pituitary. Sharp (1980) reviews literature indicating that *LH* injection stimulates secretion of progesterone (and testosterone) in laying hens, and also that ovulation in the hen is blocked by injection of anti-progesterone, but not by anti-estradiol, serum. Progesterone has a positive feedback effect, causing a preovulatory surge of *LH* in the blood plasma of the hen, which apparently triggers ovulation.

Experiments with combined injections of *FSH* and *LH* into hypophysectomized hens show that *FSH* inhibits ovulation of all but the largest follicle (Nalbandov 1976:173). Cheng and Balthazart (1982) find that in the blood plasma of female Ring Doves a depression of the *FSH* level is typically associated with every preovulatory surge of *LH*, and that an *LH* surge not acompanied by an *FSH* dip is not followed by an ovulation. Since this *FSH* depression is significantly correlated with the level of nest-building activity, they propose that nest-building activity stimulates this change and hence ovulation.

That a nest or nest-building activity is normally necessary for, or greatly facilitates, ovulation has been demonstrated in some birds. Egg laying is delayed in paired Ring Doves that are not provided with a nest bowl and nest materials (Lehrman 1965). The presence of a male Canary accelerates nest building by the female, and egg laying is greatly delayed if the females are kept without a nest cup and nest materials (Hinde 1965). Long delays in egg laying when the birds are deprived of nesting material and a nest cup have also been observed in Bengalese Finches (*Lonchura striata*) (Slater 1969). Village Weaver females will not lay eggs in the absence of either nests or males, and merely depriving the females of materials with which to line their nests stops or greatly reduces egg laying (Victoria 1969).

Is it the nest itself, or the act of nest building that stimulates ovulation? S. J. White (1975) found that paired female Ring Doves that had their nest bowls emptied of nest materials each day built actively and tended to lay eggs a little sooner than paired females that were given and permitted to keep a completed nest, or females that were allowed to build normally. Female Canaries that had their nest bowls emptied three times a day also tended to lay a little sooner than birds with complete nests (Hinde and Warren 1959). Apparently, either having a completed nest or the *act* of nest building itself helps stimulate ovulation.

What starts and maintains incubation?

During incubation, nest building and sexual activity in most species of birds usually cease or greatly diminish.

If her eggs are allowed to pile up, a domestic hen becomes broody, which is indicated by persistent sitting on the eggs, ruffling of feathers, and clucking. Hens incubate about 21 days before the eggs hatch, pigeons 18, and Ring Doves 14. During incubation the crop of pigeons and doves enlarges and forms a special secretion from its lining ("crop milk"), which the squabs are fed by regurgitation.

Apparently just sitting on eggs helps stimulate and maintain incubation. Pigeons and doves begin sexual activity anew if the eggs are removed soon after they are laid. On the other hand, if the eggs are sterile normal incubation may be prolonged as much as ten days in pigeons, and the crop sacs continue to secrete crop milk. One broody hen sat on artificial eggs for four months.

A completed nest is important for the normal establishment of incubation. S. J. White (1975) found that the presence of a nest with eggs, rather than just the eggs alone, is necessary for incubation in Ring doves to be effectively established and maintained. When the nest was removed from the nest bowl after the first egg was laid, the birds did not incubate well and hatched none of their eggs; in contrast, pairs having a complete nest hatched 67 to 100 percent of their eggs.

Previous breeding experience facilitates the development of incubation behavior. Female Ring Doves that have experience with nest building initiate incubation in subsequent breeding more readily than females having experience of courtship only (Michel 1977).

Prolactin, secreted from the anterior pituitary, stimulates incubation and broody behavior in domestic hens (Riddle et al. 1935, Saeki and Tanabe 1955) and in Ring Doves (Lehrman 1965). Over a 24-hour period the mean level of plasma prolactin in incubating bantam hens is three to four times greater than in laying hens (Sharp 1980). Riddle et al. (1935) found that prolactin was more effective in stimulating incubation in laying hens with active ovaries than in nonlaying hens, indicating that the sex hormones perform a priming action for prolactin. N. Collias (1950a) confirmed the sensitizing effect of sex hormones on external stimuli that cause broodiness in hens.

Prolactin also stimulates crop growth and secretion in pigeons and doves, and blood levels of prolactin in Ring Doves closely parallel changes in crop weight, with the highest concentrations occurring during incubation and when there are young squabs in the nest (Goldsmith and Follett 1980:161). Prolactin secretion, as indicated by crop growth and secretion of crop milk, can be stimulated in male or female pigeons by incubation of the eggs or merely by the sight of the mate sitting on the eggs ("psychological brooding") (Patel 1936).

Cheng and Silver (1975) find that both estradiol and progesterone are necessary to stimulate not only nest building but also incubation behavior by ovariectomized Ring Doves. Estradiol has a priming effect, sensitizing the dove to progesterone. If estradiol is injected into non-laying hens, the concentration of the cytoplasmic progesterone receptors increases in the hypothalamus and pituitary (Tanaka 1980). Measurements of plasma levels of various steroid hormones during the breeding cycle of the female Ring Dove show a decline in estradiol and a rise in progesterone just before ovulation (Silver 1978) (fig. 13.1). Prolactin levels, as indicated by crop-sac growth, increase somewhat later and led Lehrman (1965) to suggest that in female doves, progesterone initiates incubation while prolactin helps maintain it.

The male dove is stimulated to incubate by the eggs and the example of the female. Patel (1936) found that male pigeons castrated at or before the beginning of incubation continued to help the female incubate and at the end of the first incubation produced crop milk normally, but in subsequent reproductive cycles incubation was very light and crop changes did not occur. Evidently, testosterone has a priming effect on incubation and facilitates crop-sac growth by stimulating secretion of prolactin. However, incubation by a hypophysectomized male pigeon pretreated with estradiol and without any crop-sac development shows that prolactin is not indispensable for incubation behavior (N. Collias 1946, 1950a).

Progesterone is not necessary to stimulate incubation in male Ring Doves, nor does the onset of incubation produce significant changes in progesterone levels in the plasma of normal male doves (Silver 1978) (fig. 13.2). However, testosterone injections into castrated male Ring Doves significantly increase the concentration of progesterone receptors in the hypothalamus, but not in other brain areas, and Balthazart et al. (1980) suggest that such an increase in brain sensitivity to endogenous progesterone could help stimulate incubation by male Ring Doves.

What causes nest building to slow down and stop?

Giving a completed nest to a pair of Ring Doves (S. White 1975) or Canaries (Hinde 1958) may greatly slow down nest building behavior.

At the same time, the decline of gonadal hormone secretion during incubation also leads to a decline in nest building.

In a number of species, the birds continue to bring nest materials, particularly nest-lining materials, for some time after the eggs are laid. Incubating female Village Weavers frequently return to their nests, after a recess, with a soft grass head or a feather for the lining. The female Costa's Hummingbird (*Calypte costae*) may build up the sides of her nest considerably during incubation (H. Harrison 1979). Ring Doves will continue to gather materials and build them into the nest up to at least ten days after laying the first egg, although at a decreasing rate (S. White 1975). Some nest-building activity by the male albeit at a low level, is associated with continued secretion of testosterone during incubation (fig. 13.2). Castration of a male Ring Dove has a much more immediate effect on the male's bowing-coo and on his nest-solicitation display than on his nest-building activity; nest building after castration is also more rapidly restored by injections of testosterone (Erickson and Martinez-Vargas 1975). The female Ring Dove continues to secrete a little estradiol and progesterone, hormones that stimulate nest building, throughout the incubation period (Silver 1978) (fig. 13.1).

There is an inverse relationship between the sexual and the parental phases of bird behavior, which is clearly shown in domestic hens (N. Collias 1951). During the sexual phase, egg laying (gonadotrophin), copulation frequency (estradiol), size of comb (testosterone), and nest building (estradiol + progesterone) are maximal, whereas all become minimal when the hen starts clucking and becomes broody with the onset of incubation and parenting (fig. 13.3).

Prolactin has a strong antigonad effect in domestic fowl and pigeons, and probably in many other birds as well. If gonadotrophin along with prolactin is injected in doves, the gonads do not regress, indicating that prolactin normally exerts its antigonad effect by inhibiting secretion of gonadotrophin from the pituitary gland (O. Riddle and Bates 1939). As the level of prolactin rises in the blood during incubation, it acts to diminish the secretion of pituitary gonadotrophin and therefore the secretion of sex hormones, thus inhibiting both sexual behavior and nest-building behavior. The bird then passes from the sexual to the parental phase of breeding. But since the maintenance of prolactin secretion, incubation, and broody behavior all depend on sufficient priming with sex hormones (N. Collias 1950a), the bird will eventually come out of the parental phase of behavior. The suppressed state of the gonads, the maturing of the young, and perhaps other factors involved in control of the cyclic activity of the anterior pituitary, account for the ending of

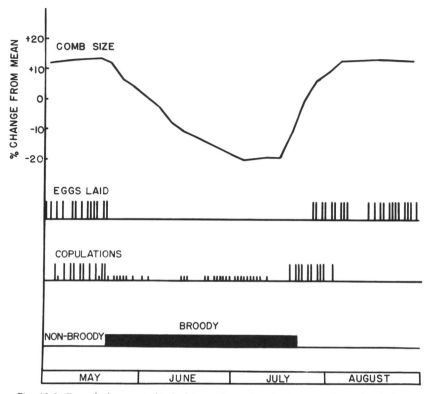

Fig. 13.3. Records for one individual hen, illustrating the inverse relationship between sexual and parental (broody) behavior in endocrine control of reproductive behavior in female Domestic Fowl. See text for details. For copulations, long vertical bars indicate observation periods when the hen copulated on exposure to a rooster, short vertical bars observation periods when she did not. (N. E. Collias, in *Comparative Psychology*, ed. C. P. Stone, 1951)

the first reproductive cycle, which may thereupon be succeeded by another reproductive cycle, or by a molt.

SUMMARY

The interaction of hormonal and external factors controlling the breeding behavior of birds is summarized in a diagram in figure 13.4. These factors form a self-regulatory and adaptive system in which the nest and nest-building behavior play important roles; the present state of knowledge about this control system is based mainly on observations of domesticated fowl, doves, and pigeons. The numbers on the diagram correspond

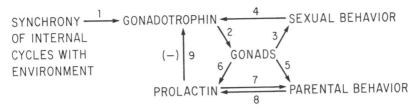

Fig. 13.4. Diagram of the interactions between hormones and behavior in the control of breeding behavior, including nest building, in birds. See "Summary" of this chapter for explanation.

to the following successive steps in the regulation of breeding behavior, including nest building:

1. Increased day-length, especially in the northern hemisphere, and suitable nesting conditions, synchronized with endogenous circannual rhythms, stimulate gonadotrophic hormone secretion from the anterior pituitary gland acting through the hypothalamus, that part of the brain to which the pituitary is attached. Among tropical birds, photoperiodism is observed to be less important than endogenous circannual cycles and suitable nesting conditions—often seasonal in occurrence—in bringing about the onset of breeding.

2. Gonadotrophins (*FSH* and *LH*), both stimulated by one hypothalamic hormone (gonadotrophic-releasing hormone, or *Gn-RH*), bring about growth and maturation of the gonads and secretion of the gonadal hormones—testosterone in the male; estradiol, progesterone, and testosterone in the female.

3. Gonadal hormones stimulate courtship and sexual behavior, and nest-building behavior.

4. In turn, courtship and sexual behavior exert a positive feedback on the secretion of gonadotrophins by the opposite sex, leading to ovulation; the nest and nest-building behavior also help stimulate ovulation and egg laying by the female.

5. Gonadal activity facilitates development of parental behavior, since priming by the sex hormones, estradiol and testosterone, increases the sensitivity of the parent birds to eggs and young. In the female Ring Dove, estradiol, in combination with progesterone, not only stimulates nest building, but also helps start incubation behavior. Sight of the eggs and the sitting female help stimulate incubation by male doves and pigeons.

6. There is some evidence that testosterone in male and estradiol in female birds may help stimulate secretion or release of prolactin by the anterior pituitary gland.

7. Prolactin stimulates incubation and maintains broody behavior in Domestic Fowl and in Ring Doves.

8. Prolactin secretion is also stimulated by the act of sitting on the eggs and, perhaps, by care of small young. This positive feedback increases the level of prolactin in the blood.

9. As the prolactin level in the blood rises, it slows down or stops the secretion of gonadotrophic hormones from the pituitary: the gonads regress, the sexual phase of the breeding cycle ends and is succeeded by the parental phase. Nest building has a lower threshold to stimulation by sex hormones than does sexual behavior, and a low level of nest-building behavior may continue for some time during incubation after sexual behavior has stopped.

As the priming effect for parental behavior of the sex hormones diminishes and as the young grow older, parental behavior declines, and the breeding cycle ends.

CHAPTER FOURTEEN

The Evolution of Gregarious Nesting

THE object of this chapter is to discuss the ecological forces that have led to the evolution of gregarious nesting, including communal building on one nest by three or more birds, and also including building of many nests close together. These two categories are not mutually exclusive.

In gregarious nesting, we meet the problem of the relationship between natural selection of individuals and of groups. There has been much controversy and misunderstanding about this relationship; different viewpoints are reviewed by Krebs and Davies (1978:8–9), by Wright (1980), and by Wade (1982). Communal nesting by several birds attending one nest is especially useful for the study of the relationship between benefits to the individual helper and benefits to the group or family. Possible mutual benefit or mutual harm, and one-sided benefits of all sorts, should be considered in their totality in explaining communal breeding.

Gregarious nesting also brings up the problem of the relationship of the breeding structure of populations to evolution. Interpopulation selection within the species refers to excessive and effective emigration of individuals from centers of population growth (Wright 1978). Sewall Wright (1931, 1978, 1980) has developed the theory, based on the shifting balance between the factors of evolution, that subdivision of a species into numerous, small, partially isolated local populations provides a trial-and-error mechanism at the population level and gives the best conditions for continuing adaptive evolution of new, harmonious genotypes.

Species of birds that nest in many different colonies during the breeding season often have a population breeding structure that seems to approximate that required by Wright's theory. The effective breeding size of a nesting colony may be much smaller than the actual numbers of birds present. For example, the number of successful breeders is often greatly reduced by intense competition for nest sites, and whole populations may fail to breed in bad years because of unsuitable nesting conditions.

There is a reciprocal effect of behavior on evolutionary mechanisms, since social behavior is often the principal and immediate force determining the breeding structure of natural populations (N. Collias 1942,

1951; N. Collias and Collias 1976). The basis for subdivision of large populations into smaller local populations may be geographical, or ecological, but it may also be social, especially in gregariously nesting birds.

Helpers at the Nest and Communal Building

A helper at the nest, according to Skutch (1976:351), is a bird that assists in the nesting of a bird other than its mate. The most common instance is of older young helping their parents to feed a younger brood; often these older young are of an age where they could breed themselves, but act as helpers instead. Helpers may assist in one or more aspects of breeding: nest construction, territorial defense, incubation, feeding of the female on her nest, or feeding the nestlings and fledged young. We are here primarily interested in communal nest building, where more than two birds help build one nest, and then in giving a brief summary of some general aspects of helping that may be useful in gaining perspective.

Communal Nest Building

The degree of involvement by helpers in nest construction varies greatly in different species of communal breeders. In the Florida Scrub Jay (*Aphelocoma c. coerulescens*), a well-known communal breeder, only the breeding pair builds (Woolfenden 1973), but in the related Gray-breasted (Mexican) Jay (*A. ultramarina*), the entire flock of eight to twenty birds may participate in nest construction, as well as in feeding the nestlings (Brown 1970). Most flocks of Gray-breasted Jays consist of two or more breeding pairs of adults plus a variable number of non-breeding yearlings and adults. Separate nests are constructed by each pair in the flock.

The tiny Bronze Mannikins (*Lonchura cucullata*) of Africa sleep together in a roofed dormitory nest. The immature birds aid in building roost nests, but the nests in which eggs are laid during the breeding season are built by the breeding pair (Woodall 1975).

In the Grey-crowned Babbler (*Pomatostomus temporalis*) of Australia, the communal groups of five to twelve birds consist of an adult pair, which mates for life, and their offspring, both young and mature. The adult pair does most of the building of the breeding nest and of dormitory nests, helped by other members of the group. Both breeding nests and dormitory nests are roofed and look alike, but a new nest is built for each breeding attempt. Nests are made of strong twigs and lined with fine grass and fur. The group roosts each night in a dormitory nest, and many of these sleeping nests are built and repaired throughout the year (H. Frith 1979).

All individuals of a group may help construct a breeding nest, but there may be intense competition within the group. In the Groove-billed Ani (*Crotophaga sulcirostris*) of the cuckoo family (Cuculidae), found in the New World tropics, a group is generally composed of from one to four monogamous pairs. All members of the group help build a single nest in which all females lay their eggs. The nest is a bulky, open structure of coarse twigs and is lined with green leaves that are brought daily until the young hatch (Skutch 1976). Each female visits the nest for several days before laying her first egg and, during these visits, frequently throws out an egg from among those that were previously laid by other females. Since the most dominant female lays last, a larger percentage of all the eggs are laid by her than by the other females. Incubation and care of the young is shared by all members of the group (Vehrencamp 1977). The gradual change from defense of individual pair territories to defense of a communal or group territory is clearly seen by comparing different species of the Crotophaginae, a subfamily of cuckoos which includes the anis (Davis 1942).

Helpers at nests of some weaverbirds are particularly important when the nest is large and complex. This was illustrated by the nest building of some of the black and red forest weaverbirds of the genus *Malimbus*, inhabiting wet tropical forests of Africa (Brosset 1978) (chap. 3). In species without helpers, *M. nitens* and *M. malimbicus*, the relatively simple nest is built in four or five hours. In contrast, the much larger and more complex nests of *M. cassini* and *M. coronatus* take these communal builders over a week to construct. Brosset suggests the helpers gain weaving skill and experience, while the breeding birds with helpers economize on energy.

Some communal builders have many nests simultaneously in one tree. White-browed Sparrow Weavers (*Plocepasser mahali*) live in small groups, often with only five to six birds. In the colonies we observed in Kenya there was an average of ten to twelve nests per colony in the tree at any one time. The birds sleep singly in different nests in the colony tree. Nests are built of dry grass stems and grass heads. Building takes much work; we counted almost a thousand pieces of nest material in one completed nest. All members of the group join in building a new nest, which may then be used for sleeping by one bird, or for breeding by the group. There is only a single incubating female in each group, but the whole group may help feed the one or two nestlings and fledged young. Shortly before a young bird is ready to leave the nest, the whole group rapidly builds a new nest, to which they attempt to lead the young one for sleeping after it leaves the brood nest. The entrance of this new nest is made large and conspicuous, as if to attract the attention of the fledged young bird.

New nests of the White-browed Sparrow Weaver usually take from five days to six weeks to build and are especially likely to be started after the rainy season begins, when the birds breed. We found no very definite association of nest-building activity with dominance status in the group. Old nests are often used by the birds as a source of materials for other nests, and so may gradually be destroyed (N. Collias and Collias 1978).

The Grey-capped Social Weaver (*Pseudonigrita arnaudi*) differs from the preceding species and many other communal breeders in that the colony tree may be occupied by several groups or families, instead of just one. Colony size varies greatly, from two to more than 60 birds. Each family has its own group of nests in the colony tree. Nest building is generally a communal affair; and when a new nest is finished, part of the group—from one to five birds—may sleep in it, or the nest may be used for breeding by the adult pair. Recently fledged young and older young from previous broods often help the parents to build, and three to six birds may help build one nest. We counted 1,760 straws or grass heads in one nest. The adult male is dominant in a group and generally does most of the building, while young birds usually do less building than do the adults. Often young birds merely pick up grass heads from the ground and drop them (N. Collias and Collias 1980).

General Aspects of Helping at the Nest

The phenomenon of "helping" in birds has been frequently termed *communal breeding, cooperative breeding,* or *group breeding.* Skutch (1935) long ago noted the occurrence of helping in various tropical species, but it was not until the subject was reviewed on a worldwide basis in 1974 at the International Congress of Ornithology in Australia (in H. Frith and Calaby 1976), that the general importance of helping among tropical and subtropical birds began to attract much attention. Well over one hundred and fifty communally breeding species have now been described—probably only a tiny fraction of those that exist. Some good recent reviews of the rapidly expanding literature on the subject are those by Brown (1974, 1978, 1983), Fry (1977), Skutch (1976), and S. Emlen (1978, 1981, 1982). There has been much confusion in discussions of communal breeding because of differences in definition of the same terms (Bertram 1982, Brown 1983).

Several selective advantages, not necessarily mutually exclusive, may have accounted for the evolution of helping and communal nesting. Both the breeding pair and the helpers may benefit from the association. For several species, although not all, the evidence indicates that having helpers may significantly improve reproductive success of the breeding pair. The parents also benefit genetically when their older young with experience as helpers become better able to survive and reproduce effectively than young who had not helped (Balda and Gabaldon 1979). Helpers may benefit in various ways: they gain valuable experience, may obtain higher social status, and can scout from a relatively secure base for available mates and vacant territories. The most dominant male helper in Florida Scrub Jays may inherit part of the parents' territory (Woolfenden 1976).

Since helpers often help to raise younger sibs, they may pass on some of their genes to the next generation through the genetic correlations involved in raising relatives (Hamilton 1963). This kin selection is one theory of the apparent altruism involved. After calculating degrees of relatedness and breeding success in Grey-crowned Babblers (*Pomatostomus temporalis*) of Australia, Brown and Brown (1981:256) concluded that "for the first year helping represents a better strategy than attempting to breed, but in later years helping is inferior to breeding if a chance to breed exists."

There are other aspects of helping that need to be considered. Many communal breeders that have been investigated appear to occupy saturated habitats, in which there often seems to be no place for mature young to go. The best strategy would seem to be for them to remain at home as helpers and to defer breeding until a place becomes available for one reason or another (Brown 1974, Koenig and Pitelka 1981). As a method of regulating population density, Skutch (1976:376) suggests that the system of helpers is an alternative, or in some cases a supplement, to territoriality.

Ecological conditions may open or close breeding opportunities for helpers in fluctuating, unpredictable environments. White-fronted Bee-eaters (*Merops bullockoides*) in Kenya are more likely to remain in groups as helpers when rainfall is low and little insect food is available, and are more likely to initiate breeding as independent pairs when conditions are favorable (S. Emlen 1982). Helping, in other places with an erratic climate such as many parts of Australia, may enable maximum reproductive effort to be made when favorable conditions permit (I. Rowley 1976). Furthermore, helping may help minimize the energy per bird required for successful breeding (L. Grimes 1976).

The reproductive rates of birds seem to be rather closely regulated by the food supply (Lack 1968, Crossner 1977), although, according to von Haartman (1971), nidicolous birds on the average rear a somewhat smaller number of young than they are capable of nourishing. Under difficult feeding conditions—for example, when under excessive harassment by predators—the presence of helpers may increase success in raising a brood, as in the White-browed Sparrow Weaver (*Plocepasser mahali*) in Kenya (N. Collias and Collias 1978). This is an extension of the idea that monogamy among birds has evolved under difficult feeding conditions where two parents are required to raise a brood (Armstrong 1955).

In populations of individually color-banded Green Woodhoopoes (*Phoeniculus purpureus*) in Kenya, one study found that only a small number of breeders produced a disproportionately large share of the next generation. Most emigrants leaving the study area were from the larger flocks (6 or more birds), that is, the ones with most helpers, and joined smaller flocks (2 to 4 birds) (Ligon 1981). Lewis (1981, 1982) found a similar picture among White-browed Sparrow Weavers in Zambia. This pattern of movements evidently gives a basis for interpopulation selection. Helpers seem to benefit largely by the opportunity to acquire breeding status.

ADVANTAGES OF BUILDING NESTS NEAR EACH OTHER

Many species of birds, particularly large water birds, nest in colonies with many nests near each other, and the group determines where and when individuals will nest as well as their daily patterns of movement. Some years ago, in reviewing the bird societies of the world, Friedmann (1935) concluded that the bulk of such gregarious breeders belong to the more primitive orders of birds. He also observed that whereas colonial nesting of this type has persisted or evolved in those species whose nesting and feeding grounds are spatially separated, birds whose reproductive area is the same as their feeding area are, on the whole, solitary nesters.

Small land birds are generally more vulnerable to predators than are larger birds. Gregarious breeding with many nests of different pairs close to each other is rare among passerine birds, being found in only 9 of the 67 families of passerine birds recognized at the time of Friedmann's review, whereas it has been estimated that about 93 percent of marine birds are colonial in this sense (Lack 1967). In the order of passerine birds, placing many nests close together occurs most notably among the Ploceidae (Sociable Weaver *Philetairus socius*, East African Social Weavers *Pseudonigrita*, Buffalo Weaver *Bubalornis albirostris*, and many species of Ploceinae or true weaverbirds), the Icteridae (Tricolor Blackbirds *Agelaius tricolor*, caciques *Cacicus*, oropendolas *Gym-*

nostinops, Zarhynchus, and *Psarocolius),* the Dulidae (Palmchat *Dulus dominicus),* the Sturnidae (Metallic or Shining Starling *Aplonis metallica,* Wattled Starling *Creatophora cinerea),* the Corvidae (Jackdaw *Corvus monedula,* Rook *C. frugilegus),* and the Hirundinidae (several species of swallows). In these colonial breeders, nesting and feeding areas are generally separate, and the birds nest where there is some special security from predators, such as on a cliff, in a very thorny tree, in the top of a tall tree with a smooth trunk, in emergent marsh vegetation over water, on a riverbank or sand bar, or close to human habitations.

Advantages facilitating the evolution of colony breeding with many nests built near each other include (1) guidance to food sources, (2) cooperative defense against enemies, (3) more complete utilization of limited nesting sites, and (4) social stimulation of breeding condition. Each of these will be considered in turn.

1. *Guidance to food sources.* The importance of guidance to a good source of food by experienced birds as a basis for colony nesting was pointed out by Peter Ward (1965) for an African weaverbird, the Red-billed Quelea (*Quelea quelea*) of acacia savanna in Africa. Whereas forest weavers are generally solitary nesters, those species nesting in savanna parkland, in cultivated country, or in marsh grassland usually breed gregariously (Chapin 1954). Crook (1962, 1964) and Lack (1968) have provided useful tabulations relating differences in sociality (dispersion of nests and nature of the pair bond) of Ploceidae to differences in diet. The forest species are insectivorous, solitary (19 of 21 species) and monogamous; the savanna species eat mainly grass seeds, breed in colonies (41 of 57 species), and are polygynous. Species that nest in grassland with few or no trees—that is, bishop birds and widowbirds—subsist largely on grass seeds, generally nest in small, grouped territories (13 of 18 species), and are polygynous. Actually, almost all species of open-country Ploceidae also eat insects (Chapin 1954), and the vast majority of species feed many insects to their nestlings, but there is no doubt of the great importance of an abundant supply of grass seeds outside the forest and of the relative scarcity of grasses inside forests. Large concentrations of birds require an abundant food supply, such as grass seeds in savannah grassland and marsh, as well as the insect life present in those habitats during the rainy season.

Many of the open-country weavers feed in flocks, searching for food that is often unevenly distributed. After some areas are exploited or cleared of seed, others are still covered with seed. A small flock of Red-billed Quelea that has found a good feeding place will attract others and swell into an enormous flock within minutes. These birds roost and

Fig. 14.1. Nesting colony of Red-billed Weavers (*Quelea quelea*) in an *Acacia tortilis* tree in tropical arid savanna, Senegal. There may be up to 1000 nests in a tree and up to 10,000,000 birds in a breeding colony. (Photo: Gérard Morel)

breed in huge aggregations (fig. 14.1). Ward observed that when a roost empties soon after dawn the birds leave in waves. "A large number of birds fly straight out of sight. Many others, however, go only a few hundred metres and settle on prominent trees or bushes; then, as subsequent waves pass overhead, they fly up in groups to join them. This is perhaps the mechanism whereby knowledge of good feeding-places is shared within the roosting population" (Ward 1965:212). This "information centre" theory of gregarious roosting and nesting was later extended by Ward and Zahavi (1973) to many other species.

In a laboratory experimental setup, naive Red-billed Quelea quickly learned to follow experienced individuals who knew the location of food and water sources (de Groot 1980). An experimental group even exploited the more profitable of two food sources, originally known only to some individuals.

Species of terns (Laridae, Sterninae) that have large nesting colonies needing more food range farther than do small colonies and tend to feed more in groups (Erwin 1978). Presumably, the larger the colony the larger the area it can search effectively for patchily and unpredictably distributed schools of fish. Inshore feeders (Gull-billed Tern *Sterna nilotica* and Least Tern S. *antillarum*) tend to have the smallest breeding colonies; mid-range feeders (Common Tern S. *hirundo* and Arctic Tern S. *paradisaea*) have intermediate-size colonies; while Roseate Terns S. *dougallii* and Royal Terns S. *maxima*, which forage farthest out to sea, have the largest colonies. Erwin analyzed the results of scientific and commercial fish collections and found a tendency for inshore fish to be more uniformly distributed than offshore fish. But in Europe, the feeding range of Gull-billed Terns decreases from small northern to large southern colonies (Møller 1982). In New Zealand, Black-billed Gulls (*Larus bulleri*) may call as they leave a colony to forage; flock leaders call more often than followers and recruit more followers than leaders that do not call; playbacks of these calls attracted the gulls (Evans 1982).

One of the critical periods in the life of a young altricial bird comes after it has fledged, when it must learn to feed itself. The more company it has, particularly of adults from whose example it can learn where and how to find food, the better its chances of survival. The amount of guidance to food sources is greatly increased if their nesting is highly gregarious and synchronized, as S. T. Emlen and N. J. Demong (1975) demonstrated for the Bank Swallow (*Riparia riparia*) in New York state.

Bank Swallows nest in colonies in numerous holes which the birds dig in earthen banks at the start of their breeding season each spring. There are usually from 10 to 300 nests in a colony. Different pairs within the same colony are highly synchronized and 67 percent of all the nests in this study fledged their young over a period of only 6 days. The advantage of this synchrony is that individuals fledging in company with many others emerge to find a steady stream of other swallows traveling to local, ephemeral, and shifting concentrations of the insect food supply. Those young, emerging late after much of the colony has been deserted, find themselves practically alone and with no guidance to good food sources.

In 12 colonies the average number of young per pair that were raised to fledging age, and the percentage of eggs laid that produced viable young at fledging (reproductive success), increased with the degree of synchrony of each colony, as measured by the standard deviation of the

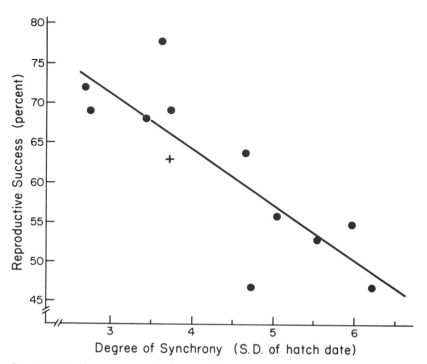

Fig. 14.2. Breeding success and colony synchrony in Bank Swallows (*Riparia riparia*). Average reproductive success (percentage of eggs laid that produced viable young at fledging) decreases with lower degree of within-colony synchrony, as measured by the standard deviation (S.D.) of hatching dates. Each dot represents a different colony; the plus sign denotes a renesting colony. (Stephen T. Emlen and Natalie J. Demong, *Science* 1975, 188:1030; © by the American Association for the Advancement of Science)

mean hatching date of the eggs in that colony (fig. 14.2). There was a highly significant correlation between the degree of synchronization within the colony and average reproductive success (r = .82, P < .001). Nests least in synchrony with the rest of the colony contained a higher proportion of starved nestlings and semi-starved fledglings. This example underscores the importance of synchronized nest construction.

In the American Bank Swallow excavation for the nest is done by the pair, insofar as known. In Europe, where the Bank Swallow is called the Sand Martin, excavation of burrows may be a communal affair, at least in colonies nesting in sand pits where all holes have to be dug anew each season. Three to six birds may be active in a single burrow and then move on to another. The same swallow may dig at several holes in succession. After the burrows are finished, there seems to be only one adult pair in attendance at each nest (Hickling 1959). House Martins

(*Delichon urbica*) may also help each other build their mud nests, and from 4 to 14 individuals have been seen working on one nest then moving on to prepare another (Lind 1964). Presumably such communal activity helps synchronize nest building throughout the colony.

2. *Cooperative defense against enemies.* The benefit of nesting aggregation as a defense against enemies depends in part on the size and aggressiveness of the birds concerned. Large, aggressive species are able to defend themselves by cooperative attacks on enemies, but small birds by aggregating might attract enemies and be more vulnerable. Dispersion and hiding of nest sites is often the best strategy for small birds to adopt against predation. Perhaps for this reason close aggregation of nests, while it is common among large birds and especially sea birds, is rare among passerine birds. In any case, breeding aggregation generally requires relatively safe nesting sites.

Among marine birds, solitary nesting is restricted to intertidal feeders whose nests are accessible to predators but widely dispersed, whereas most offshore feeders breed in large colonies in inaccessible sites. Colonies of inshore feeders tend to be smaller than those of offshore species. Many inshore feeders such as gulls and terns that nest on low-lying coasts, have colonies more accessible to predators, but the adults attack nest predators, unlike most other marine birds (Lack 1967).

Field experiments in Black-headed Gull (*Larus ridibundus*) colonies in England have shown that such predators as Herring Gulls and Carrion Crows are deterred by mass attacks of the gulls from entering the colony to prey on eggs. Although foxes are not much deterred by these mobbing attacks, the territorial spacing of the nests furnishes some protection. When well-camouflaged eggs were laid out at different densities, the risk of discovery by foxes increased sharply with increasing density. The territorial spacing of nests within the colony also helps protect the eggs and young from intraspecific predation by the gulls themselves (Tinbergen 1967).

It appears that colony nesting is favored for group defense against some predators, while spacing within the colony is regulated by the need for defense against other predators, including intraspecific predators. The success of broods in fledging young in colonies of Black-headed Gulls was much greater in the colony proper than in the more scattered nests outside the colony, where the mortality was mainly due to predation (Tinbergen 1967).

3. *More complete utilization of limited nesting sites.* Hole-nesting birds are often limited in nesting by lack of cavities (von Haartman

1957). One way to solve this problem is for a bird to make its own nesting cavity. The development of coloniality in swallows (Hirundinidae) has paralleled the development of ability to build nests (Mayr and Bond 1943). Burrow-excavators such as the Bank Swallow and mud-nest builders such as the Cliff Swallow (*Hirundo pyrrhonota*) often breed in large colonies. But swallows that utilize naturally occurring cavities, such as the Tree Swallow (*Tachycineta bicolor*) and the Violet-green Swallow (*Tachycineta thalassina*), breed in more solitary and dispersed fashion, being limited by the sporadic occurrence of such cavities.

The Barn Swallow (*Hirundo rustica*) may be found nesting in solitary pairs or in small colonies of several pairs or more. From a study of the species in New York state, where colonies ranged in size from one to thirty nests, Snapp (1976) concludes that Barn Swallows are mainly limited by nest-site availability, since the number of pairs in a colony increased with the size of the barn or other building in which they nested and with the size or number of entrances to the building. The level of predation in colonies was not very different from that of solitary nesting pairs, while nestling death due to suspected starvation was very low (ca. 2%–4%) in all colony sizes. There was no influence of colony size or synchrony within colonies on breeding success in the Barn Swallow, in contrast to the highly colonial Bank Swallow (S. Emlen and Demong 1975).

Breeding colonies of certain passerine birds nesting in isolated trees may sometimes be limited by lack of available trees. Maclean (1973:184) in a study of the Sociable Weaver in southwestern Africa observed that where suitable trees were scarce, almost all trees were occupied by nesting colonies, but where trees were numerous, only a few were occupied.

More complete utilization of limited nest sites by individuals tolerant of each other's proximity would permit a higher local population density and might confer various benefits of gregarious nesting, leading to better survival and reproduction of individuals. Behavior permitting increased gregariousness would therefore gradually spread throughout the population to the extent allowed by counterbalancing forces, such as the increased predation that might be invited by aggregation.

4. *Social stimulation of breeding condition.* Since the male and the female of all birds are behaviorally and probably hormonally sensitive to each other, there is the possibility that birds could also become sensitive to group stimulation facilitating the onset of breeding condition, and at the same time favor any other advantages of gregarious nesting balanced against the disadvantages. Another implication of social stim-

ulation is that birds coming into breeding condition would be more attracted to large groups than to small ones.

Many years ago, Darling (1938) put forth the theory that "the social group and its magnitude in birds which are gregarious at the breeding season, are themselves exteroceptive factors in the development and synchronization of reproductive condition in the members of individual pairs of birds throughout the flock." Darling documented his thesis by comparing breeding success in small and large colonies of Herring Gulls (*Larus argentatus*) and Lesser Black-backed Gulls (*L. fuscus*) on Priest Island in Scotland, but his evidence was not sufficient to verify his theory.

In later years, it was found that very small colonies of gulls, like certain other sea birds, may have a relatively large proportion of young birds that breed later in the year and compared poorly with older birds (Fisher 1963). However, Coulson and White (1960) found that, for the Kittiwake (*Rissa tridactyla*), territorial displays occurred more frequently and breeding began sooner in the more crowded parts of the colony and that the age-composition of the colonies did not account for differences in time of breeding. More recently, Parsons (1976), on the Isle of May in Scotland, observed that Herring Gulls nesting at the most common density, started laying earlier in the season than those nesting at lower or higher densities. Gulls nesting at the most common density also tended to have the highest hatching and fledging success when age differences were minimized. It seems that the phenomenon of social stimulation of breeding in gulls is real, but there is apparently an optimal degree of crowding. In the North Atlantic Gannet (*Sula b. bassana*), the mean egg-laying date is earlier, and egg laying is more synchronized in large colonies than in small ones, independently of age differences (J. Nelson 1978).

There is good experimental evidence for social stimulation of breeding from studies of various species of birds in aviaries. The presence of the mate and the nest helps stimulate ovulation in House Sparrows (Polikarpova 1940), Ring Doves (Lehrman 1965), Canaries (Warren and Hinde 1961), and Village Weavers (Victoria 1969). Vocalizations of the male are known to help stimulate ovarian development in the Budgerigar (Brockway 1965), Canaries (Mulligan et al. 1968) and Ring Doves (Lehrman and Friedman 1969).

Sounds from a Ring Dove colony piped in to pairs of Ring Doves isolated in separate rooms accelerated their time of ovulation, compared with controls not exposed to colony sounds (Lehrman and Friedman 1969). In experiments with Ring Doves, the degree of development of the female reproductive tract, which indicates the level of gonadotrophin secretion, was correlated with length of daily exposure to a courting male. Gonadotrophic secretion was affected by both the amount of stimulation per day and the number of days the stimulation was continued. A female Ring Dove exposed to two courting males would ovulate sooner than a female exposed to just one courting male (Barfield 1971).

We have attempted to analyze social stimulation of breeding in the Village Weaver (*Ploceus cucullatus*). In this polygynous species, the females will not lay eggs in the absence of either males or nests, both being necessary (Victoria 1969). Village Weavers breed in colonies with many nests in one tree. The males weave nests to which they attempt to attract unmated females by special displays and vocalizations. In Senegal, we observed that 9 small colonies, each with fewer than 10 adult males and with fewer than 20 nests, attracted a much smaller proportion of females than did 8 larger colonies (χ^2 test, P = .018). The small colonies failed to grow as the season progressed, while at their peak the large colonies contained from 60 to 270 nests (N. Collias and Collias 1969a). All the large colonies at or near their peak of growth consisted of about two-thirds resident females.

Visiting females strongly stimulate the building activities of male Village Weavers, who show a renewed burst of nest-building activity right after a group of unmated females has visited the colony. In aviary experiments, in which we systematically varied colony size but kept the sex ratio equal, more nests were built per male in moderate-size colonies, than in very small ones, both early and late in the breeding season, so extending the effective breeding period (N. Collias, Victoria, and Shallenberger 1971).

That the effect on nest building by the males was primarily due to the numbers of females, we showed by systematically varying the sex ratio. When the number of females in each colony was increased four times, while keeping the same individual males in the aviary, the average rate at which these males built nests doubled (fig. 14.3). The frequency with which they gave the nest-invitation display to females tripled. At the same time, the males built on the average only half as many nests per female, reflecting a reduction in competition between males for mates when there was an abundance of females (N. Collias, Brandman, et al., 1971).

In moderate-size colonies, compared with very small colonies, there is more intense overall stimulation to the females, more nests in the colony, and more vocalization and display by the males, and as a result the females lay eggs more frequently. Social facilitation has its greatest effect on egg laying at the onset and near the close of the breeding season. The start of egg laying depends upon the start of nest building by the males, and a moderate-size experimental colony begins breeding

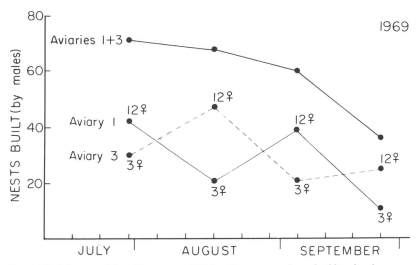

Fig. 14.3. Influence of few (3) or many (12) females on rate of nest building by the same seven male Village Weavers (*Ploceus cucullatus*) in each of two outdoor aviaries. Nine females were transferred from one aviary to the other aviary every three weeks to provide site control. (N. E. Collias, M. Brandman, J. K. Victoria, L. F. Kiff, and C. E. Rischer, *Ecology* 1971, 52:832)

earlier than a small one. Crowding the birds near the end of the breeding season results in a definite resurgence of nest building and egg laying (Victoria and Collias 1973).

Female Village Weavers often show a remarkable degree of synchrony in their egg laying. Of ten laying females in the experiment on late-season crowding, nine laid their first egg within the same two days. At least part of the synchronized egg laying traces to synchrony in starting new nests by males competing for the attention of the females. In nature, in the Lake Chad basin area, which is optimal habitat for the Village Weaver, Da Camara-Smeets (1982) found that young weavers, as a result of the synchronizing of broods, fledged together in successive waves. Such synchrony may aid their survival, perhaps by better guidance to good food sources.

SOME COMPETITIVE ASPECTS OF CROWDING NESTS

Although there are benefits to nesting in groups, there are also competitive aspects. The tendency of birds to aggregate is often balanced against intragroup aggressive behavior (N. Collias 1944, J. Emlen 1952a), as well as other possible disadvantages such as intragroup predation on the young, egg parasitism, and cuckoldry. Here, we consider only competition for nest sites, nests, and nest materials.

Territory among vertebrate animals probably evolved originally from defense of a nest site (N. Collias 1951) and is still often synonymous with such defense. Territory may have several functions, but, as in the Song Sparrow where a male is virtually undefeatable on his own territory, one of its main functions is protection against breakup of nesting by aggressive birds of the same species (Nice 1943:169). Territorial birds generally make the strongest defense of their territories when an intruder invades the nest site itself. Immediately after a territorial or border conflict between two male Village Weavers, each male will go to one of his nests and sing, the nests representing the center of each male's territory.

Competition for nest sites, nests, and nest materials is frequent among colonial birds and has been described for a wide variety of species. A good nest site is generally essential to breeding success. Among Canada Geese (*Branta canadensis*), the competition for nest sites early in the spring may be severe, and good sites may be occupied by a succession of pairs, as temporary occupants are evicted by more dominant pairs (chap. 6). Exclusion of subordinate pairs or individuals from territorial establishment, or breakup of their nesting by dominant geese in crowded situations, helps limit population density (N. Collias and Jahn 1959). In contrast to the Canada Goose, the Wood Duck (*Aix sponsa*), which normally nests in tree holes, is not territorial. The population size can be increased by supplying more nest sites in the form of nest boxes, but several pairs may try to nest in the same nest box; nesting success was inversely proportional to the number of pairs occupying a nest box (Jones and Leopold 1967).

The Waved Albatross (*Diomedea irrorata*) breeds only on Hood Island in the Galapagos and lays its one egg on the bare ground. It has no fixed nest site, even within a season (Harris 1973). An incubating bird may move its egg up to forty meters within a few days, shuffling along with the egg held loosely between the brood patch and the ground. Such behavior is commonest in crowded colonies having only a few meters between incubating birds, and may result in heavy egg losses as the birds keep trying to move away from certain neighbors.

The nest of the Black Swan (*Cygnus atratus*) of Australia is a mound of various plant materials, which the incubating bird has accumulated about itself. On islands where the swans breed in colonies, nests are often destroyed as the birds pilfer one another's nest material (H. Frith 1979:96). In Uganda, where the Marabou Stork (*Leptoptilos crumeniferus*) nests in colonies with 40 to 120 pairs in one big tree, unattended nests are quickly robbed by other Marabous. Nests that failed and were abandoned during the nesting season disappeared within a few days as neighboring birds removed the twigs, adding them to their own nests. Nevertheless, average breeding success (young per nest) in Marabou colonies increased with number and crowding of nests in a tree up to about 60 nests per tree, after which it declined. It appears that the advantages of nesting together outweigh the disadvantages to a point (Pomeroy 1978).

Stealing of nest materials is also very common in colonies of birds that weave many nests in the same tree, such as the Village Weaver in Africa (N. Collias and Collias 1959b, 1970), the Metallic Starling (*Aplonis metallica*) in northern Australia (I. Rowley 1976), and oropendolas in Central America (Skutch 1976). Skutch (1976:112) suggests that one beneficial effect of such thievery may be to discourage slovenly building, since it is not easy for a thief to detach a strand that has been properly woven into the fabric; it is the loose dangling pieces that invite pilferage.

CONTIGUOUS NESTS AND MULTICHAMBERED NESTS

Contiguous Nests

All the factors that favor colonial breeding also favor the massing of nests in physical contact with each other. The crowding of nests enables more complete utilization of safe nesting places. Birds that nest in colonies with many nests in physical contact with each other include several passerine species: the Cliff Swallow (*Hirundo pyrrhonota*) of America and the House Martin (*Delichon urbica*) found in Europe; the Little Swift (*Apus affinis*), Grey-capped Social Weaver (*Pseudonigrita arnaudi*), Chestnut Weaver (*Ploceus rubiginosus*) and Wattled Starling (*Creatophora cinerea*), all of Africa; and the Sakalava Weaver (*Ploceus sakalava*) of Madagascar. They all nest in relatively safe places—in cliffs and under the eaves of houses for the swallows and swifts, in thorny trees for the weavers and starlings, in baobab trees for the Sakalava Weaver. In addition, all these species nest in relatively open country and have domed nests, except the House Martin for whose nest a roof is furnished by overhanging eaves of houses. Any special factor, or combination of factors, that enhances security might be sufficient to increase crowding to the point of contiguity of nests that are usually separate. In India, colonies of Baya Weavers (*Ploceus philippinus*) sometimes suspend their nests from telephone wires, where they are safe from snakes and other non-avian predators (T. Davis 1971). Nests in

Fig. 14.4. A colony of Baya Weavers (*Ploceus philippinus*) with nests suspended from telephone wires, India. (Photo: T. A. Davis)

such colonies become very crowded and adjacent nests are interwoven (fig. 14.4).

The most striking examples of nest aggregation among the weaverbirds are found in arid country. Aridity favors persistence of old nests from one year to the next and also favors year-round residence of some species in the same tree. In dry, open country, the number of trees suitable for colony sites is limited. The larger the tree the more nests that can be crowded into it. In acacia trees in East Africa, we found that the percentage of nests of the Grey-capped Social Weaver in physical contact with each other was twice as great in trees over six meters high as in smaller trees (N. Collias and Collias 1977). Most nests occurred singly, but from two to twenty nests fused together were seen (figure 14.5). Similarly, nests of this species are more likely to be in contact with each other if in ant-gall acacias than in other species of acacias of the same size (chap. 9).

The Sakalava Weaver (*Ploceus sakalava*) of Madagascar, a true weaver (Ploceinae) and a seasonal breeder, builds mainly with green materials but also with bits of brown vine stem and other nongreen materials. According to Rand (1936), this species may breed in old, relined nests as well as in new nests; in this respect it differs from other true weavers

Fig. 14.5. Closely massed nests of Grey-capped Social Weavers (*Pseudonigrita arnaudi*) with ten nests in physical contact, Kenya. (N. E. and E. C. Collias, *Auk* 1977)

that have been studied. We observed greater massing of nests by the Sakalava Weaver in the drier parts of its range (N. Collias 1980). In the subdesert country of southwest Madagascar near Tulear, in two colonies in baobab trees, nests were massed together with about 50 contiguous nests in each colony (fig. 14.6). In contrast, in the more moist Ankarafantsika Forest in northwestern Madagascar, the many nests seen in three colonies were generally dispersed; 77 of 145 nests in a silk cotton tree occurred singly, and the rest in groups of only two or three nests each.

The Chestnut Weaver (*Ploceus rubiginosus*), also a seasonal breeder, builds its nests of green flexible materials during the rainy season in arid African savanna. In colonies of the Chestnut Weaver, many neighboring trees may each be occupied by hundreds of nests (fig. 14.7). Protected by a formidable barrier of thorns in an acacia or in a *Balanites agyptiaca* tree, many nests are massed together (N. Collias 1980)(fig. 14.8). In one colony, we counted 95 separate nest entrances in one continuous mass of grasses and grass stems. The Chestnut Weaver has highly synchronized breeding and compresses its breeding into a relatively short period of time (Braine and Braine 1971). The sheer number of birds in species that breed in very large synchronized colonies may exceed the capacity of local predators to consume more than a fraction of the young (Elgood and Ward 1963). This type of defense, however, requires that the species has already evolved a rather large colony size for other reasons.

An abundant food supply is necessary to support a large breeding colony of birds. Grass seeds are far more numerous in savanna than in forest, and insect abundance rises dramatically after the rains begin, when weaverbirds generally breed. The Wattled Starling (*Creatophora cinerea*) of arid African savannas feeds especially on locusts and may breed in huge numbers when there is a locust plague. Both sexes build the domed nests of twigs. A few nests are solitary, but most are combined in masses of two or three nests. The simultaneous timing within a large colony is extraordinary, and more than half the young may be reared within a space of five weeks. The birds may nest in thorn trees (*Acacia karro*) with all nests inside the outer branches, protected by a barrier of thorns (Liversidge 1961).

An important factor acting to hinder the extreme crowding of nests is the territorial reactions of the birds themselves, with their tendency to defend the vicinity of the nest with increasing vigor the more they are crowded. By removing the mud wall between contiguous nests of Cliff Swallows, John T. Emlen (1952b) found that only the nest entrance was used as a center of defense, and he proposed the theory that having

Fig. 14.6. Colony of Sakalava Weavers (*Ploceus sakalava*) with many nests massed together in a baobab tree (*Adansonia foni*), southwestern Madagascar.

Fig. 14.7. Mixed colony in a *Balanites aegyptiaca* tree with nests of Red-billed Buffalo Weavers (*Bubalornis albirostris niger*)—the large masses of twigs in the upper part of the tree—and of Chestnut Weavers (*Ploceus rubiginosus*)—the numerous small oval nests of grass, southeast Kenya. (N. E. Collias 1980)

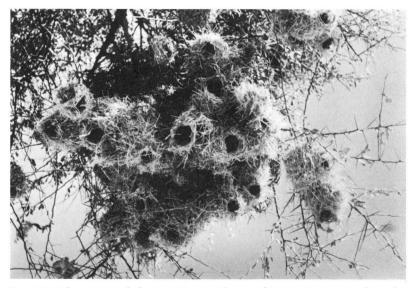

Fig. 14.8. A large group of Chestnut Weaver (*Ploceus rubiginosus*) nests massed together in a very thorny tree (*Balanites*), southeast Kenya. (N. E. Collias 1980)

enclosed nests permits the nests to be placed in physical contact, because the birds are screened from each other's territorial reactions. All of the species building contiguous nests that were discussed above build enclosed nests.

Multichambered or Compound Nests

This type of nest is common among the highly social insects but is rare among birds. There are two groups of birds building multichambered nests, those in which one pair or family builds the nest and those in which more than one family builds the nest. A good example of a species in which one pair or family builds a nest having more than one compartment is the Rufous-fronted Thornbird (*Phacellodomus rufifrons*), an ovenbird (Furnariidae) of South America. The Yellow-throated Scrub Wren (*Sericornis citreogularis*) is an Old World warbler (Sylviidae) of eastern Australia in which the pair sometimes builds more than one chamber in its large nest (H. Frith 1979).

Skutch (1969b) has studied the behavior of the Rufous-fronted Thornbird in Venezuela, a species building one of the most spectacular nests of any New World bird. It is a widely distributed species over the more arid and open parts of South America, foraging on the ground in pairs or in family groups of three to eight birds, feeding mainly on insects. The nest is built on an exposed branch of an isolated tree, often hangs prominently near human dwellings, and is occupied throughout the year. The pair builds its bulky nest of interlaced twigs, sometimes assisted by their grown offspring of the preceding nesting season. The twigs used in the nest are often two or three times as long as the bird which is six inches or fifteen centimeters long. The birds start the nest as a small platform and build it up into a bowl, which is then roofed over. To begin with, two enclosed chambers are built, one above the other; later more chambers are added, always at the top, until the nest may contain eight or nine in a vertical series and become seven feet (ca. 2 m) high (fig. 14.9). Each compartment has its own separate opening to the outside.

None of more than twenty nests of the Rufous-fronted Thornbird that Skutch investigated were occupied by more than one breeding pair. Sometimes the pair had full-grown, nonbreeding offspring, which slept in one chamber, while the parents attended eggs or nestlings in another. The eggs were always laid in the lowest, oldest chamber where the parents spend the night. Skutch (1969b:22) suggests that the Rufous-fronted Thornbirds start their nests with two chambers as a safeguard against predators, such as snakes or small mammals, giving time for the parents to escape. The nest is lined with soft, flexible materials, most

Fig. 14.9. A very long nest (over 2 m) of a family of Rufous-fronted Thornbirds (*Phacellodomus rufifrons*), Venezuela. This inaccessible nest was attached to a hanging woody vine. Built of twigs, it appeared to consist of 8 or 9 chambers, one above the other. (Skutch, *Wilson Bull.* 1969)

of which are brought while incubation is in progress. The parents lead fledged young back to the nest to sleep; sometimes they are joined by older siblings, which, however, the parents try to exclude from the nest when the parents are incubating a second brood.

Multichambered nests occupied by more than one pair or family per chamber range from normally separate nests to a massing together of nests. Where some communal feature exists, such as a common roof, we can refer to the nest mass as a compound nest. The best-known avian examples of compound nests are those of the Palmchat (*Dulus dominica*) of Hispaniola, the Monk Parakeet (*Myiopsitta monachus*) of southern South America, the Buffalo Weaver (*Bubalornis albirostris*) of sub-Saharan Africa, and the Sociable Weaver (*Philetairus socius*) of southwestern Africa. These nests are all built communally. There is relatively little information available about the breeding and nest-building behavior of the first three species at present; they all build large nests of twigs placed in trees. The Sociable Weaver's huge nest is built of straws, dry grasses, and light twigs, and is usually placed in a large acacia. Details of its construction were described in chapter 10.

The taxonomic relations of the Palmchat, sole species of its family (Dulidae), are uncertain. Its nest is usually placed in Royal Palm trees and is inhabited by several pairs and usually eight to sixteen birds. The nest consists of several separate compartments opening separately at the sides, and lined sparsely with fine grasses and shredded bark. Work on the domicile is carried on to some extent in common. Large nests are found everywhere throughout the lowlands of Hispaniola; in the mountains the Palmchat often builds a small structure, usually occupied by two pairs. Wetmore and Swales (1931), who described the nest, considered the stick nest of the Palmchat to be a safeguard against owls and other similar predators.

The nest of the Monk Parakeet has been described by Gibson (1880) and by Forshaw and Cooper (1978). This species is unique among parrots, most of which nest in holes, in that its nest consists of a large mass of dry twigs placed in the branches of a tree. Monk Parakeets prefer the thorny twigs of the Tala tree (*Celtis tala*) for constructing the nest. Nests with a single chamber, occupied by only one pair, are not uncommon. Communal nests are probably built over a number of years, as other pairs build their nests alongside of or on top of existing nests. Nest masses with up to twenty compartments have been recorded, and large nests have been estimated to weigh as much as two hundred kilograms. Some old forest trees have seven or eight of these huge masses.

Each pair of Monk Parakeets has its own separate compartment (ca. 18 cm in diameter) and entrance tunnel (35–40 cm long) opening obliquely downward at the lower side or underneath the nest. The parakeets use the nest for roosting all year. With approach of the breeding season they add to it and repair damaged sections. The pair first builds the floor, then the sides and roof of the compartment (C. Harrison 1973). The five to eight eggs are laid on a bed of twigs. The side entrances into the nest compartments of the Monk Parakeet are protected by an overhanging eave, a safeguard against an opossum (*Didelphys aurita*), which is frequently found in the upper chambers but cannot reach the lower ones (Gibson 1880).

Humphrey and Peterson (1978), in northeastern Argentina, observed Monk Parakeets building on telephone poles in association with nests of an ovenbird (Furnariidae), the Firewood Gatherer (*Anumbius annumbi*), whose nest evidently provided the stimulus for construction by the parakeets of their own nest. G. K. Cherrie (in Naumberg 1930:19, 128) observed in the Matto Grosso region of Brazil that Monk Parakeets often built in trees under the large, stick platform-nests of Jabiru Storks (*Jabiru mycteria*), and "infrequently the construction of new brood-chambers begins at the top, the structure being built downward, from the bottom of a Jabiru Stork's nest which forms a roof over all." It appears that a large mass of twigs in a tree or telephone pole may stimulate a pair of Monk Parakeets to add their nest to the mass, the normal stimulus being another nest of their own species.

The large, bristly nest of the Buffalo Weaver is usually built of thorny twigs and placed in a large acacia, baobab, or *Balanites* (fig. 14.7) tree. The thorny outer shell of the nest mass is built by the polygynous male and may contain several compartments, which are lined largely by the females. Each female has her own separate compartment opening to the side of the nest mass. Polygyny in this species has been observed in western (Crook 1958), eastern (N. Collias and Collias 1964), and southern (Kemp and Kemp 1974) Africa. There may be many nest masses in one tree. Of the West African race, Chapin (1954:289) wrote "It builds large clusters of nests in trees, three to eight combined in one great mass of thorn twigs, which may be six to eight feet in length and three to five feet thick. The individual nests are lined with grass, rootlets and feathers." The nests we saw in Kenya were similar, but the lining of individual nest compartments also included acacia leaflets, and formed semi-domed bowls inside the thorny shell of the nest mass. The whole mass has a roof almost thirty centimeters thick and a floor usually eight to ten centimeters thick under the brood chambers. Presumably, the heavy, thorny shell provides protection from monkeys, baboons, wild cats, and other mammals, as well as bird predators—although probably not from snakes.

The male Buffalo Weaver starts a new, thorny twig shell next to the old nest mass, and the new shell gradually merges into the mass as the male adds more and more twigs. The Kemps (1974) described one nest mass in South Africa consisting of thirteen chambers. The dominant male owned eight of these, on the north and west side of the mass, another male owned three chambers on the east side of the mass while two chambers of the south side did not have clear owners. Four females accepted chambers in this mass, three in the section of the chief male and one in the section of the second male. Excess and subordinate males may build satellite nests on other branches of the same tree or in trees nearby.

The nest of the White-headed Buffalo Weaver (*Dinemellia dinemelli*) shows how the more complex nest of *Bubalornis* with its complete thorny shell might have evolved (N. Collias and Collias 1964). This east African species goes about in parties of four to twelve that build domed nests of dry grass stems, the nests saddled across branches of thorn trees—often two to four grassy nests side by side in contact with each other; over all of these the birds place a loose roof of thorny twigs. *Dinemellia* also lays thorny twigs for some one to five meters along boughs leading to its nest, and these thorny pathways probably help protect the nests from some climbing mammals and from some raptorial birds.

The Sociable Weaver (*Philetairus socius*) builds a huge, apartment-style nest, illustrated in figures 2.27 and 2.28 of chapter 2 and figure 10.7 of chapter 10 and described in some detail in chapter 10. The nest mass—built of straws, dry grassheads and fine twigs—requires strong, heavy support and is generally placed on heavy boughs of the Camel-thorn (*Acacia giraffae*). There may be from one to three or more of these nest masses in a single tree. One nest mass may be over a meter thick and several meters long and contain up to a hundred or more individual chambers opening on the underside of the mass. Maclean (1973) found an average of thirteen to sixteen nest chambers in each of twenty-two nest masses distributed among fourteen trees in the Kalahari Desert. The extremes very greatly.

The very thick roof of the Sociable Weaver's nest probably helps reduce or eliminate predation on nestlings by hawks and many mammals. The fact that the nest chambers of the Sociable Weaver all open on the underside of the nest mass means they are relatively inaccessible to many predators. The Grey-capped Social Weaver builds domed nests with the entrances opening below. This species, probably the closest relative of the Sociable Weaver, often builds a second nest for a brood nest, directly beneath and fused to an older nest above it, which then functions as a thick roof for the brood nest. This behavior gives us a hint as to how the communal roof of the Sociable Weaver might have arisen in evolution.

Snakes, particularly the Cape Cobra (*Naja nivea*), are the worst enemies of the Sociable Weaver. The cobra approaches from the periphery of the nest and eats its fill of the nestlings. Maclean (1973) suggested that in large nest masses the central nests might therefore be safer. There would seem to be a selection pressure here for large size of nest mass and for synchronized nesting. Increase in size of nest mass also gives increased control over variations in environmental temperature (chap. 7).

Many factors facilitate or oppose gregarious breeding and massing together of nests among birds. The precise course taken by evolution in each case will depend on the particular combination of factors involved. Temperature control may be relatively important in places with a cold winter and hot summer, as in the Kalahari Desert. We need to look to other factors to help explain the evolution of the multichambered nest of the Palmchat in Hispaniola, a tropical Caribbean island with a mild and relatively uniform climate. The vulnerability of the top chambers in the nests of the Monk Parakeet, and probably of the Rufous-fronted Thornbird, suggests the importance of a thick communal roof for protection against predators. All species of birds known to build compound or multichambered communal nests use many twigs in their nests, particularly in the roof, and such twigs probably function as a deterrent against bird and mammal predators. The fact that entrances to nest chambers open to one side or to the underside of nests should be a deterrent to many predators. It appears that enhanced security from predation is a key feature encouraging close aggregation of the birds and leading to evolution of multichambered nests having a communal roof.

Summary

Gregarious or colony nesting can be divided into two overlapping categories: communal building of one nest by more than two birds, and building of many nests near to each other. Communal nest building is one aspect of helping at the nest by auxiliary birds. Helpers at the nest, who do not breed themselves but who assist their parents or some other pair of birds, are of common occurrence in a wide variety of species of birds throughout the tropical areas of the world. Various theories of helping and deferment of breeding by helpers include benefits to the parents or breeders, benefits to the helpers and their siblings, and benefits at the population level. There is evidence for benefits at all of these levels of natural selection.

The degree of involvement by helpers in nest construction varies greatly in different species of communal breeders: in some species, helpers do not help their parents build the nest; in many species, the adult female or the adult pair does most of the nest building, and the helpers merely reduce their labor; in species of communal breeders having large or complex nests that take a long time to build, helpers are particularly important and active.

Building of many nests near to each other is characteristic of birds whose nesting and feeding grounds are spatially well-separated. Birds whose breeding area is the same as their feeding area are often solitary nesters. Crowding many nests close together is of very general occurrence among marine birds, but is relatively rare among passerine birds. Such colony nesting, as a rule, requires safe nesting sites, such as islands, cliffs, tall and isolated trees, very thorny trees, caves, buildings, or emergent vegetation over water.

The advantages of building many nests close together include: (1) guidance to good food sources by experienced birds, (2) cooperative defense against enemies, (3) more complete utilization of limited nesting sites, and (4) social stimulation of breeding.

Social stimulation facilitates attraction of mates and synchronization of fledging times, reducing the overall period of vulnerability to predators. Social stimulation may facilitate the onset of breeding and/or prolong breeding thereby lengthening the effective breeding period in some colony nesters. There is evidence that an optimal degree of nest crowding in birds is related to breeding success, and this optimum can be expected to vary with the species.

There are benefits to nesting in groups, but there are also competitive aspects. Crowding results in increased competition for nest sites, for nests, and for nest materials, and many birds losing out in this competition may fail to breed. From a population viewpoint, such competition helps regulate the population density to the capacity of the habitat.

All the factors that favor some degree of crowding of nests also favor evolution of physical contact between nests. Under conditions conferring a relatively high degree of security from predation, and under arid conditions preserving nests from rapid deterioration, many nests may be massed together. Birds with domed nests are more likely than birds with open nests to evolve contiguity of nests, because enclosed nests help screen the birds from each other's territorial defense reactions. If a nest mass develops some communal feature enhancing protection for all, such as a thick roof of strong twigs, then a compound or apartment-style nest may evolve.

Bird Families of the World and Their Nest Types

THE following classification is taken from Van Tyne and Berger (1976), with slight modifications from Peters' *Check-list of Birds of the World* (1931–1979) and from a few other authors. Geographic distributions of families are based on the maps by Fisher and Peterson (1964). Birds are here grouped into 28 orders and 166 families. A recent count by Bock and Farrand (1980) gives 9,021 species of living and recently extinct species of birds in the world.

For those bird families that occur in North America, the orders and families adopted here largely agree with those given in the *Check-list of North American Birds*, 6th edition (American Ornithologists' Union 1983), differing mainly in that the A.O.U. check-list reduces some of the passerine families to subfamily rank. However, since most of the literature has used the old family names, we have retained these names. We have used the A.O.U. updated names for species of North American birds mentioned in the text.

The 28 orders of birds of the world include 5 orders of primitive and flightless running birds and their allies, the tinamous, 10 orders of water birds, marsh birds, and shore birds, and 13 orders of land birds. The land birds include the large order Passeriformes, small perching birds with three-fifths of all the species of birds and 66 of the families listed here.

The passerine order ends here with the family Ploceidae, or weaverbirds. Chapin (1954) included seven subfamilies in the Ploceidae: Bubalornithinae (buffalo weavers), Plocepasserinae (sparrow weavers), Passerinae (Old World sparrows), Sporopipinae (scaly-feathered finches), Ploceinae (true weavers), Estrildinae (waxbills and allies), and Viduinae (parasitic widowbirds and indigobirds). However, six of these subfamilies are nonweaving finches, and only birds in one subfamily, the Ploceinae, truly weave their nests. In line with current usage among many taxonomists, the Estrildinae is listed here as a separate family, the Estrildidae; the Viduinae are included. The Plocepasserinae, Passerinae, and Sporopipinae are sometimes united into one family, the Passeridae. We feel that the Bubalornithinae resemble the Plocepasserinae in their nest building and other behavior much more than they do the Ploceinae.

These differences in classification are in part a matter of terminology. According to recent studies with DNA hybridization, Chapin's subfamilies of Ploceidae are all closely related to each other, as well as to fringillid finches and to the sunbirds (Sibley and Ahlquist 1980).

For each family of birds we have also tabulated the main type of nest it builds (hole-nest, open nest, or domed nest), and where we have been able to find the information, whether the male or the female, or both, builds the nest. This information was taken from various general references of bird families of the world, from references of birds of important geographic areas, and, in some cases, from special references of particular groups. General references of bird families include Gilliard (1958), Austin and Singer (1971), Van Tyne and Berger (1976), and C. Harrison (1978). Reference is also made to books that include much information on nests of birds of North America (Bent 1919–1968, Headstrom 1951, H. Harrison 1975, 1979, Palmer 1962), Central and South America (Skutch 1954, 1960, 1969a, 1981, 1983, Wetmore 1926, 1965, 1968, 1972, Smithe 1966, Haverschmidt 1968, Johnson and Goodall 1965, 1967), Europe (Cramp 1977–1983, C. Harrison 1975), Africa (Mackworth-Praed and Grant 1957, 1962, 1963, 1970, 1973, McLachlan and Liversidge 1978), India and Southeast Asia (Ali and Ripley 1968–1974, Smythies 1953, Medway and Wells 1976), Australia (Cayley 1959, H. Frith 1979, Beruldsen 1980), Antarctica (Watson 1975), New Zealand (Oliver 1955, Falla et al. 1967), New Guinea (Rand and Gilliard 1968), Borneo (Smythies and Cranbrook 1981), Ceylon (G. Henry 1971), Madagascar (Rand 1936; Milon, Petter and Randrianosolo 1973), and the Hawaiian Islands (Berger 1972). Some special references are cited where relevant in the tabular part of the appendix. A bird with a cup-shaped nest built in a hole is classified with the hole-nesters. A cup-nest fastened to a leaf forming a roof overhead is classified as a domed nest.

The open nest is the most common type of nest among birds, being found in all orders, except in such typical hole-nesters as the kiwis, parrots, trogons, coraciiform, and piciform birds. Hole-nesting is of scattered occurrence in other orders, occurring in some penguins, petrels and shearwaters, some ducks, New World vultures, some small falcons, some owls, crabplovers, some alcids, owlet-frogmouths, and in over half the passerine families. The open nest occurs in about two-thirds of the families.

Domed nests are rare (6%) in nonpasserine families, but are of common occurrence in passerine families, being found in about half (52%) of the families, especially among tropical passerines. Among nonpasserines, domed nests are built by the Hammerhead Stork (*Scopus umbretta*), some rails (Rallidae), some hemipodes (Turnicidae), Monk Parakeet (*Myiopsitta monachus*), some cuckoos (Cuculidae), and some swifts (*Apodidae*). Among the passerine birds, domed nests are more frequent in families of suboscines (62%) than in the oscines, or Suborder Passeres (49%). About 48 percent of passerine families build more than one type of nest, compared with only 16 percent among nonpasserine families, suggesting more active evolution of nest-building behavior at subfamily and generic levels.

Only about four percent of the families of birds (6 families in 4 orders) contain brood parasites that build no nest of their own. Only eight (5%) of the families of birds contain nonparasitic species that build no nest.

Building by both the sexes is probably the primitive pattern in birds. Cooperation between the sexes in nest building is the rule in birds and eighty-three percent of the families contain species in which both sexes help build the nest. In only six percent of the families are there species known in which only the male builds the nest, as among the rheas and some families with reversed sex dimorphism: tinamous, jacanas, phalaropes, and painted snipe. Only the male incubates in these families. Building of the nest by the female alone is relatively common, occurring in about twenty-eight percent of the bird families. Building by the female alone is much more common in families of passerine birds (48%) than in families of nonpasserine birds (14%).

Abbreviations: H = hole-nest, O = open nest, D = domed nest, N = no nest, P = brood parasites. Lower case letters mean rare or unusual in the family. ♂ = male builds nest, ♀ = female builds nest, ♂♀ = both sexes build

STRUTHIONIFORMES
    Struthionidae—Ostriches. Africa. . . . . .O, ♂♀
RHEIFORMES
    Rheidae—Rheas. Southern part of South America. O, ♂
CASUARIIFORMES
    Casuariidae—Cassowaries. North Australia, New
      Guinea. . . . . .O, ♂
    Dromaiidae—Emus. Australia. . . . . .O
APTERYGIFORMES
    Apterygidae—Kiwis. New Zealand. . . . . .H, ♂♀
TINAMIFORMES
    Tinamidae—Tinamous. Central and South America. O, h, ♂
PODICIPEDIFORMES
    Podicipedidae—Grebes. Worldwide. . . . . .O, ♂♀
GAVIIFORMES
    Gaviidae—Loons. Holarctic. . . . . .O, ♂♀
PROCELLARIIFORMES
    Diomedeidae—Albatrosses. North Pacific and
      southern oceans. . . . . .O, ♂♀
    Procellariidae—Shearwaters and petrels. All oceans. H, O, ♂♀
    Hydrobatidae—Storm-petrels. All oceans. . . . . .H, ♂♀, ♂
    Pelecanoididae—Diving-petrels. Southern oceans. . .H, ♂♀
SPHENISCIFORMES
    Spheniscidae—Penguins. (Emperor Penguin
      [*Aptenodytes forsteri*] builds no nest.) Southern
      oceans, Antarctica. . . . . .H, O, n, ♂♀
PELECANIFORMES
    Phaethontidae—Tropicbirds. Pantropical seas. . . . . .O, ♂♀
    Sulidae—Boobies and gannets. Tropical and
      temperate seas, except North Pacific. . . . . .O, ♂♀
    Phalacrocoracidae—Cormorants. Worldwide. . . . . . .O, ♂♀
    Anhingidae—Anhingas. Pantropical. . . . . .O, ♂♀
    Pelecanidae—Pelicans. Worldwide. . . . . .O, ♂♀
    Fregatidae—Frigatebirds. Pantropical seas. . . . . . . .O, ♂♀
CICONIIFORMES
    Ardeidae—Herons and bitterns. Worldwide. . . . . . .O, ♂♀
    Balaenicipitidae—Whale-billed Storks. Central
      Africa. . . . . .O, ♂♀

Scopidae—Hammerhead Stork. Africa, Madagascar. D, ♂♀
Ciconiidae—Storks. Pantropical, a few in temperate
zones. . . . . :. . . . . .O, ♂♀
Threskiornithidae—Ibises and spoonbills.
Pantropical, few in temperate zones. . . . . .O, ♂♀

PHOENICOPTERIFORMES
Phoenicopteridae—Flamingoes. Eurasia, Africa,
North and South America. . . . . .O, ♂♀

ANSERIFORMES
Anhimidae—Screamers. South America. . . . . .O, ♂♀
Anatidae—Ducks, geese, and swans. (Black-headed
Duck [*Heteronetta atricapilla*] is parasitic.)
Worldwide. . . . . .H, O, p, ♀, ♂♀

FALCONIFORMES
Cathartidae—American vultures. New World. . . . . .H, N
Sagittariidae—Secretarybird. Africa. . . . . .O, ♂♀
Accipitridae—Hawks, kites, eagles, Old World
vultures. Worldwide. . . . . .O, ♂♀
Pandionidae—Osprey. Worldwide except South
America. . . . . .O, ♂♀
Falconidae—Falcons. (Often use other birds' nests.)
Worldwide. . . . . .N, H, O

GALLIFORMES
Megapodiidae—Megapodes (H. Frith 1979).
Australia and New Guinea to Borneo and
Philippines. . . . . .Mound-nest, h, ♂♀
Cracidae—Curassows and guans. Neotropical. . . . . . .O, ♂♀
Phasianidae—Pheasants, junglefowl, and quail.
Nearly worldwide. . . . . .O, ♀
Tetraonidae—Grouse. North America, Eurasia. . . . .O, ♀
Numididae—Guineafowl. Africa. . . . . .O, ♀
Meleagrididae—Turkeys. North and Central
America. . . . . .O, ♀
Opisthocomidae—Hoatzin. (Position uncertain;
Sibley and Ahlquist [1973] put Hoatzin in
Cuculiformes.) Amazon basin. . . . . .O, ♂♀

GRUIFORMES
Turnicidae—Hemipodes or buttonquail. Warm parts
of Old World. . . . . .O, D, ♂♀
Pedionomidae—Collared-Hemipode or Plains
Wanderer. Australia. . . . . .O
Gruidae—Cranes. Worldwide, except South
America. . . . . .O, ♂♀
Aramidae—Limpkins. Neotropical. . . . . .O, ♂♀
Rallidae—Rails, gallinules, and coots. Worldwide. . .O, D, ♂♀, ♀

Psophiidae—Trumpeters. South America (Amazon basin)......................................O, H

Heliornithidae—Finfoots. Neotropical, Africa, Southeast Asia. ....O, ♂♀

Eurypygidae—Sunbittern. Neotropical (Skutch 1947). ....O, ♂♀

Rhynochetidae—Kagu. New Caledonia. ....O, ♂♀

Cariamidae—Cariamas South America. (Naumberg 1930; D. Rimlinger, pers. commun.). ....O, ♂♀

Otididae—Bustards. Old World continents........O, ♀

Mesoenatidae—Mesites. Madagascar.............O

CHARADRIIFORMES

Jacanidae—Jacanas. Pantropical. ....O, ♂

Rostratulidae—Painted-snipe. South America, Africa, Asia, Australia.......................O, ♂

Haematopodidae—Oystercatchers. Nearly worldwide (coastal)..................................O, ♂♀

Scolopacidae—Sandpipers, snipe, and allies. (*Tringa* species may use old nests in trees.) Worldwide. ..O, ♂♀, ♀

Phalaropodidae—Phalaropes. Holarctic breeders.....O, ♂

Recurvirostridae—Avocets and stilts. Worldwide....O, ♂♀

Charadriidae—Plovers. Worldwide. ....O, ♂♀

Dromadidae—Crabplover. Indian Ocean..........H, ♂♀

Burhinidae—Thick-knees. Worldwide, except North America..................................O, ♂♀

Glareolidae—Pratincoles and coursers. Old World...O, ♂♀

Thinocoridae—Seedsnipe. Western South America (Maclean 1969)...........................O, ♂♀

Chionididae—Sheathbill. Subantarctic............H

Stercorariidae—Skuas. All oceans; breed in Arctic and Antarctic. ....O, ♂♀

Laridae—Gulls and terns. (White Tern [*Gygis alba*] has no nest.) Worldwide.....................O, n, ♂♀, ♀

Rynchopidae—Skimmers. Americas, Africa, southern Asia. ....O

Alcidae—Auks and allies. Northern oceans. ....H, O, N, ♂♀

Pteroclidae—Sandgrouse. (Maclean [1967] removed sandgrouse from Columbiformes.) Africa and Eurasia...................................O, ♂ ♀

COLUMBIFORMES

Columbidae—Pigeons and doves Worldwide. ......O, ♂♀

PSITTACIFORMES

Psittacidae—Parrots. (Generally hole-nesters; Monk Parakeet [*Myiopsitta monachus*] builds communal roofed nest.) Pantropical, few in temperate zone. H, d, ♂♀

CUCULIFORMES
   Cuculidae—Cuckoos, anis, and coucals. (Coucals
      build domed nests.) Worldwide. . . . . O, d, P, ♂ ♀
   Musophagidae—Turacos and allies. Africa. . . . . O, ♂ ♀
STRIGIFORMES
   Tytonidae—Barn owls. Worldwide, except the
      Soviet Union. . . . . N
   Strigidae—Typical owls. (Owls often use other
      birds' nests. Burrowing owls may dig their own
      burrow [Thomsen 1971].) Worldwide. . . . . H, O, N, ♂ ♀
CAPRIMULGIFORMES
   Steatornithidae—Oilbird. Northern South America. O
   Podargidae—Frogmouths. Southern Asia, Australia,
      New Guinea. . . . . O, ♂ ♀
   Nyctibiidae—Potoos. American tropics. . . . . N
   Aegothelidae—Owlet-frogmouths. Australia, New
      Guinea. . . . . H
   Caprimulgidae—Nightjars. Worldwide. . . . . N
APODIFORMES
   Apodidae—Swifts and swiftlets. Worldwide. . . . . . . H, O, D, ♂ ♀
   Hemiprocnidae—Crested-swifts. Southern Asia to
      Solomon Islands. . . . . O, ♂ ♀
   Trochilidae—Hummingbirds. New World. . . . . O, ♀
COLIIFORMES
   Coliidae—Colies, or Mousebirds. Africa (Decoux
      1978). . . . . O, ♂ ♀
TROGONIFORMES
   Trogonidae—Trogons. Pantropical, except New
      Guinea and Australia. . . . . H, ♂ ♀
CORACIIFORMES
   Alcedinidae—Kingfishers. Worldwide. . . . . H, ♂ ♀
   Todidae—Todies. Greater Antilles. . . . . H, ♂ ♀
   Momotidae—Motmots. Neotropical. . . . . H, ♂ ♀
   Meropidae—Bee-eaters. Warm parts of Old World. H, ♂ ♀
   Coraciidae—Rollers and groundrollers. (Both male
      and female of Long-tailed Groundroller
      [Uratelornis chimaera] dig nest burrow [Appert
      1968].) Warm parts of Old World. . . . . H
   Leptosomatidae—Cuckoo-roller. Madagascar. . . . . . H
   Upupidae—Hoopoe. Warm parts of Eurasia, Africa. H
   Phoeniculidae—Woodhoopoes. Africa. . . . . H
   Bucerotidae—Hornbills. Tropical Africa and Asia to
      Solomon Islands. . . . . H, ♂ ♀, ♀
PICIFORMES
   Bucconidae—Puffbirds. Neotropical. . . . . H, ♂ ♀

Galbulidae—Jacamars. Neotropical.．．．．．．．．．．．．．H, ♂♀

Capitonidae—Barbets. Pantropical, except New
　　Guinea and Australia.．．．．．．．．．．．．．．．．．．．．．．H, ♂♀

Indicatoridae—Honey-guides. (Brood parasites.)
　　Africa, southern Asia.．．．．．．．．．．．．．．．．．．．．．P

Ramphastidae—Toucans. Neotropical. ．．．．．．．．．．．H, ♂♀

Picidae—Woodpeckers. Worldwide, except New
　　Guinea and Australia.．．．．．．．．．．．．．．．．．．．．．．H, ♂♀

Jyngidae—Wrynecks. Eurasia, Africa. ．．．．．．．．．．．H, ♂♀

PASSERIFORMES (The first 13 families are often called "suboscines.")
　Suborder Eurylaimi
　　Eurylaimidae—Broadbills. Africa, India to Borneo.　D, ♂♀
　Suborder Tyranni
　　Furnariidae—Ovenbirds. Central and South
　　　America.．．．．．．．．．．．．．．．．．．．．．．．．．．．．．H, O, D, ♂♀, ♀

　　Dendrocolaptidae—Woodcreepers. Neotropical.．．．．．．H, ♂♀, ♀

　　Formicariidae—Antbirds and antpipits. Neotropical. O, h, d, ♂♀

　　Rhinocryptidae—Tapaculos. Central and South
　　　America.．．．．．．．．．．．．．．．．．．．．．．．．．．．．．H, D, ♂♀

　　Tyrannidae—Tyrant-flycatchers, becards, and allies.
　　　New World. ．．．．．．．．．．．．．．．．．．．．．．．．．．．H, O, D, ♂♀, ♀

　　Cotingidae—Cotingas and cocks-of-the-rock.
　　　Neotropical (Snow 1982).．．．．．．．．．．．．．．．．．O, ♂♀, ♀

　　Pipridae—Manakins. Neotropical.．．．．．．．．．．．．．．O, ♀

　　Phytotomidae—Plantcutters. Temperate South
　　　America.．．．．．．．．．．．．．．．．．．．．．．．．．．．．．O

　　Oxyruncidae—Sharpbill. Neotropical (Brooke et al.
　　　1983).．．．．．．．．．．．．．．．．．．．．．．．．．．．．．．．O, ♀
　Suborder status uncertain
　　Pittidae—Pittas. Old World Tropics.．．．．．．．．．．．．D, ♂♀

　　Acanthisittidae—New Zealand wrens. New Zealand. H, D, ♂♀

　　Philepittidae–Asities. Madagascar.．．．．．．．．．．．．．D
　Suborder Passeres ("Oscines" of many authors)
　　Menuridae—Lyrebirds. Southeastern Australia.．．．．．D, h, ♀

　　Atrichornithidae—Scrub-birds. Australia. ．．．．．．．．D, ♀

　　Alaudidae—larks. Worldwide, but scarcely reach
　　　South America. ．．．．．．．．．．．．．．．．．．．．．．．．O, D, ♀

　　Hirundinidae—Swallows. Worldwide. ．．．．．．．．．．．H, O, D, ♂♀, ♀

　　Campephagidae—Cuckoo-shrikes. Old World
　　　Tropics.．．．．．．．．．．．．．．．．．．．．．．．．．．．．．．O, ♂♀

　　Corvidae—Crows, magpies, and jays. Worldwide. ．．O, h, d, ♂♀

　　Cracticidae—Bellmagpies. New Guinea and
　　　Australia. ．．．．．．．．．．．．．．．．．．．．．．．．．．．．O, ♂♀

Ptilonorhynchidae—Bowerbirds. (Only in catbirds
  [*Ailuroedus*] does male help build the nest
  [Gilliard 1969].) New Guinea and Australia. . . . . .h, O, ♀, ♂♀

Paradisaeidae—Birds of Paradise. New Guinea and
  Australia (Gilliard 1969). .H, O, d, ♀

Grallinidae—Mudnest-builders. Australia, New
  Guinea. . . . . .O, ♂♀

Paridae—Titmice. Eurasia, Africa, North America. . .H, ♀

Aegithalidae—Long-tailed tits. Eurasia, Java, North
  America. . . . . .D, ♂♀

Remizidae—Penduline tits and verdins. Africa,
  Eurasia, North America. . . . . .D, ♂♀

Certhiidae—Creepers. Holarctic, Africa, India. . . . . .H, O, ♂♀

Rhabdornithidae—Philippine creepers. Philippine
  Islands. . . . . .H

Climacteridae—Australian treecreepers. Australia,
  New Guinea. . . . . .H, ♂♀

Sittidae—Nuthatches. Worldwide, except Africa and
  South America. . . . . .H, D, ♂♀

Neosittidae—Australian nuthatch. Australia. . . . . . .O, ♂♀

Dicruridae—Drongos. Old World tropics. . . . . .O, ♂♀

Oriolidae—Orioles. Warm parts of Old World. . . . .O, ♀

Pycnonotidae—Bulbuls. Africa, southern Asia. . . . . .O, ♂♀

Irenidae—Leafbirds. India, Southeast Asia, East
  Indies. . . . . .O, ♂♀, ♀

Troglodytidae—Wrens. New World, Palearctic. . . . .H, D, ♂♀, ♀

Cinclidae—Dippers. New World, Palearctic,
  southeast Asia. . . . . .H, D, ♂♀

Mimidae—Mockingbirds and thrashers. New World.O, ♂♀

Turdidae—Thrushes. Worldwide. . . . . .O, h, d, ♀, ♂♀

Sylviidae—Old World warblers, kinglets, and
  gnatcatchers. Mainly Old World, also the
  Americas. . . . . .H, O, D, ♂♀, ♀

Muscicapidae—Old World flycatchers. Old World,
  east to Hawaiian Islands. . . . . .H, O, d, ♂♀, ♀

Timaliidae—Babblers. Old World; one species in
  New World, the Wrentit (*Chamaea fasciata*). . . . .H, O, D, ♂♀

Prunellidae—Hedge-sparrows. Palearctic. . . . . .O, h, ♀

Motacillidae—Wagtails and pipits. Worldwide. . . . . .H, O, d, ♀

Bombycillidae—Waxwings. Holarctic. . . . . .O, ♂♀

Ptilogonatidae—Silky-flycatchers. North and Central
  America. . . . . .O, ♂♀

Dulidae—Palmchat (Wetmore and Swales 1931).
  (Communal and compound nest.) Hispaniola. . . . .D, ♂♀

Artamidae—Wood-swallows. Oriental, Australasia. H, O, ♂♀
Vangidae—Vanga-shrikes. Madagascar. . . . . .O, ♂♀
Laniidae—Shrikes. North America, Eurasia, Africa. O, ♂♀, ♂, ♀
Prionopidae—Helmet-shrikes. Africa. . . . . .O, ♂♀
Callaeidae—Wattlebirds, New Zealand . . . . .H, O, ♂♀
Sturnidae—Starlings and mynas. Old World,
    introduced New World. . . . . .H, o, d, ♂♀
Meliphagidae—Honeyeaters. Australia, Southern
    Africa, Hawaii. . . . . .O, h, d, ♀
Zosteropidae—White-eyes. Old World tropics. . . . . .O, ♂♀
Dicaeidae—Flower peckers, berry peckers,
    diamondbirds. Oriental, Australia. . . . . .H, O, D, ♂♀, ♀
Vireonidae—Vireos. New World. . . . . .O, ♂♀
Parulidae—Wood-warblers. New World. . . . . .H, O, D, ♀, ♂♀
Thraupidae—Tanagers and honeycreepers. New
    World. . . . . .H, O, D, ♀, ♂♀
Icteridae—American orioles, caciques, oropendolas,
    blackbirds, cowbirds (cowbirds mostly brood
    parasites). New World. . . . . .H, O, D, P, ♀, ♂♀
Emberizidae—Buntings, American sparrows,
    cardinals, grosbeaks, grassquits, and Galapagos
    finches. New World, Eurasia, Africa. . . . . .O, d, h, ♀, ♂♀
Fringillidae—Chaffinches, goldfinches, canaries,
    linnets, crossbills, and allies. New World, Eurasia,
    Africa, introduced Australia. . . . . .O, ♀
Drepanididae—Hawaiian honeycreepers. Hawaiian
    Islands. . . . . .O, h, ♂♀
Nectariniidae—Sunbirds. Old World tropics. . . . . . .D, ♀, ♂♀
Estrildidae—Waxbills, mannikins, grassfinches, and
    allies; also the parasitic viduine finches
    (Viduinae). Africa, Oriental, New Guinea,
    Australia. . . . . .D, h, P, ♂♀
Ploceidae—Old World sparrows, nonweaving
    "weaver" finches (buffalo weavers, sparrow
    weavers, social weavers, and allies), and true
    weavers. (Only the Cuckoo Finch [*Anomalospiza
    imberbis*] is a brood parasite. In Gray's Malimbe
    [*Malimbus nitens*], only the male builds [Brosset
    1978]; in Jackson's Widowbird [*Euplectes
    jacksoni*] only the female builds [Craig 1980].)
    Africa, Madagascar, Seychelles, Eurasia, Sumatra,
    and Java. The House Sparrow (*Passer domesticus*)
    has been widely introduced over the world. . . . . . .D, H, p, ♂♀, ♂, ♀

Where to Find Photographs of Bird Nests

THE following list includes books, special photographic collections, and some films. Many museums and some other ornithological research centers have reference collections of photographs that may be made available to scientists.

GENERAL (WORLDWIDE)

Barruel 1973, Campbell 1974, Gilliard 1958, Gooders 1969–71 (9 volumes), Goodfellow 1977, Grasse 1950, Hancocks 1973, Makatsch 1952, Nicolai 1974, 1982, Skutch 1976, Stresemann 1934, Thomson 1964, Van Tyne and Berger 1976, Welty 1975.

DIFFERENT GEOGRAPHIC AREAS

North America

Allen 1961, Bent 1919–1968 (21 volumes), Cruickshank 1977, Dawson 1923, Dugmore 1900, S. Grimes 1953, Grosvenor and Wetmore 1937, H. Harrison 1975, 1979, Porter 1979, Truslow and Cruickshank 1979, Wetmore 1964.

Central and South America

Dunning 1970, Haverschmidt 1968, Skutch 1954, 1960, 1969a.

Europe

Hosking 1970, Hosking and Newberry 1940, Koch 1955, Reade and Hosking 1967, von Sanden 1933.

Africa

Brosset 1974 (photos by Devez), Chapin 1932–54, N. Collias and Collias 1964, MacDonald and Loke 1965, Mackworth-Praed and Grant 1960 and 1963 (photos by V.G.L. Van Someren), V. D. Van Someren 1958.

Orient

Loke Wan-Tho 1958, Lowther 1949, MacDonald and Loke 1962.

Australia and New Guinea

Beruldsen 1980, Breeden and Slater 1968, H. Frith 1979, Gilliard 1969.

Some Special Bird Groups

Bowerbirds
Gilliard 1969

Weaverbirds
N. Collias and Collias 1964

Special Photographic Collections

Laboratory of Ornithology, Cornell University, 159 Sapsucker Woods, Ithaca, New York 14850. Complete list of slide collection available.

VIREO. Visual Resources for Ornithology. A library of bird photographs for science, art, and education. Academy of Natural Sciences, 19th and the Parkway, Philadelphia 19103.

National Photographic Index of Australian Birds. National Museum, Sydney, Australia.

Films on Weaverbirds and Their Nests

Brosset, A. 1976. *Les Malimbes.* Color, sound (French), about 20 min. Ministry of Foreign Affairs in Paris (Service du Film de Recherche Scientifique/ OFRATEME). Also available from FACSEA (French American Cultural Services and Educational Aid), 972 Fifth Avenue, New York, New York 10021. Shows four species of *Malimbus* building on their nests in the tropical rain forest of northeast Gabon.

Collias, N. E. and E. C. Collias. 1970. *Life in a Weaverbird Colony.* Color, sound, 19 min. Available from University of California at Los Angeles (Media Center) and at Berkeley (Extension), California. Breeding behavior of the Village Weaverbird *Ploceus cucullatus* in northwest Senegal.

Collias, N. E. and E. C. Collias. 1972. *The Evolution of Nests in the Weaverbirds (Ploceidae).* Color, sound, 24 min. Available from University of California at Los Angeles (Media Center) and at Berkeley (Extension), California. Survey of 18 representative species of Ploceidae and their nests, including *Malimbus cassini* and *Philetairus socius.*

Howell, T. R., G. A. Bartholomew, and F. N. White. 1977. *The World's Largest Nest.* Color, sound, 10 min. Available from University of California at Los Angeles (Media Center). Shows a spectacular variety of nests of the Sociable Weaver *Philetairus socius* and explains the ecological significance of the nest as adaptation to a desert habitat.

REFERENCES

Addicott, A. 1938. Behavior of the Bushtit in the breeding season. *Condor* 40:49–63.

Ali, Salim. 1931. The nesting habits of the Baya (*Ploceus philippinus*). *Jour. Bombay Nat. Hist. Soc.* 34:947–964.

Ali, S., and S. D. Ripley. 1968–1974. *Handbook of the Birds of India and Pakistan*. Vols. 1–10. Oxford, London and New York: Oxford Univ. Press.

Allen, A. A. 1937. Blackbirds and orioles (pp. 211–233), tanagers and finches (pp. 235–257), in *The Book of Birds*, ed. G. Grosvenor and A. Wetmore. Washington, D.C.: National Geographic Society.

————. 1961. *Stalking Birds with Color Camera*. Washington, D.C.: National Geographic Society.

Ambedkar, V. C. 1964. *Some Indian Weaver Birds. A contribution to their breeding biology*. Bombay: Bombay Univ. Press.

————. 1980. Abnormal nests of the Baya Weaver Bird *Ploceus philippinus*. *Jour. Bombay Nat. Hist. Soc.* 75 (suppl.):1205–1211.

American Ornithologists' Union. 1983. *Check-list of North American Birds*, 6th ed. Lawrence, Kansas: Allen Press.

Anderson, A. H., and A. Anderson. 1973. *The Cactus Wren*. Tucson: Univ. Arizona Press.

Appert, O. 1968. Zur Brutbiologie der Erdracke *Uratelornis chimaera* Rothschild. *Jour. für Ornithologie* 109:264–275.

Armstrong, E. A. 1955. *The Wren*. London: Collins.

Assenmacher, I., and M. Jallageas. 1980. Circadian and circannual hormonal rhythms. In *Avian Endocrinology*, ed. A. Epple and M. H. Stetson, 391–412. New York and London: Academic Press.

Austin, G. T. 1976. Behavioral adaptations of the Verdin (*Auriparus flaviceps*) in the desert environment. *Auk* 93:245–262.

Austin, O. L., and A. Singer. 1961. *Birds of the World*. New York: Golden Press.

————. 1971. *Families of Birds*. New York: Golden Press.

Baerg, W. J. 1944. Ticks and other parasites attacking Northern Cliff Swallows. *Auk* 61:413–414.

Baeyens, G. den. 1981. Magpie breeding success and Carrion Crow interference. *Ardea* 69:125–140.

Bailey, R. E. 1952. The incubation patch of passerine birds. *Condor* 54:121–136.

Balda, R. P., and G. C. Bateman. 1972. The breeding biology of the Pinon Jay. *The Living Bird* 11:5–42. Ithaca, New York: Laboratory of Ornithology, Cornell Univ.

Balda, R. P., and D. Gabaldon. 1979. Are Pinyon Jay helpers a hindrance? *Abstract 11, 49th Annual Meeting, Cooper Ornithol. Soc.*, Humboldt State Univ., Cal.

Balgooyen, T. G. 1973. Behavior and ecology of the American Kestrel (*Falco sparverius* L.) in the Sierra Nevada of California. *Univ. Calif. Publ. Zool.* 103:1–83.

Balthazart, J., J. D. Blaustein, M-F. Cheng, and H. D. Feder. 1980. Hormones modulate the concentration of cytoplasmic progestin receptors in the brain of male Ring Doves (*Streptopelia risoria*). *Jour. Endocrinol.* 86:251–261.

Barfield, R. J. 1971. Gonadotrophic hormone secretion in the female Ring Dove in response to visual and auditory stimulation by the male. *Jour. Endocrinol.* 49:305–310.

———. 1979. The hypothalamus and social behavior with special reference to the hormonal control of sexual behavior. *Poultry Science* 58:1625–1632.

Barruel, P. 1973. *Birds of the World,* trans. Phyllis Barclay-Smith. Oxford and New York: Oxford Univ. Press.

Bartholomew, G. A. 1949. The effect of light intensity and day length on reproduction in the English Sparrow. *Mus. Compar. Zool. at Harvard Col. Bull.* 101:433–476.

———. 1982. Energy metabolism. In M. S. Gordon et al., *Animal Physiology,* 4th ed., chap. 3, pp. 46–93. New York: Macmillan, and London: Collier Macmillan.

Bartholomew, G. A., and W. R. Dawson. 1979. Thermoregulatory behavior during incubation in Heermann's Gulls. *Physiol. Zool.* 52:422–437.

Bartholomew, G. A., T. R. Howell, and T. J. Cade. 1957. Torpidity in the White-throated Swift, Anna Hummingbird and the Poorwill. *Condor* 59:145–155.

Bartholomew, G. A., F. N. White, and T. R. Howell. 1976. The thermal significance of the nest of the Sociable Weaver *Philetairus socius*: summer observations. *Ibis* 118:402–410.

Bateson, P., ed. 1983. *Mate Choice.* New York: Cambridge Univ. Press.

Beck, J. R., 1970. Breeding seasons and moult in some smaller Antarctic petrels. In *Antarctic Ecology*, vol. 2, ed. M. W. Holgate, 542–550. New York and London: Academic Press.

Benson, C. W. 1960. The birds of the Comoro Islands: Results of the Brit. Ornithol. Union Centenary Exped., 1958. *Ibis* 103b:5–106.

Bent, A. C. 1942. Life histories of North American Cuckoos. Goatsuckers, Hummingbirds and their allies. *Smithsonian Inst., U.S. Nat. Mus. Bull.* 176:1–506.

Bent, A. C., ed. 1919–1968. Life histories of North American Birds. *Smithsonian Inst., U.S. Nat. Mus. Bull.* 21 vols.

Berger, A. J. 1972. *Hawaiian Birdlife.* Honolulu: Univ. of Hawaii Press.

Bernstein, M. H. 1971. Cutaneous water loss in small birds. *Condor* 73:468–469.

Berthold, A. A. 1849. Transplantation der Hoden. *Arch. für Anat. und Physiol. und Wissensch. Med.* 16:42–46.

Bertram, B.C.R. 1982. Problems with altruism. In *Current Problems in Socio-biology*, ed. King's College Sociobiology Group, 251–267. Cambridge: Cambridge Univ. Press.

Beruldsen, G. 1980. *A Field Guide to Nests and Eggs of Australian Birds.* Adelaide, Australia: Rigby Publishers.

Best, L. 1978. Field Sparrow reproductive success and nesting ecology. *Auk* 95:9–22.

Bishop, K. D. 1979–80. Birds of the volcanoes—the Scrubfowl of West New Britain. *World Pheasant Assoc. Jour.* 5:80–91.

Bock, W. J., and J. Farrand, Jr. 1980. The number of species and genera of Recent birds: a contribution to comparative systematics. *Amer. Mus. Nat. Hist. Novitates* 2703:1–29.

Bodner, T. 1980. Prefledging Prairie Falcon die-off in Colorado due to heavy tick infestation. *Wildlife Disease Assoc. Newsletter* (Jan. 1980). (Recent Literature, 1980, *Auk* 97, 3 [suppl.]:5c.)

Bonner, J. T. 1980. *The Evolution of Culture in Animals.* Princeton: Princeton Univ. Press.

Bowman, R. I. 1979. Adaptive morphology of song dialects in Darwin's finches. *Jour. Ornithol.* 120:353–389.

Bradford, J. 1954. Building in wattle, wood and turf. In *A History of Technology*, vol. 1, ed. C. Singer, E. J. Holmyard, and A. R. Hall, chap. 12, pp. 299–326. Oxford: Clarendon Press.

Braine, S. G. and J.W.S. Braine. 1971. Chestnut Weavers *Ploceus rubiginosus* breeding in West Africa. *Ostrich* 42:299–300.

Breeden, S., and P. Slater. 1968. *Birds of Australia.* New York: Taplinger Publ. Co.

Brockway, B. F. 1965. Stimulation of ovarian development and egg-laying by male courtship vocalization in Budgerigars (*Melopsittacus undulatus*). *Animal Behaviour* 13:575–598.

Brodkorb, P. 1971. Origin and evolution of birds. In *Avian Biology*, vol. 1, ed. D. S. Farner and J. R. King, chap. 2, pp. 20–56. New York and London: Academic Press.

Brooke, M. de L., D. A. Scott, and D. M. Teixeira. 1983. Some observations made at the first recorded nest of the Sharpbill *Oxyruncus cristatus*. *Ibis* 125:259–261.

Brosset, A. 1974. La nidification des oiseaux en forêt Gabonaise: architecture, situation des nids et predation. La Terre et la Vie. *Revue d'Écologie Appliquée* 28:579–610.

———. 1978. Social organization and nest-building in the forest weaver birds of the genus *Malimbus* (Ploceinae). *Ibis* 120:27–37.

Brown, J. L. 1970. Cooperative breeding and altruistic behaviour in the Mexican Jay, *Aphelocoma ultramarina*. *Animal Behaviour* 18:366–378.

———. 1974. Alternate routes to sociality in jays—with a theory for the evolution of altruism and communal breeding. *Amer. Zoologist* 14:63–80.

Brown, J. L. 1978. Avian communal breeding systems. *Ann. Rev. Ecol. Syst.* 9:123–155.

———. 1983. Cooperation—A biologist's dilemma. *Advances in the Study of Behavior* 13:1–37.

Brown, J. L., and E. R. Brown. 1981. Kin selection and individual selection in babblers. In *Natural selection and social behavior*, ed. R. D. Alexander and D. W. Tinkle, chap. 15, pp. 244–256. New York and Concord, Mass.: Chiron Press.

Bruning, D. F. 1974. Social structure and reproductive behavior in the Greater Rhea. *The Living Bird* 13:251–294. Laboratory of Ornithology, Cornell Univ., Ithaca, New York.

Burger, J. 1977. Nesting behavior of herring gulls: invasion into *Spartina* salt marsh areas of New Jersey. *Condor* 79:162–169.

———. 1978. Determinants of nest repair in Laughing Gulls. *Animal Behaviour* 26:856–861.

———. 1979. Competition and predation: Herring Gulls versus Laughing Gulls. *Condor* 81:269–277.

Burger, J., and J. Shishler. 1978. Nest site selection and competitive interactions of Herring and Laughing Gulls in New Jersey. *Auk* 95:252–266.

Butterfield, P. A., and J. H. Crook. 1968. The annual cycle of nest building and agonistic behaviour in captive *Quelea quelea* with reference to endocrine factors. *Animal Behaviour* 16:308–317.

Bütticker, W. 1969. Parasites and nest dwellers of the sand martin *Riparia riparia* (L.) in Switzerland. *Schweiz Ent. Ges.* 42:205–220.

Calder, W. A. 1971. Temperature relationships and nesting of the Calliope Hummingbird. *Condor* 73:314–321.

———. 1973. An estimate of the heat balance of a nesting hummingbird in a chilling climate. *Comp. Biochem. Physiol.* 46A:291–300.

Calder, W. A. III. 1974. Consequences of body size for avian energetics. In *Avian Energetics*, ed. R. A. Paynter, Jr., chap. 2, pp. 86–151. Publ. Nuttall Ornithol. Club, no. 15. Cambridge, Mass.

Caldwell, P. J., and G. W. Cornwell. 1975. Incubation behavior and temperatures of the Mallard Duck. *Auk* 92:706–731.

Campbell, B., 1974. *The Dictionary of Birds in Colour.* London: Peerage Books.

Campbell, B. ed. 1972. *Sexual Selection and The Descent of Man 1871–1971.* Chicago: Aldine Publ. Co.

Carpenter, F. Lynn, 1976. Ecology and evolution of an Andean Hummingbird (*Oreotrochilus estella*). *Univ. Calif. Publ. Zool.* 106:1–74.

Cayley, N. W. 1959. *What Bird Is That? A Guide to the Birds of Australia.* 3d ed. Sydney and London: Angus and Robertson.

Cerny, V. 1973. Parasite-host relationships in feather mites. *Proc. 3d Internat. Congr. Acarology*, Prague 1971, ed. M. Daniel and B. Rosicky, 761–764.

Chance, M.R.A. 1962. An interpretation of some agonistic postures: the role of "cut-off" acts and postures. *Symp. Zool. Soc. London* 81:71–89.

Chapman, F. M. 1929. *My Tropical Air Castle. Nature Studies in Panama.* New York and London: D. Appleton and Co.

Chapin, J. P. 1932. The Birds of the Belgian Congo. Part 1. *Bull. Amer. Mus. Nat. Hist.* 65.

———. 1939. The Birds of the Belgian Congo. Part 2. *Bull. Amer. Mus. Nat. Hist.* 75.

———. 1953. The Birds of the Belgian Congo. Part 3. *Bull. Am. Mus. Nat. Hist.* 75A.

———. 1954. The Birds of the Belgian Congo. Part 4. *Bull. Amer. Mus. Nat. Hist.* 75B.

Cheng, M-F. 1974. Ovarian development in the female ring dove in response to stimulation by intact and castrated male ring doves. *Jour. Endocrinol.* 63:234–239.

———. 1979. Progress and prospects in Ring Dove research: a personal view. *Advances in the Study of Behavior* 9:97–129.

Cheng, M-F, and J. Balthazart. 1982. The role of nest-building activity in the gonadotrophin secretions and the reproductive success of Ring Doves (*Streptopelia risoria*). *Jour. Compar. Physiol. Psychol.* 96:307–324.

Cheng, M-F, and R. Silver. 1975. Estrogen-progesterone regulation of nest-building and incubation behavior in ovariectomized ring doves (*Streptopelia risoria*). *Jour. Compar. Physiol. Psychol.* 88:256–263.

Clay, T. 1957. The Mallophaga of birds. In *First Symposium on Host Specificity among Parasites of Vertebrates*, ed. J. G. Baer, 120–158. Inst. Zool., Univ. de Neuchâtel, Switzerland.

Cole, L. J. 1933. The relation of light periodicity to the reproductive cycle, migration and distribution of the Mourning Dove (*Zenaidura macroura carolinensis*). *Auk* 50:284–296.

Collias, E. C. 1984. Egg measurements and coloration throughout life in the Village Weaverbird, *Ploceus cucullatus. Proc. 5th Pan-Afr. Ornithol. Congr.*, ed. J. A. Ledger, 461–475.

Collias, E. C., and N. E. Collias. 1964. The development of nest-building behavior in a weaverbird. *Auk* 81:42–52.

———. 1973. Further studies on development of nest-building behavior in a weaverbird (*Ploceus cucullatus*). *Animal Behaviour* 21:371–382.

———. 1978. Nest building and nesting behaviour of the Sociable Weaver *Philetairus socius. Ibis* 120:1–15.

———. 1980. Individual and sex differences in behavior of the Sociable Weaver *Philetairus socius. Proc. 4th Pan-Afr. Ornithol. Cong.* ed. D. N. Johnson, 243–251.

Collias, E. C., N. E. Collias, C. H. Jacobs, F. McAlary, and J. T. Fujimoto. 1979. Experimental evidence for facilitation of pair formation by bright color in weaverbirds. *Condor* 81:91–93.

Collias, N. E. 1942. Aggressive behavior among vertebrate animals; some implications and a statistical analysis. Ph. D. diss., Univ. of Chicago.

Callias, N. E. 1944. Agressive behaviour among vertebrate animals. *Physiol. Zool.* 17:83–123.

———. 1946. Some experiments on broody behaviour in fowl and pigeons. *Anat. Record* 96 (abstract 170).

———. 1950a. Hormones and behavior with special reference to birds and the mechanisms of hormone action. In *A Symposium on Steroid Hormones,* ed. E. Gordon, 277–329. Madison: Univ. of Wisconsin Press.

———. 1951. Problems and principles of animal sociology. In *Comparative Psychology,* ed. C. P. Stone, 3d ed. chap. 12, pp. 388–422. New York: Prentice-Hall.

———. 1964. The evolution of nests and nest-building in birds. *Amer. Zoologist* 4:175–190.

———. 1979. Nest and mate selection by the female Village Weaverbird. *Animal Behaviour* 27:310. (Reply to a critique by Peter Garson.)

———. 1980. Recent studies on evolution of behaviour and nest-building in weavers (Ploceidae). *Proc. 4th Pan-Afr. Ornithol. Congr.,* ed. D. N. Johnson, 233–241.

Collias, N. E., M. Brandman, J. K. Victoria, L. F. Kiff, and C. E. Rischer. 1971. Social facilitation in weaverbirds: effects of varying the sex ratio. *Ecology* 52:829–836.

Collias, N. E., and E. C. Collias. 1959a. Solar radiation and predation as factors determining evolution of nest form in weaverbirds (Ploceidae) and other tropical birds. *Bull. Ecol. Soc. Am.* 40:113–114 (abstract).

———. 1959b. Breeding behavior of the Black-headed Weaverbird, *Textor cucullatus graueri* (Hartert) in the Belgian Congo. *Ostrich* (suppl). 3:233–241.

———. 1962. An experimental study of the mechanisms of nest building in a weaverbird. *Auk* 79:568–595.

———. 1963. Evolutionary trends in nest-building by the weaverbirds (Ploceidae). *Proc. 13th Internat. Ornithol. Congr.,* Ithaca, New York, 518–530.

———. 1964. The Evolution of Nest-building in the Weaverbirds (Ploceidae). *Univ. Calif. Publ. Zool.* 73:1–162.

———. 1965. Nest-building and the bioenergetics of breeding behavior in a weaverbird. *Amer. Zoologist* 5:196 (abstract 27).

———. 1967. A quantitative analysis of breeding behavior in the African Village Weaverbird. *Auk* 84:396–411.

———. 1969a. Size of breeding colony related to attraction of mates in a tropical passerine bird. *Ecology* 50:481–488.

———. 1969b. Some experimental studies of the breeding biology of the Village Weaver *Ploceus (Textor) cucullatus* (Muller). *Proc. 3rd Pan-Afr. Ornithol. Congr. Ostrich* (suppl.) 8:169–177.

———. 1970. The behaviour of the West African Village Weaverbird. *Ibis* 112:457–480.

———. 1971a. Ecology and behaviour of the Spotted-backed Weaverbird in the Kruger National Park. *Koedoe* 14:1–27.

————. 1971b. Some observations on behavioral energetics in the Village Weaverbird. 1. Comparison of colonies from two subspecies in nature. *Auk* 88:124–133.

————. 1971c. Comparative behaviour of West African and South African subspecies of *Ploceus cucullatus*. *Ostrich* (suppl.) 9:41–52.

————. 1977. Weaverbird nest aggregation and evolution of the compound nest. *Auk* 94:50–64.

————. 1978. Cooperative breeding behavior in the White–browed Sparrow Weaver. *Auk* 95:472–484.

————. 1980. Behavior of the Grey-capped Social Weaver (*Pseudonigrita arnaudi*) in Kenya. *Auk* 97:213–226.

Collias, N. E., and E. C. Collias, ed. 1976. External Construction by Animals. In *Benchmark Papers in Animal Behavior*, vol. 4, ser. ed. Martin W. Schein. Stroudsburg, Pa.: Dowden, Hutchinson and Ross.

Collias, N. E., P. J. Frumkies, D. S. Brooks, and R. J. Barfield. 1961. *Amer. Zoologist* 1 (abstract 101).

Collias, N. E., and L. R. Jahn. 1959. Social behavior and breeding success in Canada Geese (*Branta canadensis*) confined under semi-natural conditions. *Auk* 76:478–509.

Collias, N. E., and J. K. Victoria. 1978. Nest and mate selection in the village weaverbird (*Ploceus cucullatus*). *Animal Behaviour* 26:470–479.

Collias, N. E., J. K. Victoria, E. L. Coutlee, and M. Graham. 1971. Some observations on behavioral energetics in the Village Weaverbird. 2. All-day watches in an aviary. *Auk* 88:133–143.

Collias, N. E., J. K. Victoria, and R. J. Shallenberger. 1971. Social facilitation in weaverbirds: importance of colony size. *Ecology* 52:823–828.

Conner, R. N. 1975. Orientation of entrances to woodpecker nest cavities. *Auk* 92:371–374.

Cooper, W., and J. M. Forshaw. 1977. *The Birds of Paradise and Bowerbirds*. Sydney and London: Collins.

Coulombe, H. N. 1971. Behavior and population ecology of the Burrowing Owl, *Speotyto cunicularia*, in the Imperial Valley of California. *Condor* 73:162–176.

Coulson, J. C., and E. White. 1960. The effect of age and density of breeding birds on the time of breeding of the Kittiwake, *Rissa tridactyla*. *Ibis* 102:71–86.

Cowles, R. B. 1930. The life history of *Scopus umbretta bannermani* C. Grant, in Natal, South Africa. *Auk* 47:159–176.

Cracraft, J. 1981. Toward a phylogenetic classification of the recent birds of the world (class Aves). *Auk* 98:681–714.

Craig, A.J.F.K. 1980. Behaviour and evolution in the genus *Euplectes*. *Jour. für Ornithologie* 121:144–161.

Craighead, J. J., and D. S. Stockstad. 1961. Evaluating the use of aerial nesting platforms by Canada geese. *Jour. Wildlife Mgmt.* 25:363–372.

Cramp, S., ed. 1977–1983. *Handbook of the Birds of Europe, the Middle East and North Africa.* Vols. 1–3. Oxford, London and New York: Oxford Univ. Press.

Crook, J. H. 1958. Étude sur le comportement social de *Bubalornis a. albirostris* (Vieillot). *Alauda* 26:161–195.

———. 1960. Studies on the reproductive behaviour of the Baya Weaver, *Ploceus philippinus* (L.). *Jour. Bombay Nat. Hist. Soc.* 57:1–44.

———. 1961. The Fodies (Ploceinae) of the Seychelles Islands. *Ibis* 103a (1961):517–548.

———. 1962. The adaptive significance of pair formation types in weaver birds. *Symp. Zool. Soc. London* 8:57–70.

———. 1963a. A comparative analysis of nest structure in the weaver birds (Ploceinae). *Ibis* 105:238–262.

———. 1963b. The Asian weaver birds: problems of co-existence and evolution with particular reference to behaviour. *Jour. Bombay Nat. Hist. Soc.* 60:1–48.

———. 1964. The evolution of social organisation and visual communication in the weaver birds (*Ploceinae*). *Behaviour* (suppl.) 10:1–178.

Crook, J. H., and P. A. Butterfield. 1968. Effects of testosterone propionate and luteinizing hormone on agonistic and nest building behaviour of *Quelea quelea. Animal Behaviour* 16:370–390.

Crossner, K. A. 1977. Natural selection and clutch size in the European Starling. *Ecology* 58:885–892.

Crowfoot, G. M. 1954. Textiles, basketry, and mats. In *A History of Technology,* vol. 1, ed. C. Singer, E. J. Holmyard, and A. R. Hall, chap. 16, pp. 412–447. Oxford: Clarendon Press.

Cruickshank, A. D. 1977. *Cruickshank's Photographs of Birds of America.* New York: Dover.

Cullen, E. 1957. Adaptions in the Kittiwake to cliff nesting. *Ibis* 99:275–302.

Cunningham-van Someren, G. R. 1971. *Amadina fasciata* (Gmelin) as a "nest-parasite." *Bull. Brit. Ornithol. Club* 91:135–137.

Da Camara-Smeets, M. 1982. Nesting of the Village Weaver *Ploceus cucullatus. Ibis* 124:241–251.

Darling, F. Fraser. 1938. *Bird flocks and the breeding cycle.* Cambridge: Cambridge Univ. Press, and New York: Macmillan.

———. 1952. Social behavior and survival. *Auk* 69:183–191.

Darlington, A. 1962. House Martin building nest of cement. *Brit. Birds* 55:134–135.

Darwin, C. 1871. *The Descent of Man and Selection in Relation to Sex.* Photo-reproduction in 1981 by Princeton Univ. Press, Princeton, N.J.

Davis, D. E. 1942. The phylogeny of social nesting habits in the Crotaphaginae. *Quart. Rev. Biol.* 17:115–134.

Davis, T. A. 1971. Variation in nest-structure of the Common Weaverbird *Ploceus philippinus* (L.) of India. *Forma et Functio* 4:225–239.

Dawson, W. L. 1923. *The Birds of California.* 3 vols. San Diego, Los Angeles, San Francisco: Smith Moulton Co.

Dawson, W. R., and F. E. Evans. 1960. Relation of growth and development to temperature regulation in nesting Vesper Sparrows. *Condor* 62:329–340.

Decoux, J.-P. 1978. Les régulations écologiques de la reproduction chez le colion strié (*Colius striatus nigricollis*). *L'Oiseau* 48:1–20.

De Groot, P. 1980. Information transfer in a socially roosting weaver bird (*Quelea quelea; Ploceinae*): An experimental study. *Animal Behaviour* 28:1249–1254.

de Naurois, R., and H. E. Wolters. 1975. The affinities of the São Tomé weaver *Textor grandis* (Gray, 1844). *Bull. Brit. Ornithol. Club* 95(3):122–126.

Dennis, J. V. 1971. Utilization of pine resin by the Red-cockaded Woodpecker and its effectiveness in protecting roosting and nest sites. In *The Ecology and Management of the Red-cockaded Woodpecker*, ed. R. L. Thompson, 78–86. Tallahasee, Florida: Bureau of Sport Fisheries and Wildlife and Tall Timbers Research Station.

Diamond, J. M. 1982a. Evolution of bowerbirds' bowers: animal origins of the aesthetic sense. *Nature* 297:99–102.

———. 1982b. Rediscovery of the Yellow-fronted Bowerbird. *Science* 216:431–434.

Dilger, W. C. 1962. The behavior of lovebirds. *Scientific American* 206(1):88–99.

Dixon, C. 1902. *Birds' Nests. An Introduction to the Science of Caliology*. New York: F. A. Stokes and Co., and London: G. Richards.

Dixon, W. J., and F. J. Massey, Jr. 1969. *Introduction to Statistical Analysis*. 3d ed. New York: McGraw-Hill.

Domm, L. V. 1927. New experiments on ovariotomy and the problem of sex inversion in the fowl. *Jour. Exper. Zool.* 48:31–196.

———. 1939. Modifications of sex and secondary sexual characters in birds. In *Sex and Internal Secretions*, ed. C. H. Danforth and E. Doisy, chap. 5, pp. 227–327. Baltimore, Md.: Williams and Wilkins.

Dorst, J. 1962. Nouvelle recherches biologiques sur les trochilides des hautes Andes peruviennes (*Oreotrochilus estella*). *Oiseau R.F.O.* 32:95–126.

Downing, R. L. 1959. Significance of ground nesting by Mourning Doves in Northwestern Oklahoma. *Jour. Wildlife Mgmt.* 23:117–118.

Dugmore, A. R. 1900. *Bird Homes. The nests, eggs and breeding habits of the land birds breeding in the eastern United States*. New York: Doubleday and McClure Co.

Dunning, J. S. 1970. *Portraits of Tropical Birds*. Wynnewood, Pa: Livingston.

Durango, S. 1949. The nesting associations of birds with social insects and with birds of different species. *Ibis* 91:140–143.

Elgood, J. H., and P. Ward. 1963. A snake attack upon a weaver-bird colony. Possible significance of synchronous breeding activity. *Bull. Brit. Ornithol. Club* 83:71–73.

Emerson, K. C. 1972. Checklist of the Mallophaga of North America (north of Mexico). Part 4. *Bird host list*. Dugway, Utah: Desert Test Center.

Emlen, J. T., Jr. 1952a. Flocking behavior in birds. *Auk* 69:160–170.

Emlen, J. T., Jr. 1952b. Social behavior in nesting Cliff Swallows. *Condor* 54:177–79.

———. 1954. Territory, nest building and pair formation in the Cliff Swallow. *Auk* 71:16–35.

———. 1957. Display and mate selection in the whydahs and bishop birds. *Ostrich* 28:202–213.

Emlen, S. T. 1978. The evolution of cooperative breeding in birds. In *Behavioral Ecology: An Evolutionary Approach*, ed. J. Krebs and N. Davies, 245–281. Oxford: Blackwell Scientific Publications.

———. 1981. Altruism, kinship, and reciprocity in the White-fronted Bee-Eater. In *Natural Selection and Social Behavior*, ed. R. D. Alexander and D. W. Tinkle, chap. 13, pp. 217–230. New York and Concord, Mass.: Chiron Press.

———. 1982. The evolution of helping. *Amer. Naturalist* 119:29–53.

Emlen, S. T., and N. J. Demong. 1975. Adaptive significance of synchronized breeding in a colonial bird: a new hypothesis. *Science* 188:1029–1031.

Emlen, S. T., and L. W. Oring. 1977. Ecology, sexual selection, and the evolution of mating systems. *Science* 197:215–223.

Emlen, S. T., and S. L. Vehrencamp. 1983. Cooperative breeding strategies among birds. In *Perspectives in Ornithology*, ed. A. H. Brush and G. A. Clark, Jr., 93–120. Cambridge: Cambridge Univ. Press.

Epple, A., and M. H. Stetson ed. 1980. *Avian Endocrinology*. New York and London: Academic Press.

Erickson, C. J., and M. C. Martinez-Vargas. 1975. The hormonal basis of cooperative nest-building. In *Neural and Endocrine Aspects of Behavior in Birds*, ed. P. Wright, P. G. Caryl, and D. M. Vowles, chap. 5, pp. 91–110.

Erwin, R. M. 1978. Coloniality in terns: the role of social feeding. *Condor* 80:211–215.

Evans, R. M. 1982. Foraging-flock recruitment of a Black-billed Gull colony: implications for the information center hypothesis: *Auk* 99:24–30.

Ettinger, A. O., and J. R. King. 1980. Time and energy budgets of the Willow Flycatcher (*Empidonax traillii*) during the breeding season. *Auk* 97:533–546.

Falla, R. A., R. B. Sibson, and E. G. Turbott. 1967. *A Field Guide to the Birds of New Zealand*. Boston: Houghton Mifflin Co.

Farner, D. S., and E. Gwinner. 1980. Photoperiodicity, circannual and reproductive cycles. In *Avian Endocrinology*, ed. A. Epple and M. H. Stetson, 331–366. New York and London: Academic Press.

Farner, D. S., and J. C. Wingfield. 1980. Reproductive endocrinology of birds. *Ann. Rev. Physiol.* 42:457–472.

Feare, C. J. 1976. Desertion and abnormal development in a colony of Sooty Tern *Sterna fuscata* infested by virus infested ticks. *Ibis* 118:112–115.

Feduccia, A. 1980. *The Age of Birds*. Cambridge: Harvard Univ. Press.

Feekes, F. 1981. Biology and colonial organization of two sympatric caciques, *Cacicus c. cela* and *Cacicus h. haemorrhous* (Icteridae, Aves) in Suriname. *Ardea* 69:83–108.

ffrench, R. P. 1973. *A Guide to the Birds of Trinidad and Tobago.* Wynnewood, Pa.: Livingston.

Fisher, J. 1963. Evolution and bird sociality. In *Evolution as a Process*, 2d ed., ed. J. Huxley, A. C. Hardy and E. B. Ford, 87–102. New York: Collier.

Fisher, J., and R. T. Peterson. 1964. *The World of Birds.* Garden City, New York: Doubleday and Co.

Fitch, H. S. 1963. Natural history of the Blue Racer *Coluber constrictor. Univ. Kansas Publ. Natural Hist.* 15:351–468.

Fitch, J. M., and D. P. Branch. 1960. Primitive architecture and climate. *Scientific American* 203(6):134–144.

Forshaw, J. M., and W. T. Cooper. 1978. Parrots of the World. Garden City, New York: Doubleday and Co.

Fraga, R. M. 1980. The breeding of Rufous Horneros (*Furnarius rufus*). *Condor* 82:58–68.

Friedmann, H. F. 1929. *The Cowbirds: A Study in the Biology of Social Parasitism.* Springfield, Ill.: Thomas.

———. 1935. Bird societies. In C. Murchison's *Handbook of Social Psychology*, 142–185. Worcester, Mass.: Clark Univ. Press.

———. 1950. The breeding habits of the weaverbirds. A study in the biology of behavior patterns. In *Smithsonian Report* 1949, 293-316. Washington, D.C.: Smithsonian Inst.

———. 1960. The Parasitic Weaverbirds. *Smithsonian Inst., U.S. Nat. Mus. Bull.* 223.

———. 1963. Host Relations of the Parasitic Cowbirds. *Smithsonian Inst., U.S. Nat. Mus. Bull.* 233.

———. 1968. The Evolutionary History of the Avian genus *Chrysococcyx Smithsonian Inst., U.S. Nat. Mus. Bull.* 265.

Frith, C. B. 1976. A 12-month field study of the Aldabran Fody *Foudia eminentissima aldabrana. Ibis* 188:156–178.

Frith, H. J. 1962. *The Mallee–Fowl.* Sydney and London: Angus and Robertson.

Frith, H. J., ed. 1979. *Reader's Digest Complete Book of Australian Birds.* Sydney: Reader's Digest Services.

Frith, H. J., and J. H. Calaby, ed. 1976. *Proc. 16th Internat. Ornithol. Congr.*, Canberra 1974.

Fry, C. H. 1977. The evolutionary significance of cooperative breeding in birds. In *Evolutionary Ecology*, ed. B. Stonehouse, 127–136. Baltimore, Md.: University Park Press.

Garson, P. J. 1980. Male behaviour and female choice: mate selection in the wren. *Animal Behaviour* 28:491–502.

Gibson, E. 1880. 1. Ornithological notes from the neighborhood of Cape San Antonio, Buenos Ayres. *Ibis* 14 (4th ser.):3–38.

Gilbert, A. B., and D.G.M. Wood-Gush. 1976. The effects of exogenous estrogen and progesterone on laying and nesting behavior in the hen. *Brit. Poultry Science* 17:13–15.

Gilliard, E. T. 1958. *Living Birds of the World*. Garden City, New York: Doubleday and Co.

———. 1969. *Birds of Paradise and Bower Birds*. Garden City, New York: Natural History Press.

Goldsmith, A. R., and B. K. Follett. 1980. Anterior pituitary hormones. In *Avian Endocrinology*, ed. A. Epple and M. H. Stetson, 147–166. New York and London: Academic Press.

Gooders, J., ed. 1969–1971. *Birds of the World*. Vols. 1–9. London: IPC Magazines, Ltd.

Goody, R. M. 1954. *The Physics of the Stratosphere*. Cambridge: Cambridge Univ. Press.

Goodfellow, P. 1977. *Birds as Builders*. New York: Arco Publ. Co.

Goodwin, D. 1982. *Estrildid Finches of the World*. Ithaca, N.Y.: Cornell Univ. Press.

Gordon, J. E. 1978. *Structures*. New York and London: Plenum Press.

Gordon, M. S. 1981. Introduction to the symposium: Theoretical ecology; To what extent has it added to our understanding of the natural world. *Amer. Zoologist* 21:793.

Grant, G. S. 1982. Avian incubation: egg temperature, nest humidity, and behavioral thermoregulation in a hot environment. *Ornithol. Monog.* no. 30. Amer. Ornithologists' Union.

Grasse, Pierre-P. 1950. *Traite de Zoologie*. Vol. 15, *Oiseaux, Nidification*, 561–600. Paris: Masson.

Graul, W. D. 1974. Adaptive aspects of the Mountain Plover social system. *The Living Bird* 12:69–94. Laboratory of Ornithology, Cornell Univ. Ithaca, New York.

Greenewalt, C. H. 1960. *Hummingbirds*. Garden City, New York: Doubleday and Co.

Grimes, L. G. 1973. The breeding of Heuglin's Masked Weaver and its nesting association with the Red Weaver Ant. *Ostrich* 44:170–175.

———. 1976. Co-operative breeding in African birds. *Proc. 16th Internat. Ornithol. Congr.*, Canberra 1974, ed. H. J. Frith and J. H. Calaby, 667–673.

Grimes, S. A. 1953. *An Album of Southern Birds*. Photographs by S. A. Grimes, text by A. Sprunt, Jr. Austin: Univ. of Texas Press.

Grosvenor, G., and A. Wetmore ed. 1937. *The Book of Birds*. 2 vols. Washington, D.C.: National Geographic Society.

Hall, B. P., and R. E. Moreau. 1970. *An Atlas of Speciation in African Passerine Birds*. London: Trustees of Brit. Mus. (Natural History).

Hamilton, W. D. 1963. The evolution of altruistic behaviour. *Amer. Naturalist* 97:354–356.

Hammond, M. C., and W. R. Foreward. 1956. Experiments on causes of duck predation. *Jour. Wildlife Mgmt.* 20:243–247.

Hancocks, D. 1973. *Master Builders of the Animal World*. New York: Harper and Row.

Hann, H. W. 1941. The cowbird at the nest. *Wilson Bull.* 53:211–221.

Hardy, J. W. 1963. Epigamic and reproductive behavior of the Orange-fronted Parakeet. *Condor* 65:169–199.

———. 1970. Duplex nest construction by Hooded Oriole circumvents cowbird parasitism. *Condor* 72:491.

Harris, M. P. 1973. The biology of the Waved Albatross *Diomedia irrorata* of Hood Island, Galapagos. *Ibis* 115:483–511.

Harrison, C.J.O. 1973. Nest building behaviour of quaker parrots. *Ibis* 115:124–128.

———. 1975. *A Field Guide to the Nests, Eggs and Nestlings of European Birds.* London: Collins.

———. 1978. *Bird Families of The World.* New York: Harry N. Abrams.

Harrison, H. H. 1975. *A Field Guide to Birds' Nests in the United States East of the Mississippi River.* Boston: Houghton Mifflin Co.

———. 1979. *A Field Guide to Western Birds' Nests in the United States West of the Mississippi River.* Boston: Houghton Mifflin Co.

Hasluck, P. N. 1942. *Knotting and Splicing Ropes and Cordage.* Philadelphia: D. McKay Co.

Haverschmidt, F. 1949. *The Life of the White Stork.* Leiden: E. J. Brill.

———. 1950. The nest and eggs of *Tolmomyias poliocephalus. Wilson Bull.* 62:214–216.

———. 1968. *Birds of Surinam.* Edinburgh: Oliver and Boyd.

Headstrom, R. 1951. *Birds' Nests of the West. A Field Guide.* New York: I. Washburn, Inc.

Hector, D. P. 1982. Botfly (Diptera, Muscidae) parasitism of nestling Aplomado Falcons. *Condor* 84:443–444.

Henry, G. M. 1971. *A Guide to the Birds of Ceylon.* London: Oxford Univ. Press.

Henry, V. G. 1969. Predation on dummy nests of ground-nesting birds in the southern Appalachians. *Jour. Wildlife Mgmt.* 33: 169–172.

Herrick, F. H. 1911. Nests and nest-building in birds. *Animal Behaviour* 1:159–192, 244–277, 336–373.

———. 1932. Daily Life of the American Eagle. *Auk* 49:307–323.

Hickling, R.A.O. 1959. The burrow excavation phase in the breeding cycle of the Sand Martin, *Riparia riparia. Ibis* 101:497–500.

Hicks, E. A. 1953. Observations on the insect fauna of birds' nests. *Jour. Kansas Ent. Soc.* 26:11–18.

———. 1962. Check-list and bibliography on the occurrence of insects in birds' nests. Suppl. 1. *Iowa State Jour. Sci.* 36:233–344.

———. 1971. Check-list and bibliography on the occurrence of insects in birds' nests. Suppl. 2. *Iowa State Jour. Sci.* 46:123-338.

Hinde, R. A. 1952. The behaviour of the Great Tit (*Parus major*) and some other related species. *Behaviour* (suppl.) 2:1–201.

———. 1958. The nest-building behaviour of domesticated canaries. *Proc. Zool. Soc. London,* 131 (pt. 1):1–48.

———. 1965. Interaction of internal and external factors in integration of canary reproduction. In *Sex and Behaviour*, ed. F. A. Beach, chap. 16, pp. 381–415. New York and London: J. Wiley.

Hinde, R. A., and E. Steel. 1962. Selection of nest material by female canaries. *Animal Behaviour* 10:67–75.

———. 1966. Integration of the reproductive behaviour of female canaries. *Symp. Soc. Exp. Biol.* 20:401–426.

Hinde, R. A., E. Steel, and B. K. Follett. 1974. Effect of photoperiod on oestrogen-induced nest-building in ovariectomized or refractory female canaries (*Serinus canarius*). *Jour. Reprod. Fert.* 40:383–399.

Hinde, R. A., and R. P. Warren. 1959. The effect of nest-building on later reproductive behavior in the domesticated canary. *Animal Behaviour* 7:35–41.

Hindwood, K. A. 1955. Bird-wasp nesting associations. *Emu* 55:263–274.

———. 1959. The nesting of birds in the nests of social insects. *Emu* 59:1–36.

Hodges, J. I., Jr. 1982. Bald Eagle nesting studies in Seymour Canal, southeast Alaska. *Condor* 84:125–127.

Horváth, O. 1963. Contributions to nesting ecology of forest birds. Master of Forestry Thesis, Univ. of Brit. Columbia.

———. 1964. Seasonal differences in Rufous Hummingbird nest height and their relation to nest climate. *Ecology* 45:235–241.

Hosking, E. J. 1970. *An Eye for a Bird, the Autobiography of a Bird Photographer*. London: Hutchison.

Hosking, E., and C. Newberry. 1948. *The Art of Bird Photography*. London: Country Life Limited.

Houston, D. C. 1979. Why do Fairy Terns *Gygis alba* not build nests? *Ibis* 121:102–104.

Howe, M. A. 1975. Behavioral aspects of the pair bond in Wilson's Phalarope. *Wilson Bull.* 87:248–270.

Howell, F. C. 1965. *Early Man*. New York: Time Inc.

Howell, T. R. 1979. Breeding biology of the Egyptian Plover, *Pluvianus aegyptius*. *Univ. Calif. Publ. Zool.* 113:1–76.

Howell, T. R., B. Araya, and W. R. Millie. 1974. Breeding biology of the Gray Gull, *Larus modestus*. *Univ. Calif. Publ. Zool.*, 104:1–57.

Howell, T. R., and G. A. Bartholomew. 1962. Temperature regulation in the Sooty Tern, *Sterna fuscata*. *Ibis* 104:98–105.

Howell, T. R., and W. R. Dawson. 1954. Nest temperature and attentiveness in the Anna Hummingbird. *Condor* 56:93–97.

Hudson, W. H. 1920. *Birds of La Plata*. London and Toronto: J. M. Dent and Sons.

Humphrey, P. S., and R. T. Peterson. 1978. Nesting behavior and affinities of Monk Parrakeets of southern Buenos Aires Province, Argentina. *Wilson Bull.* 90:544–552.

Humphrey-Smith, I., and D. E. Moorhouse. 1981. Host acquisition by *Ornithodoros capensis* Neumann (Ixodoidea:Argasidae). *Ann. Parasitol.* (Paris) 56:353–357.

Hutchison, J. B. 1975. Target cells for gonadal steroids in the brain: studies on steroid-sensitive mechanisms of behaviour. In *Neural and Endocrine Aspects of Behaviour in Birds*, ed. P. Wright, P. G. Caryl, and D. M. Vowles, chap. 7, pp. 123–138. Amsterdam: Elsevier.

———. 1976. Hypothalamic mechanisms of sexual behavior, with special reference to birds. *Advances in the Study of Behavior* 6:159–199.

Hutchison, J. B., and S. Lovari. 1976. Effect of male aggressiveness on behavioral transitions in the reproductive cycle of the Barbary Dove. *Behaviour* 59:296–318.

Immelmann, K. 1962. Beitrage zu einer vergleichenden Biologie australischer Prachtfinken (Spermestidae). *Zool. Jb. Sys. Bd.* 90:1–196.

———. 1965. *Australian Finches in Bush and Aviary.* Sydney and London: Angus and Robertson.

———. 1980. *Introduction to Ethology.* New York and London: Plenum Press.

Irving, L., and J. Krog. 1956. Temperature during the development of birds in Arctic nests. *Physiol. Zool.* 29:195–205.

Jackson, J. A. 1978. Competition for cavities and Red-cockaded Woodpecker Management. In *Endangered Birds*, ed. S. A. Temple, 103–112. Madison: Univ. of Wisconsin Press.

Jackson, J. A., and B. B. Nickol. 1979. Ecology of *Mediorhynchus centurorum* host specificity. *Jour. Parasitology.* 65:167–169.

Jacobs, C. H., N. E. Collias, and J. T. Fujimoto. 1978. Nest colour as a factor in nest selection by female village weaverbirds. *Animal Behaviour* 26:463–469.

Janzen, D. H. 1969. Birds and the ant × acacia interaction in Central America, with notes on birds and other myrmecophytes. *Condor* 71:240–256.

Jenni, D. A. 1974. Evolution of polyandry in birds. *Amer. Zoologist* 14:129–144.

Johnson, A. W., and J. D. Goodall. 1965, 1967. *The Birds of Chile.* 2 vols. Buenos Aires: Platt Establecimientos Graficos.

Johnston, R. F., and J. W. Hardy. 1962. Behavior of the Purple Martin. *Wilson Bull.* 74:243–262.

Johnston, R. F., and R. K. Selander. 1964. House Sparrows: rapid evolution of races in North America. *Science* 144:548–550.

Jones, R. E., and A. S. Leopold. 1967. Nesting interference in a dense population of Wood Ducks. *Jour. Wildlife Mgmt.* 31:221–228.

Kahl, M. P. 1967. Observations on the behaviour of the Hamerkop *Scopus umbretta* in Uganda. *Ibis* 109:25–32.

———. 1971. Social behavior and taxonomic relationships of the storks. *The Living Bird* 10:151–170. Laboratory of Ornithology, Cornell Univ., Ithaca, New York.

Kale, H. W. II. 1965. Ecology and bioenergetics of the Long-billed Marsh Wren *Telmatodytes palustris griseus* (Brewster) in Georgia salt marshes. *Publ. Nuttall Ornithol. Club*, no. 5. Cambridge, Mass.

Kemp, A. C. 1970. Some observations on the sealed-in nesting method of hornbills (Family Bucerotidae). *Ostrich* (suppl.) 8:149–155.

Kemp. A., and M. Kemp. 1974. Observations on the Buffalo Weaver. *Bokmakierie* 26:55–58.

Kendeigh, S. C. 1934. The role of environment in the life of birds. *Ecological Monog.* 4:299–417.

———. 1941. Territorial and mating behavior of the House Wren. *Illinois Biol. Monog.* 18:1–120.

———. 1952. Parental care and its evolution in birds. *Illinois Biol. Monog.* 22:1–358.

———. 1961. Energy of birds conserved by roosting in cavities. *Wilson Bull.* 73:140–147.

Kendeigh, S. C., V. R. Dolnik, and V. M. Gavrilov. 1977. Avian energetics. In *Granivorous Birds in Ecosystems*, ed. J. Pinowski, 127–203. Cambridge: Cambridge Univ. Press.

Kern, M. D., and A. Bushra. 1980. Is the incubation patch required for the construction of a normal nest? *Condor* 82:328–334.

Kiel, W. H., Jr. 1955. Nesting studies of the Coot in southwestern Manitoba. *Jour. Wildlife Mgmt.* 19:189–198.

Kilgore, D. L., Jr., and K. L. Knudsen. 1977. Analysis of materials in Cliff and Barn Swallow nests: relationship between mud selection and nest architecture. *Wilson Bull.* 89:562–571.

King, K. A., D. R. Blankenship, R. T. Paul, and R.C.A. Rice. 1977. Ticks as a factor in the 1975 nesting failure of Texas Brown Pelicans. *Wilson Bull.* 89:157–158.

Koch, L. 1955. *The Encyclopedia of British Birds*. London: Waverly Publ. Co.

Koenig, W. D., and F. A. Pitelka. 1981. Ecological factors and kin selection in the evolution of cooperative breeding in birds. In *Natural Selection and Social Behavior*, ed. R. D. Alexander and D. W. Tinkle, chap. 17, pp. 261–282. New York and Concord, Mass.: Chiron Press.

Koepcke, M. 1972. On the types of bird's nests found side by side in a Peruvian rain forest. *Proc. 15th Internat. Ornithol. Congr., Leiden, Netherlands,* 662–663.

Krebs, J. R., and N. B. Davies, ed. 1978. *Behavioural Ecology*. Sunderland, Mass.: Sinauer Associates.

Lack, D. 1947. *Darwin's Finches*. Cambridge: Cambridge Univ. Press.

———. 1954. *The Natural Regulation of Animal Numbers*. Oxford: Clarendon Press.

———. 1956. *Swifts in a Tower*. London: Methuen.

———. 1966. *Population Studies of Birds*. Oxford: Clarendon Press.

———. 1967. Interrelationships in breeding adaptations as shown by marine birds. *Proc. 14th Internat. Ornithol. Congr.,* Oxford 1966, 3–42.

———. 1968. *Ecological Adaptations for Breeding in Birds*. London: Methuen.

Lanyon, W. E. 1978. Revision of the *Myiarchus* flycatchers of South America. *Bull. Amer. Mus. Nat. Hist.* 164(4):429–627.

Lasiewski, R. C., and W. R. Dawson. 1967. A reexamination of the relation between standard metabolic rate and body weight in birds. *Condor* 69:13–23.

Lawton, M. F., and R. O. Lawton. 1980. Nest-site selection in the Brown Jay. *Auk* 97:631–636.

Laycock, H. T. 1979. Breeding biology of the Thickbilled Weaver. *Ostrich* 50:70–82.

Layne, D. S., R. H. Common, W. A. Maws, and R. M. Fraps. 1957. The presence of progesterone in extracts of ovaries of laying hens. *Proc. Soc. Exp. Biol. (N.Y.)* 94:528–529.

Ledger, J. A. 1980. *The Arthropod Parasites of Vertebrates in Africa South of the Sahara.* Vol. 4, *Phthiraptera (Insecta).* South African Institute for Medical Research Publications, no. 56. Johannesburg.

Lehrman, D. S. 1961. Hormonal regulation of parental behavior in birds and infrahuman mammals. In *Sex and Internal Secretions*, vol. 2, ed. W. C. Young, 1268–1382. Baltimore, Md.: Williams and Wilkins.

————. 1964. The reproductive behavior of ring doves. *Scientific American* 488 (Nov.).

————. 1965. Interaction between internal and external factors in the regulation of the reproductive cycle of the ring dove. In *Sex and Behavior*, ed. F. A. Beach, chap. 15, pp. 355–380. New York and London: J. Wiley.

Lehrman, D. S., and M. Friedman. 1969. Auditory stimulation of ovarian activity in the Ring Dove (*Streptopelia risoria*). *Animal Behaviour* 17:494–497.

Lenington, S. 1980. Female choice and polygyny in red-winged blackbirds. *Animal Behaviour* 28:347–361.

Lewis, D. M. 1981. Determinants of reproductive success of the White-browed Sparrow Weaver, *Plocepasser mahali*. *Behav. Ecol. Sociobiol.* 9:83–93.

————. 1982. Dispersal in a population of White-browed Sparrow Weavers. *Condor* 84:306–312.

Ligon, J. D. 1981. Demographic patterns and communal breeding in the Green Woodhoopoe, *Phoeniculus purpureus*. In *Natural Selection and Social Behavior*, ed. R. D. Alexander and D. W. Tinkle, chap. 14, pp. 231–243. New York and Concord, Mass.: Chiron Press.

Lill, A. 1966. Some observations on social organization and non-random mating in captive Burmese Red Jungle Fowl (*Gallus gallus spadiceus*). *Behaviour* 26:228–242.

Lind, E. A. 1964. Nistzeitliche Geselligkeit der Mehlschwalbe, *Delichon u. urbica* (L.). *Annales Zoologici Fennici* 1:7–43.

Linsdale, J. M. 1937. The Natural History of Magpies. *Pacific Coast Avifauna*, no. 25. Berkeley, Calif.: Cooper Ornithol. Soc.

Liversidge, R. 1961. The Wattled Starling (*Creatophora cinerea*) (Menschen) *Annals Cape Prov'l. Museum* 1:71–80.

————. 1963. The nesting of the Hamerkop *Scopus umbretta*. *Ostrich* 34:55–62.

Loke Wan-Tho. 1958. *A Company of Birds*. London: M. Joseph.

Loman, J. 1979. Nest tree selection and vulnerability to predation among Hooded Crows *Corvus corone cornix*. *Ibis* 121:204–207.

Lorenz, K. 1935. Companions as factors in the bird's environment. In *Studies in Animal and Human Behaviour*, vol. 1, trans. by R. Martin, 101–258. Cambridge: Harvard Univ. Press, 1970.

Lowther, E.H.N. 1949. *A Bird Photographer in India*. Oxford: G. Cumberlege, Oxford Univ. Press.

MacDonald, M. With Photographs by Christina Loke. 1962. *Birds in the Sun*. London: H. F. Witherby.

———. With Photographs by Christina Loke. 1965. *Treasure of Kenya*. New York: G. P. Putnam's Sons.

Mackworth-Praed, C. W., and C.H.B. Grant. 1957, 1960. *Birds of Eastern and North-eastern Africa*. 2 vols. London: Longmans.

———. 1962, 1963. *Birds of Southern Africa*. 2 vols. London: Longmans.

———. 1970, 1973. *Birds of West Central and Western Africa*. 2 vols. London: Longmans.

MacLaren, P.I.R. 1950. Bird-ant nesting associations. *Ibis* 92:564–566.

Maclean, G. L. 1967. Die systematische Stelling der Flughuhner (Pteroclididae). *Jour. für Ornithologie* 108:203–217.

———. 1968. Field studies on the sandgrouse of the Kalahari Desert. *The Living Bird* 7:209–235. Laboratory of Ornithology, Cornell Univ., Ithaca, New York.

———. 1969. A study of seedsnipe in southern South America. *The Living Bird* 8:33–80. Laboratory of Ornithology, Cornell Univ., Ithaca, New York.

———. G. L. 1970. The biology of larks (Alaudidae) of the Kalahari sandveld. *Zoologica Africana* 5:7–39.

———. 1973. The Sociable Weaver, Parts 1–5. *Ostrich* 44:176–261.

Makatsch, W. 1950. *Der Vogel und Sein Nest*. Akademische Verlagsgesellschaft. Leipzig: Geest and Portig.

Marais, E. N. 1938. *The Soul of the White Ant*. New York: Dodd, Mead and Co.

Marchant, S. 1960. The breeding of some southwestern Ecuadorian birds. *Ibis* 102:349–382, 584–599.

Marshall, A. G. 1981. *The Ecology of Ectoparasitic Insects*. New York and London: Academic Press.

Marshall, A. J. 1954. *Bowerbirds: Their Displays and Breeding Cycles*. Oxford: Clarendon Press.

Marshall, A. J., and J. H. de S. Disney. 1957. Experimental induction of the breeding season in the xerophilous bird. *Nature* 180:647–649.

Martinez-Vargas, M. C. 1974. The induction of nest-building in the Ring Dove (*Streptopelia risoria*): hormonal and social factors. *Behaviour* 50:123–151.

Mason, E. A. 1944. Parasitism by *Protocalliphora* and management of cavity-nesting birds. *Jour. Wildlife Mgmt.*, 8:232–247.

May, R. M. 1981. The role of theory in ecology. *Amer. Zoologist* 21:903–910.

Mayfield, H. 1960. *The Kirtland's Warbler*. Bloomfield Hills, Mich.: Cranbrook Institute of Science.

Mayfield, H. F. 1979. Red Phalaropes breeding on Bathurst Island. *The Living Bird* 17:7–40. Laboratory of Ornithology, Cornell Univ., Ithaca, New York.

Mayr, E. 1969. *Principles of Systematic Zoology*. New York and London: McGraw-Hill.

———. 1970. *Populations, Species, and Evolution*. Cambridge: Harvard Univ. Press.

Mayr, E., and D. Amadon. 1951. A classification of recent birds. *Amer. Mus. Nat. Hist. Novitates*, no. 1496:1-42.

Mayr, E., and J. Bond. 1943. Notes on the generic classification of the swallows, Hirundinidae. *Ibis* 85:334–341.

Mayr, E., and J. C. Greenway, ed. 1962. *Peters' Check-list of Birds of the World*, vol. 15. Cambridge: Harvard Univ. Press.

McCabe, R. A. 1965. Nest construction by House Wrens. *Condor* 67:229–234.

McClure, H. E., N. Ratanaworabhan, K. C. Emerson, H. Hoogstraal, N. Nadchatram, P. Kwanyuen, W. T. Atyeo, T. C. Maa, N. Wilson, and L. Wayuping. 1972. Some Ectoparasites of the Birds of Asia. *Migratory Animal Pathological Survey*. SEATO Medical Laboratory, APO San Francisco, Calif.

McDonald, P. A. 1982. Influence of pinealectomy and photoperiod on courtship and nest-building in male doves. *Physiology and Behavior* 29:813–818.

McEllin, S. M. 1979. Nest sites and population demographies of White-breasted and Pigmy Nuthatches in Colorado. *Condor* 81:348–352.

McLachlan, G. R., and R. Liversidge. 1978. *Roberts Birds of South Africa*. 4th ed. Cape Town, South Africa: John Voelker Bird Book Fund.

Medway, Lord. 1960. Cave Swiftlets. In B. E. Smythies, *The Birds of Borneo*, Edinburgh: Oliver and Boyd.

Medway, Lord, and D. R. Wells. 1976. *The Birds of the Malay Peninsula*. Vol. 5, *Conclusion and Survey of Every Species*. London: H. F. Witherby.

Meyerriecks, A. J. 1960. Comparative breeding behavior of four species of North American herons. *Publ. Nuttall Ornithol. Club*, no. 2. Cambridge, Mass.

Michel, George G. 1977. Experience and progesterone in ring dove incubation. *Animal Behaviour* 25:281–285.

Milon, P., J-J. Petter, and G. Randrianasolo. 1973. *Faune de Madagascar 35, Oiseaux*. Paris: ORSTOM, Tananarive, and CNRS.

Moenke, R. 1978. Gelbspotter *Hippolais icterina* (Vieill.) baut ein Nest aus Glasfasern. *Beitrage zur Volgelkunde* 24:101–102.

Møller, A. P. 1982. Coloniality and colony structure in Gull-billed Terns *Gelochelidon nilotica*. *Jour. für Ornithologie* 123:41–54.

Morel, G., and Marie-Yvonne Morel. 1962. La reproduction des oiseaux dans une region semi-aride: la vallée du Sénégal. *Alauda* 30:161–203.

Morel, G., Marie-Yvonne Morel, and F. Bourliere. 1957. The Black-faced Weaverbird or Dioch in West Africa. *Jour. Bombay Nat. Hist. Soc.* 54:811–825.

Moreau, R. E. 1936. Bird-insect nesting associations. *Ibis* (13th ser.) 6:460–471.

———. 1937. The comparative breeding biology of the African hornbills (Bucerotidae). *Proc. Zool. Soc. London* A, 107:331–346.

———. 1942. The nesting of African birds in association with living things. *Ibis* 84:240–263.

———. 1960. Conspectus and classification of the Ploceinae Weaverbirds. *Ibis* 102:298–321, 443–471.

Morlion, M. L. 1980. Pterylosis as a secondary criterion in the taxonomy of the African Ploceidae and Estrildidae. *Proc. 4th Pan-Afr. Ornithol. Congr.*, 27–41.

Morton, M. L. 1978. Snow conditions and the onset of breeding in the Mountain White-crowned Sparrow. *Condor* 80:285–289.

Mulligan, J., G. Neal, and F. Nottebohm. 1968. An experimental study of bird song. *Amer. Zoologist* 8:13.

Myers, L. E. 1928. The American swallow bug, *Oeciacus vicarius* Horvath (Hemptera, Cimicidae). *Parasitology* 20:159–172.

Nalbandov, A. V. Reproductive physiology of mammals and birds, 3d ed. San Francisco: W. H. Freeman.

Naumberg, E.M.B. 1930. The Birds of Matto Grosso, Brazil. *Bull. Amer. Mus. Nat. Hist.* 60:1–432.

Nelson, B. 1968. *Galapagos. Islands of Birds*. New York: W. Morrow and Co.

Nelson, J. B. 1978. *The Sulidae. Gannets and Boobies*. Oxford: Oxford Univ. Press.

Nethersole-Thompson, C., and D. Nethersole-Thompson. 1944. Nest-site selection by birds. *British Birds* 37:70–74, 88–94, 108–113.

Newton, Ian. 1979. *Population ecology of raptors*. Vermillion, S. Dakota: Buteo Books.

Nice, Margaret M. 1922. A study of the nesting of Mourning Doves. *Auk* 39:457–474.

———. 1937. Studies in the life history of the Song Sparrow, 1. *Trans. Linnaean Society of New York*.

———. 1943. Studies in the life history of the Song Sparrow, 2. *Trans. Linnaean Society of New York*, 6:1–328.

———. 1957. Nesting success of altricial birds. *Auk* 74:305–321.

———. 1962. Development of behavior in precocial birds. *Trans. Linnaean Society of New York* 8:1–211.

Nickell, W. P. 1958. Variations in engineering features of the nests of several species of birds in relation to nest sites and nesting materials. *Butler Univ. Botanical Studies* 13(2):121–140.

Nicolai, J. 1964. Der Brutparasitismus der Viduinae als ethologisches Problem. *Z. Tierpsychol.* 21:129–204.

———. 1967. Rassen- und Artbildung in der Viduinengattung *Hypochera*. *Jour. für Ornithologie* 108:308–319.

———. 1974. *Bird Life*. New York: Putnam.

———. 1982. *Fotoatlas der Vögel.* Munich: Gräfe und Verlegerdienst.

Nolan, V., Jr. 1978. The Ecology and Behavior of the Prairie Warbler *Dendroica discolor. Ornithol. Monog.* no. 26, American Ornithologists' Union.

Nordberg, S. 1936. Biologisch-ökologische untersuchungen über die vogelnidicolen. *Acta Zool. Fenn.* 21:1–168.

Ogden, J. C. 1975. Effects of Bald Eagle territoriality on nesting Ospreys. *Wilson Bull.* 87:496–505.

Ohlendorf, H. M. 1976. Comparative breeding ecology of phoebes in Trans-Pecos Texas. *Wilson Bull.* 88:255–271.

Oliver, W.R.B. 1955. *New Zealand Birds.* 2d ed. Wellington: A. H. and A. W. Reed.

Oniki, Y. 1979. Is nesting success of birds low in the tropics? *Biotropica* 11:60–69.

Orians, G. H. 1961. The ecology of blackbird (*Agelaius*) social systems. *Ecological Monog.* 31:285–312.

———. 1971. Ecological aspects of behavior. In *Avian Biology,* ed. D. S. Farner and J. R. King, chap. 11, pp. 513–546. New York and London: Academic Press.

———. 1972. The adaptive significance of mating systems in the Icteridae. *Proc. 15th Internat. Ornithol. Congr.,* ed. K. H. Voous, 389–398.

———. 1980. *Some Adaptations of Marsh-nesting Blackbirds.* Princeton: Princeton Univ. Press.

Orr, Y. 1970. Temperature measurements at the nest of the Desert lark (*Ammomanes deserti deserti*). *Condor* 72:476–478.

Palmer, R. S., ed. 1962. *Handbook of North American birds.* Vol. 1, *Loons through Flamingos.* New Haven and London: Yale Univ. Press.

Parsons, J. 1976. Nesting density and breeding success in the Herring Gull *Larus argentatus. Ibis* 118:537–547.

Patel, M. D. 1936. The physiology of formation of "pigeon's milk." *Physiol. Zool.* 9:129–152.

Paterson, R. L. 1977. An unusual Rock Dove nest. *Auk* 94:159–160.

Payne, R. B. 1967. Interspecific communication signals in parasitic birds. *Amer. Naturalist* 101:363–376.

———. 1969. Nest parasitism and display of chestnut sparrows in a colony of grey-capped social weavers. *Ibis* 111:300–307.

———. 1977. The ecology of brood parasitism in birds. *Ann. Rev. Ecol. Syst.* 8:1–28.

———. 1979. Sexual selection and intersexual differences in variance of breeding success. *Amer. Naturalist* 114:447–452.

———. 1982. Species limits in the Indigobirds (Ploceidae, *Vidua*) of West Africa: mouth mimicry, song mimicry, and description of new species. *University of Michigan Miscell. Publs. Mus. Zool.,* no. 162.

Paynter, R. A., Jr., ed. 1974. Avian Energetics. *Publ. Nuttall Ornithol. Club,* no. 15. Cambridge, Mass.

Pearson, O. P. 1953. Use of caves by hummingbirds and other species at high altitudes in Peru. *Condor* 55:17–20.

————. 1954. The daily energy requirements of a wild Anna Hummingbird. *Condor* 56:317–322.

Peckover, W. S. 1969. The Fawn-breasted Bowerbird (*Chlamydera cerviniventris*). *Proc. Papua and New Guinea Sci. Soc.*, 21:23–35.

Perrins, C. M. 1979. *British Tits*. London: Collins.

Peters, J. L. 1931-1979. *Check-list of Birds of the World*. Cambridge: Harvard Univ. Press.

Peterson, R. T. 1961. *A Field Guide to Western Birds*. Boston: Houghton Mifflin Co.

Phillips, J. R., and D. L. Dindal. 1977. Raptor nests as a habitat for invertebrates. A review. *Raptor Res.* 11:87–94.

Pitman, C.R.S. 1958. Snake and lizard predators of birds. *Bull. Brit. Ornithol. Club* 78:82–86, 99–104, 120–124.

Polikarpova, E. 1940. Influence of external factors upon the development of the sexual gland of the sparrow. *Compt. Rend. Acad. Sci. USSR* 26:91–95.

Pomeroy, D. E. 1978. The biology of Marabou Storks in Uganda, 2. Breeding biology and general review. *Ardea* 66:1–23.

Porter, E. 1979. *Birds of North America. A Personal Selection*. New York: Galahad Books. 144 pp.

Postupolsky, S. 1978. Artificial nesting platforms for ospreys and bald eagles. In *Endangered Birds*, ed. S. A. Temple, chap. 5, pp. 35–45. Madison: Univ. of Wisconsin Press.

Preston, F. W., and A. T. Norris. 1947. Nesting heights of breeding birds. *Ecology* 28:240–273.

Rand, A. L. 1936. The distribution and habits of Madagascar birds. *Bull. Amer. Mus. Nat. Hist.* 52:143–499.

Rand, A. L., and E. T. Gilliard. 1968. *Handbook of New Guinea Birds*. Garden City, New York: Natural History Press.

Reade, W., and E. Hosking. 1967. *Nesting Birds, Eggs, and Fledglings*. London: Blandford Press.

Reeves, J. J., P. C. Harrison, and J. M. Casey. 1973. Ovarian development and ovulation in hens treated with synthetic (porcine) luteinizing hormone/ follicle stimulating hormone-releasing hormone (LH-RH/FSH-RH). *Poultry Science* 52:1883–1886.

Richardson, F. 1965. Breeding and feeding habits of the black wheatear *Oenanthe leucura* in southern Spain. *Ibis* 107:1–16.

Ricklefs, R. E. 1969. An analysis of nesting mortality in birds. *Smithsonian Contrib. Zool.* 9:1–48.

Ricklefs, R. E., and F. R. Hainsworth. 1969. Temperature regulation in nestling cactus wrens: the nest environment. *Condor* 71:32–37.

Riddle, O., and R. W. Bates. 1939. Preparation assay, and actions of lactogenic hormones. In *Sex and Internal Secretions*, ed. E. Allen, C. H. Danforth, and E. Doisy, 3d ed., 1088–1120. Baltimore, Md.: Williams and Wilkins.

Riddle, O., R. W. Bates, and E. L. Lahr. 1935. Prolactin induces broodiness in fowl. *Amer. Jour. Physiol.* 111:352–360.

Ridgely, R. S. 1976. *A Guide to the Birds of Panama.* Princeton: Princeton Univ. Press.

Ripley, S. D. 1957a. Notes on the Horned Coot, *Fulica cornuta* Bonaparte. *Postilla, Yale Peabody Mus. Nat. Hist.* 30:1–8.

———. 1957b. Additional notes on the Horned Coot, *Fulica cornuta* Bonaparte. *Postilla, Yale Peabody Mus. Nat. Hist.* 32:1–2.

Rivolier, S. 1956. *Emperor Penguins,* trans. P. Wiles. London: Elek Books Ltd.

Rodriguez, J. G., ed. 1979. *Recent Advances in Acarology.* 5th Internat. Congr. Acarology, Mich. State University 1978. 2 vols. New York and London: Academic Press.

Root, R. B. 1969. The behavior and reproductive success of the Blue-Gray Gnatcatcher. *Condor* 71:16–31.

Roseberry, J. L., and W. D. Klimstra. 1970. The nesting ecology and reproductive performance of the Eastern Meadowlark. *Wilson Bull.* 82:243–267.

Rothschild, M., and T. Clay. 1957. Fleas, flukes and cuckoos. London: Collins.

Rowan, M. K., and G. J. Broekhuysen. 1962. A study of the Karoo Prinia. *Ostrich* 33:6–30.

Rowley, I. 1971. The use of mud in nest-building—a review of the incidence and taxonomic importance. Proc. 3rd Pan-Afr. Ornithol. Congr., 1969, ed. G. L. Maclean. *Ostrich* (suppl.) 8:139–148.

———. 1976. Co-operative breeding in Australian birds. *Proc. 16th Internat. Ornithol. Congr.,* Canberra, Australia, ed. H. J. Frith and J. H. Calaby, 657–666.

Rowley, J. S., and R. T. Orr. 1965. Nesting and feeding habits of the White-collared Swift. *Condor* 67:449–456.

Ruschi, A. 1949. Classification of the nests of Trochilidae (hummingbirds), trans. C. H. Greenwalt. Boletim do Museu de Biologia Prof. Mello-Leitao, Santa Teresa E. E. Santo-Brasil, no. 7.

Russell, S. M. 1969. Regulation of egg temperatures by incubating White-winged Doves. In *Physiological Systems in Semi-arid Environments,* ed. C. C. Hoff and M. L. Riedsel, 107–112. Alburquerque: Univ. New Mexico Press.

Saeki, Y., and Y. Tanabe. 1955. Changes in prolactin content of fowl pituitary during broody periods and some experiments on the induction of broodiness. *Poultry Science* 4:909–919.

Sargent, T. D. 1965. The role of experience in the nest-building of the zebra finch. *Auk* 82:48–61.

Schaeffer, V. H. 1977. Geographic variation in the placement and structure of oriole nests. *Condor* 78:443–448.

Schally, A. V. 1978. Aspects of hypothalamic regulation of the pituitary gland. *Science* 202:18–28.

Schmidt-Nielsen, K. 1979. *Animal Physiology: Adaptation and Environment.* 2d ed. Cambridge and London: Cambridge Univ. Press.

Schnell, G. D. 1973. A reanalysis of nest structure in the weavers (Ploceinae) using numerical taxonomic methods. *Ibis* 115:93–106.

Schodde, R. 1976. Evolution in the birds-of-paradise and bowerbirds, a resynthesis. *Proc. 16th Int. Ornithol. Congr.*, Canberra, ed. H. F. Frith and J. H. Calaby, 137–149.

Schodde, R., and J. L. McKean. 1973. Distribution, taxonomy and evolution of the Gardener Bowerbirds *Amblyornis* spp. in eastern New Guinea, with descriptions of two new subspecies. *Emu* 73:51–60.

Searcy, W. A. 1982. The evolutionary effects of mate selection. *Ann. Rev. Ecol. Syst.* 13:57–85.

Serventy, D. L., and H. M. Whittell. 1962. *Birds of Western Australia.* Perth: Peterson Brokensha Pty. Ltd.

Sharp, P. J. 1980. Female reproduction. In *Avian Endocrinology*, ed. A. Epple and M. H. Stetson, 435–454. New York and London: Academic Press.

Sherrod, S. K., C. M. White, and F.S.L. Williamson. 1977. Biology of the Bald Eagle (*Haliaetus leucocephalus alascanus*) on Amchitka Island, Alaska. *The Living Bird* 15:143–182. Laboratory of Ornithology, Cornell Univ., Ithaca, New York.

Shoemaker, H. 1939. Effect of testosterone propionate on behavior of the female Canary. *Proc. Soc. Exp. Biol. Med.* 41:299–302.

Short, Lester L. 1979. Burdens of the Picid hole-excavating habit. *Wilson Bull.* 91:16–28.

Sibley, C. G., and J. E. Ahlquist. 1973. The relationships of the Hoatzin. *Auk* 90:1–13.

———. 1980. The relationships of the "primitive insect eaters" (Aves: Passeriformes) as indicated by DNA X DNA hybridization. *Acta XVII Congressus Internationalis Ornithologici*, Berlin, 1215–1219.

Sick, H. 1957. Rosshaarpilze als Nestbau–Material Brasilianischer Vögel. *Jour. für Ornithologie* 98:421–431.

Sielmann, H. 1959. *My year with the woodpeckers*, trans. S. Lightman. London: Barrie & Rockcliff.

Silver, R. 1978. The parental behavior of Ring Doves. *Amer. Scientist* 66:209–215.

Sincock, J. L. and J. M. Scott. 1980. Cavity nesting of the Akepa on the Island of Hawaii. *Wilson Bull.* 92:261–262.

Skead, C. J. 1947. A study of the Cape Weaver (*Hyphantornis capensis olivaceus*). *Ostrich* 38:1–42.

Skead, C. J. 1959. A study of the Cape Penduline Tit *Anthoscopus minutus minutus. Proc. 1st Pan-Afr. Ornithol. Congr., Ostrich* (suppl.) 3:274–288.

Skead, C. J. 1967. *The Sunbirds of Southern Africa.* Cape Town and Amsterdam: Balkema.

Skowron, C., and M. Kern. 1980. The insulation in nests of selected North American songbirds. *Auk* 97:816–824.

Skutch, A. F. 1931. The life history of Rieffer's Hummingbird (*Amazilia tzacatl tzacatl*) in Panama and Honduras. *Auk* 48:481–500.

———. 1935. Helpers at the nest. *Auk* 52:257–273.

———. 1947. A nest of the Sun-bittern in Costa Rica. *Wilson Bull.* 59:38.

———. 1948. The life history of the Olivaceus Piculet and related forms. *Ibis* 90:433–449.

———. 1954. Life Histories of Central American Birds, 1. *Pacific Coast Avifauna*, no. 31. Berkeley Calif.: Cooper Ornithol. Soc.

———. 1960. Life Histories of Central American Birds, 2. *Pacific Coast Avifauna*, no. 34. Berkeley Calif.: Cooper Ornithol. Soc.

———. 1966. A breeding bird census and nesting success in Central America. *Ibis* 108:1–16.

———. 1969a. Life Histories of Central American Birds, 3. *Pacific Coast Avifauna*, no. 35. Berkeley, Calif.: Cooper Ornithol. Soc.

———. 1969b. A study of the Rufous-fronted Thornbird and associated birds. *Wilson Bull.* 81:5–43, 123–139.

———. 1973. *The Life of the Hummingbird.* New York: Crown Publishers. 95 pp.

———. 1976. *Parent Birds and Their Young.* Austin and London: Univ. of Texas Press.

———. 1981. *New Studies of Tropical American Birds. Publ. Nuttall Ornithol. Club* 19:1–281. Cambridge, Mass.

———. 1983. *Birds of Tropical America.* Austin: Univ. of Texas Press.

Sladen, W.J.L. 1958. The Pygoscelid Penguins. 2, The Adelie Penguin. *Sci. Rep. F.I.D.S.* 17:1–97.

Slater, C.J.B. 1969. The stimulus to egg-laying in the Bengalese finch. *Jour. Zool., London,* 158:427–440.

Smith, G. C., and R. B. Eads. 1978. Field observations on the Cliff Swallow, *Petrochelidon pyrrhonota* (Viellot), and the swallow bug, *Oeciacus vicarius* Horvath. *Jour. Wash. Acad. Sci.* 68:23–26.

Smith, N. G. 1980. Some evolutionary, ecological, and behavioral correlates of communal nesting by birds with wasps or bees. *Acta XVII Congressus Internationalis Ornithologici,* Berlin 1978, 2:1199–1205.

Smith, P. W. 1904. Nesting habits of the Rock Wren. *Condor* 6:109–110.

Smith, W. J. 1962. The nest of *Pitangus lictor. Auk* 79:108–111.

Smithe, F. B. 1966. *The Birds of Tikal.* Garden City, New York: *Natural Hist. Press.*

Smythies, B. E. 1953. *The Birds of Burma,* 2d ed. Edinburg and London: Oliver and Boyd.

———. 1981. The Birds of Borneo. 3d ed. rev. the Earl of Cranbrook. Kota Kinabalu, Sabah: Sabah Society, and Kuala Lumpur: Malayan Nature Society.

Snapp, Barbara D. 1976. Colonial breeding in the Barn Swallow (*Hirundo rustica*) and its adaptive significance. *Condor* 78:471–480.

Snow, D. W. 1976. *The Web of Adaptation. Bird Studies in the American Tropics.* New York: Quadrangle, New York Times Book Co.

———. 1971. Evolutionary aspects of fruit-eating by birds. *Ibis* 113:194–202.

Snow, D. W. 1981. The nest as a factor determining clutch-size in tropical birds. *Jour. Ornithol.* 119:227–30.

———. 1982. *The Cotingas.* Ithaca, New York: Cornell Univ. Press.

Snow, D. W., and B. K. Snow. 1979. The Ochre-bellied Flycatcher and the evolution of lek behavior. *Condor* 81:286–292.

Snyder, N.F.R. 1975. Breeding biology of Swallow-tailed Kites in Florida. *The Living Bird* 13:73–97. Laboratory of Ornithology, Cornell Univ., Ithaca, New York.

Steel, E., and R. A. Hinde. 1972. Influence of photoperiod on oestrogenic induction of nest–building in canaries. *Jour. Endocr.* 55:265–278.

Steimer, T., and J. B. Hutchison. 1980. Aromatization of testosterone within a discrete hypothalamic area associated with the behavioral action of androgen in the male dove. *Brain Research* 192:586–591.

———. 1981. Androgen increases formation of behaviorally effective oestrogen in dove brain. *Nature* 292:345–347.

Stein, R. C. 1963. Isolating mechanisms between populations of Traill's Flycatcher. *Proc. Am. Phil. Soc.* 107:21–50.

Steiner, H. 1955. Das Brutverhalten der Prachtfinken, Spermestidae, als Ausdruck ihres selbstandagen Familiencharakters. *Acta XI Congressus Internationalis Ornithologici*, Basel 1954, pp. 350–355. Basel: Birkhauser Verlag.

Stonehouse, B. 1970. Adaptation in polar and subpolar penguins (Sphenicidae). In *Antarctic Ecology*, ed. M. W. Holdgate, vol. 1, pp. 526–541. New York and London: Academic Press.

Storer, R. W. 1971. Classification of birds. In *Avian Biology*, vol. 1, ed. D. S. Farner and J. R. King, chap. 1, pp. 1–18. New York: Academic Press.

Stresemann, E. 1934. Sauropsida: Aves. Part 7(2), *Handbuch der Zoologie*, ed. H. Kukenthal and T. Krumbach. Berlin and Leipzig: W. de Gryter and Co.

Summers–Smith, D. 1963. *The House Sparrow.* London: Collins.

Taber, E. 1948. The relation between ovarian growth and sexual characters in Brown Leghorn chicks treated with gonadotropins. *Jour. Exp. Zool.* 107:65–102.

———. 1949. The source and effects of androgen in the male chick treated with gonadotrophins. *Amer. Jour. Anat.* 85:231–256.

Tanaka, K. 1980. Hormone receptor interactions: 2. Steroid hormones. In *Avian Endocrinology*, ed. A. Epple and M. H. Stetson, 17–31. New York and London: Academic Press.

Temple, S. A., ed. 1978. *Endangered Birds. Management Techniques for Preserving Threatened Species.* Madison: Univ. of Wisconsin Press.

Thomsen, Lise. 1971. Behavior and ecology of burrowing owls on the Oakland Municipal Airport. *Condor* 73:177–192.

Thomson, A. L., ed. 1964. *A New Dictionary of Birds.* New York: McGraw Hill.

Thompson, C. F., and B. M. Gottfried. 1976. How do cowbirds find and select nests to parasitize? *Wilson Bull.* 88:673–675.

Thorpe, W. H. 1963. *Learning and instinct in animals*, 2d ed. London: Methuen.

Tickell, W.L.N., and R. Pinder. 1975. Breeding biology of the Black-browed Albatross *Diomedea melanophris* and Grey-headed Albatross *D. chrysostoma* at Bird Island, South Georgia. *Ibis* 117:433–451.

Tinbergen, N. 1951. *The Study of Instinct*. Oxford: Clarendon Press.

———. 1967. Adaptive features of the Black-headed Gull. *Proc. 14th Internat. Ornithol. Congr.*, Oxford 1966, 43–60.

———. 1969. *Curious Naturalists*. Amer. Mus. of Nat. Hist. ed. Garden City, New York: Doubleday and Co.

Tinbergen, N., G. J. Broekhuysen, F. Feekes, J.C.W. Houghton, H. Kruuk, and E. Szulc. 1963. Egg shell removal by the Black-headed Gull, *Larus ridibundus* L., a behaviour component of camouflage. *Behaviour* 19:74–117.

Traylor, M. A., and J. W. Fitzpatrick. 1982. A survey of the tyrant flycatchers. *The Living Bird* 19:7–50. Laboratory of Ornithology, Cornell Univ., Ithaca, New York.

Trivelpiece, W., and N. J. Volkman. 1979. Nest-site competition between Adelie and Chinstrap Penguins: an ecological interpretation. *Auk* 96:675–681.

Truslow, F. K., and H. G. Cruickshank. 1979. *The Nesting Season. The Bird Photographs of Frederick Kent Truslow*. Commentary by Helen G. Cruickshank. New York: Viking Press.

Tucker, V. A. 1970. Energetic cost of locomotion in animals. *Compar. Biochem. Physiol.* 34:841–846.

———. 1973. Bird metabolism during flight: evaluation of a theory *Jour. Exp. Biol.* 58:689–709.

Turner, E. C., Jr. 1971. Fleas and lice. In *Infectious and Parasitic Diseases of Wild Birds*, ed. J. W. Davis, R. C. Anderson, L. Karstad, and D. O. Trainer, 175–184. Ames, Iowa: Iowa State Univ. Press.

Tweedie, M.W.F., and J. L. Harrison. 1954. *Malayan Animal Life*. London: Longmans.

Van Dobben, W. H. 1949. Nest building techniques of icterine warbler and chaffinch. *Ardea* 37:89–97.

Van Riper, C. III 1973. The nesting of the Apapane in lava caves on the island of Hawaii. *Wilson Bull.* 85:238 240.

Van Someren, V.G.L. 1956. Days with birds. Studies of the habits of some East African species. *Fieldiana: Zoology* 38:1–520. Chicago Natural History Museum.

Van Someren, V. D. 1958. *A Bird Watcher in Kenya*. Edinburgh: Oliver and Boyd.

Van Tets, G. F. 1965. A comparative study of some social communication patterns in the Pelicaniformes. *Ornithol. Monog.* no. 2, American Ornithologists' Union.

Van Tyne, J., and A. J. Berger. 1976. *Fundamentals of Ornithology*, 2d ed. New York and London: J. Wiley, 808 pp.

Vaurie, C. 1980. Taxonomy and geographical distribution of the Furnariidae (Aves, Passeriformes). *Bull. Amer. Mus. Nat. Hist.*, vol. 166, article 1.

Vehrencamp, S. L. 1977. Relative fecundity and parental effort in communally nesting Anis, *Crotophaga sulcirostris*. *Science* 197:403–405.

Victoria, J. K. 1969. Environmental and behavioral factors influencing egg-laying and incubation in the Village Weaverbird, *Ploceus cucullatus*. Ph.D. diss., Univ. of California, Los Angeles. Ann Arbor, Michigan: University Microfilms, Inc.

———. 1972. Clutch characteristics and egg discriminative ability of the African Village Weaverbird *Ploceus cucullatus*. *Ibis* 114:367–376.

Victoria, J. K., and N. E. Collias. 1973. Social facilitation of egg-laying in experimental colonies of a weaverbird. *Ecology* 54:399–405.

Villenga, R. E. 1970. Behavior of the male Satin Bowerbird. *Australian Bird Bander* 8:3–11.

———. 1972. Satin Bowerbirds. *Wildlife in Australia* 9:6.

———. 1980. Distribution of bowers of the Satin Bowerbird at Leura, NSW, with notes on parental care, development and independence of the young. *Emu* 80:97–102.

Vincent, J.F.V. 1982. *Structural Biomaterials*. New York: J. Wiley.

Vleck, D., C. M. Vleck, and R. S. Seymour. 1980. Megapode eggs: energy and water loss during incubation. *Amer. Zoologist* 20:906 (abstract 1021).

von Haartman, L. 1956. Der Einfluss der Temperatur auf den Brutrhythmus experimentell nachgewiesen. *Ornis. Fenn.* 33:100–107.

———. 1957. Adaptation in hole-nesting birds. *Evolution* 11:294–347.

———. 1969. The nesting habits of Finnish birds. I. Passeriformes. *Commentationes Biologicae, Societas Scientiarum Fennica* 32:1–187.

———. 1971. Population dynamics. In *Avian Biology*, vol. 1, ed. D. S. Farner and J. R. King, chap. 9, pp. 392–461. New York and London: Academic Press.

von Sanden, W. 1933. *Gudja. Leben am See der Vögel*. Königsberg (Pr.): Graf und Unzer Verlag (now in Munich, Germany).

Wade, M. J. 1982. Evolution of interference competition by individual, family and group selection. *Proc. National Acad. Science* 79:3575–3578.

Wagner, H. O. 1955. Einfluss der Poikilothermie bei Kolibris auf ihre Brutbiologie. *Jour. für Ornithologie* 96:361–368.

Wainwright, S. A., W. D. Biggs, J. D. Correy, and J. M. Gosline. 1976. *Mechanical Design in Organisms*. New York: J. Wiley.

Walkinshaw, L. H. 1941. The Prothonotary Warbler, a comparison of nesting conditions in Tennessee and Michigan. *Wilson Bull.* 53:3–21.

Walkinshaw, L. H., and W. R. Faust. 1974. Some aspects of Kirtland's Warbler breeding biology. *Jack-Pine Warbler* 52:64–75.

Wallace, A. R. 1891. *Natural Selection and Tropical Nature*. London: Macmillan.

Walsberg, G. E. 1977. Ecology and energetics of contrasting social systems in *Phainopepla nitens* (Aves: Ptilogonatidae). *Univ. Calif. Publ. Zool.* 108:1–63.

Walsberg, G. E., and J. R. King. 1978. The heat budget of incubating mountain white-crowned sparrows (*Zonotrichia leucophrys oriantha*) in Oregon. *Physiol. Zool.* 51:92–103.

Walsh, J. F., and B. Walsh. 1976. Nesting association between the Red-headed Weaver *Malimbus rubriceps* and raptorial birds. *Ibis* 18:106–108.

Ward, P. 1965. Feeding ecology of the Black-faced Dioch (*Quelea quelea*) in Nigeria. *Ibis* 107:173–214.

Ward, P., and W. Zahavi. 1973. The importance of certain assemblage of birds as "information centres" for food finding. *Ibis* 115:517–534.

Warren, R. P., and R. A. Hinde. 1959. The effect of oestrogen and progesterone on the nest-building of domesticated canaries. *Animal Behaviour* 57:209–213.

———. 1961. Roles of the male and the nest-cup in controlling reproduction in female canaries. *Animal Behaviour* 9:64–67.

Watson, G. E. 1975. *Birds of the Antarctic*, in collaboration with J. P. Angle and P. C. Harper. Washington: Amer. Geophysical Union.

Weathers, W. W., and K. A. Nagy. 1980. Simultaneous doubly labeled water ($^3HH^{18}O$) and time-budget estimates of daily energy expenditure in *Phainopepla nitens*. *Auk* 97:861–867.

Weller, M. W. 1959. Parasitic egg laying in the redhead (*Aythya americana*) and other North American Anatidae. *Ecological Monog.* 29:333–365.

———. 1968. The breeding biology of the parasitic black-headed duck. *The Living Bird* 7:169–208. Laboratory of Ornithology, Cornell Univ., Ithaca, New York.

Welty, J. C. 1975. *The Life of Birds*. Philadelphia: W. B. Saunders.

Wetmore, A. 1926. Observations on the birds of Argentina, Paraguay, Uraguay and Chile. *Bull. U.S. National Mus.* 133.

———. 1964. *Song and Garden Birds of North America*. Washington, D.C.: National Geographic Society.

———. 1965, 1968, 1972. The Birds of the Republic of Panama. *Smithsonian Miscell. Collections*, vol. 150.

Wetmore, A., and B. H. Swales. 1931. The Birds of Haiti and the Dominican Republic. *Smithsonian Inst., U.S. Nat. Mus. Bull.* 155.

Whitacre, D., and D. Ukrain. 1982. Bird in a cave. *Natural History* 91:56–61.

White, C. M., and T. Cade. 1971. Cliff-nesting raptors and Ravens along the Colville River, in arctic Alaska, *The Living Bird* 10:107–150. Laboratory of Ornithology, Cornell Univ., Ithaca, New York.

White, F. N., G. A. Bartholomew, and T. R. Howell. 1975. The thermal significance of the nest of the Sociable Weaver *Philetairus socius*: winter observations. *Ibis* 117:171–179.

White, F. N., G. A. Bartholomew, and J. L. Kinney. 1978. Physiological and ecological correlates of tunnel nesting in the European Bee-eater, *Merops apiaster*. *Physiol. Zool.* 51:140–154.

White, F. N., and J. L. Kinney. 1974. Avian incubation. *Science* 186:107–115.

White, F. N., J. Kinney, W. R. Siegfried, and A. C. Kemp. Thermal and gaseous conditions of hornbill nests. *Research Reports, National Geographic Society* (in press).

White, S. J. 1975. Effects of stimuli emanating from the nest on the reproductive cycle in the ring dove. *Animal Behaviour* 23:854–888.

White, S. J., and R. A. Hinde. 1968. Temporal relations of brood patch development, nest-building and egg-laying in domesticated canaries. *Jour. Zool. Soc. London* 155:145–155.

Whittow, G. C., and A. J. Berger. 1977. Heat loss from the nest of the Hawaiian honeycreeper "Amakihi." *Wilson Bull.* 89:480–483.

Wilson, E. O. 1971. *The Insect Societies.* Cambridge: Harvard Univ. Press.

———. 1975. *Sociobiology. The New Synthesis.* Cambridge: Harvard Univ. Press.

Wingate, D. B. 1978. Excluding competitors from Bermuda Petrel nesting burrows. In *Endangered Birds*, ed. S. A. Temple, 93–102. Madison: Univ. of Wisconsin Press.

Witschi, E. 1956. *Development of Vertebrates.* Philadelphia: W. B. Saunders. 588 pp.

Withers, P. C. 1977. Energetic aspects of reproduction by the Cliff Swallow. *Auk* 94:718–725.

Wolf, L. L., and F. R. Hainsworth. 1978. Energy: expenditures and intakes. In *Chemical Zoology* 10 (*Aves*), ed. M. Florkin and B. T. Scheer, 307–358. New York and London: Academic Press.

Woodall, P. E. 1975. On the life history of the Bronze Mannikin. *Ostrich* 46:55–86.

Wood-Gush, D.G.M. 1954. Observations on the nesting habits of Brown Leghorn hens. *Section Papers, 10th World's Poultry Congress*, 187–192.

———. 1971. *The Behaviour of the Domestic Fowl.* London: Heinemann Educational Books.

———. 1975. Nest construction by the domestic hen: some comparative and physiological considerations. In *Neural and Endocrine Aspects of Behaviour in Birds*, ed. P. W. Wright, P. G. Caryl, and D. M. Vowles, chap. 3, pp. 35–50. Amsterdam: Elsevier.

Wood-Gush, D.G.M., and A. B. Gilbert. 1964. The control of the nesting behaviour of the domestic hen. 2, The role of the ovary. *Animal Behaviour* 12:451–453.

———. 1969. Oestrogen and the pre-laying behaviour of the domestic hen. *Animal Behaviour* 17:586–589.

———. 1973. Some hormones involved in the nesting behaviour of hens. *Animal Behaviour* 21:98–103.

Woolfenden, G. E. 1973. Nesting and survival in a population of Flordia Scrub Jays. *The Living Bird* 12:25–50. Laboratory of Ornithology, Cornell Univ., Ithaca, New York.

———. 1976. Co-operative breeding in American birds. *Proc. 16th Internat. Ornithol. Congr.*, Canberra, 674–684.

Wright, S. 1978. *Evolution and the Genetics of Populations*. Vol. 4, *Variability Within and Among Natural Populations*. Chicago and London: Univ. of Chicago Press. 580 pp.

———. 1980. Genic and organismic selection. *Evolution* 34:825–843.

Zeleny, L. 1978. Nesting box programs for Bluebirds and other passerines. In *Endangered Birds*, ed. S. A. Temple, 55–60. Madison: Univ. of Wisconsin Press.

Zerba, E., and M. L. Morton. 1983. Dynamics of incubation in Montane White-crowned Sparrows. *Condor* 85:1–11.

(Page numbers in boldface type refer to illustrations.)

Library of Congress Cataloging in Publication Data

Collias, Nicholas E. (Nicholas Elias), 1914-
Nest building and bird behavior.

Bibliography: p.   Includes index.
1. Birds—Eggs and nests. 2. Birds—Behavior.
I. Collias, Elsie C. (Elsie Cole) II. Title.
QL675.C65   1984   598.2'56'4   84-42585
ISBN 0-691-08358-4   ISBN 0-691-08359-2 (pbk.)

Nicholas E. Collias is Professor of Zoology at the University
of California, Los Angeles. Elsie C. Collias is Research Associ-
ate at the University of California, Los Angeles, and the Natural History Museum of Los Angeles County.